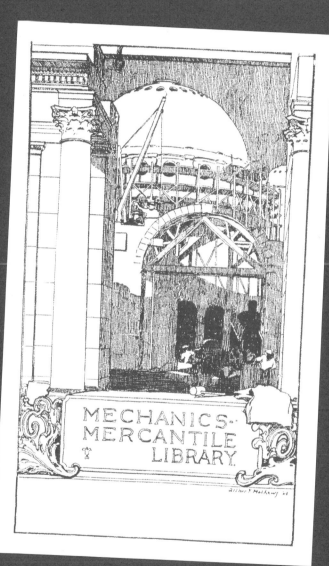

FOR KING AND COUNTRY

Also by Brian MacArthur

The Penguin Book of Twentieth-Century Speeches (ed.)

The Penguin Book of Historic Speeches (ed.)

The Penguin Book of Twentieth-Century Protest (ed.)

Requiem: Diana, Princess of Wales, 1961–97

Despatches from the Gulf War (ed.)

Deadline Sunday: Life in the Week of the *Sunday Times*

Eddy Shah: *Today* and the Newspaper Revolution

Surviving the Sword: Prisoners of the Japanese 1942–45

FOR KING AND COUNTRY

Voices from the First World War

Edited by

BRIAN MacARTHUR

Little, Brown

LITTLE, BROWN

First published in Great Britain in 2008 by Little, Brown

A CIP catalogue record for this book
is available from the British Library.

ISBN 978-0-316-02743-4

Typeset in Sabon by M Rules
Printed and bound in Great Britain by
Clays Ltd, St Ives plc

Little, Brown
An imprint of
Little, Brown Book Group
100 Victoria Embankment
London EC4Y 0DY

An Hachette Livre UK Company

www.littlebrown.co.uk

To the memory of Sapper Edward Wybrow,
511th Field Company, Royal Engineers, who died
on 2 June 1917, aged 19, and has two brothers,
the uncles I never knew

CONTENTS

INTRODUCTION

Ninety years on the Great War of 1914–18 continues to haunt the British imagination. In 2007 the ninetieth anniversary of Passchendaele, where nearly seventy thousand British and Allied soldiers were killed and over a hundred and seventy thousand wounded, was being marked. Elizabeth Grice of the *Daily Telegraph*, whose great-uncle John Cheesewright was killed in Flanders in November 1917, joined the knots of visitors to Lijssenthoek Military Cemetery as she searched among the eleven thousand white slabs for the one that bore his name.

'Why are we here in Flanders, ninety years after these soldiers were slaughtered in a swamp of mud?' she asked. 'Most of us don't remember the person we are looking for. But we have family stories of what it was like when the news came through: the official telegram, the disbelief, then the blinds of all the front windows being drawn, and a woman's hair turning white overnight when she heard that her favourite son had been killed in the Great War. We are part of the living consciousness of this apocalyptic conflict – but only just. We heard it from the people who knew. So we are looking for our connection to an event that, for us, is more than a history topic. I think we are proof that this most pitiful of wars did not end, not absolutely. It is deep in our national psyche.'

That was well put. Many of us do indeed have such family

stories and the First World War – or the Great War as it was known in contemporary parlance – really is deep in the nation's psyche. That is why ninety years on more than thirty million red poppies are still sold in November as we approach the anniversary of the armistice on 11/11/18. It is why across the country, in thousands of cities, towns and villages, a two-minute silence is observed at 11 o'clock at services of remembrance; and why thousands watch the service at the Cenotaph in London, led by the Queen and Prime Minister; and why millions watch the service and march-past of veterans on BBC television.

Enter 'First World War' on the London Library's computer and 890 titles come up. The Imperial War Museum has thousands of Great War diaries, letters, interviews and memoirs as well as its library. There are also Great War archives at Leeds University, Birmingham University and King's College, London. The greatest play of the war, R. C. Sherriff's *Journey's End*, is still performed to packed houses in London and New York. School students study the war, and especially its poetry, for school projects, GCSEs and A levels. The remains of British soldiers who died in the war ninety years ago are still being dug up in France. As the Great War historian Malcolm Brown has written, the Somme is not just a landscape of a particular war. It has also become a landscape of the mind.

Some five million British servicemen went to war between 1914 and 1918, so few families, high or low, were untouched by the slaughter. Among the high was Raymond Asquith, son of the Prime Minister, who was killed in France. 'Whatever pride I had in the past and whatever hope I had for the future, by much the largest part was vested in Raymond,' his father wrote. 'Now all that is gone.' Among the low were the three uncles I never knew, my mother's three brothers, each killed before he was twenty-one. So, even though I was born more than twenty years after the Great War ended, it has loomed in the background of my life for nearly seventy years, as it has for so many others of my generation who lost grandfathers or uncles in the fighting.

I had read all the usual books – Wilfred Owen, Rupert Brooke, Siegfried Sassoon, Robert Graves, Vera Brittain, Lyn Macdonald, Pat Barker, Sebastian Faulks – and I had seen the films. But until I started work on this anthology I did not realise how little I really knew about the Great War. So the compiling of *For King and Country* has been a journey of discovery – as I hope it will be for readers too.

Another anthologist might well have chosen utterly different contributions and this anthology concentrates on the Western Front with the sole exception of Gallipoli and does not visit other theatres of the war. The choice was deliberate. The aim is to reveal the depth of emotion felt by those who fought in the First World War. Of course, it was at the Western Front that these emotions – at first exhilaration but principally fear, horror, anger and despair – were to be found in their greatest concentration. But the soldiers' sense of humour, reflected in several contributions, was a source of strength, all the more remarkable for its backdrop. And finally, at least for some, there is the joy of victory. Overriding all is one criterion: that every contribution – those of soldiers, poets, journalists, song, letter and diary writers – is informed by its author's direct experience of the First World War. Only in the Aftermath, where a broader perspective is appropriate, are there contributions from historians born, for my purposes at least, too late.

Beyond this, the contributions that follow are those that interested me and seemed worth passing on to a new generation. Within the following pages there are stories that are so moving and so poignant that they bring tears to the eyes. Vera Brittain captures the aching regret among the survivors for a pre-war world that was lost for ever – for her a Speech Day at Uppingham, her brother's public school, 'one perfect summer idyll', as she puts it, her 'last care-free entertainment before the Flood'.

There are letters to their mothers and fathers from schoolboys written to say farewell lest they were about to die – and too often they did. 'I could not wish for a finer death . . . I died doing my duty to my God, my Country, my King,' says John Sherwin Engall, writing before the Somme in 1916. The letters speak in language that is unfamiliar today about God, duty, sacrifice and patriotism. Yet as Ruth Elwin Harris says in her collection of Billie Nevill's letters – it was Nevill who kicked a football towards the German lines on the first day of the Somme – the emotional patriotism expressed by the poet Rupert Brooke may be disparaged now but in 1914 and 1915 Brooke spoke for his generation (as Vera Brittain also testifies).

There are many stories of bravery in this anthology. As Alan Clark wrote in *The Donkeys*, 'Bravery, perfect discipline, absolute conviction of right and wrong and the existence of God; a whole code of behaviour that is now little more than an object of derision – these were to be pitted against the largest and most highly trained army in the world.' That bravery and discipline were too often ordered by an older breed of officers, as Richard Aldington writes, who possessed that 'British rhinoceros equipment of mingled ignorance, self-confidence and complacency' that was 'triple-armed against all the shafts of the mind'. Exasperatingly stupid, yes, says Aldington; but also honest and conscientious.

There is the eloquence of the well-known poets and writers – among them Brooke, Grenfell, Owen, Rosenberg, Sassoon and Sorley. Yet, under the pressures of war, unknown soldiers and officers, their archives now buried deep in the Imperial War Museum or their post-war books long forgotten, could be equally eloquent, as is shown by the contributions of, for instance, Henry Dillon, James Graystone and Maurice Gamon, or Frank Richards, Frederic Manning and Cecil Lewis.

There were surprises as my research went on. I had expected the camaraderie of the trenches but not the friendship that often developed between junior officers and their men (about which R. C. Sherriff and Sidney Rogerson write) nor, surprisingly to those of us who were not there, the camaraderie between the British and German trenches, shown most spectacularly during the Christmas truce of 1914 but also month by month as across no man's land the soldiers shared their weariness of war and their common humanity. That is why I have included letters and memoirs from German soldiers: they had the same joys, fears and sorrows as their British 'enemy'; they too were patriots. For this reason, there are also French and American contributors.

Another surprise, at least in 2007, was the brutality of the punishments meted out to the men – the 'crucifixion' on a wagon wheel for the most trifling offences, for instance. Most barbaric to modern eyes, however, were the executions whereby men convicted of cowardice or desertion were shot at dawn, three of which are described in this anthology.

As the war ground on, and especially after the Somme, the idealism of the Rupert Brooke generation was replaced by the disillusion of such writers as Siegfried Sassoon, Wilfred Owen and C. E. Montague of the *Manchester Guardian* and other critics horrified by the continuing slaughter. They are amply represented in the following pages, as are those – see, for instance, Charles Carrington on Esprit de Corps – who believed that Sir Douglas Haig had been unjustly vilified as Commander-in-Chief and that matters were not so bad as the Sassoons and Owens would have had us believe. As the historian Hugh Cecil has pointed out, death sentences were frequently set aside, most of the five million British soldiers who took part survived, the British losses were less than those of the French, Germans or Russians – and the British Army achieved an overwhelming victory in the summer and autumn of 1918.

Anthologists rely on the work of others; I hope that I have made sufficient acknowledgement to the authors whose work I have chosen. Writing this book has left me with an abiding sense of awe at the dedication to duty and discipline and the gallantry of the men who so often seem to have been senselessly sacrificed in the slaughter and squalor of the trenches of the Western Front. I hope that sense of awe will be shared by the reader.

1914

On 28 June 1914 Archduke Franz Ferdinand, the heir to the Austro-Hungarian throne, and his wife were assassinated at Sarajevo in Bosnia-Hercegovina. The assassination provided Austria with an excuse to declare war on Serbia on 28 July, very much encouraged by Germany. Russia, which vied with Austria for influence in the Balkans, sided with Serbia.

The Great Powers – Britain, Germany, Russia and France – had been limbering up for war for years. An intensely militaristic Germany was engaged in an arms race with Britain and determined to overturn British naval supremacy. There was deep-rooted hostility between France and Germany. Europe was divided into two hostile camps: the Triple Alliance of Germany, Austria and Italy, and the Triple Entente of Russia, France and Britain. It only needed a spark to light the fuse of war.

Throughout the tense days of July a flurry of telegrams passed among the royal cousins George V of Britain, Kaiser Wilhelm II of Germany and Tsar Nicholas II of Russia, but they were powerless to stop the momentum towards war. On 3 August Germany declared war on France and violated Belgian neutrality when its army crossed the Belgian border. Britain, which had sworn to protect Belgium, accordingly declared war on Germany on 4 August. Two days later Austria declared war on Russia and France. A well-oiled military machine swung into action as the railways carried the troops to the various fronts.

Woodrow Wilson, the American president, declared neutrality, but Britain was joined by the Dominions of Canada, Australia, New Zealand and South Africa, who were later joined by Japan, Italy, Portugal and Romania. Eventually in 1917 the United States and Greece entered the war on the Allies' side. Turkey and Bulgaria joined Germany and Austro-Hungary. So, as the military historian John Keegan has written, 'the states of Europe proceeded, as if in a dead march and a dialogue of the deaf, to the destruction of their continent and its civilisation'. One after another events gradually overwhelmed 'the capacity of statesmen and diplomats to control and contain them – they were bound to the written note, the encipherment routine, the telegraph schedule'. The potential of the telephone and the radio evaded them altogether.

There was a mood of despair in both London and Berlin as the clocks ticked down to midnight on the evening of 4 August. As Sir Edward Grey, the Foreign Secretary, looked from his window and saw the lamps being lit, he murmured: 'The lamps are going out all over Europe. We shall not see them lit again in our time.' Herbert Asquith, the Liberal Prime Minister, was in the Prime Minister's room in the House of Commons sitting at his writing desk. His wife entered the room and sat down beside him. As she later recalled, she wondered what he was thinking of. His sons? Her son was too young to fight. Did they all have to fight? 'I got up and leaned my head against his', she said, 'and we could not speak for tears.' The British Ambassador in Berlin paid a farewell visit to the Chancellor and found him agitated. 'Just for a word Britain is going to make war on a kindred nation that asks only friendship. Just for a word: "neutrality"! Just for a scrap of paper!'

Addressing Parliament two days later, Asquith said that war had been declared to fulfil an obligation (to Belgium) and to vindicate the principle that small nationalities were not to be crushed, in defiance of international good faith, by the arbitrary will of a strong, overmastering power. Both sides expected that the war would be over by Christmas.

At the outset the young were enthusiastic to fight for a cause they believed to be just. Their idealism was captured by poets (as later was the growing disillusion with the conduct of the war by Douglas Haig and his generals). In a poem published in *The Times*, Thomas Hardy spoke of the 'faith and fire' within the men who were marching to war: victory crowned the just, he said. Rupert Brooke thanked God who had 'matched us with this hour . . . and wakened us from sleeping'. Meanwhile Julian Grenfell declared that he 'adored' war. He was killed seven months later.

Yet idealism was accompanied by an outbreak of anti-German xenophobia. The chief victim was the First Sea Lord, Prince Louis Alexander Battenberg, who, although related to Britain's Royal Family and a naturalised British subject, was widely seen as being of German origin. After a whispering campaign he offered his resignation to Winston Churchill, who was then the First Lord of the Admiralty. Many Germans left for Germany. Those who remained had to register and many were interned. German names were anglicised – Bernstein became Curzon, Rosenheim Rose. In Paris the Rue d'Allemagne became Rue Jean Jaurès. In Berlin, meanwhile, the Hotel Westminster became the Hotel Lindenhof and chauffeurs became *schauffoers*.

On the Eastern Front Russia invaded East Prussia on 17 August and Austria-Hungary invaded Russian Poland (Galicia) on 23 August, but Germany had its greatest success of the war to the east when it defeated the Russians at the Battle of Tannenberg at the end of August.

To the west the Germans swept through Belgium, leaving behind allegations of atrocities and the ancient university town of Louvain devastated. Using the plan devised by General Schlieffen of invading France via Belgium and Luxemburg, crossing the lower Seine, wheeling east and attacking the French fortresses from the rear, the Germans thought that France would be defeated within six weeks. The first engagement between the British Expeditionary Force (BEF), uniquely in Europe composed of professional soldiers, and the Germans occurred at Mons on 23 August. Although outnumbered by six divisions to four, the British, ordered to hold the Mons–Condé canal, at first overwhelmed the Germans. But the French Army to the right of the British was falling back and there were no troops to the left. Sir John French, the BEF's commander-in-chief, was forced to order a retreat.

On 26 August the British stood and fought at Le Cateau. They held the Germans up and got away. But over fourteen gruelling days the retreat from Mons took the British and French armies to the outskirts of Paris. On 1 September the German Army was only thirty miles from Paris and about to achieve Schlieffen's objective. So the French were astonished when the German First Army, under General von Moltke, the German chief of staff, started moving south across the River Marne to support the German Second Army, thus exposing his flank. This the French attacked on 5 September, starting the Battle of the Marne, in which the Germans were forced to retreat to the River Aisne. General Joffre, the French commander-in-chief, became a national hero for saving Paris and forcing the Germans to retreat.

There were important consequences. Not only was Paris saved, but the plan to conquer France in six weeks had failed; and Germany now had to fight on two fronts – the Western as well as the Eastern. The slaughter that was to characterise the First World War had also begun. There were 250,000 Allied casualties at the Marne. In the three weeks since the war began, each side had lost 500,000 men.

The next major encounter between the two armies was at Ypres near the Channel coast in Flanders between 19 October and 22 November. The Germans had moved to Ypres intending to outflank the British while the British arrived at Ypres intending to outflank the Germans. After the British and French withstood the Germans the battle ended in stalemate. But everywhere the

Germans held the high ground dominating the shallow crescent of trenches that became known as the Ypres Salient. By the end of this First Battle of Ypres – there were to be two more – fewer than half of the 160,000 men of the BEF had survived. But the two-million-strong French Army suffered more: its estimated losses in the first four months were more than 500,000 men, of whom 360,000 were killed. The Germans lost even more men.

The Western Front now stretched four hundred miles from the Channel to Switzerland with both sides dug into trenches behind barbed wire and protected by machine guns (both in use for the first time). The line would not move more than ten miles either way in the next three years. Another 'first' was the use of gas on the battlefield by the Germans on 27 October, when they fired three thousand shrapnel shells containing a nose and eye irritant.

On the home front the Defence of the Realm Acts began dismantling some of the ancient liberties so nostalgically described by A. J. P. Taylor in his *English History, 1914–1945*:

Until August 1914 a sensible, law-abiding Englishman could pass through life and scarcely notice the existence of the state, beyond the post office and the policeman. He could live where he liked and as he liked. He had no official number or identity card. He could travel abroad or leave his country for ever without a passport or any sort of official permission. He could exchange his money for any other currency without restriction or limit. He could buy goods from any country in the world on the same terms as he bought goods at home. For that matter, a foreigner could spend his life in this country without permit and without informing the police.

Unlike the countries of the European continent, the state did not require its citizens to perform military service. An Englishman could enlist, if he chose, in the regular army, the navy, or the territorials. He could also ignore, if he chose, the demands of national defence. Substantial householders were occasionally called on for jury service. Otherwise, only those helped the state who wished to do so. The Englishman paid taxes on a modest scale: nearly £200 million in 1913–14, or rather less than 8 per cent of the national income.

The state intervened to prevent the citizen from eating adulterated food or contracting certain infectious diseases. It imposed safety rules in factories, and prevented women, and adult males in some industries, from working excessive hours. The state saw to it that children received education up to the age of 13. Since 1 January 1909, it provided a meagre pension for the needy over the age of 70. Since 1911, it helped to insure certain classes of workers against sickness and unemployment. This tendency towards more state action was increasing. Expenditure on the social services had roughly doubled since the Liberals took office in 1905. Still, broadly speaking, the state acted only to help those who could not help themselves. It left the adult citizen alone.

That was the world that was to be swept away over the next four years. The number of men who joined up in 1914 was 1,186,357.

On Christmas Eve England was attacked from the air for the first time by a small German biplane which dropped a small bomb on Dover but no harm was caused. On that same day there was the Christmas truce, perhaps the most extraordinary event of the war, when soldiers on both sides left their trenches, greeted each other, exchanged gifts and celebrated Christmas in no man's land.

In his book *The Donkeys* (suggesting that the British soldiers were lions led by donkeys), the military historian and Tory MP Alan Clark argued that after the battles of the autumn British commanders spent the lives of their men with 'profligacy' in trying to reproduce the sort of conditions of open warfare and 'cavalry country' that they met on the Aisne. Their handling of operations gave no confidence that had their wish been granted they would have been any more efficient or imaginative than they were in coping with the siege-like conditions that now set in:

'So it was that as the leaves fell and the ground turned to mud and the German howitzers with their twelve-horse teams plodded patiently up to the line, the British Army was poised over an abyss. It could be saved only by reckless squandering of the virtues which, like its delusions, sprang from a background of peace and a stable, ordered society. Bravery, perfect discipline, absolute conviction of right and wrong and the existence of God; a whole code of behaviour that is now little more than an object of derision – these were to be pitted against the largest and most highly trained army in the world.'

HERBERT ASQUITH

'What we are fighting for'

On 6 August Asquith went to the House of Commons to explain why Britain had gone to war and to make the 'unusual demand' for a Note of Credit of £100 million.

> I am entitled to say, and I do say on behalf of this country –
> I speak not for party, but for the country as a whole – we
> made every effort that a Government could possibly make
> for peace. This war has been forced upon us.
>   And what is it that we are fighting for? No one knows
> better than the members of the Government the terrible and
> incalculable sufferings economic, social, personal, political,
> which war, especially war between the Great Powers of the
> world, must entail. There is not a man among us sitting on
> this bench in these trying days – more trying, perhaps, than
> any body of statesmen for a hundred years has had to pass
> through – who has not during the whole of that time had
> clearly before his vision the almost unequalled suffering
> which war, even in a just cause, must bring about, not only
> to us who are for the moment living in this country and in
> the other countries of the world, but to posterity and to the
> whole prospects of European civilisation. Every step we
> took, we took with that vision before our eyes, and with a

sense of responsibility which it is impossible to describe. Unhappily in spite of all our efforts to keep the peace, and with that full and overpowering consciousness of the results of the issue if we decided in favour of war, nevertheless we have thought it to be our duty as well as the interest of this country to go to war. The House may be well assured it was because we believe, and I am certain the country will believe, we are unsheathing our swords in a just cause.

If I am asked what we are fighting for, I can reply in two sentences. In the first place, to fulfil a solemn international obligation – an obligation which, if it had been entered into between private persons in the ordinary concerns of life, would have been regarded as an obligation not only of law, but of honour, which no self-respecting man could possibly have repudiated.

I say, secondly, we are fighting to vindicate the principle in these days when material force sometimes seems to be the dominant influence and factor in the development of mankind, that small nationalities are not to be crushed, in defiance of international good faith, by the arbitrary will of a strong and overmastering power. I do not believe any nation ever entered into a great controversy – and this is one of the greatest history will ever know – with a clearer conscience and stronger conviction that it is fighting, not for aggression, not for the maintenance even of its own selfish interest, but in defence of principles the maintenance of which is vital to the civilisation of the world, and with the full conviction, not only of the wisdom and justice, but of the obligations which lay upon us to challenge this great issue.

JEROME K. JEROME

'The instinct that Germany was "The Enemy"'

Jerome, author of *Three Men in a Boat*, written in 1889 and still in print, was fifty-six in 1914 and was turned down when he tried to enlist. But he became an ambulance driver with the French Army and went to the Western Front. In this extract from his autobiography, he describes the mood of England when war was declared.

Sir Edward Grey has been accused of having 'jockeyed' us into the war – of having so committed us to France and Russia that no honourable escape was possible to us. Had the Good Samaritan himself been our Foreign Secretary, the war would still have happened. Germany is popularly supposed to have brought us into it by going through Belgium. Had she gone round by the Cape of Good Hope, the result would have been the same. The Herd instinct had taken possession of us all. It was sweeping through Europe. I was at a country tennis tournament the day we declared war on Germany. Young men and maidens, grey-moustached veterans, pale-faced curates, dear old ladies: one and all expressed relief and thankfulness. 'I was so afraid Grey would climb down at the last moment' – 'It was Asquith I was doubtful of. I didn't think the old man had the grit' – 'Thank God, we shan't read "Made in Germany" for a little time to come"'. Such was the talk over the tea-cups.

It was the same whichever way you looked. Railway porters, cabmen, workmen riding home upon bicycles, farm labourers eating their bread and cheese beside the hedge: they had the faces of men to whom good tidings had come.

For years it had been growing, this instinct that Germany was 'The Enemy'. In the beginning we were grieved. It was the first time in history she had been called upon to play the part. But that was her fault. Why couldn't she leave us alone – cease interfering with our trade, threatening our command of the sea? Quite nice people went about saying: 'We're bound to have a scrap with her. Hope it comes in my time' – 'Must put her in her place. We'll get on all the better with her afterwards'. That was the idea everywhere: that war would clear the air, make things pleasanter all round, afterwards. A party, headed by Lord Roberts, clamoured for conscription. Another party, headed by Lord Fisher, proposed that we should seize the German Fleet and drown it. Books and plays came out one on top of another warning us of the German menace. Kipling wrote, openly proclaiming Germany, The Foe, first and foremost.

In Germany, I gather from German friends, similar thinking prevailed. It was England that, now secretly, now openly, was everywhere opposing a blank wall to German expansion, refusing her a place in the sun, forbidding her the seas, plotting to hem her in.

The pastures were getting used up. The herds were becoming restive.

RUPERT BROOKE

'Peace'

Rupert Brooke was born in 1887 and educated at Rugby and King's College, Cambridge. His first volume of poems was published in 1911. On the outbreak of war he was given a commission in the Royal Naval Division.

Now God be thanked Who has matched us with His hour,
And caught our youth, and wakened us from sleeping,
With hand made sure, clear eye, and sharpened power,
To turn, as swimmers into cleanness leaping,
Glad from a world grown old and cold and weary,
Leave the sick hearts that honour could not move,
And half-men, and their dirty songs and dreary,
And all the little emptiness of love!

Oh! We, who have known shame, we have found release there,
Where there's no ill, no grief, but sleep has mending,
Naught broken save this body, lost but breath;
Nothing to shake the laughing heart's long peace there
But only agony, and that has ending;
And the worst friend and enemy is but Death.

VERA BRITTAIN

'One perfect summer idyll'

Vera Brittain's autobiographical *Testament of Youth* was a best-seller when it was published in 1933, it was a TV serial in 1979 and it is still in print. The book is at its most moving when she describes her relationship with Roland Leighton, her brother Edward's closest school friend (especially when read now in the knowledge of what was to happen to both during the war).

Speech Day, Uppingham
As the headmaster strode, berobed and majestic, onto the platform of the School Hall, I was in the midst of examining with appreciation my Speech Day programme, and especially the page headed 'Prizemen, July 1914', of which the first seven items ran as follows:

Nettleship Prize for English Essay	R. A. Leighton
Holden Prize for Latin Prose	1st, R. A. Leighton
	2nd, C. R. B. Wrenford
Greek Prose Composition	R. A. Leighton
Latin Hexameters	R. A. Leighton
Greek Iambics	R. P. Garrod
Greek Epigram	R. A. Leighton
Captain in Classics	R. A. Leighton

But, still automatically responsive to school discipline, I hastily put down the programme as the headmaster began, with enormous dignity, to address the audience.

I do not recall much of the speech, which ended with a list of the precepts laid down for boys by a famous Japanese general – a monument of civilisation whose name I forget, but whose qualities were evidently considered entirely suitable for emulation by young English gentlemen. I shall always, however, remember the final prophetic precept, and the breathless silence which followed the Headmaster's slow, religious emphasis upon the words:

'If a man cannot be useful to his country, he is better dead.'

For a moment their solemnity disturbed with a queer, indescribable foreboding the complacent mood in which I watched Roland, pale but composed, go up to receive his prizes.

I have written so much of Uppingham Speech Day because it was the one perfect summer idyll that I ever experienced, as well as my last care-free entertainment before the Flood. The lovely legacy of a vanished world, it is etched with minute precision on the tablets of my memory. Never again, for me and for my generation, was there to be any festival the joy of which no cloud would darken and no remembrance invalidate.

Alfred Lichtenstein

'Prayer Before Battle'

According to the historian Niall Ferguson, the German Alfred Lichtenstein, who was born in 1889 and died in September 1914, has a good claim to have been the first of the anti-war poets.

> *God protect me from misfortune,*
> *Father, Son and Holy Ghost,*
> *May no high explosives hit me,*
> *May our enemies, the bastards,*
> *Never take me, never shoot me,*
> *May I never die in squalor*
> *For our well-loved fatherland.*

Look, I'd like to live much longer,
Milk the cows and stuff my girlfriends
And beat up that lousy Josef,
Get drunk on lots more occasions
Till a blissful death o'ertakes me.
Look, I'll offer heartfelt prayers,
Say my beads seven times daily,
If you, God, of your gracious bounty,
Choose to kill my mate, say Huber
Or else Meier, and let me off.

But suppose I have to take it
Don't let me get badly wounded.
Send me just a little leg wound
Or a slight gash on the forearm
So I go home as a hero
Who has got a tale to tell.

Captain Henry Dillon

Mons

Exhilarated by the battle, Captain Dillon, a thirty-three-year-old captain in the 52nd Oxfordshire and Buckinghamshire Light Infantry, wrote in a letter:

August 29: I am very fit and everything is going top hole. We have done a great march – it has been fearful work, 25 hours with hardly a stop once and it has been going on so far almost continuously for days. One's feet throb so one can hardly stick it at times. We have bumped into the absolute flower of the German army and have laid them absolutely in thousands. In one place they lie in heaps of 50 to 100 for three miles. Of course we have had some losses but I think there are probably 20 or more Germans to every Englishman. The swine are doing all sorts of low down things. In one case they drove civilian women and children in front of them, – our men would not fire but rushed at them with their bayonets and fought till they were all killed, which was inevitable on account of the numbers. On another occasion they dressed in French uniforms and came up shouting 'Vive l'Angleterre' and actually started talking French to our people and then when they were all up they suddenly opened fire. This happened to a picket of about 50 men so it was not very serious. We have had the best of them everywhere . . .

I am awfully glad to hear the Russians have come as it will have a great moral effect on the Germans. The swine are at their old tricks again. The cavalry I mentioned who advanced on us in the early morning had on English great coats and caps. In an advance of one of the Guards regiments some Germans dropped apparently wounded and as the Guards advanced over them they jumped up and shot the officers. In another case they hoisted a white flag and then opened fire. It was annoying to lose a lot of men without firing a shot back. We never let off a rifle all day. Anyhow we are up on them as far as our losses are concerned.

CORPORAL BERNARD JOHN DENORE

The Retreat from Mons

Bernard Denore, a corporal in the 1st Royal Berkshire Regiment, covered some 250 miles on foot in the retreat from Mons:

August 31st: Again we were rearguard, but did little fighting. We marched instead staggering about the road like a crowd of gipsies. Some of the fellows had puttees wrapped round their feet instead of boots; others had soft shoes they had picked up somewhere; others walked in their socks, with their feet all bleeding. My own boots would have disgraced a tramp, but I was too frightened to take them off, and look at my feet. Yet they marched until they dropped, and then somehow got up and marched again.

One man (Ginger Gilmore) found a mouth-organ, and, despite the fact that his feet were bound in blood-soaked rags, he staggered along at the head of the company playing tunes all day. Mostly he played 'The Irish Emigrant'. Which is a good marching tune. He reminded me of Captain Oates. An officer asked me if I wanted a turn on his horse, but I looked at the fellow on it, and said, 'No thanks.'

The marching was getting on everyone's nerves, but, as I went I kept saying to myself, 'If you can, force your heart and nerve and sinew.' Just that, over and over again. That night we spent the time looking for an Uhlan [cavalry] regiment, but didn't get in touch with them, and every time we stopped we fell asleep; in fact we slept while we were marching, and consequently kept falling over.

September 1st: We continued at the same game from dawn till dark, and dark till dawn – marching and fighting and marching. Every roll call there were fewer to answer – some were killed, some wounded, and some who had fallen out were missing. During this afternoon we fought for about three hours – near Villers-Cotterets I think it was, but I was getting very mixed about things, even mixed about the days of the week. Fifteen men in my company were killed, one in a rather peculiar fashion. He was bending down, handing me a piece of sausage, and a bullet ricocheted off a man's boot and went straight into his mouth and out of the top of his head. We got on to the road about 200 yards only in front of a German brigade, and then ran like hell for about a mile.

September 3rd: The first four or five hours we did without a single halt or rest, as we had to cross a bridge over the Aisne before the Royal Engineers blew it up. It was the most terrible march I have ever done. Men were falling down like nine-pins. They would fall flat on their faces on the road, while the rest of us staggered round them, as we couldn't lift our feet high enough to step over them, and, as for picking them up, that was impossible, as to bend meant to fall.

What happened to them, God only knows. An aeroplane was following us most of the time dropping iron darts; we fired at it a couple of times, but soon lost the strength required for that. About 9 a.m. we halted by a river, and immediately two fellows threw themselves into it.

Nobody, from sheer fatigue, was able to save them, although one sergeant made an attempt, and was nearly drowned himself.

I, like a fool, took my boots off and found my feet were covered with blood. I could find no sores or cuts, so I thought I must have sweated blood.

As I couldn't get my boots on again I cut the sides away, and when we started marching again, my feet hurt like hell.

We marched till about 3 p.m. – nothing else, just march, march, march. I kept repeating my line, . . . 'If you can, force, etc.' Why, I didn't know. A sergeant irritated everyone who could hear him by continually shouting out: 'Stick it, lads. We are making history.'

The Colonel offered me a ride on his horse, but I refused, and then wished I hadn't, as anything was preferable to the continuous marching.

We got right back that afternoon among the refugees again. They were even worse off than we were, or, at least, they looked it. We gave the kids our biscuits and 'bully', hoping that would help them a little; but they looked so dazed and tired there did not seem to be much hope for them. At 8 p.m. we bivouacked in a field and slept till dawn. Ye gods! what a relief.

I discovered that the company I was in covered 251 miles in the Retreat from Mons, which finished on September 5th, 1914.

THE TIMES, AUGUST 1914

The Retreat from Mons

The Times's correspondent Arthur Moore was cycling around the back roads near Amiens when he rode into the chaos of a great battle and obtained the newspaper's first big scoop of the war. 'Scattered remnants of British forces were trying to regain their units. It was the Fourth Division turning after the retreat from Mons.' The history of *The Times* adds: 'Moore was greatly alarmed by what he saw and heard it bore no relation to the official communiqués.' The report caused an uproar.

It is important that the nation should know and realize certain things. Bitter truths, but we can face them. We have to cut our losses, to take stock of the situation, to set our teeth.

First let it be said that our honour is bright. Amongst all the straggling units that I have seen, flotsam and jetsam of the fiercest fight in history, I saw fear in no man's face. It was a retreating and a broken army, but it was not an army of hunted men. Nor in all the plain tales of officers, non-commissioned officers and men did a single story of the white feather reach me. No one could answer for every man, but every British regiment and every battery of which any one had knowledge had done its duty. And never has duty been more terrible.

The German advance has been one of almost incredible rapidity. The British Force fought a terrible fight – which may be called the action of Mons, though it covered a big front – on Sunday. The German attack was withstood to the utmost limit, and a whole division was flung into the fight at the end of a long march and had not even time to dig trenches. The French supports expected on the immediate right do not seem to have been in touch, though whether or not they were many hours late I cannot say.

Further to the right, along the Sambre and in the angle of the Sambre and the Meuse, the French, after days of long and gallant fighting, broke. Namur fell and General Joffre was forced to order a retreat along the whole line. The Germans, fulfilling one of the best of all precepts in war, never gave the retreating army one single moment's rest. The pursuit was immediate, relentless, unresting. Aeroplanes, Zeppelins, armoured motors, and cavalry were loosed like an arrow from the bow, and served at once to harass the retiring columns and to keep the German Staff fully informed of the movements of the Allied Forces.

The British Force fell back . . . Regiments were grievously injured, and the broken army fought its way desperately with many stands, forced backwards and ever backwards by the sheer unconquerable mass of numbers of an enemy prepared to throw away three or four men for the life of every British soldier. Where it is at present it might not be well to say even if I knew, but I do not know, though I have seen to-day in different neighbourhoods some units of it. But there are some things which it is eminently right that I should say . . .

Our losses are very great. I have seen the broken bits of many regiments. Let me repeat that there is no failure in discipline, no panic, no throwing up the sponge. Every one's temper is sweet, and nerves do not show. A group of men, it may be a dozen, or less or more, arrives, under the command of whoever is entitled to command it. The men are battered with marching, and ought to be weak with hunger, for, of course, no commissariat could cope with such a case, but they are steady and cheerful, and wherever they arrive make straight for the proper authority, report themselves, and seek news of their regiment.

I saw two men give such reports, after saluting smartly. 'Very badly cut up, Sir,' was the phrase one used of his regiment. The other said, 'Very heavy loss, I'm afraid, Sir,' when asked if much was left . . .

Apparently every division was in action. Some have lost nearly all their officers. The regiments were broken to bits, and good discipline and fine spirit kept the fragments together, though they no longer knew what had become of the other parts with which they had once formed a splendid whole.

Certain things about the fighting seem clear. One is the colossal character of the German losses. I confess that when I read daily in official bulletins in Paris of how much greater the German losses were than those of the Allies I was not much impressed. Much contemplation of Eastern warfare, where each side claims to have annihilated the other, has made me over-sceptical in such matters. But three days among the combatants has convinced me of the truth of the story in this case . . .

The German commanders in the north advance their men as if they had an inexhaustible supply. Of the bravery of the men it is not necessary to speak. They advance in deep sections, so slightly extended as to be almost in close order, with little regard for cover, rushing forward as soon as their own artillery has opened fire behind them on our position. Our artillery mows long lanes down the centres of the sections, so that frequently there is nothing left of it but its outsides. But no sooner is this done than more men double up rushing over the heaps of dead, and remake the section. Last week, so great was their superiority in numbers that they could no more be stopped than the waves of the sea. Their shrapnel is markedly bad, though their gunners are excellent at finding the range.

On the other hand their machine guns are of the most deadly efficacy, and are very numerous. Their rifle shooting is described as not first-class, but their numbers bring on the infantry till frequently they and the Allied troops meet finally in bayonet tussles. Superiority of numbers in men and guns, especially in machine guns; a most successfully organized system of scouting by aeroplanes and Zeppelins; motors carrying machine guns, cavalry; and extreme mobility are the elements of their present success . . .

To sum up, the first great German effort has succeeded. We have to face the fact that the British Expeditionary Force, which bore the great weight of the blow, has suffered terrible losses and requires immediate and immense reinforcement. The British Expeditionary Force has won indeed imperishable glory, but it needs men, men, and yet more men. The investment of Paris *cannot be banished from the field of possibility.* I saw rolling stock being hurriedly moved to-day from Amiens. *Proximus ardet Ucalegon. We want reinforcements and we want them now.* Whether the Chief of the German General Staff, after reckoning up his losses, will find that he has enough men left to attempt a further assault with any hope of success is more doubtful. His army has made a colossal effort and moved with extraordinary speed. It is possible that its limits have been reached.

WALTER BLOEM

Advancing from Mons

Walter Bloem was a well-known German novelist serving as a reserve captain in the 12th Brandenburg Grenadiers. *The Advance from Mons*, in which this piece appears, was published in 1916.

My nerves seemed to brace themselves up for the great test. At least the hour had struck; so be it. I saluted, turned Alfred about and trotted back to my company: 'B Company is to attack, lads! It's a raging hell in front, but we've got to go through it. I rely on you all.' Dismounting, I gave the order: 'B Company extend to the right – double!' My 'staff' came out to me and together we moved out in front of the company, the whole line emerging from the group of houses in excellent order and past the battalion commander, who saluted his *'morituri'* [We who are about to die].

In front of us, now scarcely a hundred yards off, a long line of little puffs of white cloud floated in the air, and below them a small forest of black fountains of smoke and dirt. Death, I'm ready for you! Here is my forehead, here is my heart! Strike, if you wish! And as I went into it, a shout of triumph, a wild, unearthly singing surged within me, uplifting and inspiring me, filling all my senses. I had overcome fear; I had conquered my mortal bodily self. And I glanced back on my little army; they were following, a long line of high-held foreheads, of strong, gallant hearts. Bless you, children – my children!

Nearer and nearer the barrage, to the messengers of death. Welcome! welcome! Strange, though, that of a sudden no more shells were coming. All was quiet in front of us. No treacherous white lambs frolicking in the sky, no explosions, no miniature volcanoes; the black smoke and cloud of dust was gradually clearing away in front. Just a pause in the fight, no doubt; any moment the storm would break again and burst over us with redoubled fury. We were already crossing the zone where for half an hour volley after volley of shells had ploughed up the field, bits of shell, empty shells, dud-shells – shrapnel that had not burst – lying all about, with every here and there a mutilated Fusilier among them.

On, on to the village edge! Now our own guns were coming into action, howitzer-batteries, and their high-explosive shells passed over us and crashed into the roofs of the village, rusty-red clouds of smoke and debris towered up into the sky. The church-spire cracked like a bit of timber, and toppled on one side. On, on!

Strange, though, still no enemy shells. Where were they? Had they gone, cleared out? Was it possible? And as I marched on, sweating, across the torn-up acres and saw death retreating away from us, the nervous reaction that overcame me was so intense that I suddenly laughed, laughed outright at the way I had braced myself up to such a high pitch of heroism!

Behind me, too, I heard talking and giggling, and looking round saw my staff grinning, and then they too burst out laughing. Turning my head still further I saw the whole line of B Company were laughing, the corners of their mouths almost reaching their ears. We all felt the same. Who would have imagined how amazingly comic it is having worked oneself up with heaven-inspired ardour to meet Death like a true hero, for her not to come to the trysting-place? No doubt about it now, she had definitely gone, away over the far horizon. I almost wept with joy and laughter.

St Vincent Morris

'The Eleventh Hour'

St Vincent Morris was still at school and too young to join the Army when war was declared. His frustration at not being able to fight finds an outlet in this sonnet. Morris was gazetted in 1915 to the Nottinghamshire and Derbyshire Regiment, or the 'Sherwood Foresters', transferred to the Royal Flying Corps and died of wounds after his aircraft crashed in April 1917.

Is this to live? – to cower and stand aside
While others fight and perish day by day?
To see my loved ones slaughtered, and to say:
'Bravo! Bravo! how nobly you have died!'
Is this to love? – to heed my friends no more,
But watch them perish in a foreign land
Unheeded, and to give no helping hand,
But smile, and say, 'How terrible is war!'

Nay, this is not to love, nor this to live!
I will go forth; I hold no more aloof;
And I will give all that I have to give,
And leave the refuge of my father's roof.
Then, if I live, no man shall say, think I,
'He lives, because he did not dare to die!'

'HUSH! HERE COMES A WHIZZ-BANG'

As the 1960s musical *Oh! What a Lovely War* demonstrated, songs became the voice of the soldiers fighting the Great War. They were often obscene: it was during the war that use of the word 'fucking' became universal. The tunes were frequently adapted from music-hall hits and this example was a pre-1914 pantomime song sung to the air 'Hush! Here Comes the Dream Man':

Hush! Here comes a whizz-bang,
Hush! Here comes a whizz-bang,
Now you soldiers, get down those stairs
Down in your dug-outs and say your prayers.
Hush! Here comes a whizz-bang,
And it's making straight for you:
And you'll see all the wonders of no man's land
If a whizz-bang (bump!) hits you.

ERNST LISSAUER

'Hymn of Hate Against England'
(translated by Barbara Henderson)

As the English denounced the Germans, so the Germans
denounced the English. Ernst Lissauer, a German poet serving as
an army private, wrote an anti-English poem called 'Hassgesang
gegen England', or 'Hymn of Hate Against England'. This
became a pamphlet that sold in millions, was taught in schools,
memorised in the trenches and became a second national anthem
in Germany. When it drifted over from the enemy lines, British
soldiers would join in and sing with great gusto:

> *French and Russians they matter not;*
> *A blow for a blow, and a shot for a shot;*
> *We love them not, we hate them not . . .*
> *We have but one and only hate,*
> *We love as one, we hate as one,*
> *We have one foe and one alone.*
> *He is known to you all, he is known to you all!*
> *He crouches behind the dark gray flood,*
> *Full of envy, of rage, of craft, of gall,*
> *Cut off by waves that are thicker than blood . . .*
> *We will never forgo our hate,*
> *We have all but a single hate,*
> *We love as one, we hate as one.*
> *We have one foe, and one alone – England.*

P. S.: CAPTAIN ERIC FISHER WOOD

"Oo do we 'ite?'

Wood, an American major who served in the British Army, noted
this example of the English soldiers' robust sense of humour.

The German 'Hymn of Hate' also bids fair to become one of England's national songs, just as derisive 'Yankee Doodle', first composed and played by the musicians of British troops early in the American Revolution, was later, on the occasion of their final surrender at York Town, played 'at them' by the bands of the Continental Army and subsequently became one of America's national songs, having today a popularity rivalled only by that of 'Dixie'. It is truly an extraordinary sight to see some English county regiment on the march singing the 'Hymn of Hate' at the top of their lungs, and at the chorus to hear some clear tenor voice call out "Oo do we 'ite?' and then the whole battalion's reply in a voice of thunder – 'England!'

THOMAS HARDY

'Men Who March Away' ('Song of the Soldiers')

'Men Who March Away', a call to action by Thomas Hardy (1840–1928), was published in *The Times* on 9 September.

> *What of the faith and fire within us*
> *Men who march away*
> *Ere the barn-cocks say*
> *Night is growing gray,*
> *Leaving all that here can win us;*
> *What of the faith and fire within us*
> *Men who march away?*
>
> *Is it a purblind prank, O think you,*
> *Friend with the musing eye,*
> *Who watch us stepping by*
> *With doubt and dolorous sigh?*
> *Can much pondering so hoodwink you!*
> *Is it a purblind prank, O think you*
> *Friend with the musing eye?*

Nay. We shall see what we are doing,
Though some may not see –
Dalliers as they be –
England's need are we;
Her distress would leave us rueing:
Nay. We well see what we are doing,
Though some may not see!

In our heart of hearts believing
Victory crowns the just,
And that braggarts must
Surely bite the dust,
Press we to the field ungrieving,
In our heart of hearts believing
Victory crowns the just.

Hence the faith and fire within us
Men who march away
Ere the barn-cocks say
Night is growing gray,
Leaving all that here can win us;
Hence the faith and fire within us
Men who march away.

ELIZABETH BRIDGES

'For England'

Elizabeth Bridges, who later wrote under her married name of Daryush, was the daughter of Robert Bridges, the Poet Laureate.

Use me, England,
In thine hour of need,
Let thy ruling
Rule me now in deed.

Sons and brothers
Take for armoury,
All love's jewels
Crushed, thy warpath be!

Thou hast given
Joyous life and free,
Life whose joy now
Anguisheth for thee.

Give then, England,
If my life thou need,
Gift yet fairer,
Death, thy life to feed.

LAURENCE BINYON

'For the Fallen'

Laurence Binyon (1869–1943) wrote this poem in September, only seven weeks after the declaration of war. Even though omitted from several anthologies of Great War poetry, it is the most-quoted example as the fourth verse is frequently used on soldiers' headstones and is still spoken ninety years later at official celebrations of Armistice Day:

With proud thanksgiving, a mother for her children,
England mourns for her dead across the sea
Flesh of her flesh they were, spirit of her spirit,
Fallen in the cause of the free.

Solemn the drums thrill: Death august and royal
Sings sorrow up into immortal spheres.
There is music in the midst of desolation
And glory that shines upon our tears.

They went with songs to the battle, they were young,
Straight of limb, true of eye, steady and aglow,
They were staunch to the end against odds uncounted,
They fell with their faces to the foe.

They shall grow not old, as we that are left grow old:
Age shall not weary them, nor the years condemn.
At the going down of the sun and in the morning
We will remember them.

They mingle not with their laughing comrades again;
They sit no more at familiar tables at home;
They have no lot in our labour of the daytime:
They sleep beyond England's foam.

But where our desires are and our hopes profound,
Felt as a well-spring that is hidden from sight,
To the innermost heart of their own land they are known
As the stars are known to the Night.

As the stars that shall be bright when we are dust,
Moving in marches upon the heavenly plain,
As the stars that are starry in the time of our darkness,
To the end, to the end, they remain.

'IT'S A LONG WAY TO TIPPERARY'

(Words: Jack Judge; music: Harry Williams)

'Tipperary' was introduced to the British Army by the Connaught Rangers, who were stationed in that part of Ireland before the war. It was written in 1912 by Jack Judge, a market stallholder, for a bet. The *Daily Mail* reporter George Curnock heard the Rangers singing the song at Boulogne in August 1914 and his report ensured its enduring popularity.

Up to mighty London came an Irishman one day,
As the streets are paved with gold, sure everyone was gay;
Singing songs of Piccadilly, Strand and Leicester Square,
Till Paddy got excited, then he shouted to them there –

Chorus:
It's a long way to Tipperary,
It's a long way to go;
It's a long way to Tipperary,
To the sweetest girl I know!
Goodbye Piccadilly,
Farewell Leicester Square,
It's a long long way to Tipperary
But my heart's right there!

Paddy wrote a letter to his Irish Molly O
Saying, 'Should you not receive it, write and let me know!'
'If I make mistakes in spelling, Molly dear', said he
'Remember it's the pen that's bad, don't lay the blame on
    me.'

Chorus:
It's a long way to Tipperary (etc.)

Molly wrote a neat reply to Irish Paddy O,
Saying, 'Mike Maloney wants to marry me, and so
Leave the Strand and Piccadilly, or you'll be to blame,
For love has fairly drove me silly – hoping you're the
    same!'

Chorus:
It's a long way to Tipperary (etc.)

That's the wrong way to tickle Marie,
That's the wrong way to kiss!

Don't you know that over here, lad,
They like it best like this!
Hooray pour le Français!
Farewell, Angleterre!
We didn't know the way to tickle Marie,
But we learned how, over there!

JULIAN GRENFELL

'I adore War'

Julian Grenfell, the eldest son of a Liberal and later Conservative MP who became Lord Desborough, was educated at Eton and Balliol College, Oxford. He was commissioned in the Royal Dragoons in 1910 and served in India. He was twenty-six when this letter was written in October and he died of wounds in May 1915:

I adore War. It is like a big picnic without the objectlessness of a picnic. I have never been so well or so happy. Nobody grumbles at one for being dirty. I have only had my boots off once in the last 10 days, and only washed twice. We are up and standing to our rifles by 5 a.m. when doing this infantry work, and saddled up by 4.30 a.m. when with our horses. Our poor horses do not get their saddles off when we are in trenches.

The wretched inhabitants here have got practically no food left. It is miserable to see them leaving their houses, and tracking away, with great bundles and children in their hands. And the dogs and cats left in the deserted villages are piteous.

October 3rd, 1914 . . . I have not washed for a week, or had my boots off for a fortnight. But we cook good hot food in the dark, in the morning before we start, and in the night when we get back to our horses; . . . It is all the best fun. I have never never felt so well, or so happy, or enjoyed anything so much. It just suits my stolid health, and stolid nerves, and barbaric disposition. The fighting-excitement vitalizes everything, every sight and word and action. One loves one's fellow man so much more when one is bent on killing him. And picnic-ing in the open day and night (we never see a roof now) is the real method of existence.

There are loads of straw to bed-down on, and one sleeps like a log, and wakes up with the dew on one's face. The stolidity of my nerves surprises myself. I went to sleep the other day when we were lying in the trenches, with the shrapnel bursting within 50 yards all the time and a noise like nothing on earth. The noise is continual and indescribable. The Germans shell the trenches with shrapnel all day and all night; and the Reserves and ground in the rear with Jack Johnsons (heavy shells), which at last one gets to love as old friends. You hear them coming for miles, and everyone imitates the noise; then they burst with a plump and make a great hole in the ground, doing no damage unless they happen to fall into your trench or on to your hat. They burst pretty nearly straight upwards. One landed within 10 yards of me the other day, and only knocked me over and my horse. We both got up and looked at each other, and laughed. It did not even knock the cigarette out of my mouth . . . Our men are splendid, really splendid. One marvels at them. We shall beat those German swine by sticking it out . . .

We took a German Officer and some men prisoners in the wood the other day. One felt hatred for them as one thought of our dead; and as the Officer came by me, I scowled at him, and the men were cursing him. The Officer looked me in the face and saluted me as he passed, and I have never seen a man look so proud and resolute and smart and confident, in his hour of bitterness. It made me feel terribly ashamed of myself . . .

JULIAN GRENFELL

'Into Battle'

> The naked earth is warm with spring,
> And with green grass and bursting trees
> Leans to the sun's gaze glorying,
> And quivers in the sunny breeze;
> And life is colour and warmth and light,
> And a striving evermore for these;
> And he is dead who will not fight;
> And who dies fighting has increase.
>
> The fighting man shall from the sun
> Take warmth, and life from the glowing earth;
> Speed with the light-foot winds to run,
> And with the trees to newer birth;
> And find, when fighting shall be done,
> Great rest, and fullness after dearth.
>
> All the bright company of Heaven
> Hold him in their high comradeship,
> The Dog-Star, and the Sisters Seven,
> Orion's Belt and sworded hip.
>
> The woodland trees that stand together,
> They stand to him each one a friend;
> They gently speak in the windy weather;
> They guide to valley and ridge's end.
>
> The kestrel hovering by day,
> And the little owls that call by night,

Bid him be swift and keen as they,
As keen of ear, as swift of sight.

The blackbird sings to him, 'Brother, brother,
If this be the last song you shall sing,
Sing well, for you may not sing another;
Brother, sing.'

In dreary, doubtful, waiting hours,
Before the brazen frenzy starts,
The horses show him nobler powers;
O patient eyes, courageous hearts!

And when the burning moment breaks,
And all things else are out of mind,
And only joy of battle takes
Him by the throat, and makes him blind,

Through joy and blindness he shall know,
Not caring much to know, that still
Nor lead nor steel shall reach him, so
That it be not the Destined Will.

The thundering line of battle stands,
And in the air death moans and sings;
But Day shall clasp him with strong hands,
And Night shall fold him in soft wings.

F. E. SMITH

'A necessity for five cigars'

How the other half lived. F. E. Smith (later Lord Birkenhead) (1872–1930), one of the outstanding advocates and parliamentarians of his day, was initially in charge of press censorship but then served from 1914–15 as a staff officer with the Indian Corps.

In May 1915 Asquith made him Solicitor General. This plaintive letter to his wife Margaret Furneaux explains his longing for cigars:

> October 21, 1914: Would you send me my waterproof that Marshall Hall gave me? It rains every day and it would be most useful. Also, my angel, do send me from the Stores every 20 (or perhaps 18) days a box of my cigars. I can live, as I am doing, on bully beef. I can drink, as I am doing, cocoa and tea. But I cannot, and I will not, as long as my bank will honour my cheques, wash them down, so to speak, with nothing but a pipe. I can smoke two pipes a day and not more, which leaves me with a necessity for five cigars, or say seven (two to a friend) and honestly the support of my system requires this. This is most important and quite serious. Tell the Stores not to print any indication the boxes are cigars. Have printed yourself some gummed labels as follows:
>
> Army Temperance Society
> Publications Series 9
>
> And put these and nothing else on the outside. These precautions are very necessary, as again as always stolen by the men if they escape the officers.

FRITZ PHILIPPS

Farewell Letter

An agricultural student at Jena University, Fritz Philipps was twenty-five when this farewell letter was written. He was killed seven months later.

> Farewell Letter, only to be opened if I am killed.

I am going with all my heart, freely and willingly, into the war, never doubting but that Germany will bring it to a favourable and victorious end. I wish that there may be no laying down of arms until we have won a real world-victory. I need scarcely say that I hate war in itself, but for that very reason I will fight and take part in this great affair and willingly die, if I can contribute to the transformation of world war into world peace ... Do not have my body brought home even if that is possible; let me lie there where I have fought and fallen. Do not put on any mourning for me; let nobody feel any constraint; but rejoice that you too have been allowed to offer a sacrifice on the altar of the Fatherland.

'KEEP THE HOME FIRES BURNING'

(Music: Ivor Novello; words: Lena Guilbert Ford)

Ivor Novello was only twenty-one and a Royal Naval Air Service pilot when he wrote the tune and the memorable phrase of the chorus of this song in 1914. The words were written by Lena Guilbert Ford, an American poet who was living in London. Novello went on to write songs and West End revues that boosted the morale of Londoners and troops on home leave. After the war he wrote several hit musicals.

There is a snapshot of Ivor Novello in 1918 in Robert Graves's *Goodbye to All That*: 'He and his young stage-friends were all sitting or lying on cushions scattered about the floor. Feeling uncomfortably military, I removed my spurs (I was a temporary field-officer at the time) in case anyone got pricked. Novello had joined the Royal Navy Air Service but, his genius being officially recognized, was allowed to keep the home fires burning until the boys came home.'

They were summoned from the hillside,
They were called in from the glen,

And the country found them ready
At the stirring call for men.
Let no tears add to their hardship,
As the soldiers pass along,
And although your heart is breaking
Make it sing this cheery song.

Chorus:
Keep the Home fires burning,
While your hearts are yearning,
Though your lads are far away they dream of home.
There's a silver lining
Through the dark cloud shining,
Turn the dark cloud inside out,
Till the boys come home.

Overseas there came a pleading,
'Help a Nation in distress!'
And we gave our glorious ladies;
Honour bade us do no less.
For no gallant son of Britain
To a foreign yoke shall bend,
And no Englishman is silent
To the sacred call of Friend.

Chorus:
Keep the Home fires burning (etc.)

CAPTAIN HENRY DILLON

'Out of the darkness a great moan'

In August Captain Dillon had been buoyed up by the British Army's early prowess at Mons. Two months later he was filled with a 'great rage', as he reports in this vivid letter. His letters were passed on to the War Office, which appreciated his power of description. His use of a rifle rather than a sword was noted, suggesting that it would be more useful to arm officers with rifles and teach bayonet exercises.

October 24: The night came on rather misty and dark, and I thought several times of asking for reinforcements, but I collected a lot of rifles off the dead, and loaded them and put them along the parapet instead. All of a sudden about a dozen shells came down and almost simultaneously 2 machine guns and a tremendous rifle fire opened on us. It was the most unholy din. The shells ripped open the parapet and trees came crashing down. However I was well underground and did not care much, but presently the guns stopped, and I knew then that we were for it. I had to look over the top for about 10 minutes however under their infernal maxims before I saw what I was looking for. It came with a suddenness that was the most startling thing I have ever known. The firing stopped, and I had been straining my eyes so for a moment I could not believe them, but fortunately I did not hesitate long. A great grey mass of humanity was charging running for all God would let them straight on to us not 50 yards off, – about as far as the summer house to the coach-house. Everybody's nerves were pretty well on edge as I had warned them what to expect, and as I fired my rifle the rest all went off almost simultaneously. One saw the great mass of Germans quiver. In reality some fell, some fell over them, and others came on. I have never shot so much in such a short time, could not have been more than a few seconds and they were down. Suddenly one man, I expect an officer, jumped up and came on; I fired and missed, seized the next rifle and dropped him a few yards off. Then the whole lot came on again and it was the most critical moment of my life. Twenty yards more and they would have been over us in thousands, but our fire must have been fearful, and at the very last moment they did the most foolish thing they possibly could have done. Some of the leading people turned to the left for some reason, and they all followed like a great flock of sheep. We did not lose much time I can give you my oath. My right hand is one huge bruise from banging the bolt up and down. I don't think one could have missed at the distance and just for one short minute or two we poured the ammunition into them in boxfuls. My rifles were red hot at the finish, I know, and that was the end of that battle for me.

The firing died down and out of the darkness a great moan came. People with their arms and legs off trying to crawl away; others who could not move gasping out their last moments with the cold night wind biting into their broken bodies and lurid red glare of a farm house showing up clumps of grey devils killed by the men on my left further down. A weird awful scene; some of them would raise themselves on one arm or crawl a little distance, silhouetted as black as ink against the red glow of the fire. Well, I suppose if there is a God, Emperor Bill will have to come to book some day. When one thinks of the misery of these wounded and later on wives, mothers and friends, and to think that this great battle where there may have been half a million on either side, is only on a front of about 25 miles, and that this sort of thing is now going on a front of nearly 400. To think that this man could have saved it all.

The proposition is almost too vast to get a grip of. It is ruining thousands of lives, from the Bay of Biscay through France, Germany, Russia, India, and right to Siberia, poor wives and people are waiting to hear. It really is the greatest calamity the world has ever seen. Our losses in the battle were 6 officers killed and five wounded, and we have not had time to find out how many men, but I should think about 400. There are not many of the original lot left now.

Our Colonel is all right. I am the only Captain and the rest subalterns. It all fills me with a great rage. I know I have got to stop my bullet some time, and it is merely a question of where it hits one whether it is dead or wounded. We fight every day and I am in support today in a trench with the shells coming along at intervals. The order may come at any minute to support an attack which is going on, and then it is just a chance. I don't care one farthing as far as I am concerned, but the whole thing is an outrage on civilisation. The whole of this beautiful country devastated. Broken houses, broken bodies, blood, filth and ruin everywhere. Can any unending everlasting Hell fire for the Kaiser, his son, and the party who caused this war repair the broken bodies and worse broken hearts which are being made? – Being made this very minute within a few hundred yards of where I am sitting.

Alfred Edward Housman

Epitaph on Army of Mercenaries

Alfred Edward Housman (1859–1936) was educated at Bromsgrove School and St John's College, Oxford. He was professor of Latin at University College London, and then Cambridge. His most famous poem is 'A Shropshire Lad'. He wrote this epitaph after the First Battle of Ypres:

These, in the days when heaven was falling,
The hour when earth's foundations fled,
Followed their mercenary calling
And took their wages and are dead.

Their shoulders held the sky suspended;
They stood, and the earth's foundations stay;
When God abandoned, these defended,
And saved the sum of things for pay.

RUDOLF BINDING

'An endless reproach to mankind'

Rudolf Binding's sketches from the battlefront were written contemporaneously and later published as *A Fatalist at War*. He took the field with one of the Jungdeutschland divisions in October. The following was written in Flanders the next month:

> November 22: As matters stand now, not only here but all along the line, both we and the enemy have so crippled ourselves by in-fighting that we cannot get in a blow properly, we cannot get the momentum for a thrust; we get in our own way with every movement of any importance. Once again I observe that, here at least, the art of war is not noticeable. It may be an incredible achievement to create this endless, unbroken line from the Alps to the sea as a monstrous whole; but it is not my idea of strategy . . .
>
> Only a month ago this country might have been called rich; there were cattle and pigs in plenty. Now it is empty; not a wine-cellar in any town that has not been requisitioned for the Germans. Not a grocer, corn-chandler, or dairy but must sell their goods to the Germans only. We have taken every horse, every car; all the petrol, all the railway-trucks, all the houses, coal, paraffin, and electricity, have been devoted to our exclusive use. I buy all the necessities and comforts I want for myself and my man, give the shopman a requisition order signed by myself, and he bows me out. I take fifteen bottles of the best claret and a few of old port from the cellars of Chevalier van der B – they only drink wine and milk in this country and gin in the pubs – and do not even tip the butler two franks. I take the oats and straw, the pigs, cattle, chickens, vegetables, tinned fruit, potatoes, and apples that belong to the inhabitants who have fled or been evacuated.

They do not even get a chit to give them any formal right to claim. Whom could I give it to?

If we were making rapid progress and there were problems to be solved that claimed one's whole energy one might not think backwards so much. As it is the horizon is bounded in front as with a mighty wall that neither deeds nor thoughts can surmount, and only behind us can we see a little patch of blue sky.

November 27: When one sees the wasting, burning villages and towns, plundered cellars and attics in which the troops have pulled everything to pieces in the blind instinct of self-preservation, dead or half-starved animals, cattle bellowing in the sugar-beet fields, and then corpses, corpses, and corpses, streams of wounded one after another – then everything becomes senseless, a lunacy, a horrible bad joke of peoples and their history, an endless reproach to mankind, a negation of all civilization, killing all belief in the capacity of mankind and men for progress, a desecration of what is holy, so that one feels that all human beginnings are doomed in this war.

We will probably lie here for a few days more. The battle, which has lasted nine times twenty-four hours without effecting a decision, has immobilized both Fronts close to one another. Now forces will be massed for the attack. Our Army has Ypres as its objective. There is no doubt that the English and French troops would already have been beaten by trained troops. But these young fellows we have only just trained are too helpless, particularly when the officers have been killed. Our light infantry battalion, almost all Marburg students, the best troops we have as regards musketry, have suffered terribly from enemy shell-fire. In the next division, just such young souls, the intellectual flower of Germany, went singing into an attack on Langemarck, just as vain and just as costly.

George Adam, *The Times*

A belt of misery and ruin

As Paris correspondent of *The Times* George Adam made the first of several visits to the fronts in France and Belgium in November. His book *Behind the Scenes at the Front*, from which this extract is taken, was published in 1915:

> In the course of my journeyings along the front I have seen enough with my own eyes, and through the lens of the aerial photographer, to be able to state with certainty that there runs right across Western Europe, for some 500 miles, a belt some ten miles wide of misery and ruin: of villages pounded to pieces by high explosives, burned to charred fragments by incendiary shells; of towns with battered squares and crumbling churches; of isolated, unroofed, desolate farmhouses. In attempting to convey an impression of this ten-mile belt I shall be careful only to describe what I myself have seen; and if my descriptions differ from those which have already been published, they do not call into question the accuracy of other records. To those who witnessed the flames shooting up over the roof of Rheims Cathedral there can have been no doubt at the time that the cathedral was destroyed. A very eminent French statesman informed me, indeed, that it had been razed to the ground. Seen a week or so after the fire had consumed the outer timber roofing, both descriptions seemed to be very far from the reality. To use the word 'destruction' in giving an account of the state of the cathedral is to leave one's vocabulary beggared in recording the work of the Germans in many other towns and villages. The mark of the incendiary, the havoc of shell, is to be seen in much greater completeness (than at Rheims) at Ypres and the villages we still defend in Belgium.

There are many villages so battered and smashed as to have, perhaps, no more than the framework of two or three houses left standing, where the peasants and farmers, on their return to the village after the passage of the Germans, have for a time been unable to locate with certainty the sites of their own homes. In these spots something has been destroyed which it will be difficult to replace. Sentiment, association, and interest, which centred on those villages, have been scattered as though they were dust before the wind. The tragedies there did not afford the grandiose spectacle of the red flames shooting up over Rheims; they did not wring a cry of horror from the world; they were intimate, small, and infinitely sorrowful. The glories of the rose-window of Rheims may have belonged to all the world, but the clock which was snatched by a marauding Bavarian from an old woman's cottage at Vassincourt meant more to her than the whole of Rheims Cathedral to the lovers of beauty all the world over.

In Clermont-en-Argonne the Germans carried their work of incendiarism to the highest pitch of cruelty. The town, a stronghold of medieval days, lies at the eastern entrance to the Argonne. The opening of railway communication deprived the road which it defended of its strategical importance, and the town, after long years of decay, had just begun to realize, when the war broke out, that its picturesque position in the heart of one of the loveliest stretches of forest country in France, its terraced streets, had a value to the traveller in search of beauty. It had its little devices for spreading the fame of the loveliness of Argonne through France; its 1,200 inhabitants hoped at a later date to go still farther afield, and bring the foreigner to admire its charms. Then the foreigner came, in the shape of the 121st and 122nd Würtemberg Regiments, under the command of General von Durach and Prince Wittgenstein.

My own observation leads me to believe that the Prussians have been completely outdone by the Bavarians and the Würtemberg troops in the genial German work of sacking and incendiarism. It would be unfair to place upon the two German noblemen who were in command at Clermont the responsibility for beginning the scenes which attended the sack of the town. It was carried out without method, and apparently without instructions. A brutish soldier, having made himself a cup of coffee over a methylated spirit stove, apparently thought that it would be rather amusing to burn the house down. He started by upsetting the stove, and then, presumably anxious for more light, obtained the assistance of one or two kindred souls in spreading it. The idea seemed good, and soon all the fire-lighting machinery of the German Army was in full blast. The place was besprinkled with the little black patches of gunpowder which have figured in nearly all the big German bonfires, and with petrol. The kind-hearted Würtemberger, so far as can be ascertained, was good enough to allow the inhabitants to leave their burning houses. They were, at any rate, not shot down as they ran for refuge. While the town below was getting well alight, some earnest churchgoers climbed up the hill to the beautiful old church. One with a musical soul sat down to the organ while his comrades danced crazily up and down the aisles. This did not end their fun. A church, of course, could not be allowed to escape. Having set fire to their dancing-hall, they hurried down the hill again to join in the pillaging that was going on.

I found one of the inhabitants of Clermont. She was an old woman, scavenging along the ruined street for any little object which might go to the rebuilding of her home. As my car stopped, she raised herself slowly from the heap of stones over which she was bending, and turned the uncurious face of utter misery towards me. The heap she had been turning over was her house. She had been proud of it, with all the pride of the old peasant woman whose savings in life were represented by a son with the army, the stone and mortar of her dwelling-place, her handwoven linen, two clocks, a breviary with a silver clasp, and a few sticks of furniture. She had at first thought that her decent old age had won her favour in the Würtemberger's eye, for before putting the torch to her home they had removed the furniture, the clocks, the breviary, and the linen. But once the fire was well alight she saw her mistake, as the soldiers went through the pile of her household belongings in the street, tucked the clocks under their arms, tore the silver clasp from the breviary, and then threw the book back among the furniture, which before they left was blazing away merrily. They appear to have been on the move, and fearful lest they might not be able to return to complete their work, as they passed the baskets of linen they shoved their bayonets through them.

'KEEP YOUR HEAD DOWN, ALLEYMAN'

(Tune: 'Hold Your Hand Out Naughty Boy' by C. W. Murphy and Worton David)

'Alleyman' was the soldiers' version of the French 'Allemand', a German, in this parody of the music-hall hit of 1914.

The original song:

Hold your hand out naughty boy,
Hold your hand out naughty boy!
Last night in the pale moonlight,
I saw you! I saw you!
You were spooning in the park
With a nice girl in the dark,
And you said you'd never kissed a girl before
Hold your hand out naughty boy.

The soldiers' parody:

Keep your head down, Alleyman,
Keep your head down, Alleyman,
Last night, in the pale moonlight
We saw you, we saw you,
You were mending broken wire
When we opened rapid fire,
If you want to see your father in that Fatherland
Keep your head down, Alleyman.

THE TIMES, 10 NOVEMBER, PERSONAL COLUMN

'Pauline – Alas, it cannot be. But I will dash into the great venture with all that pride and spirit an ancient race has given me . . .'

MÈRE MARIE GEORGINE

'Crucifying people'

Some commentators were sceptical about the truth of German atrocities in Belgium. But this powerful account by Mother Marie Georgine, of the Ursuline Convent at Tildanck in Wespelaer, suggests that they did occur. The previous entry in the nun's diary reports that a curé had been found in a grave with four or five civilians, stripped entirely and with his nose and ears cut off.

November 24th: Yesterday we received news for one of the lay sisters that her two brothers, a brother-in-law, a sister-in-law, two children in one family, one a baby of a few days old and one child in another had all been killed during the passage of the troops at Tamines in Hainault. It seems that the people had taken refuge in the Church and the soldiers made the men come out shooting them all after which they committed further horrors. In all about 6[00] to 700 people were killed. The women and young girls were stripped and then made to march in between the troops. The Curé was crucified against a wall and when he complained of thirst they amused themselves by shooting him down the middle so that he had a row of bullet holes like buttons in the middle of his body. They seem to have a fiendish delight in crucifying people especially priests. A woman was here the other day who saw one crucified near Namur and one of the Haecht nuns who was taken prisoner also saw the body of a priest who had evidently been crucified from the holes in hands and feet. I was told the other day that they had crucified children against doors and walls at Charleroi, but that I cannot vouch for. They had pierced the hands of the Curé of Bruken, but do not seem to have crucified him. Perhaps he expired before they had time to do more. From all accounts they played pitch and toss with his body flinging it in and out of the cart as they went along; but it is impossible to know all the details of the treatment he was subjected to. At the beginning of the War one of our workmen was shot on his way here and as they saw he was not yet dead from his movements, they trampled on him with their great boots and then buried him (still alive) where he lay. They did the same to a young girl at Wespelaer and burnt the house over the head of an old man and his daughter. Half the horrors they have committed will never be known even after the War, for people are buried all over the place and half the time it is not known who they are and where they come from.

ALAN SEEGER

Table d'hôte

Alan Seeger, the 'American Rupert Brooke', who was to write the best-known American poem of the war ('I have a rendezvous with Death'; see page 144), graduated from Harvard in 1912 and went to France to learn how to write poetry. He joined the French Foreign Legion in August.

In this letter he describes the importance to the French, even in war, of eating:

> We are not, in fact, leading the life of men at all, but that of animals, living in holes in the ground and only showing our heads outside to fight and to feed.
>
> Amid the monotony of this kind of existence the matter of eating assumes an importance altogether amusing to one who gives it only very secondary consideration in time of peace. It is in fact the supreme if not the only event of the day. In France the soldier is very well cared for in this respect. In cantonment and under all normal conditions he receives ordinarily coffee and an ample day's ration of good bread the first thing in the morning; then at 10 and at 5 he is served with soup, meat and a vegetable, excellently cooked, coffee and wine, not to mention such little occasional luxuries as chocolate, confitures, brandy, etc.
>
> In the trenches this programme is necessarily modified by the distance from the kitchens and the impossibility of passing back and forth in daylight on account of the artillery fire. When we first came to the trenches we made the mistake of having our kitchen too near in the woods. Whether it was the smoke that gave it away or one of the hostile aeroplanes that buzz continually over our heads the Germans soon found its range and with one man killed and half a dozen wounded the cooking brigade was forced to move back to the château and take up its quarters at a point in the woods at three or four kilometres from the line of the trenches.
>
> Since then the matter of *ravitaillement* is arranged as follows: every morning at 3 o'clock a squad of men leaves the trenches and returns before daybreak with the day's provisions – bread and coffee, cheese and preserved foods, such as cold meat, pâtés, sardines, etc. The ration is very small,

but the nature of life in the trenches is not such as to sharpen one's appetite. In the evening another squad leaves immediately after sundown. Every one waits eagerly to hear the clink of the pails returning in the dark. It is a good meal, a soup, or stew of some kind, as hot as can be expected in view of the distance from the kitchen fires, coffee and wine, and we all gather about with our little tins for the distribution.

These nightly trips to the kitchen are sometimes a matter of considerable difficulty, for frequent changes of position often find us unfamiliar with the course of the paths through the woods, which are newly cut, impassably muddy and ill defined. Notwithstanding the danger of going astray in swamp and thicket and the labor of bringing back a heavy load in the dark it is considered a privilege to be assigned to this duty because it gives a little activity to relieve the day's tedium. Single file, with rifle strapped to shoulders, we flounder on, wet to the ankles, the black forest all around, each man carrying half a dozen canteens besides his other burdens. Our water comes from a spring down by the château.

To supplement the regular rations with little luxuries such as butter, cheese, preserves and especially chocolate is a matter that occupies more of the young soldier's thoughts than the invisible enemy. Our corporal told us the other day that there wasn't a man in the squad who wouldn't exchange his rifle for a jar of jam. It is true that we think more about securing these trifles than we do about keeping our rifles clean. Nor is it an easy matter to get such things. The country where we are now has been thoroughly fought over, so that the poor inhabitants and their stocks of goods have suffered severely from the continual passing of troops in action. The countryside is stripped as a field by locusts.

ALFRED CHATER

Camaraderie

The Old Harrovian Alfred Chater was a twenty-four-year-old captain with the 2nd Gordon Highlanders. He wrote this description of the occasional sense of shared comradeship between the two sides in a letter to his girlfriend, Joyce Francis:

> It's not so very cold up in the trenches and we are allowed to have fires in braziers although we don't get an opportunity of getting very much fuel. Things up there are very quiet – in my part of the line the trenches are only 50 or 60 yards apart in some places, and we can hear the Germans talking. They often shout to us in English and we respond with cries of 'waiter'! There was one fellow who had a fire with a tin chimney, sticking up over the parapet, and our men were having shots at it with their rifles. After such a shot the German waved a stick or rang a bell according to whether we hit the chimney or not! There are lots of amusing incidents up there and altogether we have quite a cheery time, our worst trouble is the wet and mud which is knee-deep in some places.

JAMES CAMERON

Attack on Scarborough

On 14 December British naval intelligence learned that the German 1st Cruiser Squadron had left the River Jade behind Heligoland with four battle cruisers, five light cruisers and three flotillas of destroyers. Cameron describes the first attack on Britain since Napoleon:

> The morning of December 16 broke reluctantly through a thick, pervasive mist that was very nearly a fog; such sun as there was fought weakly and was lost behind the dank grey

haze and smirr from the east. On the cliffs beyond Scarborough
the Chief Coastguard Officer, whose name was Arthur Dean,
glanced seaward at exactly five minutes past eight; to his astonishment he saw two cruisers loom in through the vapour from
behind the Castle Hill towards South Bay. When they were at
six hundred yards' range from the Castle itself they opened fire
with all guns on the starboard side. They made a passage at
half-speed across South Bay, deliberately and without interfer-
ence of any kind, firing as they went; then they turned on their
wakes and returned, firing now from the port side.

Scarborough, with its remote and detached population of
elderly ladies, retired gentlemen, hoteliers, boarding-house
keepers, and the tradesmen and commerce to serve them,
was breakfasting, opening its shutters, reading its post, going
to school, when it was abruptly hurled headlong into the
war by death screaming in from the sea. The coast-guard
had no time to sound any warning when the first shells
whipped into the town and tore it down in sections with
horrifying and unbecoming noise – disintegrating half of the
Grand Hotel on the cliff head, carrying away the gable end
of the Town Hall, crashing into shop-fronts and bedrooms,
bringing blood and destruction to hundreds of those both
too young to comprehend what could conceivably be the
reason, or too old to care. The boarding-houses on St
Nicholas Cliff collapsed, a whole row of cottages in Stalby
Road became brick and rubble in a moment. Mr John Hall,
J.P., was dressing for the day when a shell howled through
his walls and blew him, and his bedroom with him, into
limbo. Out to sea, but only just out to sea, the cruisers
coughed their missiles into the awakening town, and the
mists swirling around them grew thicker with gun-smoke.

At almost exactly the same hour two cruisers appeared off
Whitby, twenty miles to the north. Their first shell smashed
into a field behind the Abbey, on the East Cliff. It had probably been aimed at the railway station, which lay at a bend

of the harbour east of the town. Another demolished the west bay of the Abbey. A great smoking gap appeared in the houses of Esk Terrace. People swarmed into the streets, at once aghast and inquisitive; even while the whine and thud of the shells continued the children of Grimsby were busy collecting warm and abrasive fragments of shrapnel.

The same thing happened at Hartlepool, yet another twenty miles up the North Sea coast. There the Germans had the uncommon fluke to hit the gasworks, which with one explosion deprived the town of all artificial light (all that day they lined up for the telegraph-counter in the post office, temporarily fitted with oil-lamps, to cable relations of their safety). Furthermore they sent a casual shell clean through the local branch of Lloyds Bank.

The German cruisers kept this up for exactly half an hour, then quietly turned eastwards and homewards into the deepening grey mist, unchallenged. As they left they strewed mines behind them. (When, shortly afterwards, they were located by the Royal Navy they were not removed, but plotted and actually reinforced as a screen, leaving a fifteen-mile gap between Whitby and Scarborough.)

Behind them, the three towns were left picking up their dead and wounded and staring humbly at the torn masonry, at the buildings opened up like dolls' houses, at the shattered streets. Nothing in England like this had ever been known before. The bombardment of civil towns was a conception absolutely new, not to be grasped or understood in a long half-hour of bewilderment and shock.

In those thirty minutes nearly five hundred people of the three towns had been quickly killed.

By now, too late, the hunt was up. The 3rd Battle Squadron was rushed from the Forth to prevent the Germans' escape northward; cruisers and destroyers of the Harwich Striking Force set out to join the 2nd Battle Squadron. Commodore Keyes, the British Naval Commander, was ordered to take his submarines from their stations off Terschelling into the Heligoland Bight to intercept the enemy on their way back. Between the Germans and Germany were four British battle-cruisers and six of the most powerful battleships in the world.

Then the weather, already deteriorating fast, closed in; visibility dropped from seven thousand yards at sea to five, to four thousand. The British fleet groped desperately round in the mist; by and by the visibility diminished to a thousand yards. The German raiding vessels slipped scatheless home.

PRIVATE BOB HARKER

The Mud

Throughout the war the mud of the trenches was a constant subject in soldiers' letters and diaries. Private Harker served with the 1st Battalion, the Honourable Artillery Company, and was training to be an officer. He was killed by a sniper in March 1915.

The men have to stand in mud and water in some places up to their knees continuously and other fellows get a short length perhaps not quite so bad. We had a lot of very heavy rain and were wet both above and below. The mud up there is extraordinary. It has a lot of clay and mineral matter in it and it goes into a thick paste like bird lime with tremendous suction in which feet stick. Five men in another section got stuck and bogged in a communication trench up to the firing line and it was 7 hours before we got 3 of them out. I volunteered to go back and get some spades and was very glad to find the way with little trouble, another fellow came with me. After getting the spades we could not dig the stuff with them and got the men out by kneeling on faggots out of a hedge and scraping the mud out away from their legs and feet with our hands. Luckily we got them out before dawn otherwise (as the trench had fallen in and was enfiladed by the German trenches) they would have been in great danger in daylight of being shot. Four of us tugged at each man.

The mud sticks on to one's clothes, overcoat, trousers and equipment in half-inches of depth and we have almost double the weight to carry, it is almost impossible to keep one's rifle in working order as it all gets coated and clogged. And it takes hard work for 2 days to get all shipshape after our return to rest billets.

THE CHRISTMAS TRUCE

As the three following accounts demonstrate, the Christmas truce of 1914 was perhaps the most extraordinary event of the war. The account of events on Christmas Eve by Sergeant A. Lovell of the 3rd Battalion, the Rifle Brigade, was published on the front page of the London *Evening News* in early January. Captain Alfred Chater of the Gordons and Captain Sir Edward Hulse of the Scots Guards, educated at Eton and Balliol College, Oxford, and killed in action in March 1915 at the age of twenty-five, describe the events of Christmas Day and Boxing Day.

SERGEANT A. LOVELL

Christmas Eve

Last night as I sat in my little dugout, writing, my chum came bursting in upon me with: 'Bob! Hark at 'em.' And I listened. From the German trenches came the sound of music and singing. My chum continued: 'They've got Christmas trees all along the top of their trenches! Never saw such a sight.'

I got up to investigate. Climbing the parapet, I saw a sight which I shall remember to my dying day. Right along the whole of the line were hung paper lanterns and illuminations of every description, many of them in such positions as to suggest that they were hung upon Christmas trees. And as I stood in wonder a rousing song came over to us; at first the words were indistinguishable, then, as the song was repeated again and again, we realized that we were listening to 'The Watch on the Rhine'. Our boys answered with a cheer, while a neighbouring regiment sang lustily the National Anthem. Some were for shooting the lights away, but almost at the first shot there came a shout in really good English, 'Stop shooting!' Then began a series of answering shouts from trench to trench. It was incredible. 'Hallo! Hallo! you English, we wish to speak.' And everyone began to speak at once. Some were rational, others the reverse of complimentary. Eventually some sort of order obtained, and lo! A party of our men got out from the trenches and invited the Germans to meet them halfway and talk.

And together in the searchlight they stood, Englishman and German, chatting and smoking cigarettes together midway between the lines. A rousing cheer went up from friend and foe alike. The group was too far away from me to hear what was said, but presently we heard a cheery 'Good night. A Merry Christmas and a Happy New Year to you all', with which the parties returned to their respective trenches.

After this we remained the whole night through singing with the enemy song for song.

CAPTAIN ALFRED CHATER

Christmas Day

Dearest Mother,
I am writing this in the trenches in my 'dug out' – with a wood fire going and plenty of straw it is rather cosy although it is freezing hard and real Christmas weather.

I think I have seen one of the most extraordinary sights today that anyone has ever seen. About 10 o'clock this morning I was peeping over the parapet when I saw a German, waving his arms, and presently two of them got out of their trenches and came towards ours – we were just going to fire on them when we saw they had no rifles so one of our men went out to meet them and in about two minutes the ground between the two lines of trenches was swarming with men and officers of both sides, shaking hands and wishing each other a Happy Christmas. This continued for about half an hour when most of the men were ordered back to the trenches. For the rest of the day nobody has fired a shot and the men have been wandering about at will on the top of the parapet and carrying straw and firewood about in the open. We have also had joint burial parties with a service for some dead – some German and some ours – who were lying out between the lines. Some of our officers were taking groups of English and German soldiers. This extraordinary truce has been quite impromptu – there was no previous arrangement and of course it had been decided that there was not to be any cessation of hostilities.

I went out myself and shook hands with several of their officers and men, from what I gathered most of them would be as glad to get home again as we should. We have had our pipes playing all day and everyone has been wandering about in the open unmolested but not of course as far as the enemy's lines. The truce will probably go on until someone is foolish enough to let off his rifle – we nearly messed it up this after-noon, by one of our fellows letting off his rifle skywards by mistake but they did not seem to notice it so it did not matter.

Boxing Day
27th: I am writing this back in billets – the same business continued yesterday and we had another parley with the Germans in the middle we exchanged cigarettes and auto-graphs and some more people took photos. I don't know how long it will go on for – I believe it was supposed to stop yesterday but we can hear no firing going on along the front today except a little distant shelling. We are, at any rate having another truce on New Year's Day as the Germans

want to see how the photos come out! Yesterday was lovely in the morning and I went for several quite long walks about the lines. It was difficult to realise what that means but of course in the ordinary way there is not a sign of life above ground and everyone who puts his head up gets shot at. It is really very extraordinary that this sort of thing should happen in a war in which there is so much bitterness and ill-feeling. The Germans in this part of the line are certainly sportsmen if they are nothing else.

CAPTAIN SIR EDWARD HAMILTON WESTROW HULSE, BART

Flanders
28/12/14
Dearest Mother
We stood to arms as usual at 6.30 a.m. on the 25th, and I noticed that there was not much shooting; this gradually died down, and by 8 a.m. there was no shooting at all, except for a few shots on our left (Border Regt.). At 8.30 a.m. I was looking out, and saw four Germans leave their trenches and come towards us; I told two of my men to go and meet them, *unarmed* (as the Germans were unarmed), and to see that they did not pass the halfway line. We were 350–400 yards apart at this point. My fellows were not very keen, not knowing what was up, so I went out alone, and met Barry, one of our ensigns, also coming out from another part of the line. By the time we got to them, they were ¾ of the way over, and much too near our barbed wire, so I moved them back. They were three private soldiers and a stretcher-bearer, and their spokesman started off by saying that he thought it only right to come over and wish us a happy Christmas, and trusted us implicitly to keep the truce. He came from Suffolk, where he had left his best girl and a 3½ h.p. motor-bike! He

told me he could not get a letter to the girl, and wanted to send one through me. I made him write out a postcard in front of me, in English, and I sent it off that night.

They protested that they had no feeling of enmity towards us at all, but that everything lay with their authorities, and that being soldiers they had to obey. I believe that they were speaking the truth when they said this, and that they never wished to fire a shot again. They said that unless directly ordered, they were not going to shoot again until we did . . .

On my return at 10 a.m. I was surprised to hear a hell of a din going on, and not a single man left in my trenches; they were completely denuded (against my orders), and nothing lived! I heard strains of '*Tipperary*' floating down the breeze, swiftly followed by a tremendous burst of '*Deutschland über Alles*' and as I got to my own Coy. H.-qrs. dug-out, I saw, to my amazement, not only a crowd of about 150 British and Germans at the half-way house which I had appointed opposite my lines, but six or seven such crowds, all the way down our lines, extending towards the 8th Division on our right. I bustled out and asked if there were any German officers in my crowd, and the noise died down (as this time I was myself in my own cap and badges of rank).

I found two, but had to talk to them through an interpreter, as they could neither talk English nor French . . . I explained to them that strict orders must be maintained as to meeting half-way, and everyone unarmed; and we both agreed not to fire until the other did, thereby creating a complete deadlock and armistice (if strictly observed) . . .

Meanwhile Scots and Huns were fraternizing in the most genuine possible manner. Every sort of souvenir was exchanged, addresses given and received, photos of families shown, etc. One of our fellows offered a German a cigarette; the German said, 'Virginian?' Our fellow said, 'Aye, straight-cut': the German said, 'No thanks, I only smoke Turkish!' (Sort of 10/- a hundred me!) It gave us all a good laugh.

A German N.C.O. with the Iron Cross, – gained, he told me, for conspicuous skill in sniping, – started his fellows off on some marching tune. When they had done I set the note for *'The Boys of Bonnie Scotland, where the heather and the bluebells grow'*, and so we went on singing everything from *'Good King Wenceslas'* down to the ordinary Tommies' song, and ended up with *'Auld Lang Syne'*, which we all, English, Scots, Irish, Prussian, Wurtembergers, etc., joined in. It was absolutely astounding, and if I had seen it on a cinematograph film I should have sworn that it was faked! . . .

From foul rain and wet, the weather had cleared up the night before to a sharp frost, and it was a perfect day, everything white, and the silence seemed extraordinary, after the usual din. From all sides birds seemed to arrive, and we hardly ever see a bird generally. Later in the day I fed about 50 sparrows outside my dug-out, which shows how complete the silence and quiet was.

On my left was the bit of ground over which we attacked on the 18th, and here the lines are only from 85 to 100 yards apart.

The Border regiment were occupying this section on Christmas Day and Giles Loder, our Adjutant, went down there with a party that morning on hearing of the friendly demonstrations in front of my Coy., to see if he could come to an agreement about our dead, who were still lying out between the trenches. The trenches are so close at this point, that of course each side had to be far stricter. Well he found an extremely pleasant and superior stamp of German officer, who arranged to bring all our dead to the half-way line. We took them over there, and buried 29 exactly half way between the two lines. Giles collected all personal effects, pay-books and identity discs, but was stopped by the

Germans when he told some men to bring in the rifles; all rifles lying on their side of the half-way line they kept carefully! . . .

They apparently treated our prisoners well, and did all they could for our wounded. This officer kept on pointing to our dead and saying, 'Les Braves, c'est bien dommage' . . .

When George heard of it he went down to that section and talked to the nice officer and gave him a scarf. That same evening a German orderly came to the half-way line, and brought a pair of warm, woolly gloves as a present in return for George.

RICHARD ALDINGTON

The Public-school Boy

Almost without exception, and certainly early in the war, British officers were recruited from the dozen most famous public schools. Already in this anthology, two writers (Julian Grenfell and Edward Hulse) were from Eton and Balliol, another from Harrow (Alfred Chater) and another (Rupert Brooke) from Rugby. They had a fierce loyalty to their schools and a fierce pride in being British.

They were patriots in a way that many today would find incomprehensible. 'Never such innocence again', Philip Larkin wrote decades later.

Richard Aldington (1892–1962) was embittered by his experience of the war and expressed that bitterness in his 1929 novel *Death of a Hero*, from which this extract about the 'usual' English public-school boy is taken. Winterbourne represents Aldington.

Evans was the usual English public-school boy, amazingly ignorant, amazingly inhibited, and yet 'decent' and good-humoured. He had a strength of character which enabled him to carry out what he had been taught was his duty to do. He accepted and obeyed every English middle-class prejudice and taboo. What the English middle classes thought and did was right, and what anybody else thought and did was wrong. He was contemptuous of all foreigners. He appeared to have read nothing but Kipling, Jeffery Farnol, Elinor Glyn, and the daily newspapers. He disapproved of Elinor Glyn, as too 'advanced'. He didn't care about Shakespeare, had never heard of the Russian Ballets, but liked to 'see a good show'. He thought *Chu Chin Chow* was the greatest play ever produced, and the Indian Love Lyrics the most beautiful songs in the world. He thought that Parisians lived by keeping brothels, and spent most of their time in them. He thought that all Chinamen took opium, then got drunk, and ravished white slaves abducted from England. He thought Americans were a sort of inferior Colonials, regrettably divorced from that finest of all institutions, the British Empire. He rather disapproved of 'Society', which he considered 'fast', but he held that Englishmen should never mention the fastness of Society, since it might 'lower our prestige' in the eyes of 'all these messy foreigners'. He was ineradicably convinced of his superiority to the 'lower classes', but where that superiority lay Winterbourne failed to discover. Evans was an 'educated' pre-War public-school boy, which means that he remembered half a dozen Latin tags, could mumble a few ungrammatical phrases in French, knew a little of the history of England, and had a 'correct' accent. He had been taught to respect all women as if they were his mother; would therefore have fallen an easy prey to the first tart who came along, and probably have married her. He was a good runner, had played at stand-off half for his school and won his colours at cricket. He could play fives, squash rackets, golf, tennis, water-polo, bridge, and vingt-et-un, which he called 'pontoon'. He disapproved of baccarat, roulette, and *petits chevaux*, but always went in for the Derby sweepstake. He could ride a horse, drive a motor-car, and regretted that he had been rejected by the Flying Corps.

He had no doubts whatever about the War. What England did must be right, and England had declared war on Germany. Therefore, Germany must be wrong. Evans propounded this somewhat primitive argument to Winterbourne with a condescending air, as if he were imparting some irrefutable piece of knowledge to a regrettably ignorant inferior. Of course, after ten minutes' conversation with Evans, Winterbourne saw the kind of man he was, and realised that he must continue to dissimulate with him as with every one else in the Army. However, he could not resist the temptation to bewilder him a little sometimes. It was quite impossible to do anything more. Evans possessed that British rhinoceros equipment of mingled ignorance, self-confidence, and complacency which is triple-armed against all the shafts of the mind. And yet Winterbourne could not help liking the man. He was exasperatingly stupid, but he was honest, he was kindly, he was conscientious, he could obey orders and command obedience in others, he took pains to look after his men. He could be implicitly relied upon to lead a hopeless attack and to maintain a desperate defence to the very end. There were thousands and tens of thousands like him.

R. C. Sherriff

The Public-school Boys

When R. C. Sherriff (1896–1975) was interviewed for the Army in 1914 he was asked what school he had been to. Then he was told it was not a public school, even though it had been founded by Queen Elizabeth in 1567. He was recruited to the ranks and it was 'a long hard pull' before he was accepted as an officer. His play *Journey's End*, the classic drama of the Great War, ran for 594 performances when it was staged at the Savoy Theatre in 1928. Sherriff writes here, in an extract from the fiftieth-anniversary anthology *Promise of Greatness*, about the leadership qualities of the boys from the public schools:

Without raising the public school boy officers onto a pedestal it can be said with certainty that it was they who played the vital part in keeping the men good-humoured and obedient in the face of their interminable ill treatment and well-nigh insufferable ordeals.

The colonels of battalions were mainly professional soldiers, survivors of the old Regular Army. They were good men who shared the hardships of the fighting soldier. But the junior officers – the commanders of companies and lieutenants in charge of platoons – were predominantly from the public schools, and it was they who lived in close personal touch with the soldiers in the ranks. They led them, not through military skill, for no military skill was needed. They led them from personal example, from their reserves of patience and good humour and endurance. They won the trust and respect of their men, not merely through their willingness to share the physical privations, but through an understanding of their spiritual loneliness. Many of the younger ones had never been away from home before. Their lives had been spent in a simple and secluded way with their parents, young brothers and sisters, a few intimate friends from the neighbourhood who shared their interests and recreations, including perhaps the girl they were courting. They knew little or nothing of the world beyond, and they found no true comradeship with the strange men that the war had chosen for them to serve with. They were desperately homesick, with a pathetic yearning for their own people in the towns and villages of England.

These boys were only happy, perhaps, when they were on sentry duty alone, with the moon and the stars for their companions. It was the duty of the officer on watch to visit these sentry posts. If you could break through their shyness, they would sometimes talk to you of their homes, and you could lead them on to tell you of their work and small achievements, their hopes and ambitions if, one day, they returned. You might be able to help them see a glimmer of light at the end of the dark tunnel that enclosed them.

It was on such quiet nights of communion between man and officer that the foundations of final victory were laid, not in the planning rooms at Army headquarters. And it was in this way that the public school boy officer could play so true a part.

When a man surrendered himself to the Army machine, his individuality was exchanged for a number. When he put on his uniform and wrapped up his civilian clothes, he wrapped up with them his personal initiative and the right to think. 'Think!' shouted a sergeant to a recruit who had had the effrontery to use the word. 'For a common soldier it's mutiny to think!'

But the common soldier naturally expected something in return for all that he surrendered. He expected leadership, an officer who thought for him – better still an officer who thought with him.

The general had lost all personal touch with the common soldier. He lived in a remote French chateau miles behind the line. The soldiers never saw him, never even knew his name. If some of them had come around the trenches, talked to the men in their dugouts, made the men realize that they all were in it together, then they might have become legendary heroes, as men like Montgomery and Alexander became to the soldiers of the Second World War. As it was, the generals gave nothing to the common soldier to gain his respect or affection. They were a menace lurking in the background, always concocting a new devil's brew with the same old poisonous ingredients.

And so the common soldier turned instinctively to his own company officers for the leadership that he required, to the young officers who lived with him and talked to him as a human being like themselves and helped him hold onto a shred of pride and self respect.

Fortunately, the great majority of these young officers were worthy of the trust imposed on them. If they had behaved, in miniature, as the generals behaved, then God knows what would have happened in the end.

In those days, in England, there were class distinctions that everyone recognized and accepted without resentment so long as they were not abused. In civilian life the humble workman was content to obey a foreman who had risen from his own class so long as the boss was socially a cut above the foreman.

By the same token, a common soldier would obey the sergeants and the sergeants major who had risen from the ranks, but when it came to his officer, commissioned by the king, he expected something more. What it was he could never have defined in words. But if the officer had it, then the soldier instinctively recognized it, and that indefinable something was what was instilled into a boy at the public school.

It had nothing to do with wealth or privilege. Very few of the public school boys came from the landed gentry or distinguished families. For the most part they came from modest homes, the sons of local lawyers, doctors, or schoolmasters – hardworking professional men. Some were the sons of country clergymen who lived on the verge of poverty and sold their precious family heirlooms for the money to send their boy to a public school.

Too often the sacrifice was in vain. The Army ordained that officers should wear distinctive tunics, cut differently from the private soldier. When they led an attack, this made it easy for the Germans to pick them out and shoot them down before they turned their attention to the men. At the Battle of the Somme, thirty young officers went in with our battalion, and only four survived.

These public school boy officers were not soldiers in the ordinary meaning of the word. Very few of them would have wanted to stay on in the Army when the war was done. They only wanted to get the thing over and return to the jobs they had planned to do. But while the thing was on, they did their best, not realizing at the time what a vital part they were playing. The common soldier liked them because they were 'young swells', and with few exceptions the young swells delivered the goods.

1915

According to Lyn Macdonald, the great oral historian of the First World War, 1915, seen in harsh hindsight, appears to be a saga of such horrors, of such mismanagement and muddle, that it is easy to see why it coloured the views of succeeding generations and gave rise to prejudices and myths that have been applied to the whole war. It was also the year when there first surfaced disenchantment with the conduct of the war by Sir John French, the British commander-in-chief, Sir Douglas Haig, commander of the First Army, and Britain's generals. C. E. Montague, the distinguished *Manchester Guardian* journalist whose *Disenchantment* was not published until four years after the war, wrote that after the Battle of Loos those who had been a year in the Army knew that the skeletons of the British soldiers now half hidden by nettles and grass in no man's land had gone 'foredoomed' into a battle lost before a shot was fired.

In his book *The Donkeys* Alan Clark quoted from the diary of Germany's 15th Reserve Regiment to confirm that the advancing English columns at Loos offered such a target as had never been seen before or even thought possible. One German battalion commander said later that the impression made on him and his fellow soldiers as they witnessed the slaughter was so 'revolting and nauseating' that after the British retreat had begun they ceased fire. As the survivors of the 'field of corpses' rose and began to crawl back to their lines, 'no shot was fired at them from the German trenches . . . so great was the feeling of compassion and mercy for the enemy after such a German victory'.

For the Allies, as John Keegan writes, it was a 'doleful' year on the Western Front. Much blood was spilt for little gain and any prospect of success postponed until 1916. The Germans fortified their defences until they were almost impregnable; meanwhile the French failed in their aim of repulsing the Germans in Artois and Champagne and recapturing the plain of Douai and access to its railways. The British made no progress either. There were battles at Neuve Chapelle, where they made their first major organised attack of the war and at first overwhelmed the Germans; at Ypres where the Germans first used poison gas, but the French held the line; and at Aubers Ridge (the British) in May and Vimy Ridge (the French), also in May, where the French gained the summit only to lose it when the Germans counter-attacked.

Each side drew their own conclusions from these indecisive battles. The Germans gave up their attempt to take Ypres and decided instead to demolish it by constant bombardment (by the end of the war the town was rubble and its famous Cloth Hall wrecked, though it has now been rebuilt). Haig concluded that the German defences were so strong that long, methodical bombardment was necessary before infantry were sent into attack.

At Loos in September Haig ordered a four-day artillery bombardment in which 250,000 shells were fired before the troops went over the top. He also used gas but it was blown back to the British trenches by the wind and as a result there were 2600 casualties. The carnage as the hapless British troops advanced has already been described. Loos was a disaster which might have been avoided if Sir John French had not withheld reinforcements of the British line after the early breakthrough. French was replaced by Haig in December 1915.

Gas was used frequently as a weapon after Ypres, where, at sunrise on 22 April, the Germans fired 5700 canisters containing 168 tons of chlorine gas at the French troops. It was a 'cynical and barbarous' disregard of the usages of civilised war, said Sir John French. The poet Wilfred Owen later described the white eyes writhing in the face of a man exposed to phosgene gas, and saw 'the blood come gargling from the froth-corrupted lungs, obscene as cancer, bitter as the cud of vile, incurable sores on innocent tongues'. Chlorine gas was later superseded by mustard gas, the cause of the most casualties. In the American Army out of nearly 58,000 gas casualties, 26,828 were known to have been due to mustard gas. Chlorine gas led to slow death by asphyxiation, often over days, with victims conscious to within minutes of the end. Death from mustard gas took up to four or five weeks – the pain was so great that victims had to be strapped to their beds.

The biggest military event for the British, Australians and New Zealanders was the Gallipoli campaign in the Dardanelles, which lasted from February until January 1916. Winston Churchill's aim was to knock Turkey out of the war, open the supply route to Russia through the Black Sea, and persuade the neutral Balkan states to join the Allies. The plan was that the British and French fleets would destroy the defences of the Dardanelles while troops conquered the Gallipoli peninsula. They would then advance on Constantinople (now Istanbul), the Turkish capital, and Turkey would surrender when the city fell. As what follows demonstrates, the campaign was a disaster – the troops were eventually evacuated and Churchill resigned (he then commanded a battalion in France before returning to Lloyd George's government).

On the home front Herbert Asquith became head of a coalition with the Tories. By March two out of three undergraduates at Oxford and Cambridge had volunteered to serve and public opinion was becoming strongly in favour of conscription, the more so as the casualty lists lengthened. The popular romantic novelist Baroness Orczy set up an 'Active Service League', which encouraged the women of England to influence sweethearts, brothers, sons and friends to offer their services to the country. They pledged not to be seen in public with any man who had refused his country's call. It was now that a white feather began to be presented to young men not in khaki (sometimes to men on leave from the front). One advertisement in *The Times* said: 'Jack, F. G. – if you are not in khaki by the 20th I shall cut you dead – Ethel M.'

The first Zeppelin air raid on Britain occurred in January. German U-boats started attacking British shipping in February. Women were now fully established as workers in factories and a miners' strike was only narrowly averted, though more than five million days were lost to strikes in 1915 and 1916. The opening hours of public houses were altered so that they were shut in the afternoon, a law intended to encourage work that lasted into the 1990s.

There were two great dramas. The first was the sinking of the *Lusitania* in May by a U-boat in which 1100 passengers drowned, including 128 Americans. Then, in October, there was the execution in Belgium by the Germans of the British nurse Edith Cavell ('Patriotism is not enough'), who had been convicted of helping Allied prisoners to escape to Holland and Britain.

The poet Rupert Brooke died in April on his way to Gallipoli, not in battle but of blood poisoning. He was buried in an olive grove – a 'corner of a foreign field that is for ever England' – on the Greek island of Skyros.

By the end of the year the French had suffered two million casualties, of whom 600,000 died.

IAN HAY

K

Ian Hay was the pen name of John Hay Beith (1876–1952), a Scottish novelist and playwright. Hay wrote *The First Hundred Thousand*, published in 1915, the 'unofficial chronicle of a unit of K (1)', a section of the army of one hundred thousand volunteers that Kitchener requested in September 1914. Hay served as an officer

with the Argyll and Sutherland Highlanders. This 'poem' captures
the mood of the volunteers as they set off for France early in 1915.

A slap at Kaiser Bill

We do not deem ourselves A 1,
We have no past: we cut no dash:
Nor hope, when launched against the Hun,
To raise a more than moderate splash.

But yesterday, we said farewell
To plough; to pit; to dock; to mill.
For glory? Drop it! Why? Oh, well –
To have a slap at Kaiser Bill.

And now today has come along.
With rifle, haversack, and pack, We're off, a hundred
  thousand strong.
And – some of us will not come back.

But all we ask, if that befall
Is this. Within your hearts be writ
This single-line memorial: –
He did his duty – and his bit!

KARL ALDAG

New Year's Eve

For Karl Aldag, a twenty-five-year-old German philosophy student,
the Christmas truce lasted until New Year's Eve. He wrote this
letter on 3 January and was killed twelve days later.

New Year's Eve was very queer here. An English officer came
across with a white flag and asked for a truce from 11
o'clock till 3 to bury the dead (just before Christmas there

were some fearful enemy attacks here in which the English lost many in killed and prisoners). The truce was granted. It is good not to see the corpses lying out in front of us any more. The truce was moreover extended. The English came out of their trenches in no-man's-land and exchanged cigarettes, tinned-meat and photographs with our men, and said they didn't want to shoot any more. So there is an extraordinary hush, which seems quite uncanny. Our men and theirs are standing up on the parapet above the trenches.

That couldn't go on indefinitely, so we went across to say that they must get back into their trenches as we were going to start firing. The officers answered that they were sorry, but their men wouldn't obey orders. They didn't want to go on. The soldiers said they had had enough of lying in wet trenches, and that France was done for.

They really are much dirtier than we are, have more water in their trenches and are more sick. Of course they are only mercenaries, and so they are simply going on strike. Naturally we didn't shoot either, for our communication trench leading from the village to the firing-line is always full of water, so we are very glad to be able to walk on the top without any risk. Suppose the whole English army strikes, and forces the gentlemen in London to chuck in the whole business! Our lieutenants went over and wrote their names in an album belonging to the English officers.

Then one day an English officer came across and said that the Higher Command had given orders to fire on our trench and that our men must take cover, and the (French) artillery began to fire, certainly with great violence but without inflicting any casualties.

On New Year's Eve we called across to tell each other the time and agreed to fire a salvo at 12. It was a cold night. We sang songs, and they clapped (we were only 60–70 yards apart); we played the mouth-organ and they sang and clapped. Then I asked if they hadn't got any musical instruments, and they produced some bagpipes (they are the Scots Guards, with the short petticoats and bare legs) and they played some of their beautiful elegies on them, and sang, too. Then at 12 we all fired salvos *into the air!* Then there were a few shots from our guns (I don't know what they were firing at) and the usually so dangerous Very lights crackled like fireworks, and we waved torches and cheered. We had brewed some grog and drank the toast of the Kaiser and the New Year. It was a real good 'Sylvester', just like peace-time!

'When This Bloody War Is Over'

Sung to the tune of the hymn 'What a Friend We Have in Jesus', this song was popular during the American Civil War:

> *When this bloody war is over,*
> *No more soldiering for me.*
> *When I get my civvy clothes on,*
> *Oh, how happy I shall be!*
> *No more church parades on Sunday,*
> *No more putting in for leave*
> *I shall kiss the Sergeant-Major*
> *How I'll miss him: how he'll grieve.*

Sometimes the last four lines of this verse were sung as:

> *No more going in the trenches,*
> *No more asking for a pass*
> *You can tell the Sergeant-Major*
> *To stick his passes up his arse.*

or:

> *I shall sound my own reveille,*
> *I shall make my own tattoo;*

No more NCOs to curse me,
No more bloody Army stew.

When this bloody war is over
Guards' fatigues will be no more
We'll be spooning with the wenches
As we did in days of yore.
NCOs will then be navvies,
Privates own their motor cars,
No more 'stirring' and saluting,
No more tea dished out in jars.

Some units sang the additional verse:

N.C.O.s will smoke their woodbines,
Privates puff their big cigars.
No more standing-to in trenches,
Only one more church-parade;
No more shivering on the firestep,
No more Tickler's marmalade.

WALTER AMBROSELLI

A philosophy student from Leipzig, Walter Ambroselli wrote this account of bravery on both sides of the battlefront on 19 January. He was killed on 19 May, aged twenty-one.

Our Pioneers, who are more feared than anybody because of their bombs, worked with axes and wire-cutters in front of and among us, and just then I witnessed, with admiration, a heroic deed. A Pioneer caught sight of a Frenchman in the trench who was just about to fire. The Pioneer quickly pulled the stopper out of the fuse, raised his bomb, and was just going to throw it. At that very moment some German comrades came between him and his objective. He could not throw the bomb without hitting them; so he kept it in his hand, and in a few seconds it exploded, blowing him to pieces.

Many of the ghastly things that happened during this attack I couldn't possibly tell you. It makes me sick to think of them. One was ready to weep over the misery of it all, as when for instance, comrades close to us fell, with a last pathetic look at us. Then, as we forced our way through the deep narrow trench, what a horrible sight met our eyes! In a place where a trench-mortar shell had burst, there lay, torn to pieces, about eight of the Alpine Chasseurs – some of the finest French troops – in a great, bloody heap of mangled human bodies; dead and wounded; on the top a corpse without a head or torso; and underneath some who were still alive, though with limbs torn off or horribly mutilated. They looked at us with bleeding, mournful eyes. The crying and moaning of these poor, doomed, enemy soldiers went to our hearts. We couldn't get out of the trench to avoid this pile of bodies. However much our hearts shrank from trampling over them with our hob-nailed boots, we were forced to do it!

Our Corporal and a few men of our section were still together, but we had got separated from the rest of the platoon. That often happens in hand-to-hand fighting, as companies have to spread out, and individual sections, platoons, companies and even regiments, get all mixed up. We were now, with the 12th and 8th, under the command of a Captain of the 52nd, attacking a hill from which a French gun was still firing. We swarmed up it from every side. There we finally discovered a French Artillery Major, alone with his gun – fetching the ammunition himself, loading and firing. When we got there, he was just trying to shoot the first one of our men – Corporal Finder of the 2nd Company – with his revolver. The Corporal was too quick for him, however, and sent a bullet through the Major's head. The shot was not immediately fatal.

Exerting all his remaining strength the brave enemy officer dragged himself to the telephone in order to send warning to the enemy rear-line. We were just in time to stop him. Then he collapsed. I fetched two French stretcher bearers out of a hole which we had already captured, so that they might carry the Major out of the line of fire. Without a groan, but also without vouchsafing a glance in my direction, he let himself be carried down into a quarry where there were already a lot of wounded.

Two days later I read in the printed Order-of-the-Day issued by the Army Corps that, in accordance with the personal instructions of the Kaiser, who had been present at the battle, this hero had been buried with full military honours, escorted by officers of even higher rank, behind the line.

WILFRED EWART

'The swift stirrings of war'

Wilfred Ewart (1892–1922) served with the Scots Guards from 1915 to 1918. On 23 February 1915 he was billeted a mile behind the trenches when, after an inspection by the Brigadier-General of the newly arrived draft, he learned that the evening would offer his first experience of the trenches.

It is time to start on the first trip to the trenches. Nor, with the sombre winter's evening falling, is the prospect a particularly inviting one, despite a natural curiosity and the excitement born of long anticipation. There lies before us a two-mile walk, a long night's work and, for the newly joined ensign, a number of unique experiences.

It is four o'clock. We parade in the road – it is said a German machine gun sprays the first crossing – and set off. Soon we take to the fields. The men have spades and rifles to carry, and it is not long before we struggle knee-deep in mud and fall over strands of barbed wire and into holes. Having drawn extra tools from a shattered barn, we take to crawling.

'Zip!' There is no mistaking the sound; the first bullet I have heard in the war whistles overhead with a peculiar clear-cut twang. One feels interested rather than frightened, for obviously the sergeant and the men take bullets as a matter of course. We are in the machine-gun zone. The sergeant says: 'You had better double along. Keep down here, sir.' Bright moonlight makes these three hundred yards of exposed ground as clear as day.

A little farther on an engineer officer is waiting to point out the work to be done. Two sections of trench have to be linked up by a third which is to run over the crest of a small hill. After getting the men strung out in a long irregular line and setting the N.C.O.s their appointed task, I make my way along a rough breastwork which has been built up as a temporary protection. The English front-line trench is on the forward face of the little hill. Here I find an old machine-gun emplacement in which occasionally to sit down and rest, whence may be obtained a view of the working party on one side and across to the German lines on the other. No Man's Land spreads in between.

Many a night subsequently was I to look out over a similar scene, but never did the details of the picture impress themselves so vividly on my mind as upon that first visit to the trenches. And suddenly out of the long silence there came the obscure reminders, the swift stirrings of war: the faint clink of spades away down in the trench where the men are working, stertorous masculine breathings, a muttered exclamation, an occasional curse. Sometimes a stray bullet whistles out of the darkness and goes singing on its way; sometimes a party of soldiers, heavily burdened, tramps by, crouching low. Often – about the middle of the night – a machine gun speaks with its metallic 'clack-clack', or the sharp crack of a rifle comes from near at hand, or somewhere afar off a great gun booms sullenly. Then silence, and one listens intently. Always there is a feeling of tenseness and expectancy. Only the 'click-clack' of our picks and shovels at work and eighty yards away the answering 'thud-thud' of the German wiring parties driving in their stakes!

Then, rising and creeping to the parapet of the little fort, I peer over, my head and body partly concealed by the sandbags. The ground slopes sharply away to the confused region of moonlight and shadows. At first the eyes cannot probe this dusky space. Yet after a few minutes you make men out – flitting here and there, fetching, carrying, digging, working like demons, bent figures silhouetted in the moonlight. They look rather like Cossacks from famous pictures of 1812. And occasionally the non-commissioned officers can be heard cursing those grey soldiers of the Fatherland. There is a partial truce between us. By night everybody works at that part of the line; by day everybody fights desultorily.

And, looking out for the first time across that country so dark and shadowy, so pregnant with fate for us all, the strange baffling mystery of it confronts one. Now and again the crack of a rifle breaks the stillness, and at intervals there comes to the ear the infernal 'clack-clack' of a machine gun, than which there is no sound more sinister in war. 'Twas on such a clear moonlit night, when a fresh wind blew to the nostrils the first scents of spring, that a man working in the midst of his fellows fell silently to the ground – dripping blood – nor ever spoke again. That is the impenetrable problem, the everlasting mystery of it; experience can go no further. The interminable lines of watching men stretching away into the dim distance towards the battlefield of Ypres, where the guns boom and the machine guns chatter all night long – the interminable lines of watching men quenching their fears (of each other) as best they may, awaiting their chance to kill, to wound – for why? For what? 'For some idea dimly understood?' The same blood, indeed, the same God, the same humanity, the same mentality, the same love of life, the same dread of death – one could not hate them, one could only wonder – and pity.

And as I watched that night, there came to my ears the sound of a man singing. Do you know the curious quality of a man's voice heard at a distance? Strangely the voice rose and fell on the wings of the night; it was joined by others, and the Germans began to sing 'The Watch on the Rhine' and the Austrian National Hymn. This, as I learned later, happened every Sunday evening. On an off-night they would have been 'strafed', but now all was still. And often afterwards there would come from the enemy trenches – generally, as I subsequently learned, to screen some particularly important work they were engaged upon – strains of wild, windy music, like the sighing of pine forests, such songs as the Southern Germans love. And every now and then there came, too, the sound of a mouth-organ, cheap and bizarre, to remind one of a *café chantant* in Paris, or – why, I know not – of the hot mid-day in some London street.

Soon after midnight our task is finished, and we trudge back to billets beneath the waning moon, towards a darkness in which there is as yet no hint of dawn.

CHARLES MORAN

The Chivalry of Arms

Charles Moran served with the 1st Battalion, the Royal Fusiliers, from the autumn of 1914 to the spring of 1917. His job, he said, was to keep men in the line. What was happening in their minds? How were they standing up to fear and danger. He described his conclusions in *The Anatomy of Courage*. In this extract Moran's company commander has told him that Gordon, a fellow officer, was anxious to get back to the line. Moran subsequently became Winston Churchill's physician.

Most of us were quite content to do nothing; we were in no hurry to go back to the mud and monotony of the trenches, and I wanted to know if Gordon's restlessness was genuine, why he preferred the trenches to that peaceful existence in a village that might have been in England. I questioned Hill, but he was not very helpful. He told me that Gordon was in his College Boat at Oxford; he seemed to have an idea at the back of his mind that he had not yet pulled his weight, though already, early in the war, he had been severely wounded in the neck. Bow had done this, and Four that, and now the crew was down to three. He had an obsession about this boat; he was secretly bent on bringing some credit to it. Gordon was not an easy man to get to know, but when I saw more of him I was satisfied that this was the real aggressive spirit, so strange to most of us who had been out for some time and never went out of our way to look for trouble. There it was beneath the stolid exterior, covered up by all the negatives the average young Briton of his type thinks valuable.

One day after our return to the salient while he was at the transport, his company was rather heavily shelled. When he returned and learnt what had happened he said nothing, but seemed put out; Hill thought he was brooding on it. Then one night, without a word to anyone, he went out on patrol taking a corporal with him. He did not come back. He had gone in his leather waistcoat, without a coat or anything that might give away his unit if he were captured. He had emptied his pockets of letters and papers. People said that to go off like that without telling anyone was a silly thing to do, but that he was a good fellow and would be a loss. Months later a communication came from Germany through the American Red Cross. I print it because it gave me new heart at a time when I was less certain of things:

'On the morning of the 24th January on the Ypern front, near four big holes caused by the bursting of shells, north-west of the Bellevarde Farm, and about 30 metres distant from the German front measuring from the west to the east, an Englishman was buried, a German officer in charge. The body had lain for a fortnight or three weeks before our front (here followed a full description with minute details about studs and underclothing). The wounds consisted of a shot in the heart so that death was instantaneous. Since the burial was carried out by the young officer in charge, although at a great personal risk as he was under fire at the time, and since his only object was to give his enemy an honourable burial, in the hope that this action would be of some comfort to the relatives of the dead man, I beg that this description may be sent to the English troops on the Ypern front.'

Mark that minute description of the clothing, though Gordon was buried in no man's land after dark. Mark those comfortable words 'The wounds consisted of a shot in the heart, so that death was instantaneous.' I am glad to think that Gordon was decently buried by a gallant enemy. This was a man without fear who had brought from Oxford the young clean zest of his kind into the mixed business of war. Providence did well to revive the ancient chivalry of arms for his going out.

WILFRID WILSON GIBSON

'Because he bore my name'

Wilfrid Gibson (1878–1962) was a friend of Rupert Brooke and associated with him in publishing the first anthology of *Georgian Poetry* in 1912. He served briefly as a private in the infantry on the Western Front.

They ask me where I've been,
And what I've done and seen;

But what can I reply,
Who know it wasn't I,
But some one just like me,
Who went across the sea,
And with my head and hands
Killed men in foreign lands, . . .
Though I must bear the blame
Because he bore my name?

HENRY WILLIAMSON

A Fox Under My Cloak

It is for his nature stories, such as *Tarka the Otter*, that Henry Williamson (1895–1977) is best known. But he served on the Western Front and described his experience in several semi-autobiographical novels, including *A Fox Under My Cloak*, which contains this passage attacking the incompetence of Field Marshal Sir John French, commander of the British Expeditionary Force. Phillip Maddison is the alter ego of Williamson. French was later replaced by Douglas Haig.

The reserves, which the First Army commander fighting the battle had requested, again and again, to be two thousand yards behind the British front line, were then six miles back, and in no fit condition to march on until they had rested.

They had been kept back deliberately by Field-Marshal Sir John French.

The field-marshal was sixty-three years of age . . . He had reached the time of life when a man reflects rather than acts; and for over a year of war he had been continually frustrated. He had lived with grief: the flower of his army had been destroyed. Anxiety gnawed him, a fox under his cloak . . .

General Haig, who was to fight the battle, had more than once suggested that [the reserves] be moved nearer. He was supported by General Foch, commanding the 10th French Army on his right, who had proposed to the field-marshal that they be brought to within two thousand yards of the corps reserves (which, in fact, did not exist: for the six divisions of the two corps comprising Haig's First Army were all to be used in the assault; and he had no reserves whatsoever).

General Haig once more urged that the two divisions be held ready, by daybreak of zero day, to move forward directly into the battle of pursuit. To this the field-marshal had replied merely that he did not agree: he, as commander-in-chief, would keep the whole of the general reserve in the Lillers area, sixteen miles back, until the course of the battle was known . . . General Haig persisted. He wrote yet again, repeating his request for the general reserve to be well up behind the assault – 'On the line Noeux-les-Mines-Beuvy by daylight on 25 September'. To this the field-marshal, committed in the first place by politicians to a battle he had no belief in – fearing to send untried troops in forlorn hope, yet wishing to support his First Army commander with the loyalty of a good soldier – replied 'Two divisions . . . will be in the area referred to in your letter by daybreak on the 25th September'.

They were indeed there, shortly after daybreak, but in no condition to move forward.

The field-marshal, with only his personal aides, had left his headquarters at St Omer unexpectedly to visit the Château Philomel three miles south of Lillers on the evening before the battle. From the château there was no communication by wire with his armies; and only the civilian French telephone system to St Omer. Sir Douglas Haig sent, at 7 a.m. the next morning, a staff-officer by motor car to inform the field-marshal of the success of the assault by the 47th London and 15th Scottish divisions towards Loos and Hill 70, and to ask that the two reserve divisions be put in immediately.

Again at 8.45 a.m. General Haig sent another messenger, to report that all the brigades of the 1st and 4th Corps were either in the German trenches or on the move there; and to request that the reserve divisions be pushed in at once. Two valuable hours had already been lost.

At 9.30 a.m. the field-marshal replied by telegraph that the divisions would 'move forward to First Army trenches as soon as the situation requires and admits'.

At 11.30 a.m. the field-marshal visited Sir Douglas Haig and told him, at last, that he would arrange to put the reserve divisions under his orders.

From First Army at Hinges he motored to Noeux-les-Mines, where he arrived about noon. There he saw the corps general under whose command the divisions had been placed. Having discussed the general situation with him, the field-marshal, at 12.30 p.m., gave the corps general the order to move his divisions forward. Five and three-quarter most valuable hours had wasted away.

Fifty minutes later, at 1.20 p.m., the corps general informed Sir Douglas Haig that the reserve divisions 'were under him and marching to the areas ordered, but were delayed on the road'. Sir Douglas Haig, a devout man, had meanwhile spent some minutes in the privacy of his room praying on his knees.

At the same time, from various parts of the front, according to many regimental officers, the Germans were on the run. Some had thrown away arms and equipment: field-gun batteries had been abandoned. It was only when they saw that the British had paused after their efforts, and were not being reinforced, that they halted, and came back to their vacant trenches, and took up the fight once more.

Messages sent back took a long time to deliver, owing to clogging mud, and the mêlée of movement upon degraded soil; thus Sir Douglas Haig believed for some hours that his First Army was 'on the crest of the wave of victory, that it had broken through the second and last line of defence in two central and vital places, Cité St. Elie and Hulluch; and that a break-through at Haisnes and Cité St. Auguste was imminent'.

The truth was the First Army had spent itself, like a wave with none behind to gather its waters and follow on.

And the jetsam of that wave was two out of every three men in the battalions of the original assault fallen, broken or dead, to the ground.

ALFONS ANKENBRAND

'Now I am free to dare anything'

Alfons Ankenbrand, a theology student at Freiburg, was twenty-one when he wrote this letter in March anticipating death. He was killed six weeks later.

'So fare you well, for we must now be parting' – so run the first lines of a soldier-song which we often sang through the streets of the capital. These words are truer than ever now, and these lines are to bid farewell to you, to all my nearest and dearest, to all who wish me well or ill, and to all that I value and prize.

Everybody must be prepared now for death in some form or other. Two cemeteries have been made up here, the losses have been so great I ought not to write that to you, but I do so all the same, because the newspapers have probably given you quite a different impression. They tell only of our gains and say nothing about the blood that has been shed, of the cries of agony that never cease. The newspaper doesn't give any description either of how the 'heroes' are laid to rest, though it talks about 'heroes' graves' and writes poems and suchlike about them. Certainly in Lens I have attended funeral-parades where a number of dead were buried in one large grave with pomp and circumstance. But up here it is pitiful the way one throws the dead bodies out of the trench and lets them lie there, or scatters dirt over the remains of those which have been torn to pieces by shells.

I look upon death and call upon life. I have not accomplished much in my short life, which has been chiefly occupied with study. I have commended my soul to the Lord God. It bears His seal and is altogether His. Now I am free to dare anything. My future life belongs to God, my present one to the Fatherland, and I myself still possess happiness and strength.

Fatherland! Home! How often have I revelled in your woods and mountains! Now you have need of your sons, and I too have heard the call and have come, stepped into the ranks, and will be true to the last.

> *'So fare you well, my parents and belov'd ones,*
> *For the last time we press each other's hands.*
> *If here on earth it is the final parting,*
> *We hope to meet in yonder Better Land.'*

It is painful to die far away from home, without a loving eye to look down upon one. A grave at home surrounded with love, to which loved ones come to weep and pray, is granted to few soldiers. But hush! The Heavenly Father has commanded the Guardian Angel to console the dying; he bends lovingly over him and shows him already the crown the unfading crown, which awaits him above.

> *'And now will I boldly fight,*
> *Even should I die to-night.'*

IAN HAY

Guess Who's Come to See Us

This extract is taken from Hay's *The First Hundred Thousand*:

One more picture, to close the record of our trivial round.

It is a dark, moist, and most unpleasant dawn. Captain Blaikie stands leaning against a traverse in the fire-trench, superintending the return of a party from picket duty. They file in, sleepy and dishevelled, through an archway in the parapet, on their way to dug-outs and repose. The last man in the procession is Bobby Little, who has been in charge all night.

Our line here makes a sharp bend round the corner of an orchard, and for security's sake a second trench has been cut behind, making, as it were, the cross-bar of a capital A. The apex of the A is no health resort. Brother Bosche, as already explained, is only fifty yards away, and his trench-mortars make excellent practice with the parapet. So the Orchard Trench is only occupied at night, and the alternative route, which is well constructed and comparatively safe, is used by all careful persons who desire to proceed from one arm of the A to the other.

The present party are the night picket, thankfully relinquishing their vigil round the apex.

Bobby Little remained to bid his company commander good-morning at the junction of the two trenches.

'Any casualties?' An invariable question at this spot.

'No, sir. We were lucky. There was a lot of sniping.'

'It's a rum profession,' mused Captain Blaikie, who was in a wakeful mood.

'In what way, sir?' enquired the sleepy but respectful Bobby.

'Well' – Captain Blaikie began to fill his pipe – 'who takes about nine-tenths of the risk, and does practically all the hard work in the Army? The private and the subaltern – you and your picket, in fact. Now, here is the problem which has puzzled me ever since I joined the Army, and I've had nineteen years' service. The farther away you remove the British soldier from the risk of personal injury, the higher you pay him. Out here, a private of the line gets about a shilling a day. For that he digs, saps, marches, and fights like a hero. The motor-transport driver gets six shillings a day, no danger, and lives like a fighting cock. The Army Service

Corps drive about in motors, pinch our rations, and draw princely incomes. Staff Officers are compensated for their comparative security by extra cash, and first chop at the war medals. Now – why?'

'I dare say they would sooner be here, in the trenches, with us,' was Bobby's characteristic reply.

Blaikie lit his pipe – it was almost broad daylight now – and considered.

'Yes,' he agreed, 'perhaps. Still, my son, I can't say I have ever noticed Staff Officers crowding into the trenches (as they have a perfect right to do) at four o'clock in the morning. And I can't say I altogether blame them. In fact, I shall say: "There goes a sahib – and a soldier!" and I shall take off my hat to him.'

'Well, get ready now,' said Bobby. 'Look!'

They were still standing at the trench junction. Two figures, in the uniform of the Staff, were visible in Orchard Trench, working their way down from the apex – picking their steps amid the tumbled sandbags, and stooping low to avoid gaps in the ruined parapet. The sun was just rising behind the German trenches. One of the officers was burly and middle-aged; he did not appear to enjoy bending double. His companion was slight, fair-haired, and looked incredibly young. Once or twice he glanced over his shoulder, and smiled encouragingly at his senior.

The pair emerged through the archway into the main trench, and straightened their backs with obvious relief. The younger officer – he was a lieutenant – noticed Captain Blaikie, saluted him gravely, and turned to follow his companion.

Captain Blaikie did not take his hat off, as he had promised. Instead, he stood suddenly to attention, and saluted in return, keeping his hand uplifted until the slim, childish figure had disappeared round the corner of a traverse.

It was the Prince of Wales.

STODDARD KING

'Love Song'

> *All night long I hear them calling*
> *Calling sweet and low,*
> *Calling till it seems*
> *The world is full of dreams,*
> *Just to call you back to me:*
> *There's a long, long trail a-winding*
> *Into the land of my dreams,*
> *Where the nightingales are singing*
> *And a white moon beams.*
> *There's a long, long night of waiting,*
> *Until my dreams all come true,*
> *Till the day when I'll be going*
> *Down that long, long trail with you.*

SIR JOHN FRENCH

'A barbarous disregard of civilised war'

On 22 April 1915 the Germans launched an attack in which
poison gas was first used in warfare, initiating the Second Battle
of Ypres. This account was written some two months later by Sir
John French, Commander-in-Chief of the British Expeditionary
Force:

> Headquarters, June 15, 1915
> I much regret that during the period under report the fight-
> ing has been characterized on the enemy's side by a cynical
> and barbarous disregard of the well-known usages of civi-
> lized war and a flagrant defiance of the Hague Convention.
>   All the scientific resources of Germany have apparently
> been brought into play to produce a gas of so virulent and
> poisonous a nature that any human being brought into con-

tact with it is first paralysed and then meets with a lingering and agonizing death.

The enemy has invariably preceded, prepared and supported his attacks by a discharge in stupendous volume of these poisonous gas fumes whenever the wind was favourable.

Such weather conditions have only prevailed to any extent in the neighbourhood of Ypres, and there can be no doubt that the effect of these poisonous fumes materially influenced the operations in that theatre, until experience suggested effective counter measures, which have since been so perfected as to render them innocuous.

The brainpower and thought which has evidently been at work before this unworthy method of making war reached the pitch of efficiency which has been demonstrated in its practice shows that the Germans must have harboured these designs for a long time.

As a soldier I cannot help expressing the deepest regret and some surprise that an Army which hitherto has claimed to be the chief exponent of chivalry of war should have stooped to employ such devices against brave and gallant foes.

It was the commencement of the second battle of Ypres on the evening of April 22nd that the enemy first made use of asphyxiating gas. Following a heavy bombardment, the enemy attacked the French Division at about 5 p.m., using asphyxiating gases for the first time. Aircraft reported that at about 5 p.m. thick yellow smoke had been seen issuing from the German trenches between Langemarck and Bixschoote. The French reported that two simultaneous attacks had been made east of the Ypres–Staden Railway, in which these asphyxiating gases had been employed.

What follows almost defies description. The effect of these poisonous gases was so virulent as to render the whole of the line held by the French Division mentioned above practically incapable of any action at all. It was at first impossible for any one to realize what had actually happened. The smoke and fumes hid everything from sight, and hundreds of men were thrown into a comatose or dying condition, and within an hour the whole position had to be abandoned, together with about fifty guns.

I wish particularly to repudiate any idea of attaching the least blame to the French Division for this unfortunate incident. After all the examples our gallant Allies have shown of dogged and tenacious courage in the many trying situations in which they have been placed throughout the course of this campaign it is quite superfluous for me to dwell on this aspect of the incident and I would only express my firm conviction that if any troops in the world had been able to hold their trenches in the face of such a treacherous and altogether unexpected onslaught, the French Division would have stood firm.

W. A. QUINTON

Writhing, Shaking, Gasping

W. A. Quinton served with the 1st Battalion of the Bedfordshire Regiment. He wrote a memoir of his experiences in 1929 so that his son should understand the futility of war.

Unlike Sir John French, he suffered personally from the gas attack and wrote a particularly vivid account of its effects.

Every man was issued with a body belt, which seemed rather an unusual thing. It would have been much more welcome had it been an extra overcoat apiece. Anyhow we soon found out the reason for this curious addition to our kit. The enemy had commenced to use poisonous gas. The French had had a dose, and the Canadians, holding part of the line some miles to our right, had been subjected to this new

horror only the day previously. Rum jars filled with water
were placed at intervals along our trench, with strict orders
that it was to be used only in the event of an attack by gas.
'Soak your body belt in water, and hold it over your nose
and mouth.'

We did not know much about this new form of warfare
and before we had actually experienced it I'm afraid we
treated the matter very lightly. We had the common sense to
know that this gas, whatever it was, was released from
cylinders in the German trenches and drifted with the wind.
There seemed to be no wind at all this morning. What little
there was, if any, was blowing towards the enemy, so we
were safe from gas at the present anyway. That night we
were relieved by A and B Coys and we again took our turn
in the support lines, which were, by the way, about 50 yards
behind the front line.

Next morning, while busily engaged in our various tasks,
filling sandbags etc., the enemy stirred into sudden activity.
His heavy guns opened fire, and shells of sizes began to fall
around us. We did not need any orders to 'stand to'. Hastily
donning our equipment and grabbing our rifles, we cringed
in our trench, partly sheltered by the hill. To the rear of us
was a small wood. Enemy 'heavies' were crashing into it,
uplifting the young trees bodily, and splintering the trunks of
the larger ones with a sickening tearing sound. Above the
din of the bursting shells we could hear the crack of rifles
and machine guns. What was happening in the front line?
We received orders to be ready to go forward. Our section
was grouped at the end of one of the communication
trenches leading to the firing line, ready to race through it to
the assistance of the front line, as soon as they should
require assistance. They did not seem to be suffering so
much from shell fire, but we in the supports were getting it
with a vengeance.

Three of our section were already hors-de-combat: Reed,

from Luton, laughed like a maniac, as he dropped his rifle and grabbed his right forearm with his left hand. 'I've got it!' Within a second or two, blood was streaming down the back of his hand. He did not stop to bind himself up, or allow one of us to do it, but was quick to avail himself of a wounded man's privilege and clear out. 'S'long, you fellows', and off he went. Whether he got through that hail of shells falling in the open country behind us, and eventually out of the danger zone, I do not know: but he had missed something we had yet to come.

On our immediate right was a battalion of the 'Dorsets' forming part of our brigade. From this direction came the sound of exploding bombs. We knew, but could not see, that they must be at grips with the enemy. Suddenly over the top of our front line we saw what looked like clouds of thin grey smoke rolling slowly along with the slight wind. It hung to the ground reaching to the height of 8 or 9 feet, and approached so slowly that a man walking could have kept ahead of it. GAS! The word quickly passed round. Even now it held no terror for us, for we had not yet tasted it. From our haversacks we hastily drew the flannel belts, soaked them in water and tied them round our mouths and noses. The trench in which we crouched was being smashed to pieces. The sand-bag walls we had been so busily engaged on when the bombardment started were already unrecognisable. Men were getting buried alive, as yards of our parapet caved in on them.

Suddenly, through the communication trench came rushing a few khaki-clad figures. Their eyes glaring out of their heads, their hands tearing at their throats, they came on. Some stumbled and fell, and lay writhing in the bottom of the trench, choking and gasping, whilst those following trampled over them. If ever men were raving mad with terror, these men were. They raced on, those who could, through our support trenches (or what was left of them), through that wood behind and out into the open country. Many never reached the open country; many never even reached the wood. Through that rain of 'coal-boxes' [heavy shells] most of them were blown to pieces.

What was left of our section still crouched at the support end of the communication trench. Our front line, judging from the number of men who had just come from it, had been abandoned, and we now waited for the first rush of the Germans. But they did not come. Our biggest enemy was now within a few yards of us, in the form of clouds of gas. We caught our first whiff of it. No words of mine can ever describe my feelings as we inhaled the first mouthful. We choked, spit, and coughed, my lungs felt as though they were being burnt out, and were going to burst. Red hot needles were being thrust into my eyes. The first impulse was to run. We had just seen men running to certain death, and knew it, rather than stay and be choked in to a slow and agonising death. It was one of those occasions when you do not know *what* you are doing. The man who stayed was no braver than the man who ran away. We crouched there, ter-rified – stupefied. We lay with our noses in the mud, fighting for breath, forgetful of the bursting shells. I felt myself chok-ing. I could not stand it much longer. I would have to get up and run.

A large shell burst on the parapet just where we were sheltered. We were almost buried beneath the falling earth. Young Addington, a chap about my own age, was screaming at the top of his voice and trying to free his buried legs. He got free, and before we could stop him he rushed off – God knows where! We then saw the reason for his screams. His left arm was blown off above the elbow. He left a trail of blood over my tunic as he climbed over me in his mad rush to get away. (Had we but known it, we were doing about the worst thing we could have done by putting our noses to the ground, for the gas being heavier than air, clung to the earth and hung about in the trenches and hollows, and we were acting as if dealing with smoke.)

At last the order came to advance to the front line. Glad to move, whether backward or forward, we staggered through the trench leading to our objective, but after a few yards we were at a standstill again, for here the trench was absolutely blocked with dead and dying. We clambered over them, and here and there could be seen a wounded man struggling to free himself from the dead who lay over him. All this at a glance as we struggled onwards, for we must reach the front-line trench before the enemy got possession. We half expected to find them in it and to be greeted with a shower of bombs. Reaching the trench, we ran along it, and spreading ourselves out, manned the firing step. We opened fire across No Man's Land to let the Germans know that our front line was still occupied and showing fight. What was left of 'A' company, who had been holding this trench, lay in the bottom of it, overcome with the gas.

Black in the face, their tunics and shirt fronts torn open at the necks in their last desperate fight for breath, many of them lay quite still while others were still wriggling and kicking in the agonies of the most awful death I have ever seen. Some were wounded into the bargain, and their gaping wounds lay open, blood still oozing from them. One poor devil was tearing at his throat with his hands. I doubt if he knew, or felt, that he had only one hand, and that the other was just a stump where the hand should have been. This stump he worked around his throat as if the hand was still there, and the blood from it was streaming over his bluish-black face and neck. A few minutes later and he was still except for the occasional shudders as he breathed his last. All this was taken in at a glance, for we had other work to think about. It was a good job we had, for what human being could have stood by and seen such sights without wanting to end the sufferings of such poor devils with a bullet.

ANONYMOUS

'Blind panic'

An eyewitness wrote this account of the German attack:

> Utterly unprepared for what was to come, the [French] divisions gazed for a short while spellbound at the strange phenomenon they saw coming slowly toward them.
>
> Like some liquid the heavy-coloured vapour poured relentlessly into the trenches, filled them, and passed on.
>
> For a few seconds nothing happened; the sweet-smelling stuff merely tickled their nostrils; they failed to realize the danger. Then, with inconceivable rapidity, the gas worked, and blind panic spread.
>
> Hundreds, after a dreadful fight for air, became unconscious and died where they lay – a death of hideous torture, with the frothing bubbles gurgling in their throats and the foul liquid welling up in their lungs. With blackened faces and twisted limbs one by one they drowned – only that which drowned them came from inside and not from out.
>
> Others, staggering, falling, lurching on, and of their ignorance keeping pace with the gas, went back.
>
> A hail of rifle fire and shrapnel mowed them down, and the line was broken. There was nothing on the British left – their flank was up in the air. The northeast corner of the salient around Ypres had been pierced. From in front of St Julien away up north towards Boesinghe there was no one in front of the Germans.

BRUCE BAIRNSFATHER

'A colossal, rushing swish in the air'

Bruce Bairnsfather (1888–1959) joined the Army but left to train as an artist. On the outbreak of war he joined the Royal

Warwickshire Regiment, was commissioned and went to the Western Front. He described his part in the Second Battle of Ypres, where he was a victim of chlorine gas, in his book *Bullets and Billets*. He subsequently created the character Old Bill and was the most popular British cartoonist of the war. His work appeared in the *Bystander* and *Punch*. In the Second World War he was official cartoonist to the American forces in Europe.

It was now just about four o'clock in the morning. A faint light was creeping into the sky. The rain was abating a bit, thank goodness! We topped the rise and rushed on down the road as fast as was possible under the circumstances. Now we were in it! Bullets were flying through the air in all directions. Ahead in the semi-darkness, I could just see the forms of men running out into the fields on either side of the road in extended order, and beyond them a continuous heavy crackling of rifle-fire showed me the main direction of the attack. A few men had gone down already, and no wonder – the air was thick with bullets.

The machine-gun officer of one of the other regiments in the brigade was shot right through the head as he went over the brow of the hill. I found one of his machine-gun sections later and appropriated them for our own use. After we had gone down the road for about two hundred yards I thought that my best plan was to get over to the left a bit, as the greatest noise seemed to come from there. 'Come on you chaps,' I shouted, 'we'll cross this field, and get to the hedge over there.' We dashed across, intermingled with a crowd of Highlanders, who were also making to the left. Through a cloud of bullets, flying like rice at a wedding, we reached the other side of the field. Only one casualty – one man with a shot in the knee.

Couldn't get a view of the enemy from the hedge, so I decided to creep along further to the left still, to a spot I saw on the left front of a large farm which stood about two hundred yards behind us. The German machine guns were now busy and sent sprays of bullets flicking up the ground all around us. Lying behind a slight fold in the ground we saw them whisking through the grass, three or four inches above our heads. We slowly worked our way across to the left, past an old, wide ditch full of stagnant water and into a shallow gully beyond. Dawn had come now and in the cold grey light I saw our men out in front of me advancing in short rushes towards a large wood in front.

The Germans were firing star shells into the air in pretty large numbers, why, I couldn't make out, as there was quite enough light now to see by. I ordered the section out of the gully and ran across the open to a bit of old trench I saw in the field. This was the only suitable spot I could see for bringing our guns to bear on the enemy, and assist in the attack. We fixed up a couple of machine guns and awaited a favourable opportunity. I could see a lot of Germans running along in front of the wood towards one end of it. We laid our aim on the wood, which seemed to me the chief spot to go for. One or two of my men had not managed to get up to the gun position as yet. They were ammunition carriers and had had a pretty hard job with it.

I left the guns to run back and hurry them on. The rifle-fire kept up an incessant rattle the whole time, and now the German gunners started shelling the farm behind us. Shell after shell burst beyond, in front of, and on either side of the farm. Having got up the ammunition, I ran back towards the guns past the farm . . . All movement in the attack had now ceased but the rifle and shell fire was as strong as ever. My corporal was with the two guns and had orders to fire as soon as an opportunity arose . . . Shells were crashing into the roof of the farm and exploding round it in great profusion. Every minute one heard the swirling rush overhead, the momentary pause, saw the cloud of red dust, then 'Crumph!' That farm was going to be extinguished, I could plainly see.

I went along the edge of the dried-up moat at the back towards my guns. I couldn't stand up any longer. I lay down on the side of the moat for five minutes. Twenty yards away the shells burst round and in the farm, but I couldn't care; rest was all I wanted.

What about my sergeant and those other guns? I thought as I lay there. I rose and cut across the open space again to the two guns.

'You know what to do here, Corporal?' I said. 'I am going round the farm over to the right to see what's happened to the others.'

I left him and went across to the farm. As I went I heard the enormous ponderous, gurgling, rotating sound of large shells coming. I looked to my left. Four columns of black smoke and earth shot up a hundred feet into the air, not eighty yards away. Then four mighty reverberating explosions that rent the air. A row of four 'Jack Johnsons' [heavy shells] had landed not a hundred yards away, right amongst the lines of men, lying out firing in extended order. I went on and had nearly reached the farm when another four came over and landed fifty yards further up the field towards us.

They'll have our guns and section, I thought rapidly, and hurried on to find out what had become of my sergeant.

The shelling of the farm continued: I ran past it between two explosions and raced along the old gully we had first come up. Shells have a way of missing a building and getting something else near by. As I was on the sloping back of the gully I heard a colossal rushing swish in the air and then didn't hear the resultant crash . . . All seemed dull and foggy; a sort of silence, worse than all the shelling, surrounded me. I lay in a filthy stagnant ditch covered in mud and slime from head to foot. I suddenly started to tremble all over. I couldn't grasp where I was. I lay and trembled . . . I had been blown up by a shell. I lay there some little time, I imagine, with a most peculiar sensation.

All fear of shells and explosions had left me. I still heard them dropping about and exploding, but I listened to them and watched them as calmly as one would watch an apple fall off a tree. I couldn't make myself out. Was I all right or all wrong? I tried to get up, and then I knew. The spell was broken. I shook all over and had to lie still, with tears pouring down my face.

I could see my part in this battle was over.

LIEUTENANT ERNEST SHEPHARD

'Rats in a trap'

Second Lieutenant Shephard was only seventeen when he enlisted in the Dorset Regiment Army Special Reserve. His diary reports that on Hill 60 on 1 May it was a 'very hot' day but 'fairly quiet' in the trenches. Then, at 2 p.m., fighting started. He was killed in January 1917.

Saturday 1st May: Fighting started on our left about 2 p.m., our Artillery heavily shelled the enemy trenches in front of Hill 60. At 6 p.m. started the most barbarous act known in modern warfare. We had just given orders guarding against the gases the Germans use. These orders had just reached one platoon when the enemy actually started pumping out gas onto us. This gas we were under impression was to stupefy only. We soon found out at a terrible price that these gases were deadly poison. First we saw a thick smoke curling over in waves from enemy trenches on left. The cry was sent up that this was gas fumes. The scene that followed was heartbreaking. Men were caught by fumes and in dreadful agony, coughing and vomiting rolling on ground in agony. Very shortly after gas was pumped over thus, the enemy were seen running from their own trenches (a part of), as the fumes blew back to them. Had order reigned and this fact been generally known we should doubtless have charged and chanced consequences of new gas. As soon as cleared the enemy attacked, but were held off by those of us left, until the Devons came up from the support dug outs and reinforced us. Men caught by fumes badly were at this stage dying, and we fully realised our desperate position. I ran round at intervals and tied up lots of men's mouths, placed them in sitting positions, and organised parties to assist them to the support dug outs. When not doing this I was rushing ammunition along the trenches, bombs, star lights etc. Telephonic communication with our artillery was broken and consequently they did not open fire until after we had borne the brunt of the attacks. The enemy sent over trench mortar shells and bombs thick and fast, but our lads stuck it well, and the fighting slackened towards dawn at 3 a.m. When we found our men were dying from fumes we wanted to charge, but were not allowed to do so. What a start for May. Hell could find no worse the groans of scores of dying and badly hurt men, the chaos which however soon gave way to discipline, the fierce fighting and anxiety.

The fumes did not catch me badly, as I was prepared and when I smelt gas and felt sick I continued to draw in breath through my wet cloth round mouth and exhale thro' nose. Lots of men were unprepared, quite a coincidence we were. I felt groggy at times but kept very busy and scraped thro'.

Sunday, 2nd May: The bitterest Sunday I have known or ever wish to know.

Hardly know who is dead yet, but several of my best chums are gone under. Had we lost as heavily while actually fighting we would not have cared as much, but our dear boys died like rats in a trap, instead of heroes as they all were. The Dorset Regiment's motto now is, 'No Prisoners'. No quarter will be given when we again get to fighting. I feel quite knocked up, as we all are, and crying with rage. A lot of men are missing having crawled over back of trench when gassed and enemy shelled them as they crawled away. We spent a morning looking for these, a few were just living, majority dead.

Of those who are still living very few are expected to recover. We found our dead everywhere where they had crawled to get out of the way.

Hill 60 quite apart from our losses is a terrible sight. Hundreds of bodies and all over the place terribly mutilated, a large number of our own men, and larger number of Hun. Stench is awful as they cannot be buried, never quiet enough to do that. So they lie as they fell, silent spectators of modern warfare.

MRS M. HALL

'Our skin was perfectly yellow'

Mrs Hall, one of the contributors to Max Arthur's bestselling book *Forgotten Voices of the Great War*, describes work in a munitions factory where the women were one big, happy family:

I'd never been in a factory before, but the crisis made you think. I thought well, my brothers and my friends are in France, so a friend and I thought to ourselves, well, let's do something. So we wrote to London and asked for war work. And we were directed to a munitions factory at Perivale in London. We had to have a health examination because we had to be very physically fit – perfect eyesight and strong. We had to supply four references, and be British-born of British parents.

We worked ten hours a day, that's from eight in the morning till quarter to one – no break, an hour for dinner, back again until half-past six – no break. We single girls found it

very difficult to eat as well as work because the shops were
closed when we got home. We had to do our work and try to
get food, which was difficult. I remember going into a shop
after not having milk for seven days and they said, 'If you
can produce a baby you can have the milk' – that was it! I
went into a butcher's shop to get some meat because we
were just beginning to be rationed and I said, 'That looks
like a cat.' And he said, 'It is.' I couldn't face that.

It was a perfect factory to work in: everybody seemed
unaware of the powder around them, unaware of any
danger. Once or twice we heard, 'Oh so and so's gone.'
Perhaps she'd made a mistake and her eye was out, but
there wasn't any big explosion during the three years I was
there. We worked at making these little pellets, very inno-
cent-looking little pellets, but had there been the slightest
grit in those pellets, it would have been 'Goodbye.'

We had to do a fortnight on and a fortnight off. It was terribly hard, terribly monotonous, but we had a purpose.
There wasn't a drone in that factory and every girl worked
and worked and worked. I didn't hear one grumble and
hardly ever heard of one that stayed home because she had
her man in mind, we all had. I was working with sailors'
wives from three ships that were torpedoed and sank.
Aboukir, *Cressy* and *Hogue*, on the 22nd of September
1914. It was pitiful to see them, so we had to cheer them up
as best we could, so we sang. It was beautiful to listen to.

After each day when we got home we had a lovely good
wash. And believe me the water was blood-red and our skin
was perfectly yellow, right down through the body, legs and
toenails even, perfectly yellow. In some people it caused a
rash and a very nasty rash all round the chin. It was a shame
because we were a bevy of beauties, you know, and these
girls objected very much to that. Yet amazingly even though
they could do nothing about it, they still carried on and
some of them with rashes about half an inch thick but didn't

seem to do them any inward harm, just the skin. The hair, if it was fair or brown it went a beautiful gold, but if it was any grey [sic], it went grass-green. It was quite a twelve-month after we left the factory that the whole of the yellow came from our bodies. Washing wouldn't do anything – it only made it worse.

Each day we really and truly worked as I've never seen women work like it in my life before or since. It was just magic, we worked and we stood and we sat and we sang. If anyone had come into that factory they would never have believed it could have gone on, because we were such a happy band of women working amongst such treacherous conditions. And there was the cold. I am certain I'd never known brass to be so cold as it was in those factory nights.

But we were just one big happy family. It was amazing and I shall never forget it as long as I live, the way those women worked and talked and chatted about their ordinary everyday experiences, their boys at the Front, but mind you, it was the boys at the Front that we worried about and thought about and that's what made us work like that.

I used to be in Kent quite a lot and I used to see all the troop trains coming – the Red Cross on them, non-stop night and day. I went to Chatham Hospital to see a brother of mine, who was there, from the Front and I saw all the soldiers come in from Hill 60.

Never shall I forget the sight as long as I live. They were unhealthy, they were verminous, and they used to say, 'It's Hell.' That was their words, only a few more adjectives with it, but that's their words, 'It was Hell.' But I know that they were glad to see women at home and the nurses who looked after them. There they were, soldiers lying in Chatham Hospital from that battle scene, and how grateful they were for a kindly word from their womenfolk.

The Death of Rupert Brooke

W. Denis Browne

'England's truest singer'

Rupert Brooke died at 4.46 with the sun shining all round his cabin, and the cool sea breeze blowing through the door and the shaded windows. No one could have wished a quieter or a calmer end than in that lovely bay, shielded by the mountains and fragrant with sage and thyme.

All our ships were under orders to sail for Turkey the next morning at 6 a.m. So – we decided to bury him the same night on the island. We felt sure he would not have wished to be buried at sea, and if we had left his coffin on the French ship until we could reclaim it, we might never have seen it again; for they were bound for Asia, we for Europe. Under the circumstances then we decided to bury him on Skyros that evening, and found a most lovely olive grove about a mile up the valley from the sea.

We buried him there by cloudy moonlight. He wore his uniform and on the coffin were his helmet, belt and pistol (he had no sword). We lined the grave with flowers and olive, and laid an olive wreath on the coffin. The chaplain, who saw him in the afternoon, read the service, very simply; the firing party fired three volleys and the bugles sounded the Last Post.

And so we laid him to rest. He once said in a chance talk that he would like to be buried in a Greek Island. He could have no lovelier one than Skyros, and no quieter resting-place.

On the grave, we (his brother officers) heaped blocks of white marble; the men of his company made a great wooden cross for his head with his name on it, and his platoon put a smaller one at his feet. On the back of the large cross our Greek interpreter wrote a Greek inscription in pencil, which means:

Here lies
The servant of God
Sub-Lieutenant in the
English Navy
Who died for the
Deliverance of Constantinople from
the Turks

The next morning we sailed and had no chance of re-visiting his grave.

But no words of mine can tell you the sorrow of those whom he has left behind him here. None of us knew him without loving him, but those who knew him chiefly as a poet of the rarest gifts, the brightest genius, know that the loss is not only ours, but the world's. He was just coming into his own; what he had written had reached a zenith of perfection that marked him as belonging to the very finest.

It was so hard that he should die the day before we opened battle – cut off by disease, when he had given himself to England, of which his last poems have shown him to be the truest singer.

Denis Browne was killed a fortnight later.

RUPERT BROOKE

'The Soldier'

Winston Churchill wrote Brooke's obituary for *The Times* and Dean Inge read the poet's 'The Soldier' from the pulpit of St Paul's Cathedral on Easter Sunday:

If I should die, think only this of me
That there's some corner of a foreign field
That is for ever England. There shall be

In that rich earth a richer dust concealed;
A dust whom England bore, shaped, made aware,
Gave, once, her flowers to love, her ways to roam,
A body of England's breathing English air,
Washed by the rivers, blest by suns of home.

And think, this heart, all evil shed away,
A pulse in the eternal mind, no less
Gives somewhere back the thoughts by England given;
Her sights and sounds; dreams happy as her day;
And laughter, learnt of friends; and gentleness,
In hearts at peace, under an English heaven.

DAILY MAIL

'The Sinking of the *Lusitania*'

As A. J. P. Taylor noted, the use of the U-boat in war had not
been foreseen. The Germans declared a blockade of the British
Isles in 1915. When a German U-boat sank the *Lusitania*, which
was carrying some munitions but also a hundred Americans, the
Daily Mail spoke for England.

We chronicle today the foulest of the many foul crimes that
have stained the German arms. The great Cunard liner
Lusitania, the pride of two continents and a household word
among Britons and Americans all over the earth, was torpedoed yesterday off the Irish coast. She sank rapidly and with
a loss of life that must, we fear, inevitably prove heavy.

There is but one word for such an infamy. It is not an act
of war, it is a case of sheer, cowardly murder. Before she
sailed from New York the German Embassy in Washington
advertised in the American papers that all travellers crossing
the Atlantic would embark at their own risk. Many of the
1,200 passengers who had booked their berths in the
Lusitania were warned by mysterious telegrams that she

would be sunk. The warning was disregarded. It seemed incredible that even the German pirates would attack a liner that served no military purpose and was known to be carrying hundreds of neutral non-combatants, women and children as well as men. But the Americans and ourselves have still to learn the character of our German foe. He is free from all the restraints of humanity. He is a stabbing, slashing, trampling, homicidal maniac, dead to all sense of respect for the laws of God and man, a wild and cunning beast that has broken loose and must be caught and killed before there can again be any peace or security in the world. The premeditation of his latest atrocity merely adds to its fiendishness.

To the American people who have suffered from this felon's blow equally with ourselves we address no words of impertinent counsel. But we do venture to offer them from the bottom of our hearts a message of the profoundest sympathy. It is at such times as these that the essential kinship of the English-speaking peoples is made unmistakably manifest. We share their indignation, their loathing and contempt for the assassins who sneak under the waters and wage a campaign of murder against unarmed and defenceless passenger ships, merchant vessels, and fishing trawlers; and we promise them that, so far as in us lies, the deaths of these American citizens shall be avenged.

For the British Government and the British people there is one clear moral to be drawn from what has happened. It is that we must fall upon Germany tooth and nail, fight her with her own weapons, decline any longer to be bound by restrictions that she herself repudiates, and gather up all our resources to crush this brood of vipers into impotence.

We shall suffer much, we shall lose men by the thousands, and ships, it may be, by the score, but in the end, please God, we shall have cleansed Europe and the world of a venomous pest.

ERNST TOLLER

A Dead Man

Ernst Toller (1893–1939) enlisted in the 1st Bavarian Foot Artillery
Regiment in 1915, was sent to the Western Front and asked for a
transfer to the front-line trenches because, as a Jew, he thought he
was being victimised by his platoon commander. He served at
Verdun and in 1916 suffered a nervous breakdown and was discharged. He became a socialist and pacifist and supported the
German Revolution of October 1918. He suffered under the Nazis
and committed suicide in New York in May 1939.

One night we heard a cry, the cry of one in excruciating
pain; then all was quiet again. Someone in his death agony,
we thought. But an hour later the cry came again. It never
ceased the whole night. Nor the following night. Naked and
inarticulate the cry persisted. We could not tell whether it
came from the throat of German or Frenchman. It existed in
its own right, an agonized indictment of heaven and earth.
We thrust our fingers into our ears to stop its moan; but it
was no good: the cry cut like a drill into our heads, dragging
minutes into hours, hours into years. We withered and grew
old between those cries.

Later we learned that it was one of our own men hanging
on the wire. Nobody could do anything for him; two men
had already tried to save him, only to be shot themselves.
We prayed desperately for his death. He took so long about
it, and if he went on much longer we should go mad. But on
the third day his cries were stopped by death.

I saw the dead without really seeing them. As a boy I
used to go to the Chamber of Horrors at the annual fair, to
look at the wax figures of emperors and kings, of heroes and
murderers of the day. The dead now had the same unreality,
which shocks without arousing pity.

I stood in the trench cutting into the earth with my pick. The point got stuck, and I heaved and pulled it out with a jerk. With it came a slimy, shapeless bundle, and when I bent down to look I saw that wound round my pick were human entrails. A dead man was buried there.

A – dead – man.

What made me pause then? Why did those three words so startle me? They closed upon my brain like a vice; they choked my throat and chilled my heart. Three words, like any other three words.

A dead man – I tried to thrust the words out of my mind; what was there about them that they should so overwhelm me?

A – dead – man –

And suddenly, like light in darkness, the real truth broke in upon me; the simple fact of Man, which I had forgotten, which had lain deep buried and out of sight; the idea of community, or unity.

A dead man.

Not a dead Frenchman.

Not a dead German.

A dead man.

All these corpses had been men; all these corpses had breathed as I breathed; had had a father, a mother, a woman whom they loved, a piece of land which was theirs, faces which expressed their joys and their sufferings, eyes which had known the light of day and the colour of the sky. At that moment of realization I knew that I had been blind because I had wished not to see; it was only then that I realized, at last, that all these dead men, Frenchmen and Germans, were brothers, and I was the brother of them all.

After that I could never pass a dead man without stopping to gaze on his face, stripped by death of that earthly patina which masks the living soul. And I would ask, who were you? Where was your home? Who is mourning for you now? But I never asked who was to blame. Each had defended his own country; the Germans Germany, the Frenchmen France; they had done their duty . . .

HENRI BARBUSSE

'Not made for human slaughter'

When Henri Barbusse's novel *Le Feu*, translated as *Under Fire*, was published in 1916 it won France's most prestigious literary prize, the Prix Goncourt. It influenced both Siegfried Sassoon and Wilfred Owen. Barbusse served on the Western Front in Artas and Picardy from 1914 until early 1916. *Under Fire* was written in hospitals after he was wounded. In this extract Barbusse describes the humanity of the men as they prepare to go over the top.

Stooping or kneeling we bestir ourselves; we buckle on our waist-belts; shadowy arms dart from one side to another; pockets are rummaged. And we issue forth pell-mell, dragging our knapsacks behind us by the straps, our blankets and pouches.

Outside we are deafened. The roar of gunfire has increased a hundredfold, to left, to right, and in front of us. Our batteries give voice without ceasing.

'Do you think they're attacking?' ventures a man. 'How should I know?' replies another voice with irritated brevity.

Our jaws are set and we swallow our thoughts, hurrying, bustling, colliding, and grumbling without words.

A command goes forth – 'Shoulder your packs!'
'There's a counter-command,' shouts an officer who runs down the trench with great strides, working his elbows, and the rest of his sentence disappears with him. A counter-command! A visible tremor has run through the files, a start which uplifts our heads and holds us all in extreme expectation.

But no; the counter-order only concerns the knapsacks. No pack; but the blanket rolled round the body, and the trenching-tool at the waist. We unbuckle our blankets, tear them open and roll them up. Still no word is spoken; each has a steadfast eye and the mouth forcefully shut. The corporals and sergeants go here and there, feverishly spurring the silent haste in which the men are bowed: 'Now then, hurry up! Come, come, what the hell are you doing? Will you hurry, yes or no?'

A detachment of soldiers with a badge of crossed axes on their sleeves clear themselves a fairway and swiftly delve holes in the wall of the trench. We watch them sideways as we don our equipment.

'What are they doing, those chaps?' – 'It's to climb up by.'

We are ready. The men marshal themselves, still silently, their blankets crosswise, the helmet-strap on the chin, leaning on their rifles. I look at their pale, contracted, and reflective faces.

They are not soldiers, they are men. They are not adventurers, or warriors, or made for human slaughter, neither butchers nor cattle. They are labourers and artisans whom one recognises in their uniforms. They are civilians uprooted, and they are ready. They await the signal for death or murder; but you may see, looking at their faces between the vertical gleams of their bayonets, that they are simply men.

Each one knows that he is going to take his head, his chest, his belly, his whole body, and all naked, up to the rifles pointed forward, to the shells, to the bombs piled and ready, and above all to the methodical and almost infallible machine-guns – to all that is waiting for him yonder and is now so frightfully silent – before he reaches the other soldiers that he must kill. They are not careless of their lives, like brigands, nor blinded by passion like savages. In spite of the doctrines with which they have been cultivated they are not inflamed. They are above instinctive excesses. They are not drunk, either physically or morally. It is in full consciousness, as in full health and full strength, that they are massed there to hurl themselves once more into that sort of madman's part imposed on all men by the madness of the human race. One sees the thought and the fear and the farewell that there is in their silence, their stillness, in the mask of tranquillity which unnaturally grips their faces. They are not the kind of hero one thinks of, but their sacrifice has greater worth than they who have not seen them will ever be able to understand.

They are waiting; a waiting that extends and seems eternal. Now and then one or another starts a little when a bullet, fired from the other side, skims the forward embankment that shields us and plunges into the flabby flesh of the rear wall.

The end of the day is spreading a sublime but melancholy light on that strong unbroken mass of beings of whom some only will live to see the night. It is raining – there is always rain in my memories of all the tragedies of the great war. The evening is making ready, along with a vague and chilling menace; it is about to set for men that snare that is as wide as the world.

ROBERT GRAVES

'Bloody warts'

The poet and novelist Robert Graves (1895–1985) went straight from Charterhouse to the Royal Welch Fusiliers, where he became a captain. He wrote *Goodbye to All That* in 1929 and it became a modern classic. In 1914 not only was there a gulf between officers and other ranks but there was also a gulf between the long-serving regular officers and the raw young recruits from the public schools, as Graves vividly recalls in this passage from his book. The 'Surrey-man' was Hilary Drake-Brockman, another subaltern.

The Second Battalion was peculiar in having a battalion mess instead of company messes: another peacetime survival. The Surrey-man said grimly: 'It's supposed to be more sociable.'

We went together into the big *château* near the church. About fifteen officers of various ranks were sitting in chairs reading the week's illustrated papers or, the seniors at least, talking quietly. At the door I said: 'Good morning, gentlemen,' the new officer's customary greeting to the mess. No answer. Everybody glanced at me curiously. The silence that my entry had caused was soon broken by the gramophone, which began carolling:

We've been married just one year,
And Oh, we've got the sweetest,
We've got the neatest,
We've got the cutest
Little oil stove.

I found a chair in the background and picked up the *Field*. The door burst open suddenly, and a lieutenant-colonel with a red face and angry eye burst in. 'Who the blazes put that record on?' he shouted to the mess. 'One of the bloody warts, I expect. Take it off, somebody! It makes me sick. Let's have some real music. Put on the "Angelus".'

Two subalterns (in the Royal Welch a subaltern had to answer to the name of 'wart') sprang up, stopped the gramophone, and put on 'When the Angelus is ringing'. The young captain who had put on 'We've been married' shrugged his shoulders and went on reading; the other faces in the room remained blank.

'Who's that?' I whispered to the Surrey-man.

He frowned. 'That's Buzz Off,' he muttered. 'The second-in-command.'

Before the record had finished, the door opened and in

came the colonel; Buzz Off reappeared with him. Everybody jumped up and said in unison, 'Good morning, sir,' this being his first appearance that day.

Instead of returning our loyal greeting and asking us to sit down, he turned spitefully to the gramophone: 'Who on earth puts this wretched 'Angelus' on every time I come into the mess? For heaven's sake play something cheery for a change!' With his own hands he took off the 'Angelus', wound up the gramophone, and put on 'We've been married just one year'. At that moment a gong rang for lunch, and he abandoned his task.

We filed into the next room, a ball-room with mirrors and a decorated ceiling, and took our places at a long, polished table. The senior sat at the top, the junior competed for seats as far away from them as possible. Unluckily I got a seat at the foot of the table, facing the colonel, the adjutant, and Buzz Off. Not a word was spoken down my end, except an occasional whisper for the salt or the beer – very thin French stuff. Robertson, who had not been warned, asked the mess-waiter for whisky. 'Sorry, sir,' said the mess-waiter, 'it's against orders for the young officers.' Robertson was a man of forty-two, a solicitor with a large practice, and had stood for Parliament in the Yarmouth division at the previous election.

I saw Buzz Off glaring at us and busied myself with my meat and potatoes.

He nudged the adjutant. 'Who are those two funny ones down there, Charley?' he asked.

'New this morning from the militia. Answer to the names of Robertson and Graves.'

'Which is which?' asked the colonel.

'I'm Robertson, sir.'

'I wasn't asking you.'

Robertson winced but said nothing. Then Buzz Off noticed something.

'T'other wart's wearing a wind-up tunic.' Then he bent forward and asked me loudly: 'You there, wart! Why the hell are you wearing your stars on your shoulder instead of your sleeve?'

My mouth was full, and everybody had his eyes on me. I swallowed the lump of meat whole and said: 'Shoulder stars were a regimental order in the Welsh Regiment, sir. I understood that it was the same everywhere in France.'

The colonel turned puzzled to the adjutant: 'Why on earth is the man talking about the Welsh Regiment?' And then to me: 'As soon as you have finished your lunch you will visit the master-tailor. Report at the orderly room when you're properly dressed.'

In a severe struggle between resentment and regimental loyalty, resentment for the moment had the better of it. I said under my breath: 'You damned snobs! I'll survive you all. There'll come a time when there won't be one of you left in the battalion to remember this mess at Laventie.'

JOHN WILLIAMS

The White Feather

Admiral Charles Fitzgerald founded the Order of the White Feather in August 1914 with the aim of coercing men to join up by persuading women to present them with a white feather if they were not wearing a uniform. A white feather was a symbol of cowardice from cock fighting, where it was believed that a cockerel with a white feather in its tail was a poor fighter.

With public sentiment swinging strongly towards conscription, it had become embarrassing for any fit-looking young man to be seen not wearing khaki. There had been social pressure on men to 'join up' ever since the early volunteering days of 1914, when the popular romantic novelist, Baroness Orczy, had sent a jingoistic appeal to the *Daily Mail*, addressed to the 'Women and Girls of England'. 'Your hour has come!' she exhorted them. 'Together we have laughed and cried over that dauntless Englishman the Scarlet Pimpernel and thrilled with enthusiasm over the brave doings of his League. Now we shall form ourselves into an Active Service League, its sole object: influencing sweethearts, brothers, sons and friends to recruit. Pledge: I hereby pledge myself most solemnly in the name of my King and Country, to persuade every man I know to offer his services to his country, and I also pledge myself never to be seen in public with any man who being in every way free and fit has refused to respond to his country's call.' Twenty thousand women joined the League, receiving special badges, and the King himself acknowledged the movement.

By mid-1915 the lost illusions about the short duration of the war, and the lengthening casualty lists, had intensified this attitude. It was increasingly felt that unenlisted men were dodging their clear-cut duty and leaving all the sacrifice to their brothers in khaki: they were not 'doing their bit'. And it was now that the 'white feather' activity began, said to have been originated by an admiral in Folkestone who urged young women to present men in civilian dress with white feathers. As the idea caught on, any young man not in khaki – who may well have been rejected as medically unfit or have neglected to wear the armlet issued to him to show that he had enlisted or was in a 'starred' occupation – was liable to be dubbed by irresponsible females with the 'Order of the White Feather'. Typical of the treatment accorded to the man still in 'civvies' was an advertisement appearing in *The Times* in July: 'Jack, F. G. – if you are not in khaki by the 20th I shall cut you dead – Ethel M.' War widows and mothers who had lost sons would stop young civilians in the streets and demand why they were not doing their duty. Young women formed leagues pledging themselves not to marry young men who had not joined up. Males of service age were publicly insulted, like the two young men in a London tram who, as an observer noted, were assailed by three girls with the words: 'Why don't you fellows enlist? Your King and Country want you. We don't.' Thereupon one girl stuck a white feather in one of the men's buttonholes.

MICHAEL MACDONAGH

As a reporter on *The Times*, where he had worked for twenty years, Michael MacDonagh was well placed to describe life on the home front in London:

September 9, 1915: I had another novel War experience last night. I was writing in my study about twenty minutes to eleven o'clock when the roar of bombs and guns broke upon my meditations, and, stepping out upon a little balcony of the room at the back of the house, commanding a wide sweep of the sky north-east, I saw an amazing spectacle. High in the sky was a Zeppelin picked out of the darkness by search-lights – a long, narrow object of a silvery hue! I felt like what a watcher of the skies must feel when a new planet swims into his ken. For it was my first sight of an enemy airship!

The raider was striking at the very heart of London – in the City between St. Paul's Cathedral and the Mansion House and Bank. This I found when I went out this morning to see the effects of the bombardment. In Wood Street and Silver Street, behind Cheapside and quite close to Guildhall, there were gutted and smouldering warehouses, some other premises less damaged, and there were deep holes in the roadways. At last, I thought, the War has begun to knock the London we know and love about our ears! Making my way across Moorgate Street and down London Wall, I came to the place where a bomb dropped in front of a motor-omnibus bound for Liverpool Street Station, and blew it to pieces. Twenty people were on board, including the driver

and conductor. Nine were instantly killed and eleven seriously injured. The driver had both his legs blown off and
died on his way to hospital. The door of a block of offices
was pointed out to me where the housekeeper standing on
the steps was killed. The roadway was strewn with the glass
of shattered windows. Entering Liverpool Street Station, I
saw a section of the permanent way that was wrecked by a
bomb. The same raider dropped a bomb in Bartholomew
Close, which smashed the windows of Bart's Hospital, and
narrowly missed the ancient church of St. Bartholomew-the-
Great. The crowds of visitors to the extensive area of the
raid were more curious than angry, I thought.

The casualties of the raid were thirty-eight killed (including two policemen) and one hundred and twenty-four
wounded. Property destroyed is valued at over half a million
sterling. No independent reports of the raid is permitted in
the newspapers.

LIEUTENANT R. P. HAMILTON

'Small beans of human beings'

Robert Hamilton, a subaltern with the London Regiment, was
twenty-five when he wrote this reflective piece. 'Governor' was
his sixteen-year-old cousin James Peyton. Hamilton was killed in
September.

But of big things here there is no such thing as criticism.
You've either done well or done badly; and the only escape
is to lay low. The King's Regulations are such that, if an
officer obeys an order from a superior officer, knowing it to
be unwise, or in obeying that order fatal consequences
occur, he is to blame equally with the officer who gave the
order. On the other hand if an officer refuses to obey an
order, he is shot or sent home. Which means, you see, that
you get the fruits of your action whatever it may be. All this

tends to make one lose one's personality and think always of the job; and Governor dear, men dying so often and so near makes you think very small beans of human beings, and although when making runs at home or talking to you – often – I become a wonderful person to me, out here you get too near the bottom of things to boost any. Cavalry gents and gunners and such-like people, who can go for graceful strolls between whiles miles behind the lines with nicely-creased trousers and brown shoes may still preserve the cocky hold of their heads; but give 'em two or three months in the trenches, with men near them splashed to mincemeat, and they won't think overmuch inwardly. There's no danger for the most conceited of infantrymen to think overmuch of 'emselves, provided they have a continuous dose of trench.

LIEUTENANT F. C. HITCHCOCK

'Men blown to pieces'

Lieutenant Hitchcock served with the 2nd Battalion, the Leinster Regiment, from 1915 to 1918 and kept a diary. This is his entry from Hooge for 12 August:

Dawn broke at 4 a.m. and within half an hour I had two casualties. Pte. Bowes was killed by an explosive bullet in the head, and Pte. Duffey was wounded by an enfilade bullet from the Bellewaarde Farm. We buried Bowes in a disused trench behind our line. One could now make out the country all round perfectly, and what an appalling sight it was. Everywhere lay the dead. The ridge in our rear was covered with dead men who had been wiped out in the final assault of the German position; their faces were blackened and swollen from the three days' exposure to the August sun, and quite unrecognisable. Some of the bodies were badly dismembered; here and there a huddled up heap of khaki on the brink of a shell-crater told of a direct hit. Haversacks, tangled heaps of webbing equipment, splintered rifles, and broken stretchers, lay scattered about. The ground was pitted with shell-holes of all sizes. A few solitary stakes and strands of barbed wire was all that was left of the dense mass of German entanglements by our artillery. Several khaki figures were hanging on these strands in hideous attitudes. In front of us, in No-Man's-Land, lay a line of our dead, and ahead of them on the German parapet lay a Durham Light Infantry officer. They had advanced too far, and had got caught by a withering machine gun fire from Bellewaarde Wood. There was not a blade of grass to be seen in No-Man's-Land or on the ridge, the ground had been completely churned up by the shells, and any of the few patches of grass which had escaped had been burnt up by the liquid fire. Some 50 yards away, around the edge of the Bellewaarde Wood, ran the sand-bagged parapet of the German line on its serpentine course towards the shattered remains of Hooge.

The wood itself had suffered severely from the shell-fire. Most of the trees were badly splintered, and some had been torn up by the roots. There was little foliage to be seen on any of the trees. All that was left of the once bushy-topped trees which lined the Menin Road were shattered stumps, and the telegraph poles stood drunkenly at all angles. Although numbers of the Durhams and the York and Lancs lay about in the open, yet our trench was full of German belonging to the Wurtembergers.

They lay in the dug-outs, where they had gone to seek refuge from our guns, in fours and in fives. Some had been killed by concussion, others had had their dug-outs blown in on top of them, and had suffocated. Our gunners had done their work admirably, and the strong cover made with railway lines and sleepers and with trunks of trees had collapsed under the fierce onslaught of our shells. The faces of the enemy dead, who had thus been caught or pinned down by the remnants and shattered timber of their death-traps, wore agonised expressions.

Here and there, where portions of the trench had been obliterated by the shells, legs and arms in the German field-grey uniform stuck out between piles of sand-bags. Thousands of rounds of fired and unexpended cartridges lay about the parapets, and grounded into the bottom of the trench. German Mausers, equipment, helmets, and their peculiar skin-covered packs lay everywhere. The ground was littered with portions of the enemy uniforms saturated in blood. Serving in the Ypres salient one was not unaccustomed to seeing men blown to pieces and, there-fore, I expected to see bad sights on a battle-field, but I had never anticipated such a dreadful and desolate sight as the Hooge presented, and I never saw anything like it again during my service at the front. The reason that Hooge was such a particularly bloody battle-field was due to the fact that it covered such a small area in the most easterly por-tion of the salient, and was not spread out over miles of open country like those battle-fields on the Somme in 1916. Hooge had been continually under shellfire since the First Battle of Ypres in October, and the ridge which we had dug into had been captured and recaptured five times since April.

At 5 a.m. some shells fell all along our line. Then all was silent and we realised the meaning of those dozen shells which traversed our line from left to right, ranging shots for a pukka bombardment. Within fifteen minutes of the burst of the last shot, a steady bombardment started all along our line.

The enemy gunners carried out their work in a most sys-tematic manner. They fired by a grouping system of five shells to a limited area, under 12 yards. Then they burst shrapnel over this area. This plan for shelling our position was undoubtedly successful, as three out of the five shells hit our trench, obliterating it, blowing in the parapet on top of the occupants, or exposing them to a deadly hail from shrapnel shells. Our casualties were beginning to mount up. A direct hit with a 5.9 knocked out six men of the Machine-Gun Section, Burlace, Cleary, and Scully being killed. As there was no communication trench, the walking wounded 'chanced their arms' going back over the ridge which was being raked by shrapnel fire, but the badly wounded had to lie in the bottom of the trench and wait until the cover of darkness to be carried back by the stretcher bearers. Some of these stretcher cases were, unfortunately, hit for a second time and killed.

At 3 p.m. exactly the enemy started a second bombardment of our line. All along our trench they put down a terrific barrage of shells of every description. High explosives and crumps exploded on our parapets, leaving burning and smoking craters, and torn flesh, and above, screeching and whining shrapnel burst over us. We were shelled in a worse position, and it seemed that every enemy gun around the Salient was turned on to our 400 yards of trench on the left of the Menin Road. Shells from the Bellewaarde direction enfiladed us, and blew in our few traverses; shells from the Hill 60 direction ploughed great rifts in our parados, and broke down our only protection from back-bursts, and now and then some horrible fragments of mortality were blown back from the ridge with lyddite wreaths.

The blackened bodies of our dead, and the badly wounded, lay about at the bottom of the trench, and it was impossible to move without treading on them. Every few minutes the call for the stretcher bearers would be heard. Then along came Morrissey with his first-aid bag, closely followed by Reid. 'Steady, me lad,' they'd say to a man who had lost his leg, but could still feel the toes of the lost limb tingling, ''tis a grand cushy one you've got. Sure you're grand entirely, and when darkness sets in we'll carry you off to the dressing station, and then ye'll get your ticket for Blighty.' How they stuck it, those company stretcher bearers, Morrissey, Reid, Dooley, and Neary.

ROLAND LEIGHTON

'What price victory?'

Roland Leighton and Vera Brittain, whom we last met at Speech Day at Uppingham in the summer of 1914, became engaged when Leighton was on leave in August. On 14 September, after his return to France, he sent this eloquent letter to Vera describing conditions in the trenches north of Albert:

This afternoon I am very sleepy, almost too sleepy to write. It is partly the warm weather and chiefly perhaps not getting more than 4 hours' sleep at night and being too busy to get any rest in the day. I have been rushing round since 4 a.m., superintending the building of dug-outs, drawing up plans for the draining of trenches, doing a little digging myself as a relaxation, and accidentally coming upon dead Germans while looting timber from what was once a German fire trench. This latter was captured by the French not so long ago and is pitted with shell-holes each big enough to bury a horse or two in. The dug-outs have been nearly all blown in, the wire entanglements are a wreck, and in among [this] chaos of twisted iron and splintered timber and shapeless earth are the fleshless, blackened bones of simple men who poured out their red, sweet wine of youth unknowing, for nothing more tangible than Honour or their Country's Glory or another's Lust of Power. Let him who thinks that War is a glorious golden thing, who loves to roll forth stirring words of exhortation, invoking Honour and Praise and Valour and Love of Country with as thoughtless and fervid a faith as inspired the priests of Baal to call on their own slumbering deity, let him look at a little pile of sodden grey rags that cover half a skull and a shin bone and what might have been Its ribs [*sic*], or at this skeleton lying on its side, resting half-crouching as it fell, supported on one arm, perfect but that it is headless, and with the tattered clothing still draped around it; and let him realise how grand and glorious a thing it is to have distilled all Youth and Joy and Life into a foetid heap of hideous putrescence. Who is there who has known and seen who can say that Victory is worth the death of even one of these?

ARTHUR WIMPERIS

'I'll Make a Man of You'

Its suggestive chorus made this song very popular and it helped the campaign to recruit more men for the war:

The army and the navy need attention
The outlook isn't healthy you'll admit,
But I've got a perfect dream of a new recruiting scheme
Which I really think is absolutely it.
If only other girls would do as I do
I believe that we could manage it alone,
For I turn all suitors from me but the sailor and the
    Tommy
I've an army and a navy of my own.

Chorus:
On Sunday I walk out with a soldier,
On Monday I'm taken by a Tar
On Tuesday I'm out with a baby Boy Scout,
On Wednesday a Hussar,

On Thursday I gang oot wi' a Scottie,
On Friday, the Captain of the crew,
But on Saturday I'm willing
If you'll only take the shilling,
To make a man of every one of you.

I teach the tenderfoot to face the powder
That adds an added lustre to my skin,
And I show the raw recruit how to give a chaste salute,
So when I'm presenting arms he's falling in,
It makes you almost proud to be a woman
When you make a strapping soldier of a kid,
And he says 'You put me through it and I didn't want to
    do it,
But you went and made me love you, so I did.'

Chorus:
On Sunday I walk out with a Bo'sun
On Monday a Rifleman in green,
On Tuesday I choose a 'sub' in the 'Blues',
On Wednesday a Marine;
On Thursday, a Terrier from Tooting
On Friday, a Midshipman or two,
But on Saturday I'm willing
If you'll only take the shilling,
To make a man of every one of you.
[QE]

The soldiers' rude version was:

[QS]
On Monday I touched her on the ankle,
On Tuesday I touched her on the knee,
On Wednesday I confess, I lifted up her dress.
On Thursday I saw it, gorblimey,

On Friday I put me 'and upon it,
On Saturday she gave my balls a treat,
On Sunday after supper, I whopped me fucker up 'er
And now I'm paying forty bob a week! Gorblimey.

New recruits were given a shilling for expenses when they signed up.

LEONARD THOMPSON

Gallipoli

The Dardanelles Campaign, which lasted from February 1915 to January 1916, was an attempt to seize the Turkish Dardanelles Strait, which connects the Sea of Marmara with the Aegean Sea, with the aim of pushing Turkey out of the war and relieving pressure on Russia.

There were heavy losses after landings on the Gallipoli peninsula in April and August. All forces were withdrawn from December. There were 250,000 casualties. Winston Churchill resigned from the Admiralty. The failure of the campaign meant that the Western Front became the decisive arena of the war.

Leonard Thompson was a discontented farm worker from Suffolk who joined the Army in March 1914, became a machine-gunner in the 3rd Essex Regiment and was 'damned glad' for seven shillings a week. His account of his experiences at Gallipoli appears in Ronald Blythe's classic study of rural Suffolk, *Akenfield*:

We arrived at the Dardanelles and saw the guns flashing and heard the rifle-fire. They heaved our ship, the *River Clyde*, right up to the shore. They had cut a hole in it and made a little pier, so we were able to walk straight off and on to the beach. We all sat there – on the Hellespont! – waiting for it to get light. The first things we saw were big wrecked Turkish guns, the second a big marquee. It didn't make me think of the military but of the village fêtes. Other people must have thought like this because I remember how we all rushed up to it, like boys getting into a circus, and then found it all laced up. We unlaced it and rushed in. It was full of corpses. Dead Englishmen, lines and lines of them, with their eyes wide open. We all stopped talking. I'd never seen a dead man before and here I was looking at two or three hundred of them. It was our first fear. Nobody had mentioned this. I was very shocked. I thought of Suffolk and it seemed a happy place for the first time.

Later that day we marched through open country and came to within a mile and a half of the front line. It was incredible. We were there – at the war! The place we had reached was called 'dead ground' because it was where the enemy couldn't see you. We lay in little square holes, myself next to James Sears from the village. He was about thirty and married. That evening we wandered about on the dead ground and asked about friends of ours who had arrived a month or so ago. 'How is Ernie Taylor?' – 'Ernie? – he's gone.' 'Have you seen Albert Paternoster?' – 'Albert? – he's gone.' We learned that if 300 had 'gone' but 700 were left, then this wasn't too bad. We then knew how unimportant our names were.

I was on sentry that night. A chap named Scott told me that I must only put my head up for a second but that in this time I must see as much as I could. Every third man along the trench was a sentry. The next night we had to move on to the third line of trenches and we heard that the Gurkhas were going over and that we had to support their rear. But when we got to the communication trench we found it so full of dead men that we could hardly move. Their faces were quite black and you couldn't tell Turk from English. There was the most terrible stink and for a while there was nothing but the living being sick on to the dead. I did sentry again that night. It was one-two-sentry, one-two-sentry all

along the trench, as before. I knew the next sentry up quite
well. I remembered him in Suffolk singing to his horses as he
ploughed. Now he fell back with a great scream and a look
of surprise – dead. It is quick, anyway, I thought. On June
4th we went over the top. We took the Turks' trench and
held it. It was called Hill 13. The next day we were relieved
and told to rest for three hours, but it wasn't more than
half an hour before the relieving regiment came running
back. The Turks had returned and recaptured their trench.
On June 6th my favourite officer was killed and no end of us
butchered, but we managed to get hold of Hill 13 again. We
found a great muddle, carnage and men without rifles shouting 'Allah! Allah!', which is God's name in the Turkish
language. Of the sixty men I had started out to war from
Harwich with, there were only three left.

We didn't feel indignant against the Government. We
believed all they said, all the propaganda. We believed the
fighting had got to be done. We were fighting for England.
You only had to say 'England!' to stop any argument. We
shot and shot. On August 6th they made a landing at Suvla
Bay and we took Hill 13 again, and with very few casualties
this time. We'd done a good job. The trench had been lost
yet again, you see. When we got back for the third time we
found a little length of trench which had somehow missed
the bombardment. There were about six Turkish boys in it
and we butchered them right quick. We couldn't stay in the
trench, we had to go on. Then we ran into machine-gun fire
and had to fall flat in the heather, or whatever it was.
Suddenly my mate caught fire as he lay there. A bullet had
hit his ammunition belt. Several people near jumped up and
ran back, away from the burning man and the machine-
gun fire. I could hear the strike of the gun about a foot
above my head. I lay between the burning man and friend
of mine called Darky Fowler. Darky used to be a shepherd
Helmingham way. I put my hand out and shook him, and

said 'Darky, we've got to go back. We *must* go back!' He never answered. He had gone. I lay there thinking how funny it was that I should end my life that night. Then my mate began to go off like a firework – the fire was exploding his cartridges. That did it! I up and ran.

LIEUTENANT JOHN HUGH ALLEN

'Shall I go to heaven or hell, sir?'

Lieutenant John Allen, a New Zealander educated at Jesus College, Cambridge, and commissioned in the Worcestershire Regiment, sent this letter to his family from Gallipoli, where he was killed on 6 June:

> Before I came here and fought in a war, I read casualty lists with sympathy but without intense emotion. But nothing can convey to you how dreadful is the sight of the suffering, badly wounded man – nothing can convey it to you. I heard two short surprised coughs, and saw a man bend and fall. A friend darted to him, opened his tunic, and said to him: 'You're done, Ginger, you're done; they've got you.' This frankness really seemed the most appropriate and sincere thing. They bandaged him up, with the lint every soldier carries inside his tunic; then, knowing evidently that I had a medicine chest with sedatives, he asked for me. By a stroke of providence I was given a beautiful pocket-case with gelatine lamels [discs] of a number of drugs. It cost twenty-seven shillings – and under present circumstances worth ten times the money. By the light of the moon – useful for once – I read and tore off the perforated strip. While I was with him he said some remarkable things. I had only known him a day or so, but spotted him at once as a first-rate soldier. He said: 'Shall I go to heaven or hell, sir?' I said with perfect confidence: 'To heaven.' He said: 'No, tell me as man to man.' I repeated what I had said. He said: 'At any rate I'll say my

prayers,' and I heard him murmuring the common meal grace. A little later he made up a quite beautiful prayer – 'Oh, God, be good and ease my pain – if only a little'; and then: 'I thought I knew what pain was.' All the while it was unbearable to see what he suffered. Someone digging in the trench hard by said: 'He's sinking.' He said: 'What's that?' I said: 'He means the trench.' And then, slowly drawn out: 'I didn't mean to groan, but' – in a long-drawn-out groan – 'I must.' It was intolerable. They carried him back to this trench on a blanket. He remains here twenty-four hours, till a stretcher can be brought up in the dark to convey him through the communication trench to the supports.

KEITH MURDOCH

'Ghastly bungling'

The Australian journalist Keith Murdoch (1886–1952), father of Rupert, was outraged by what he saw at Gallipoli, where he thought thousands of soldiers were being sacrificed by incompetent British commanders. He wrote an eight-thousand-word report which was read by Lloyd George, who was now Prime Minister. The report had an almost instant effect. General Sir Ian Hamilton was relieved of his command and within days Lord Kitchener, Secretary for War, agreed to evacuation.

What I want to say to you now very seriously is that the continuous and ghastly bungling over the Dardanelles enterprise was to be expected from such a general staff as the British Army possesses, so far as I have seen it. The conceit and complacency of the red feather men are equalled only by their incapacity. Along the lines of communications, and especially at Mudros, are countless high officers and conceited young cubs who are plainly only playing at war. What can you expect of men who have never worked seriously, who have lived for their appearance and for social distinction and self-satisfaction, and who are now called on to conduct a gigantic war? Kitchener has a terrible task in getting pure work out of these men, whose motives can never be pure, for they are unchangeably selfish. I want to say frankly that it is my opinion, and that without exception of Australian officers, that appointments to the general staff are made from motives of friendship and special influence. Australians now loathe and detest any Englishman wearing red . . .

OSKAR MEYER

Longing for Peace

Oskar Meyer, a philosophy student from Kiel, wrote this letter from the Vosges on 29 August. He was killed, aged twenty-four, in April 1916.

Fourteen days in the Line! Much has happened during that time. Many times our trench was under heavy French shell-fire, and our battalion has had heavy losses, though the 6th Company has come off comparatively lightly. We lay on a very steep hill-side, which was difficult to shoot at, and many of the boomers intended for us fell into the valley below, where there is still plenty of room!

The French attacked several times, and are still holding some small sections of our line. Some of our saps are less than ten yards apart. At first we threw bombs at each other, but then we agreed not to throw any more, and not to go on firing. Latterly we exchanged cigars, cigarettes, money, letters, etc. We looked out over the parapet in broad daylight and gazed innocently at one another. The French gave our men some photographs of their big guns. One of them photographed our most advanced post, after having shaken him warmly by the hand! We had several quiet days in that spot. If a Frenchman had orders to throw bombs several times during the night, he agreed with his 'German comrade' to throw them to the left and right of the trench. At night the French perched themselves on the parapet and smoked cigarettes, which are visible for a long distance.

While we were on such good terms, our Pioneers were able to do a lot of useful work and constructed a new advance-post without being fired at. Naturally the French Pioneers were not idle either.

The whole incident shows that the French soldiers have a great longing for peace, just as we have, and that if it depended on them, peace would have been made long ago. We too hope that the time may not be very long now.

CHARLES HAMILTON SORLEY

'Purged of all false pity'

Captain Charles Hamilton Sorley of the 7th Battalion, the Suffolk Regiment, educated at Marlborough College, was one of England's most promising writers when he was killed by a sniper in France in October. This extract is taken from a letter written in August and is followed by Sorley's final sonnet:

... out in front at night in that no-man's land and long graveyard there is a freedom and a spur. Rustling of the grasses and grave tap-tapping of distant workers: the tension and silence of encounter, when one struggles in the dark for moral victory over the enemy patrol: the wail of the exploded bomb and the animal cries of wounded men. Then death and the horrible thankfulness when one sees that the next man is dead: 'We won't have to carry him in under fire, thank God; dragging will do': hauling in of the great resistless body in the dark, the smashed head rattling: the relief, the relief that the thing has ceased to groan: that the bullet or bomb that made the man an animal has now made the animal a corpse. One is hardened by now: purged of all false pity: perhaps more selfish than before. The spiritual and the animal get so much more sharply divided in hours of encounter, taking possession of the body by swift turns.

'When you see millions . . .'
When you see millions of the mouthless dead
Across your dreams in pale battalions go,
Say not soft things as other men have said,
That you'll remember. For you need not so.
Give them not praise. For, deaf, how should they know
It is not curses heaped on each gashed head?
Nor tears. Their blind eyes see not your tears flow.
Nor honour. It is easy to be dead.
Say only this, 'They are dead.' Then add thereto,
'Yet many a better one has died before.'
Then, scanning all the o'ercrowded mass, should you
Perceive one face that you loved heretofore,
It is a spook. None wears the face you knew.
Great death has made all his for evermore.

VERA BRITTAIN

'Vera to Roland', Buxton, 10 September 1915

Vera Brittain sent to her fiancé Roland Leighton this poignant insight into the effects of the war on the lives of wounded soldiers and girlfriends:

What do you think of this for an 'agony' in the 'Times'? 'Lady, fiancé killed, will gladly marry officer totally blinded or otherwise incapacitated by the War.'

At first sight it is a little startling. Afterwards the tragedy of it dawns on you. The lady (probably more than a girl or she would have called herself 'young lady'; they always do) doubtless has no particular gift or qualification, and does not want to face the dreariness of an unoccupied and unattached old maidenhood. But the only person she loved is dead; all men are alike to her and it is a matter of indifference whom she marries, so she thinks she may as well marry someone who really needs her. The man, she thinks, being blind or maimed for life will not have much opportunity of falling in love with anyone and even if he does will not be able to say so. But he will need a perpetual nurse, and she if married to him can do more for him than an ordinary nurse and will perhaps find some relief for her sorrow in devoting her life to him . . . It is purely a business arrangement, with an element of self-sacrifice which redeems it from utter sordidness. Quite an idea, isn't it!

LIONEL SOTHEBY

On Gaining Great Happiness

Lionel Sotheby was one of the 1131 Etonians who were killed in the Great War. He put a letter in a sealed envelope to be opened in the event of his death. After he died in 1915, his family broke the seal.

To my Parents, School, dear Friends, and Brother:
These few words are meant to embody a farewell . . . In bidding farewell, I feel no remorse, as indeed I have been resigned to the future paved out for me by One Who knows best . . . Think me not pessimistic; I am one who would sooner die a glorious end than live for years and die as is one's wont in ordinary life. I have been spared often, but my time will assuredly come; I sense it now. That is why I write.

Eton will be to the last the same as my Parents and dear Friends are to me . . .

Never have such wonderful and heroic private soldiers

assembled in such masses as today. To die with such is an honour. To die for one's school is an honour . . . To die for one's country is an honour. But to die for right and fidelity is a greater honour than these. And so I feel it now. When it is an honour to die, then be not sad; rather rejoice and be thankful that such an opportunity was given to me. I beg of you all, mourn for me not and bewail me not, but pray. Life is but a passing image; so let it be with me.

Farewell; I shall think of you all to the last, even as I think of you now.

'Greater promotion there is not than promotion into the wide unknown.'

'Floreat Etona.'

'Remain Calm and quiet, for all is well.'

The cables are cut and I slip away, fading into pinky mists as at early dawn, remembering you all.

From beyond I call with love and affection.

Farewell.

FRANK RICHARDS

The Fate of a Deserter

Many critics rate *Old Soldiers Never Die* by Frank Richards (1883–1961; real name Francis Philip Woodruff) as the finest memoir of the Great War written by a private. Richards, an orphan, served with the Royal Welch Fusiliers and saw Robert Graves and Siegfried Sassoon at close quarters and both writers helped him with his book.

Whilst we were there Private Jones of my company arrived back with an escort. He had been a deserter since the 24th September. Jones was a grand front-line soldier, but when out of action was continually in trouble; a few days before the 24th he had the whole of his field punishment washed out for gallant work on patrols. A man doing field punishment never received any pay, and when the company were paying out Jones went in front of the young officer who was paying out to receive his, but was refused. Jones: 'I beg your pardon, sir. I am not now on Number Ones and I am entitled to pay, the same as the remainder of the company.' The young officer, who was not a Royal Welch Fusilier, but attached to us from the East Surreys, replied: 'I know that, Jones, but I am afraid if I give you any pay you will be getting in trouble again.' Jones then told him that he hadn't received any pay for twelve months and that it would be impossible for him to get in any trouble with five francs. But the officer wouldn't give him any. 'All right,' said Jones, 'no bloody fighting.' Jones spent the remainder of the day in the guard-room until he paraded that night to march off with the Company. Going down the La Bassée Road Jones fell out and when the roll was called in the assembly trenches he was absent. We old hands who knew him very well knew when he said to the officer 'No bloody pay, no bloody fighting' that he would keep his word. There was only one penalty for being absent from an attack, and that was death.

During the time he was awaiting his court-martial he lived like an owl and drank like a lord. He was sentenced to death, but owing to his gallant conduct on numerous occasions in the line and other extenuating circumstances in his case, the sentence was altered to ten years imprisonment. Jones was one of the few men that were sent away to serve their sentences. Seven months later one of our chaps met him on the Somme: he was then a full sergeant in one of our service battalions. He had been sent to England to serve his sentence and after being three weeks in prison was took in front of the Governor, who asked him if he would like to go back out to the front. 'I don't mind,' said Jones, 'as long as I don't have to go back to my old battalion.' Three days later he was released and sent back out with a draft to one of our service battalions where he was made a full sergeant two months later. I knew several cases like this. Good soldiers were not kept very long in prison after the year 1915.

ALAN SEEGER

'I have a rendezvous with Death'

Alan Seeger's rendezvous with death occurred on 23 July 1916, when he was killed, aged twenty-nine, by machine-gun fire while charging German trenches at Belloy-en-Santerre.

I have a rendezvous with Death
At some disputed barricade,
When Spring comes back with rustling shade
And apple-blossoms fill the air –
I have a rendezvous with Death
When Spring brings back blue days and fair.

It may be he shall take my hand
And lead me into his dark land
And close my eyes and quench my breath –
It may be I shall pass him still.
I have a rendezvous with death
On some scarred slope of battered hill,
When Spring comes round again this year
And the first meadow-flowers appear.

God knows 'twere better to be deep
Pillowed in silk and scented down,
Where Love throbs out in blissful sleep,
Pulse nigh to pulse, and breath to breath,
Where hushed awakenings are dear . . .
But I've a rendezvous with Death
At midnight in some flaming town,
When Spring trips north again this year,

And I to my pledged word am true,
I shall not fail that rendezvous.

LOOS

The British advanced on the Germans at Loos on 26 September and
were decimated – of the fifteen thousand infantry of the 21st and
24th Divisions, more than eight thousand were killed or wounded.
Three weeks later, sixteen thousand British soldiers had been killed
and twenty-five thousand had been wounded. The Germans were
astonished at the recklessness and the fortitude of the British. The
following accounts of the action were written in the diaries of the
German 153rd Regiment and the 15th Reserve Regiment.

153rd Regiment
Dense masses of the enemy, line after line, appeared over the
ridge, some of their officers mounted on horseback and
advancing as if carrying out a field-day drill in peacetime.
Our artillery and machine-guns riddled their ranks as they
came on. As they crossed the northern front of the Bois
Hugo, the machine-guns there caught them in the flank and
whole battalions were annihilated. The English made five
consecutive efforts to press on past the wood and reach the
second-line position,
Ten columns of extended line could clearly be distinguished, each one estimated at more than a thousand men,
and offering such a target as had never been seen before, or
even thought possible. Never had the machine-gunners such
straightforward work to do nor done it so effectively. They
traversed to and fro along the enemy's ranks unceasingly. The
men stood on the fire-steps, some even on the parapets, and
fired triumphantly [*jauchsend*] into the mass of men advancing across the open grassland. As the entire field of fire was
covered with the enemy's infantry the effect was devastating
and they could be seen falling literally in hundreds.

15th Reserve Regiment

In spite of it [the intensity of the fire] the extended columns continued their advance in good order and without interruption. When they reached the Lens road one of our companies advanced from the Hulluch trench in an attempt to divert the attack, but only a small party of the enemy swung round to meet it, the mass took no notice and went on regardless past the southern front [of the village]. Here they came under the enfilade fire both of the troops lining the position and of a battery of artillery concealed in the village. Their losses mounted up rapidly and under this terrific punishment the lines began to get more and more confused. Nevertheless they went on doggedly right up to the wire entanglement. Confronted by this hopeless impenetrable obstacle and faced by continuous machine-gun and rifle fire the survivors began to turn and retire in confusion, though scarcely one in ten that had come forward seemed to go back again.

W. WALKER

How Easy to Scorn the Coward

Private Walker joined the colours (13th Northumberland Fusiliers) in September 1914 and went to France with the 21st Division a year later. He described how he was wounded during the Battle of Loos in this article which he wrote for *Everyman* magazine. A machine-gun bullet went through his elbow joint, requiring ten months in hospital, after which he was unfit for active service.

There began to burst above us some kind of shell. We flopped on our stomachs when this began. The ground was a quagmire, but mud was better than blood, and we wallowed in the friendly filth. After a while the cannonade quietened and word came along that we were to advance.

We did not appear to have an officer anywhere near us. The fellows near me were strangers. Hunger, thirst, and sleeplessness made me faint and weak.

The mud on my greatcoat made it monstrously heavy, so that it flapped like lead against my legs, making the going utterly wearisome. I would willingly have died just then. The ground was so uneven that headway was difficult to make, not uneven by nature either, but by the huddled heaps of men's bodies. The ground had been bitterly contested.

Hill 70 rose above us darkly. It scarcely deserves the name of hill; quite a moderate rise, but that night it appeared intensely black and forbidding against the flaring lights that gleamed intermittently in the sullen sky beyond it. So far we had seen no enemy. They were over the hill. Would to God, I prayed, they would stop over. Never was I more out of love with war than that first night at the Front. Arrived at the foot of the hill we got orders to lie down. My watch said two o'clock.

Shall I attempt to hide my feelings as I lay there? Why should I? They were the common property of the whole host. How easy it is to sit in an armchair and scorn the coward who flees the conflict.

I confess that I lay in that welter of mud devising schemes of escape; of getting back to the rear on some flimsy pretext or other. I even thought of going sick if I could have found a pain other than in my heart and nerve.

Bullets started dropping all around us like heavy thunder rain. The men on both sides of me lay snoring in exhausted slumber. I felt lonely and wretched. At last I fell asleep. 'The next b— I catch asleep I'll put a bullet through him.' By the flame light I could see the large face of an officer with the badge of the D.L.I. in his cap. No one spoke, so he snarled again: 'The next. Do you hear?' he grated. 'Yes, sir,' someone muttered. No sooner had he walked off than we all dropped off to sleep again till the grey morning dawned.

It was Sunday, if it mattered. The sun peeped brightly over the hill. Except for a general murmuring from the serried and prostrate ranks, there was scarcely a sound. In the early light an appalling scene lay before us. The ground was strewn with dead and dying men. Pieces of horse and gun equipment and the motley gear of war lay everywhere.

Behind the blackening cocks of hay lay men in the attitude of firing, now dead. One lay not two yards from my feet, a giant Scotsman stretched out in the posture of crucifixion. Leaning against a wall was a young fair lad of the Lincolnshires, kneeling as if in prayer; his hands clasped, his twisted face crimson from an ugly gash in his temple.

There was no food to be had – indeed food was far from my thoughts. I was thinking of the battle before us. We got the order to advance up the hill. There was no officer near us, so an aged sergeant, who ought to have been at home with his wife, took charge of us. Our unreadiness to fight was obvious. Our greatcoats impeded our progress; we were still without ammunition in our rifles; our bayonets were still in the frogs.

As we slowly advanced the Germans began sending over all kinds of stuff. The hill gave us fair cover and we weren't long in gaining the La Bassee road. Here we took off our greatcoats, loaded up, fixed bayonets, and made ready to advance.

At six o'clock, word came along that a general advance was to be attempted; already some had left the shelter of the roadway and were running over the open plateau. 'Come on, lads, we've got to do it,' cried stout-hearted old Sergeant J–. We braced ourselves and leapt on to the open field. Misery makes heroes of us all. The darkness of cowardice that had so clouded my mind and filled me with self-despair had fled. I marvelled at my carelessness. Possibly it was the reaction of exhaustion upon my brain. I neither know nor care, but there it was.

The shell-fire was deafening enough, but the clatter that commenced with our further advance was abominable. It was as if the enemy were attacking with a fleet of motorcycles – it was the hellish machine guns. I saw no foe.

Where he was I couldn't gamble: somewhere in front, how distant or how near no one seemed to know. The firing was indescribably fierce; an invisible hail of lead winged past my ears unceasingly; one flicked my sleeve. How pitiful it is to recall. Our chaps fell like grass under the mower, mostly shot in the guts; so well had he got our range. Groans and shouting were added to the clamour.

A bullet hit me; I feel its sharp sting yet; it felled me to the ground. I imagined the shot was in the head at first, but I soon found out its position when I essayed to crawl back to the road: it had pierced a hole through my right elbow. There was nothing for it but to walk, and, although the fire was growing intense, I managed to dodge the rest.

How heavily we had suffered could be gauged by the bleeding mass of men that lay in the shelter of the roadside. One old man who used to play the pipes in my company was shot just above the belt and was sobbing hysterically for water. A stretcher bearer forbade anyone to give it to him.

Poor old beggar, he should never have been there: he was sixty all but six months, so he used to say. How he raved for water. On my other side a young lad was attempting to staunch the blood which flowed from his opened cheek with a filthy rag. I fainted.

It took me a long time to get to the casualty clearing station. There appeared to be hundreds of wounded all making for the same place. As I passed along, a shell burst on a field-gun battery which had just galloped into a new position. There did not seem to be anything but brown dust and rubbish left. Flame and explosion surrounded me.

On arrival at the dressing station, came inoculation

against tetanus; two delirious days spent in a ruined byre awaiting the ambulance. First I was taken to Arques, then to Rouen, and from thence to England, where, at Stratford-on-Avon, soft beds and kind hearts awaited me.

C. E. MONTAGUE

The Regular Officer

C. E. Montague (1867–1928) worked on the *Manchester Guardian* for thirty-five years until 1925. He was briefly on the front line in March 1916 and became an intelligence officer in July 1916 and was a censor and official soldier-writer. He wrote a novel on the war, *Rough Justice*, and in 1922 *Disenchantment*, a collection of essays that are a scathing indictment of the complacency of the English regular officer. In this extract Montague recalls how idealism perished in the trenches after the Battle of Loos:

> The winter after the battle of Loos a sentry on guard at one part of our line could always see the prostrate skeletons of many English dead. They lay outside our wire, picked clean by the rats, so that the khaki fell in on them loosely – little heaps of bone and cloth half hidden now by nettles and grass. If the sentry had been a year in the army he knew well enough that they had gone foredoomed into a battle lost before a shot was fired. After the Boer War, you remember, England under the first shock of its blunders, had tried to find out why the staff work was so bad. What it found, in the words of a famous report, was that the fashion in sentiment in our Regular army was to think hard work 'bad form'; a subaltern was felt to be a bit of a scrub if he worried too much about discovering how to support an attack when he might be more spiritedly employed in playing polo.
>
> And so the swathes of little brown bundles, with bones showing through, lay in the nettles and grass.
>
> Consider the course of the life of the British Regular officer

as you had known him in youth – not the pick, the saving few, the unconquerably sound and keen, but the average, staple article made by a sleek, complacent, snobbish, safe, wealth-governed England after her own image. Think of his school; of the mystic aureole of quasi-moral beauty attached by authority there to absorption in the easy thing – in play; the almost passionate adoration of all those energies and dexterities which, in this world of evolution towards the primacy of the acute, full brain, are of the least possible use as aids to survival in men and to victory in armies. Before he first left home for school he may have been a normal child who only craved to be given some bit, any odd bit, of 'real work', as an experience more thrilling than games. Like most children, he may have had a zestful command of fresh, vivid, personal speech, his choice of words expressing simply and gaily the individual working of his mind and his joy in its work. Through easy contacts with gardeners, gamekeepers and village boys he often had established a quite natural unconscious friendliness with people of different social grades. He was probably born of the kind that pries young, that ask, when they play on sea sands, why there are tides, and what goes on in the sky that there should be rain. And then down came the shades of the prison-house. To make this large, gay book of fairy tales, the earth, dull and stale to a child importunately fingering at its covers might seem a task to daunt the strongest. But many of the teachers of our youth are indomitable men. They can make earth's most ardent small lover learn from a book what a bore his dear earth can be, with her strings of names of towns, rivers and lakes, her mileages *à faire mourir*, and her insufferable tale of flax and jute. With an equal firmness your early power of supple and bright-coloured speech may be taken away and a rag-bag of feeble stock phrases, misfits for all your thoughts, and worn dull and dirty by everyone else, be forced upon you instead of the treasure you had.

You may leave school unable to tell what stars are about you at night or to ask your way to a journey's end in any country but your own. Between your helpless mind and most of your fellow-countrymen thick screens of divisions are drawn, so that when you are fifteen you do not know how to speak to them with a natural courtesy; you have a vague idea that they will steal your watch if you leave it about. Above all, you have learned that it is still 'bad form' to work; that the youth with brains and no money may well be despised by the youth with money and no brains; that the absorbed student or artist is ignoble or grotesque, that to be able to afford yourself 'a good time' is a natural title to respect and regard; and that to give yourself any 'good time' that you can is an action of spirit. So it went on at prep school, public school, Sandhurst, Camberley. That was how Staff College French came to be what it was. And as it was what it was, you can guess what Staff College tactics and strategy were and why all the little brown bundles lay where they did in the nettles and grass . . .

These apprehensions were particularly apt to arise if you had spent an hour that day in seeing herds of the English 'common people' ushered down narrowing corridors of barbed wire into some gap that had all the German machine-guns raking its exit, the nature of Regular officers' pre-war education in England precluding the prompt evolution of any effectual means on our side to derange the working of this ingenious abattoir. We had asked for it all. We had made the directing brains of our armies the poor things that they were. Small blame to them if in this season of liquidation they failed to produce assets which we had never equipped them to earn – mental nimbleness, powers of individual observation, quickness to cap with counterstrokes of invention each new device of the fertile specialists opposite. Being as we had moulded them, they had probably done pretty well in doing no worse.

What's done we partly may compute
But know not what's resisted.

Who shall say what efforts it may have cost some of those
poor custom-ridden souls not to veto, for good and all, an
engine of war so far from 'smart' as the tank, or to accept
any help at all from such folk as the new-fangled, untradi-
tional airmen, some of whom took no shame to go forth to
the fray in pyjamas. Not they alone, but all of ourselves,
with our boastful chatter about the 'public school spirit', our
gallant, robust contempt for 'swats' and 'smugs' and all who
invented new means to new ends and who trained and used
their brains with a will – we had arranged for these easy
battues of thousands of Englishmen, who, for their part, did
not fail. Tomorrow you would see it all again – a few hundred square yards of ground gained by the deaths, perhaps,
of 20,000 men who would

Go to their graves like beds, fight for a plot
Which is not tomb enough and continent
To hide the slain.

So it would go on, week after week, sitting after sitting of
the dismal court that liquidated in the Flanders mud our
ruling classes' wasted decades, until we either lost the war
outright or were saved from utter disaster by clutching at aid
from French brains and American numbers. Like Lucifer
when he was confronted with the sky at night, you 'looked
and sank',

Around the ancient track marched, rank on rank,
The army of unalterable law.

What had we done, when we could, that the stars in their
courses should fight for us now? Or left undone, of all that

could provoke this methodical universe of swinging and returning forces to shake off such dust from its constant wheels?

JOHN MCCRAE

'In Flanders Fields'

Major McCrae's poem, which appeared anonymously in *Punch* on 8 December, was the most popular of the war. It is one reason the British Legion chose the poppy as its symbol of remembrance.

McCrae (1872–1918) was a Canadian physician who fought in 1914 but was then assigned to the Medical Corps. He died of pneumonia on active duty in 1918.

> *In Flanders fields the poppies blow*
> *Between the crosses, row on row*
> *That mark our place; and in the sky*
> *The larks, still bravely singing, fly*
> *Scarce heard amid the guns below.*
>
> *We are the dead. Short days ago*
> *We lived, felt dawn, saw sunset glow,*
> *Loved and were loved, and now we lie*
> *In Flanders fields.*
>
> *Take up our quarrel with the foe:*
> *To you from failing hands we throw*
> *The torch; be yours to hold it high.*
> *If ye break faith with us who die*
> *We shall not sleep, though poppies grow*
> *In Flanders fields.*

FLANDERS

Letter found on the body of an unknown German officer:

> After crawling out through the bleeding remnants of my
> comrades, and through the smoke and debris, wandering
> and running in the midst of the raging gunfire in search of
> refuge, I am now awaiting death at any moment. You do not
> know what Flanders means. Flanders means endless human
> endurance. Flanders means blood and scraps of human
> bodies. Flanders means heroic courage and faithfulness even
> unto death.

REVEREND STIRLING GAHAN

Edith Cavell – 'Patriotism is not enough'

The English nurse Edith Cavell, who was born in Norfolk in 1865,
was the first matron of the Berkendael Medical Institute in Brussels,
which became a Red Cross hospital during the war. She was
arrested by the Germans in August and convicted of assisting up to
two hundred Allied prisoners to escape to Holland and Britain. The
Reverend Stirling Gahan, the British chaplain in Brussels, reports
on a meeting with Cavell on the eve of her execution:

> On Monday evening, October 11th, I was admitted by spe-
> cial passport from the German authorities to the prison of
> St. Gilles, where Miss Edith Cavell had been confined for ten
> weeks.
>   The final sentence had been given early that afternoon.
>   To my astonishment and relief I found my friend perfectly
> calm and resigned. But this could not lessen the tenderness
> and intensity of feeling on either part during that last inter-
> view of almost an hour.
>   Her first words to me were upon a matter concerning

herself personally, but the solemn asseveration which accompanied them was made expressedly [*sic*] in the light of God and eternity.

She then added that she wished all her friends to know that she willingly gave her life for her country, and said: 'I have no fear nor shrinking; I have seen death so often that it is not strange or fearful to me.'

She further said: 'I thank God for this ten weeks' quiet before the end. Life has always been hurried and full of difficulty. This time of rest has been a great mercy. They have all been very kind to me here. But this I would say, standing as I do in view of God and eternity, I realize that patriotism is not enough. I must have no hatred or bitterness towards any one.'

We partook of the Holy Communion together, and she received the Gospel message of consolation with all her heart. At the close of the little service I began to repeat the words, 'Abide with me,' and she joined softly in the end.

We sat quietly talking until it was time for me to go. She gave me parting messages for relations and friends. She spoke of her soul's needs at the moment and she received the assurance of God's Word as only the Christian can do.

Then I said 'Good-by,' and she smiled and said, 'We shall meet again.'

The German military chaplain was with her at the end and afterwards gave her Christian burial.

PASTOR LE SEUR

The Execution

The chaplain appointed by the Germans to minister to prisoners sentenced to execution was Pastor Paul le Seur, who describes the last moments of Edith Cavell's life. A statue of Cavell stands near the National Gallery in London.

In the cell a flickering gas-flame was burning. Two large bouquets of withered flowers, which had been standing there for ten weeks, awakened the impression of a vault. The condemned lady had packed all her little property with the greatest care in a handbag.

I accompanied her through the long corridors of the great prison. The Belgian prison officials stood there and greeted her silently with the highest respect. She returned their greetings silently. Then we boarded the motor-car which awaited us in the yard. A few moments later the Catholic priest, P. Leyendecker, and the other condemned person, M. Baucq, an architect about 35 years of age, came out at the same door. Baucq went up to each one of the German sentries who were standing about, gave them his hand, and said in Flemish: 'Let us bear no grudge.' Then the two motorcars drove out in the early morning hour. I sat beside Edith Cavell in order to accompany her – to her own burial.

When we arrived at the Tir National, a company at full war strength (two hundred and fifty men) stood there, in accordance with the regulations, under the command of a staff-officer. A Military Court Councillor, Dr. Stoeber, with his secretary, Capt. Behrens in command of St. Gilles prison, an officer from the Commander's office, and a medical man, Dr. Benn, were on the spot. We clergymen led the condemned persons to the front. The company presented their rifles, and the sentence was about to be read aloud in German and in French, when M. Baucq called out with a clear voice in French: 'Comrades, in the presence of death we are all comrades.' He was not allowed to say anything more. The sentence was read out, and then the clergymen were permitted to have a last word with the condemned persons. I thought I had to make this as brief as possible. I took Miss Cavell's hand and only said (of course in English) the words: 'The grace of our Lord Jesus Christ and the love of God and the Communion of the Holy Ghost be with you for ever. Amen.'

She pressed my hand in return, and answered in those words: 'Ask Mr. Gahan to tell my loved ones later on that my soul, as I believe, is safe, and that I am glad to die for my country.'

Then I led her a few steps to the pole, to which she was loosely bound. A bandage was put over her eyes, which, as the soldier who put it on told me, were full of tears.

Then a few seconds passed, which appeared to me like eternity, because the Catholic clergyman spoke somewhat longer with M. Baucq, until he also stood at his pole.

Immediately the sharp commands were given, two salvoes crashed at the same time – each of eight men at a distance of six paces – and the two condemned persons sank to the ground without a sound. My eyes were fixed exclusively on Miss Cavell, and what they now saw was terrible. With a face streaming with blood – one shot had gone through her forehead – Miss Cavell had sunk down forwards, but three times she raised herself up without a sound, with her hands stretched upwards. I ran forward with the medical man, Dr Benn, to her. He was doubtless right when he stated that these were only reflex movements.

The bullet-holes, as large as a fist in the back, proved, in addition, that without any doubt she was killed immediately. I only mention this fact because untrue rumours have been connected with it. A few minutes later the coffins were lowered into the graves, and I prayed over Edith Cavell's grave, and invoked the Lord's blessing over the poor corpse. Then I went home, almost sick in my soul.

GITZ RICE

'I Want to Go Home'

Soldiers writing home or keeping diaries often mentioned the singing. Bombardier Dudley Gyngell, serving with the London Division of the Royal Field Artillery, described concerts in the camp canteens, the long rooms hung with paper flags and flowers, the haze of cigarette smoke, the laughter and the jokes. And a man on the platform singing a song from Blighty. 'In my mind I can feel the far-off home, as many another there does, while there's a smile in his eye and a joke on his lips perhaps he is thinking "Shall I ever see them again – my mother and my girl?"' The composer Gitz Rice served as a Canadian lieutenant and fought at Ypres, the Somme and Vimy Ridge. He also wrote 'Dear Old Pal of Mine'. This was one of those songs:

I want to go home,
I want to go home,
I don't want to go in the trenches no more,
Where whizz-bangs and shrapnel they whistle and roar
Take me over the sea
Where the Alleyman can't get at me.
Oh my,
I don't want to die,
I want to go home.

I want to go home,
I want to go home,
I don't want to visit la Belle France no more,
For oh the Jack Johnsons they make such a roar.
Take me over the sea
Where the snipers they can't snipe at me.
Oh my,
I don't want to die,
I want to go home.

CHRISTOPHER STONE

'All zig-zag'

Christopher Stone (1888–1959) was an Old Etonian who enlisted as a private in 1914 and was commissioned into the 22nd Royal Fusiliers in 1915. By 1918 he was a major and second-in-command.

He wrote more than a thousand letters to his wife Alyce. This one describes the organisation of the trenches. Stone became famous after the war as the first 'disc-jockey'. As co-editor of the *Gramophone*, with Compton Mackenzie, he was invited by the BBC to present a programme of gramophone records. After the first he received six thousand letters; he was as well known as royalty and film stars.

Cambrin trenches, 17th December, 1915.
My darling one, this is written by the light of a hurricane lamp in a dug out; the Huns are by way of sending some fizz-bangs in this direction and we can hear them pounding and screaming somewhere not far from our heads. But these small shells wouldn't do us much harm even if they got a direct hit. I can't pretend to you that I really enjoyed my first night in the trenches, though there was everything in my favour; a calm luminous night, and no particular strafing going on; a bunk in a dug out to sleep in, and, if the truth must be known, my boots off . . .

Later in fact 2 a.m. of the 18th. The Major and I are alone here. He is on duty and I am more or less. I have just come in from a tour of the firing line. It would interest you as an experience: but I suppose it shall soon bore me to death. I have on my new long waders, thigh gum-boots and a mackintosh and my India-rubber gloves, so am quite proof against the mud. It's a lovely warm night with a bit of moon-light; light enough to see your way without a torch. Most of the trenches have foot boards laid down in them which keeps them fairly clean but greasy. I go up a communication trench first of all up the centre of our 'section' and pass C Coy. headquarters where Black is asleep. MacDougall is said to be out in front by himself examining the wire. I go on to the fire trenches and then turn right-handed. It's all zig-zag work of course: a bay and then a traverse, a bay and a tra-verse, endlessly from the North Sea to the Swiss frontier without a break! In about every third bay there are two sentries standing on the firing step and looking over the parapet. At the corners of the bays there are often glowing braziers and men sleeping round them or half asleep: and you pass the entrance to dug outs and hear men murmuring inside, and the hot charcoal fumes come out. On and on: sometimes I clamber up beside the sentries and look out. There's little to see, rough ground, the barbed wire entanglement about 15 yards away, the vague line of German trenches. If a flare goes up it lights the whole place for 30 seconds and is generally followed by a good deal of rifle fire. You see the flash at the muzzle of the rifle. If you hear a machine gun you duck your head. The bullets patter along the parapet when they do what they call traversing: backwards and forwards they patter – quite a unique mud here that nearly pulls off my boots – 100 yards out towards the Germans, and at the end find 3 or 4 bombers on guard in case the Bosch tries to come across. From this point you can look back at our own front line in both directions; but it's not a very healthy spot as there's a Bosch sniper who has it in his special care, and there's always a chance of being hit in the back by one of our own excited sentries. I crawl back to the less exciting firing line and go to see the parapet where a shell fell today. It burst inside the trench and buried a man and pretty well filled up the entrance to a dug out. The man who was buried was rather badly wounded; and his particular pal who was talking to him and was slightly wounded, wouldn't let anyone else dig him out – it was his privilege . . .

The place is alive with rats and mice: a rat ran over the CO's face last night – ugh! I was luckier, but still it isn't at all pleasant.

There's a most persistent blighter of a Bosche who has got his rifle sighted on the doorway of this dugout and abut every five minutes as I sit here I hear the ping of a bullet in the mud. He does no harm but I suppose he thinks it frightens us. It's wonderful, how they know that this is the headquarters: they shelled us at lunch-time today; but did us no harm, and it was rather fun sitting here eating and telephoning to the gunners to tell them to strafe. They soon shut up the Bosches.

WINSTON CHURCHILL

Douglas Haig

Winston Churchill made this assessment of Sir Douglas Haig as he became the British Commander-in-Chief.

Alike in personal efficiency and professional credentials, Sir Douglas Haig was the first officer of the British Army. He had obtained every qualification, gained every experience and served in every appointment requisite for the General Command. He was a Cavalry Officer of social distinction and independent means, whose whole life had been devoted to military study and practice. He had been Adjutant of his regiment; he had played in its polo team; he had passed through Staff College; he had been Chief Staff Officer to the Cavalry Division in the South African war; he had earned a Brevet and decorations in the field; he had commanded a Column; he had held a command in India; he had served at the War Office; he had commanded at Aldershot the two divisions which formed the only organized British army corps, and from this position he had led the First British Army corps to France. He had borne the principal fighting part in every battle during Sir John French's command. At the desperate crisis of the first Battle of Ypres, British battalions and batteries, wearied, outnumbered and retreating, had been inspired by the spectacle of the Corps Commander riding slowly forward at the head of his whole staff along the shell-swept Menin Road into close contact with the actual fighting line.

1916

On the Western Front 1916 was dominated by two mighty battles – at Verdun, the longest of the war from February to December, and at the Somme from 1 July to 18 November.

In *The Price of Glory* Alistair Horne describes Verdun as the grimmest battle in a grim war. General von Falkenhayn, the German chief of staff, planned to 'bleed France white' and force her out of the war. On 21 February 1400 guns on an eight-mile front started the biggest bombardment yet seen. A million shells were fired on the first day. For the French it was a matter of fierce national pride that Verdun should not fall. *Ils ne passeront pas* – They shall not pass – became their battle cry (and was later to be used by La Pasionaria – political leader Dolores Ibárruri – in the Spanish Civil War). Pétain was eventually sent to take command, and beat back the Germans. He became a national hero and made his reputation (which was later destroyed during the Second World War). The Germans lost 430,000 men. The French lost 542,000.

At Verdun the term 'air force' began to have meaning. As Horne says, never since the Middle Ages and the invention of the longbow had the battlefields of Europe seen the kind of single combat that was now occurring in the skies. 'When the champions of either side met to fight spectacular duels in and out of the clouds, the rest of the war seemed forgotten; even the men in the trenches paused to watch as the hosts of Greece and Troy stood by when Hector and Achilles fought.'

Sir Douglas Haig had now reached the summit and was in command of the greatest army that the Empire had ever put in the field or was ever to amass in the future – and which in a single day on the Somme was to lose more men than any other army in the history of the world. Ninety years later, that is why to say two words – the Somme – is to conjure up visions of (now) unimaginable slaughter. One famous episode demonstrating the spirit that inspired some of the officers – and which suggested that the attack was going to be a walkover – involved Captain Nevill of the 8th East Surreys who bought four footballs and offered a prize to the platoon which first kicked its football up to the German front line. Captain Nevill was killed instantly as he jumped into no man's land. Using the lessons learned from the battles of 1915, Haig had bombarded the German lines for five days before sending his soldiers over the top. But the Germans were well prepared and there were 57,470 Allied casualties on the first day, including 19,240 dead.

It was at the Somme on 15 September that the British first used a new weapon: the tank. But tanks were as yet untried and there were too few for them to be effective. When the battle ended after twenty weeks there had been no Allied breakthrough, although in places the front had advanced about five miles. By the end the British had suffered 420,000 casualties, the French 200,000 and the Germans 450,000.

Strategically, according to A. J. P. Taylor, the Battle of the Somme was an unredeemed defeat for the Allies: it was at the Somme that idealism perished. The enthusiastic volunteers were enthusiastic no longer. 'They had lost faith in their cause, in their leaders, in everything except loyalty to their fighting comrades.' For Britain it was the greatest military tragedy of its history.

A nation that goes to war must expect deaths among the young men it sends, says John Keegan, and there was a willingness for sacrifice before and during the Somme that explains, in part, its horror.

'The sacrificial impulse cannot, however, alleviate its outcome. The regiments of Pals and Chums which had their first experience of war on the Somme have been called an army of innocents and that, in their readiness to offer up their lives in circumstances none anticipated in the heady days of volunteering, it undoubtedly was.'

Jutland, fought in the North Sea in June, was another big battle of 1916. It was the only major action between the British and German fleets during the war. Both sides claimed victory: the British forced the Germans to flee back to port; the Germans sank more ships.

On the home front David Lloyd George succeeded Herbert Asquith as Prime Minister in December. Compulsory military service for single men was introduced in January and British summer time, by which clocks were put forward an hour, allowing vital war work to continue for an extra hour in daylight, was introduced in May. The first raid on Britain by a German aeroplane occurred in November. There were big audiences for music halls and theatres, now subject to an entertainment tax, and nightclubs were popular but, supposedly in the name of economy, museums and art galleries were closed. On Boxing Day, the Government authorised the Board of Agriculture to take possession of unoccupied lands for growing food. So the allotment was born. Soon every bit of spare land – undeveloped building sites, front and back gardens of empty houses, parts of parks and commons, golf courses and tennis courts – was being used to grow vegetables.

JOHN WILLIAMS

The Home Front

On the Western Front 1916 was the year of the Battle of the Somme. Meanwhile in Britain the war was proving to be a great social equaliser:

> Though people were still taking holidays, old posters advertising 'Lovely Lucerne' and 'Gay Boulogne' struck an ironic note on shabby station walls. There was a call for economy

in dress, and smart clothes, along with evening dress in theatres, were now 'bad form'. Errand boys were disappearing, and professional men were carrying home their household groceries. Suburban housewives were cleaning their own doorsteps. Cars were being laid up; whisky was weaker and more expensive; and owing to the call-up the postal service was less efficient. As a sign of full employment, tramps had vanished from the countryside, and it was said that there were now no poor in England except the 'new poor' – writers, musicians and so on. To signalise the new prosperity, eating out was popular: the large London cafés were nightly crowded with customers seeking a little glitter and relaxation after a day's work amid the city's wartime drabness.

While theatres and music halls, now subject to amusement tax, continued to draw big audiences eager for distraction, in the sphere of reading people were discarding light fiction in favour of more serious works on the war and similar themes. But, ostensibly in the name of economy, the Home Office now decreed the closing of museums and picture galleries, regardless of the itinerant crowds of servicemen and others who might have been glad of these amenities. Critics of the closure contrasted it with the proliferation of London's night clubs, of which were said to be a hundred and fifty in Soho. Here toothbrush-moustached young subalterns danced with their 'flapper' girl-friends to the new jazz which had just crossed the Atlantic. Meanwhile, the 'pub' had begun to decline, due to the regulation of hours for serving liquor. War was proving a great equaliser, mixing the social classes (as in the munitions factories) and breaking down old etiquettes – on the trams and buses, for instance, in which junior officers who in 1914 would not have dreamed of using such plebeian transport were now everyday travellers cheerfully handing their fares to the 'conductorettes'. It was also transforming fashion by removing commonplace materials from civilian use. Women ceased wearing tight stays as the necessary steel was commandeered by the Air Board, and the machines for making the eyelets were likewise requisitioned. City men had to abandon their top hats because, owing to the commandeering of hay and straw they could no longer maintain the horses which drew their cabs to the City, and their tall hats would have come to grief in the buses and tubes.

Amid the all-embracing restrictions of the Defence of the Realm Act – and these were now more multifarious than ever – civilians were subject to strange small prohibitions whose purpose was not easily seen. In February the chiming and striking of London's public clocks was banned between sunset and sunrise, and some months later it was forbidden to whistle for cabs between 10 p.m. and 7 a.m. More useful was the famous daylight saving order introduced in May at the suggestion of the London master-builder, William Willet. When Willet had earlier proposed his scheme for advancing Greenwich time by one hour in summer he had been regarded as a crank, but now the value of his 'summer-time' plan was seen – the idea was even taken up in Germany. With the clocks thus put forward, the need for artificial lighting was reduced and vital war work could continue for an extra hour in daylight. Additional time for healthful recreation was also available. Meanwhile, as the great battles of 1916 raged across the Channel, at Verdun and later on the Somme, the war impinged deeper than before into the public consciousness. It was reported in May that the Christian name 'Verdun' was frequently being given at British baptisms: a recognition of the fearful and prolonged struggle being waged by the French around that beleaguered citadel. And at the beginning of July the rumbling of the guns was heard in the peaceful English countryside to bring home to Britons – and among them Lloyd George, who apparently heard them at his house at Walton Heath – the reality of the great British offensive just opened on the Somme.

Vera Brittain

The Smell of the Dead

Vera Brittain's fiancé, Roland Leighton, was killed on 23 December 1915. Three weeks later she was with Leighton's parents. In this letter to her brother Edward she describes the 'terrible' reality of an officer's death when his 'things' are returned home:

All Roland's things had just been sent back from the front through Cox's; they had just opened them and they were all lying on the floor. I had no idea before of the after-results of an officer's death, or what the returned kit, of which so much has been written in the papers, really meant. It was terrible. Mrs Leighton and Clare were both crying as bitterly as on the day we heard of His death, and Mr Leighton with his usual instinct was taking all the things everybody else wanted and putting them where nobody could ever find them. (His doings always seem to me to supply the slight element of humour which makes tragedy so much more tragic.) There were His clothes – the clothes in which He came home from the front last time – another set rather less worn, and under-clothing and accessories of various descriptions. Everything was damp and worn and simply caked with mud. And I was glad that neither you nor Victor nor anyone else who may some day go to the front was there to see. If you had been you would have been overwhelmed by the horror of war without its glory. For though he had only worn the things when living, the smell of those clothes was the smell of graveyards and the Dead. The mud of France which covered them was not ordinary mud; it had not the usual clean pure smell of earth, but it was as though it were saturated with dead bodies – dead that had been dead a long, long time. All the sepulchres and catacombs of Rome could not make me realise mortality and decay and corruption as vividly as did the smell of those clothes. I know now what he meant when he used to write of 'this refuse-heap of a country' or 'a trench that is nothing but a charnel-house'. And the wonder is, not that he temporally lost the extremest refinements of his personality as Mrs Leighton says he did, but that he ever kept any of it at all – let alone nearly the whole. He was more marvellous than even I ever dreamed.

'If the Sergeant Steals Your Rum'

The chorus of the original song, written by Harry Dent and Tom Goldburn, was:

> *Though your heart may ache awhile,*
> *Never mind!*
> *Though your face may lose its smile,*
> *Never mind!*
> *For there's sunshine after rain,*
> *And then gladness follows pain.*
> *You'll be happy once again,*
> *Never mind.*

This is how that chorus was parodied by the soldiers:

> *If the sergeant steals your rum,*
> *Never mind!*
> *If the sergeant steals your rum,*
> *Never mind!*
> *Though he's just a bloody sot,*
> *Just let him take the lot,*
> *If the sergeant steals your rum,*
> *Never mind!*

> *If old Jerry shells the trench,*
> *Never mind!*
> *If old Jerry shells the trench,*

Never mind!
Though the blasted sandbags fly
You have only once to die,
If old Jerry shells the trench
Never mind!

If you get stuck on the wire,
Never mind!
If you get stuck on the wire,
Never mind!
Though the light's as broad as day
When you die they stop your pay,
If you get stuck on the wire,
Never mind!

SIEGFRIED SASSOON

'You were glad and kind and brave'

In this poignant diary entry Siegfried Sassoon (1886–1967), one of the truly great poets of the First World War, mourns the death of Lieutenant David Thomas, 'a gentle soldier, perfect and without stain'. Sassoon's poem 'The Kiss' was first published in the *Cambridge Magazine* in May 1916.

This morning came the evil news from the trenches – first that 'Tracker' Richardson had died of wounds after being knocked over by a shell last night in front of the trenches; this was bad. But they came afterwards and told that my little Tommy had been hit by a stray bullet and died last night. When last I saw him, two nights ago, he had his notebook in his hand, reading my last poem. And I said good night to him, in the moonlit trenches. Had I but known! – the old human-weak cry. Now he comes back to me in memories, like an

angel, with the light in his yellow hair, and I think of him at
Cambridge last August when we lived together four weeks in
Pembroke College in rooms where the previous occupant's
name, Paradise, was written above the door.

So, after lunch, I escaped to the woods above Sailly-
Laurette, and grief had its way with me in the sultry thicket,
while the mare champed her bit and stamped her feet, tethered to a tree: and the little shrill notes of birds came piping
down in the hazels, and magpies flew overhead, and all was
peace, except for the distant mutter and boom of guns. And
I lay there under the smooth bole of a beech-tree, wonder-
ing, and longing for the bodily presence that was so fair.

Grief can be beautiful, when we find something worthy to
be mourned. To-day I knew what it means to find the soul
washed pure with tears, and the load of death was lifted
from my heart. So I wrote his name in chalk on the beech-
tree stem, and left a rough garland of ivy there, and a yellow
primrose for his yellow hair and kind grey eyes, my dear, my
dear. And to-night I saw his shrouded form laid in the earth
with his two companions (young Pritchard was killed this
evening also). In the half-clouded moonlight the parson
stood above the graves, and everything was dim but the
striped flag laid across them. Robert Graves, beside me, with
his white whimsical face twisted and grieving. Once we
could not hear the solemn words for the noise of a machine-
gun along the line; and when all was finished a canister fell
a few hundred yards away to burst with a crash. So Tommy
left us, a gentle soldier, perfect and without stain. And so he
will always remain in my heart, fresh and happy and brave.

For you were glad, and kind and brave;
With hands that clasped me, young and warm;
But I have seen a soldier's grave,
And I have seen your shrouded form.

'The Kiss'
To these I turn, in these I trust –
Brother Lead and Sister Steel.
To this blind power I make appeal,
I guard her beauty clean from rust.

He spins and burns and loves the air,
And splits a skull to win my praise;
But up the nobly marching days
She glitters naked, cold and fair.

Sweet Sister, grant your soldier this:
That in good fury he may feel
The body where he sets his heel
Quail from your downward darting kiss.

F. P. Crozier

Shot at Dawn

Judged by his book *A Brass Hat in No Man's Land*, Commander Frank Percy Crozier was an officer of the 'biff-'em' type caricatured by Evelyn Waugh as Brigadier Ritchie-Hook in his *Sword of Honour* trilogy. More than three hundred men were shot at dawn by the British Army during the Great War. Crozier was present at several executions and here he describes one of them.

The prisoner – Crocker – is produced. Cap off he is marched by the sergeant-major to the centre. The adjutant reads the name, number, charge, finding, sentence and confirmation by Sir Douglas Haig. Crocker stands erect. He does not flinch. Perhaps he is dazed: who would not be? The prisoner is marched away by the regimental police while I, placing myself at the head of the battalion, behind the band, march back to billets. The drums strike up, the men catch step. We all feel bad but we carry out our war-time pose. Crocker didn't flinch, why should we? After tea the padre comes to see me. 'Might I see Crocker?' he asks. 'Of course, Padre, but don't be too long-winded,' I say seriously, 'after you have done anything you can for him tell his company commander. But I don't think his people should be told. He can go into the "died" return. War is all pot-luck, some get a hero's halo, others a coward's cross. But this man volunteered in '14. His heart was in the right place then, even if his feet are cold in '16. What do you say?' 'I quite agree,' answers the good man, much too overcome to say more.

Now, in peace time, I and the rest of us would have been very upset indeed at having to shoot a colleague, comrade, call him what you will, at dawn on the morrow. We would not, in ordinary circumstances, have slept. Now the men don't like it but they have to put up with it. They face their ordeal magnificently. I supervise the preliminary arrangements myself. We put the prisoner in a comfortable warm place. A few yards away we drive in a post, in a back garden, such as exists with any villa residence. I send for a certain junior officer and show him all. 'You will be in charge of the firing party,' I say, 'the men will be cold, nervous and excited, they may miss their mark. You are to have your revolver ready, loaded and cocked; if the medical officer tells you life is not extinct you are to walk up to the victim, place the muzzle of the revolver to his heart and press the trigger. Do you understand?' 'Yes, Sir,' came the quick reply. 'Right,' I add, 'dine with me at my mess to-night.' I want to keep this young fellow engaged under my own supervision until late at night, so as to minimise the chance of his flying to the bottle for support. As for Crocker, he leaves this earth, in so far as knowing anything of his surroundings is concerned, by midnight, for I arrange that enough spirituous liquor is left beside him to sink a ship. In the morning, at dawn, the snow being on the ground, the battalion forms up on the public road.

Inside the little garden on the other side of the wall, not ten yards distant from the centre of the line, the victim is carried to the stake. He is far too drunk to walk. He is out of view save from myself, as I stand on a mound near the wall. As he is produced I see he is practically lifeless and quite unconscious. He has already been bound with ropes. There are hooks on the post; we always do things thoroughly in the Rifles. He is hooked on like dead meat in a butcher's shop. His eyes are bandaged – not that it really matters, for he is already blind. The men of the firing party pick up their rifles, one of which is unloaded, on a given sign. On another sign they come to the *Present* and, on the lowering of a handkerchief by the officer, they fire – a volley rings out – a nervous ragged volley it is true, yet a volley. Before the fatal shots are fired I had called the battalion to attention. There is a pause, I wait. I see the medical officer examining the victim. He makes a sign, the subaltern strides forward, a single shot rings out. Life is now extinct. We march back to breakfast while the men of a certain company pay the last tribute at the graveside of an unfortunate comrade. This is war.

To this sad story there was a sequel. Some months later one of my officers was on leave, and as he had recently been awarded the D.S.O. was entertained to luncheon by his Club. At the function there were present some young business men who had not volunteered for war service. One of these asked my officer if it were true that 'one of your men had been executed for desertion, and if so did he not think it was a very discreditable affair for the battalion and a disgrace to the city?' 'Well,' my officer replied, 'the unfortunate man volunteered to serve his country in the field; you have not done even that yet. He went through the trials of a truly terrible winter in the trenches. He endured bombardment, mud, exposure, cold, frost, trench-feet, sleepless nights and daily drudgery under conditions in which man was never intended to play a part (he had to play a part the whole time to keep going at all). This quite unnatural test broke his spirit. His brain was probably affected. In despair he quitted the line. Why don't you and your other slacking and profiteering friends join up and have a shot at doing better than this unhappy comrade of ours? If you can't stand the test and are executed because you are not endowed with the steel-like qualities which make for war efficiency, I shall think better of you than I do now. Our dead comrade, whom we had to kill with our own hands and rifles *pour encourager les autres,* is a hero compared with you. He tried and failed. He died for such as you! Isn't it time you had a shot at dying for your country?'

Sylvia Pankhurst

Crucifixion

Even for trivial offences the punishment for soldiers was brutal. Field Punishment No. 1 consisted of being strapped to a wagon wheel in the crucifixion position. Handcuffs and fetters were used. A soldier who had witnessed the punishments wrote to Sylvia Pankhurst from France. She published his letter in *Dreadnought* 'but no action was taken'.

A soldier wrote to me describing No. 1 field punishment, as he had endured it at 5th Base Remounts, Calais. His offence was being twenty minutes late from the evening roll call. During his fourteen days' punishment he passed the night, with others thus victimised, in a barbed wire-enclosed compound, having no bed, and only a couple of blankets in which to wrap himself. From 5.30 a.m. to 5 p.m. he was sent out to dig with pick and shovel. During this time only brief meal times were permitted. There were two intervals of half an hour, in which he was compelled to carry a bag containing 95 lbs. of stones, on one shoulder, round and round the camp. At 6 p.m. he was marched into a place which gave him the impression of a butcher's slaughter house, wherein were iron rings, straps, hand-cuffs and ropes, a crucifix and stocks for the torturing of unfortunate men. One of his eight companions in this agony was strapped to the crucifix. He was himself strapped into the stocks. The others were tied up to beams, their feet flung far apart, attached to iron rings in the floor, their hands fastened above their heads. So they remained for two hours, and thereafter were turned back into the comfortless compound, to weary the night through, without bed or bedding, as best they could. The soldier continued:

'I have seen men who have had to be taken out of these torturing stocks and carried into hospital. At No. 16 Veterinary Base, Calais, the soldiers doing No. 1 field pun-ishment are strapped on to the crucifix in the main road (regardless of the weather) and they are compelled to hang there in this degrading manner in full view of the French people for two hours a day . . .

'Men who have forfeited good positions, home, and practically everything they possess, for such paltry offences as I have described, are treated in this shameful manner.'

OTTO HEINEBACH

Goodbye

Otto Heinebach, aged twenty-three, was a philosophy student in Berlin before the war. He wrote this farewell letter on 18 February before the Battle of Verdun. He was wounded the next day and died in September.

I say good-bye to you, my dear Parents and Brothers and Sisters. Thanks, most tender thanks for all that you have done for me. If I fall, I earnestly beg of you to bear it with fortitude. Reflect that I should probably never have achieved complete happiness and contentment. Perhaps my life would, to the very end, have been cleft by the impossibility of reconciling desire and fulfilment, struggle and attainment, yearning and actuality. This is the tragedy of moderately gifted natures, who never being able to reach the heights of creative genius, come eventually, through constant self-criticism, to complete disaster – and I have always been of a melancholy temperament.

I say good-bye to you too, my dear friend, my Friedel. If I am killed, reflect that nobler, far finer men than I have fallen victims to the dark destiny of the race. You know that I would rather, far rather, not die, but the decision does not rest with me. We might have enjoyed more delightful times together – now we may be called upon to renounce them. But you too must keep a good heart if you should have news of my death, and honour my memory by continuing to strive after knowledge, knowledge as we two have understood it, which does not shrink from the verge of an abyss and to which no truth is too appalling. May the intellectual conscience ever remain a disgrace in our eyes.

Farewell. You have known and are acquainted with all the others who have been dear to me and you will say good-bye to them for me. And so, in imagination, I extinguish the lamp of my existence on the eve of this terrible battle. I cut myself out of the circle of which I have formed a beloved part. The gap which I leave must be closed; the human chain must be unbroken. I, who once formed a small link in it, bless it for all eternity. And till your last days remember me, I beg you, with tender love. Honour my memory without gilding it, and cherish me in your loving, faithful hearts.

JACQUES MEYER

Solidarity

The historian Alistair Horne describes Verdun as the 'grimmest battle in that grim war, perhaps in history itself'. It lasted ten months and involved almost three-quarters of the French Army. The fortress of Verdun was the battlefield with 'the highest density of dead per square yard that has probably ever been known,' Horne wrote in *The Price of Glory*.

For the French Verdun became a household name for fortitude, heroism and suffering. When the fighting ended in December, there were 542,000 French casualties, about half of whom were killed. The hero of Verdun was the French commander Henri Philippe Pétain, who in 1940 was to head the infamous Vichy Government which collaborated with the Nazis and who died in disgrace in 1951.

Jacques Meyer had been accepted for the École Normale Supérieure in Paris eight days before war was declared but he immediately enlisted, along with all his class, was commissioned in the infantry and wounded on the Somme. After the war he became a journalist and broadcaster as well as a historian of the Great War. This extract is from an essay he wrote in *Promise of Greatness*:

> The solidarity among the men – old and young, soldiers and the officers near them – was never more important than at Verdun. This moral force, said Pétain, consisted 'less of ardour than of hardy determination, and lay mainly in an inflexible will to defend their families and their goods against the invader.' And this was true for Verdun, the simplest fellow felt obscurely that he had a *mission* to protect what was for him, quite unpretentiously, 'the sacred soil of our country', a mission which, at the worst moments, the chiefs did not hesitate to call sacrificial. But unlike what devolved after the

unsuccessful 1915 offensives, the men at Verdun were no longer haunted by the feeling that they were dying for nothing. For the first and only time, in fact, between the Germans' invasion arrested at the Marne in September, 1914, and their do-or-die onslaught stopped at the same river in May, 1918, the Germans were attempting a widescale attack, with the aim of '"bleeding" the French Army', in Von Falkenhayn's phrase. And once again, as the first time, the soldiers knew they had to dam the mounting tide by raising a wall of their own bodies against it, 'so that they will not pass'. 'They will not pass' became the motto of Verdun.

As for those who had to go to earth, immobile and passive and awaiting the worst under the infernal pounding, it seemed impossible to expect them to rise, exhausted, from the debris of their departure points or shell holes when the enemy attack finally rolled in, following the flamethrowers, and fire on an attacker who thought our positions were deserted, their occupants crushed. And yet almost every time, despite the lack of possible help, with their distress signals unseen, their guns plugged up, the machine guns jammed, the survivors pulled themselves up to try to check the flood. For aside from a rare and understandable panic, these men seemed still to prefer death or capture to the safety of flight.

The image that formed of this 'war within the war' came to create a sort of myth of Verdun. That special aura was the basis of a state of mind among the soldiers which can be divided into three successive stages. When a man went up there, he felt a dim fear. When he left, he no longer was afraid of being afraid. When he left for good, he carried a sense of pride away in his memory. An officer recounts that once he was reading his men the day's communiqué, and it told about a German reverse near the Thiaumont farm where his regiment had stayed. 'Don't say nothing about our losses,' growled a *bonhomme*. But he was the only one to grumble. The others had a little flame of pride in their eyes: 'That's us, it is!' Human beings draw their pride from their worst sufferings.

GILES E. M. EYRE

'They *shall* not pass'

When 2nd Lieutenant Giles Eyre was billeted with a French family, Madame introduced him to her grandson, who said that at Verdun he had become an old man overnight. Eyre translated for his comrades thus:

Day after day pounded by artillery, peering with bleary eyes through the dust and smoke, the earth rocking drunkenly, trenches flattened out and smashed. And then the Boche attacks. Wave after wave of grey figures scramble from their trenches and run forward, howling like maniacs. They fall upon us. Tr – tr – tr – go our mitrailleuses [a multi-barrelled 'volley gun']. The enemy wavers, pauses, gaps appear in his ranks, his men fall in heaps, and the survivors pause, hesitate, then scramble down to cover. And the guns start battering at us again. We are blasted out from our trench-line by sheer weight of metal and cling on in shell-holes, sleepless, tired, almost dead, bewildered, sickened. Our senses reel with the din, the concussion and the impact of projectiles. And the grey hordes attack again and again! By day and by night the struggle goes on. We fight hand to hand with bayonet, teeth and bare hands, and they drive us back. Then our soixante-quinzes [75mm field guns] commence to cough. Reinforcements come up and we counterattack. It is a hellish nightmare, a horror of struggling figures. Knife, bludgeon and grenade come into play. Ours fall in swathes, but we leap over our dead and dying, careless of everything but the enemy in front. We fight like fiends out of Hades and reconquer the

position. And then the Boche starts all over again! Night after
night, day after day this mad saraband with Death goes on
and never ceases! Painfully strengthening a position but to
lose it, attacking to regain it. The stench, the reek of blood,
the countless unburied bodies and the heaps of wailing
wounded, praying and cursing, asking for water, shelter, protection and help, are enough to shatter any man's sanity. We
come out and go back to the caves for a rest, but the shell-fire,
the aeroplanes, they follow us, and anon we go back again
into that flaming hell. As my *copains* disappear in this mael-
strom fresh faces come up to take their places, and in their
turn, within a few days or maybe hours, they melt away like
snow in the sunshine. And I linger on unscathed physically,
but spiritually bruised and broken! Mon Dieu! C'est pas la
guerre! C'est la mort partout et pour tous!' with a weary gesture, and then with new energy he continues: 'But with all this
we have sworn "they *shall* not pass", and if it has to take
every man France has to do it Verdun will remain ours to the
very end. They may batter and bend us, but break we shall
not! I have seen battalion upon battalion of ours, line, chasseurs, Moroccans, Senegalese, Legionnaires and what not,
enter the very maws of hell at Douaumont and the Mort
Homme singing as if going to a marriage feast. I have seen the
remnants come back dirty, tattered, blood-soaked, exhausted,
staggering with fatigue, hardly able to keep on their feet, but
still as game as ever. It is like a road to Calvary, the way from
Verdun Town to the front. Strewn with the shattered bodies of
our manhood, soaked with their blood, but still ours to fight
for and keep!' His eyes flashed and his cheeks flushed in his
excitement as he spoke.

I had always looked on the French soldier with tolerant
good-natured contempt, but the sight of this twenty-two-year-
old veteran, in his faded horizon-blue uniform, war-weary,
sickened, but with unquenched spirit, made me think of the
brave French chivalry of old, and I realized that their famed

martial ardour and Furia Francesa still burnt brightly and strongly in the breasts of their descendants.

COMMANDANT SYLVAIN RAYNAL

'Vive la France'

Commandant Sylvain Raynal, aged forty-nine, had been wounded in 1915 and could walk only with difficulty. For officers who could not go to the front, the War Ministry offered posts as commanders of forts. Raynal went to Vaux at Verdun. He was captured in June but became a Commander of the Légion d'honneur.

Dawn began to break. On every side, we questioned the skyline; invariably not a sign. About 3 a.m. there was still nothing, neither from the south, nor from the right. But from the casemate, Bourges-Left, they warned me that a small body of about the strength of a platoon were sheltering in shellholes not far from the fort. And almost at once the same observers informed me that under a terrible fire, which had decimated them, this little body had thrown down its weapons and was being led off prisoners by the Germans. That was all we saw of the counterattack of 6th June.

During this day, 6th June, the Boche became more active against our barricades. It was as if he guessed the drama which was being played out within, and in actual fact the sufferings of my men, above all the wounded, increased terribly. Thirst, that horrible thirst raged.

I was in my command post with Sous-Lieutenant Roy, and my devoted sapper could find in his resourceful spirit no further remedy. Sounds of groans reached us. Mingled with the groans another noise struck our ear, that of a hesitant footstep and of hands rustling against the wall.

The door suddenly opened. There stood a terrifying apparition. It was a wounded man, his naked chest swathed in bloody bandages. He leant with one hand against the door frame, and thrusting out a leg, went down on one knee. He held out to me his other hand in a supplicating gesture, and in a whisper, muttered: 'Mon commandant, something to drink.'

I went over to him and raised him up. 'I have no water, my brave fellow. Do as I do – hope. They are coming to our rescue.'

Still groaning, my wounded man dragged himself back to the aid-post. I looked at Roy. Like my own, his eyes were clouded . . .

It was the end. Unless a miracle happened, this would be the last night of our resistance. My men, who drank no more, ate no more, slept no longer, only held themselves upright by a prodigy of will.

I summoned my officers to my command post. Every one of these brave men now despaired. They saw no salvation for their men, who must be preserved for the sake of the country, except by immediate surrender. But suddenly the guns outside began to bark, and the barking grew to a tempest. They were French guns. The fort was not touched, but the vicinity was being violently barraged. The flame of hope once more sprang up.

'Listen, comrades. That is the French artillery. It has never fired so strongly. It is the preparation for an attack. Go to your positions. Tomorrow morning, if we have not been delivered, I promise to submit to cruel necessity.'

Warmed by my words, the officers returned to their posts. About six p.m. our gun-fire abruptly ceased, and the night passed away in complete calm, more nerve-racking for me than the storm of battle. Not a sound, not a hint of movement. I thought of the promise I had made. Had I the right to prolong resistance beyond human strength and to compromise uselessly the life of these brave men who had done their duty so heroically? I took a turn in the corridors. What I saw was frightening. Men were overcome with vomiting due to urine in the stomach, for so wretched were they that they had reached the point of drinking their own urine. Some lost consciousness. In the main gallery a man was licking a little wet streak on the wall . . .

7th June! Day broke and we scarcely noticed it. For us it was still night, a night in which all hope was extinguished. Aid from outside, if it came, would come too late.

ALISTAIR HORNE

The Camaraderie of the Air

Horne writes of the new role played in aerial warfare by air-forces, as opposed to solitary flyers:

In the combat tactics of the early days, however, the French shone, for this was a form of warfare ideally suited to their individualistic temperament (though, later, it was to be the cause of grievous losses). 'We are the refuge,' said a French airman, 'of all those who fear too close a confinement of the spirit, the discipline of the corps of troops . . .' Never since the Middle-Ages and the invention of the long-bow had the battlefields of Europe seen this kind of single combat. When the champions of either side met to fight spectacular duels in and out of the clouds, the rest of the war seemed forgotten; even the men in the trenches paused to watch as the hosts of Greece and Troy stood by when Hector and Achilles fought. Accompanying this person-alised warfare, there returned a chivalry and a sporting instinct that had all but vanished with the advent of the army of the masses. A remarkable *camaraderie* grew between enemies. Once a German pilot dropped one of his expensive fur gloves during a raid over a French air-field. The next day he returned to drop the other; with a note begging the finder to keep it, as he had no use for only one glove. With medieval courtesy, the recipient dropped a thank-you note over the donor's base. Fewer flyers took after the cold killer, von Richthofen, than after Boelcke and Navarre, who both hated killing and aimed whenever possible for the engine instead of the pilot. The death of a renowned foe usually brought mourning rather than triumph to the victorious camp; when Boelcke himself was killed (in collision with his best friend), planes from every British airfield within range dropped wreaths on his base, regardless of the risk involved. But though this sense of chivalry endured throughout the war, Verdun was to spell the end of the solo flying ace and single combat. It was at Verdun that the word '*Airforce*' first began to have a meaning.

CLIFFORD GRAY

'If You Were the Only Girl in the World'

According to Elgar, this was the perfect tune. The song was introduced in April at the première of *The Bing Boys Are Here* at the Alhambra Theatre in Leicester Square. The soldiers added their own, less sentimental words to those of Clifford Gray (1887–1941):

If you were the only girl in the world,
And I was the only boy,
Nothing else would matter in the world today,
We would go on loving in the same old way.
A Garden of Eden just made for two
With nothing to mar our joy,
There would be such wonderful things to do,
I would say such wonderful things to you,
If you were the only girl in the world,
And I was the only boy.

The Tommies' version was:

If you were the only Boche in the trench,
And I had the only bomb,
Nothing else would matter in the world today,
I would blow you into eternity.
Chamber of Horrors, just made for two,
With nothing to spoil our fun;
There would be such a heap of things to do,
I should get your rifle and bayonet too,
If you were the only Boche in the trench,
And I had the only gun.

CECIL LEWIS

A Mother's Farewell – 20 March 1916

Cecil Lewis (1898–1997) was a fighter pilot when the average life expectancy for his kind was three weeks. But he survived the war and also served in the second. After lying about his age, he joined the Royal Flying Corps in 1915 and flew solo after only eighty minutes of in-air instruction. Only later, when Lewis came to write his memoir, *Sagittarius Rising*, did Lewis realise what torment it had been for his mother to bid farewell as he left for France.

My mother came down to say good-bye. She behaved as all good mothers should, gave me a cigarette-case, talked of everything except the Front, abjured me to write regularly, said she was not going to worry as I was quite certain to come through all right, and said good-bye at the station without breaking down. Seventeen is not a grateful age. So much is taken for granted. The parent's care and solicitude become a burden to be cast off. So I record with some remorse how little that parting meant. I was full of the new life, and utterly failed to grasp the blank my going would leave, the daily searching through the long casualty lists, the daily listening for the knock which might mean a word, a line, some message, however meagre, from 'somewhere in

France'. I was rather relieved to have her gone, for I dreaded a scene. I was as certain as she that I should come through all right, and that being so, why get emotional over a temporary separation? But, all the same, the truth was that the average length of a pilot's life at that time was three weeks. I was hopelessly inequipped and inexperienced. Later, no pilot was allowed to cross the lines before he had done sixty hours' flying – I had done thirteen. There was every excuse for a last farewell; but, mercifully, we did not know it. It is only now I can look back, judge of the hazards, and get a vague idea of the miracle that passed me through those years unscathed. She had made me have my photograph taken, too, and I hated it! The only one I cared about showed the 'Wings' prominently; but, of course, she liked another, in profile, where they did not show at all – liked the expression, she said. Sentimental, mothers were; but she was proud too. I was not to know that photo was to stand on her desk if 'anything happened', for her to say, 'This was my son!' and try to find something to justify a belief in the worthiness of my death when, in her heart, she knew that the world could never be richer or nobler for butchering a million of its sons.

CHARLES DOUIE

'A city of the dead'

When he was posted to the 1st Dorset Regiment at the end of 1915, Charles Douie was nineteen. The battalion was on the Somme from the end of 1915 to May 1917, apart from two months in the Béthune sector in August and September 1916. This is an extract from his book *The Weary Road, Recollections of a Subaltern of Infantry*, published in 1918:

After several days and nights of considerable strain I found myself in command of A Company, as my company commander had been sent by the colonel for a month's rest at the

Fourth Army School, after a year's continuous trench warfare from the Menin road to the Frise marshes. Throughout
the afternoon experienced soldiers (among whom I was not
numbered) could tell that news of our impending attack had
reached the German Intelligence, as we were subjected to a
harassing fire, and registration by new guns on our support
and communication trenches took place. I was in a state of
inexperienced optimism, and firmly believed that the
Germans were wasting ammunition which they would need
during the night. I expected that the mine, whose explosion
was to be the signal for our attack, would blow the village of
La Boiselle high into the air, and that the survivors, if there
were any, would soon be prisoners in our hands. As the
hour of attack approached I became less sanguine. The night
was still in a degree which no night had been before. The
broken posts and wire which marked the boundaries of no
man's land and the white chalk of the mine craters were
agleam in the moonlight, and it was so clear that I could dis-
cern the ruins and broken tree stumps of the village. Yet no
shot was fired while a hundred men crawled through our
wire into shell-holes in front. Behind them the trenches were
lined with men, for the 'stand-to-arms' had been passed
down. The deathly silence did not augur well, and as the
colonel passed down the line I noticed grave anxiety on his
face. Then at last the silence was broken by a machine-gun
firing from the dim ruins of Ovillers and sweeping our parapets from end to end. Then again there was silence. Two
minutes to go. One minute. A thought flickered for a
moment in my mind that many now very much alive would
within a brief minute be dead. The thought passed. Half a
minute. Time. The mine exploded. It seemed to me a very
small mine. The earth throbbed. Then again, but for one
moment only, there was an unearthly stillness. This was succeeded by a weird sound like rustling leaves for a fraction of
a second; then with the noise of a hurricane the shells

passed, and the whole outline of the German positions was seared with the appalling lightning and thunder of our artillery. There were a thousand flashes, and a lurid light spread over the battlefield, the light seen only in that most dreadful spectacle, a night bombardment. The thunder of the guns was such that speech was impossible. But there was no time to observe the scene, as in an inferno of flashes and explosions the German counter-barrage broke on our lines.

The intensity of the counter-barrage showed beyond a doubt that the German batteries had been standing to their guns and that every detail of our attack was known. The craters and trenches of La Boiselle were evacuated and full of wire in which those of our men who got through the entanglements were at once caught and impaled. Of Germans there were none to be seen until their bombers closed in from each side. From end to end of no man's land a hell of machine-gun fire was raging; the trenches were quite untenable.

The signal to retire was given. But our wounded were everywhere, and time and again the survivors went out to bring them in. It seemed incredible that anything could live in that barrage of gun and rifle-fire, with the German bombers in full counter-attack, yet our men would not be denied. Two men refused to leave friends who were dying; by some miracle they survived and brought back a wounded man. A young subaltern stayed behind to help a wounded man out of the German trench and in the act was killed on the wire.

Gradually the fire slackened, and only the rat-tat of the machine-guns and the whine of innumerable bullets disturbed the stillness of the night. I could hear the German transport far behind their lines. I was very tired. For five nights in six I had had no rest. At last the 'stand-down' came. Yet there were still two hours to day.

Dawn came at last. The ruins of the village and the surrounding trench lines became distinct, and it was day. On the German wire there were dark specks, among them the dead subaltern and my faithful orderly. Behind me lay a city of the dead, before me men, my friends, who yesterday had been so full of life and now lay silent and unheeding in death. Anger and bitterness were in my heart against those who had wrought this destruction, an anger which could find no expression in words.

SERGEANT LESLIE COULSON

'Who made the Law?'

Leslie Coulson, the son of a Fleet Street journalist, himself became a journalist with Reuters and an assistant editor of the *Morning Post*. He enlisted in September 1914 as a private in the Royal Fusiliers and served at Gallipoli. He was killed on the Somme in October 1916. This eloquent indictment of the politicians and commanders who relished the war was found among his possessions:

Who made the Law that men should die in meadows?
Who spake the word that blood should splash in lanes?
Who gave it forth that gardens should be bone-yards?
Who spread the hills with flesh, and blood, and brains?
Who made the Law?

Who made the Law that Death should stalk the village?
Who spake the word to kill among the sheaves,
Who gave it forth that death should lurk in hedgerows,
Who flung the dead among the fallen leaves?
Who made the Law?

Those who return shall find that peace endures,
Find old things old, and know the things they knew,

Walk in the garden, slumber by the fireside,
Share the peace of dawn, and dream amid the dew –
Those who return.

Those who return shall till the ancient pastures,
Clean-hearted men shall guide the plough-horse reins,
Some shall grow apples and flowers in the valleys,
Some shall go courting in summer down the lanes –
THOSE WHO RETURN.

But who made the Law? The Trees shall whisper to him:
'See, see the blood – the splashes on our bark!'
Walking the meadows, he shall hear bones crackle,
And fleshless mouths shall gibber in silent lanes at dark.
Who made the Law?

Who made the Law? At noon upon the hillside
His ears shall hear a moan, his cheeks shall feel a breath,
And all along the valleys, past gardens, croft, and
Homesteads,
HE who made the Law
    He who made the Law,
He who made the Law shall walk along with Death
    WHO made the Law?

MRS HUMPHRY WARD

Women at Work

Mrs Humphry Ward (1851–1920) was born Mary Arnold in Tasmania. Her uncle was Matthew Arnold and her sister Julia married Leonard Huxley, the father of Julian and Aldous. She married Humphry Ward, a Fellow of Brasenose College, Oxford, and eventually became a writer and educational benefactor, establishing the Mary Ward Adult Education Centre, which still flourishes today.

During the war the former American president Theodore Roosevelt asked her to write a series of articles explaining what was happening in Britain which was published as *England's Effort*, an appeal to the United States to join the war. This extract describes the changing role of British women based on her meeting with a factory manager:

'As to the women!' – he throws up his hands – 'they're saving the country. They don't mind what they do. Hours? They work ten and a half, or with overtime, twelve hours a day, seven days a week. At least that's what they'd like to do. The Government are insisting on one Sunday – or two Sundays – a month off. I don't say they're not right. But the women resent it. "We're not tired!" they say. And you look at them! – they're not tired. If I go down to the shed and say – "Girls! – there's a bit of work the Government are pushing for – they say they must have – can you get it done?" Why, they'll stay and get it done, and then pour out of the works laughing and singing. I can tell you of a surgical dressing factory near here, where for nearly a year the women never had a holiday. They simply wouldn't take one. "And what'll our men at the front do if we go holiday-making?" Last night (the night of the raid) the warning came to put out lights. We daren't send them home. They sat in the dark among the machines, singing "Keep the home fires burning" – "Tipperary" – and the like. I tell you, it made one a bit choky to hear them. They were thinking of their sweethearts and husbands, I'll be bound! – not of themselves.'

In another minute or two we were walking through the new workshops. Often as I have now seen this sight, so new to England, of a great engineering workshop, filled with women, it stirs me at the twentieth time little less than it did at first. These girls and women of the Midlands and the North are a young and comely race. Their slight or rounded figures, among the forest of machines, the fair or golden hair of so many of them, their grace of movement, bring a strange touch of beauty into a scene which has already its own spell. Etchers like Muirhead Bone, or Joseph Pennell, have shown us what can be done in art with these high workshops, their intricate distances, the endless criss-cross of their belting, and their ranged machines. But the coming in of the girls, in their close khaki caps and overalls, shewing the many pretty heads, and slender necks, and the rows of light bending forms, spaced in order, beside their furnaces or lathes, as far as the eye can reach, has added a new element – something flower-like – to all this flash of fire and steel, and to the grimness of war underlying it.

For the final meaning of it all is neither soft nor feminine! These girls – at hot haste – are making fuses, and cartridge-cases, by the hundred thousand, casting, pressing, drawing – and – in the special danger-buildings – filling certain parts of the fuse with explosive. There were about 4,000 of them, to 5,000 men, when I saw the shop, and their number has no doubt increased since. For the latest figures shew that about 15,000 fresh women workers are going into the munition works every week. The men are steadily training them, and without the teaching and cooperation of the men – without, that is, the surrender by the men of some of their most cherished trade customs – the whole movement would have been impossible. As it is, by the sheer body of the work the women have brought in, by the deftness, energy, and enthusiasm they throw into the simpler but quite indispensable processes, thereby setting the unskilled man free for the Army, and the skilled man for work which women cannot do, Great Britain has become possessed of new and vast resources of which she scarcely dreamed a year ago; and so far as this war is a war of machinery – and we all know what Germany's arsenals have done to make it so – its whole aspect is now changing for us. The 'eternal feminine' has made one more startling incursion upon the normal web of things!

GILES E. M. EYRE

Old Fritz

Rifleman 2nd Lieutenant Giles Eyre describes another instance of the camaraderie that occasionally occurred between the two sides:

The night was quiet, and the ensuing dawn brought out a perfect summer day. In the early morning, while we were warily coaxing a small fire to burn without smoke, patiently slicing our wood to the thickness of match-sticks, a voice, with a marked Yankee twang, hailed us from the Hun sap.

'Hey there, you guys, are you the Royal Rifles?'
'Yes, and who the 'ell are you, Squarehead?' yowled back Marriner.

'We are from Holstein, here,' answered the German, 'but the Bavarians will be relieving us to-night. I guess you yobs have some corned beef, biscuits and jam to spare there, *hein*?'

'We might,' answered Marriner. 'What will you give us for them?'

'Some cigars, Schnapps, and Johann here will play you tunes on his violin. If you take it easy to-day, we do the same. You don't bomb, we don't bomb, that right, eh?'

'All right, Yank, chuck us over your cigars and the Schnapps, whatever it is, and over comes some bully and jam,' replied our negotiator, and then, aside to me: 'What the 'ell is Schnapps anyway. D'ye eat it or what?'

'No, old scrounger, you heave it down your throat. It's kind of whisky-like liquor!'

'Now that's the ticket! Who would think old Fritz is keen to give it away, eh?' Marriner mused, pleasurably.

We looked up as three or four bundles came sailing over and fell in and on the sap edge.

'Duck your nuts, boys,' urged Oldham cautiously. 'Old Fritz may have something up his sleeve.'

However, nothing untoward happened. We retrieved the bundles. Fat cigars, and a couple of soda-water bottles, filled with yellowish spirit.

'All A1, old cock,' replied Marriner cheerfully.

'Here comes our whack,' and over we slung sundry tins of jam, bully, Maconochie [canned beef stew] and packets of Army biscuits.

Quiet reigned over all.

'Now this is what I call a bit of all right,' purred Marriner contentedly as he squatted down, drawing at a cigar and occasionally having a swig of Schnapps.

'If all the bloody Huns were as decent, we could have a cushy time out here, hurt nobody and let the Kaiser and our brass hats fight it out amongst themselves. But, of course, that bloke over there is civilized, he's lived in America!'

MORNING POST

A Mother Speaks Out

After 'A Little Mother's' letter was published in the *Morning Post*, it was reprinted as a pamphlet and seventy-five thousand copies were sold within a week. The Queen was 'deeply touched'. The letter was published later in Robert Graves's *Goodbye to All That*.

To the Editor of *The Morning Post*:
Sir, As the mother of an only child – a son who was early and eager to do his duty – may I be permitted to reply to

Tommy Atkins, whose letter appeared in your issue of the 9th inst.? Perhaps he will kindly convey to his friends in the trenches, not what the Government thinks, not what the Pacifists think, but what the mothers of the British race think of our fighting men. It is a voice which demands to be heard, seeing that we play the most important part in the history of the world, for it is we who 'mother the men' who have to uphold the honour and traditions not only of our Empire but of the whole civilized world.

To the man who pathetically calls himself a 'common soldier', may I say that we women, who demand to be heard, will tolerate no such cry as 'Peace! Peace!' where there is no peace. The corn that will wave over land watered by the blood of our brave lads shall testify to the future that their blood was not spilt in vain. We need no marble monuments to remind us. We only need that force of character behind all motives to see this monstrous world tragedy brought to a victorious ending. The blood of the dead and the dying, the blood of the 'common soldier' from his 'slight wounds' will not cry to us in vain. They have all done their share, and we, as women, will do ours without murmuring and without complaint. Send the Pacifists to us and we shall very soon show them, and show the world, that in our homes at least there shall be no 'sitting at home warm and cosy in the winter, cool and "comfy" in the summer'. There is only one temperature for the women of the British race, and that is white heat. With those who disgrace their sacred trust of motherhood we have nothing in common. Our ears are not deaf to the cry that is ever ascending from the battlefield from men of flesh and blood whose indomitable courage is borne to us, so to speak, on every blast of the wind. We women pass on the human ammunition of 'only sons' to fill up the gaps, so that when the 'common soldier' looks back before going 'over the top' he may see the women of the British race at his heels, reliable, dependent, uncomplaining.

The reinforcements of women are, therefore, behind the 'common soldier'. We gentle-nurtured, timid sex did not want the war. It is no pleasure to us to have our homes made desolate and the apple of our eye taken away. We would sooner our lovable, promising, rollicking boy stayed at school. We would have much preferred to have gone on in a light-hearted way with our amusements and our hobbies. But the bugle call came, and we have hung up the tennis racquet, we've fetched our laddie from school, we've put his cap away, and we have glanced lovingly over his last report which said 'Excellent' – we've wrapped them all in a Union Jack and locked them up, to be taken out only after the war to be looked at. A 'common soldier', perhaps, did not count on the women, but they have their part to play, and we have risen to our responsibility. We are proud of our men, and they in turn have to be proud of us. If the men fail, Tommy Atkins, the women won't.

Tommy Atkins to the front,
He has gone to bear the brunt.
Shall 'stay-at-homes' do naught but snivel and but sigh?
No, while your eyes are filling
We are up and doing, willing
To face the music with you – or to die!

Women are created for the purpose of giving life, and men to take it. Now we are giving it in a double sense. It's not likely we are going to fail Tommy. We shall not flinch one iota, but when the war is over he must not grudge us, when we hear the bugle call of 'Lights out', a brief, very brief, space of time to withdraw into our secret chambers and share, with Rachel the Silent, the lonely anguish of a bereft heart, and to look once more on the college cap, before we emerge stronger women to carry on the glorious work our men's memories have handed down to us for now and all eternity.

Yours etc.,
A Little Mother.

'APRÈS LA GUERRE FINI'

(Tune: 'Sous les Ponts de Paris')

This was a parody of 'Sous les Ponts de Paris' and in several cases (see pages 424–5) turned out to be true:

Après la guerre fini,
Soldat Anglais parti;
Mamselle Fransay boko pleuray
Après la guerre fini.

Après la guerre fini,
Soldat Anglais parti,
Mademoiselle in the family way,
Après la guerre fini.

Après la guerre fini,
Soldat Anglais parti;
Mademoiselle can go to hell
Après la guerre fini.

HELEN THOMAS

Parting

Helen Thomas (née Noble) (1877–1967) was the wife of the Welsh poet Edward Thomas (see page 201), who was killed at the Battle of Arras in April 1917. In this extract from *World Without*

End, she writes about the hours before Edward, who has been on leave, returns to the front. 'David' is Edward Thomas, 'Jenny' is Helen and 'Elizabeth' their daughter.

. . . I sit and stare stupidly at his luggage by the wall, and his roll of bedding, kit-bag, and suitcase. He takes out his prismatic compass and explains it to me, but I cannot see, and when a tear drops on to it he just shuts it up and puts it away. Then he says, as he takes a book out of his pocket, 'You see, your Shakespeare's *Sonnets* is already where it will always be. Shall I read you some?' He reads one or two to me. His face is grey and his mouth trembles but his voice is quiet and steady. And soon I slip to the floor and sit between his knees, and while he reads his hand falls over my shoulder and I hold it with mine.

'Shall I undress you by this lovely fire and carry you upstairs in my khaki overcoat?' So he undoes my things, and I slip out of them; then he takes the pins out of my hair, and we laugh at ourselves for behaving as we so often do, like young lovers. 'We have never become a proper Darby and Joan, have we?'

'I'll read to you till the fire burns low, and then we'll go to bed.' Holding the book in one hand, and bending over me to get the light of the fire on the book, he puts his other hand over my breast, and I cover his hand with mine, and he reads from *Antony and Cleopatra*. He cannot see my face, nor I his, but his low tender voice trembles as he speaks the words so full for us of poignant meaning. That tremor is my undoing. 'Don't read any more. I can't bear it.' All my strength gives way. I hide my face on his knee, and all my tears so long kept back come convulsively. He raises my head and wipes my eyes and kisses them, and wrapping his greatcoat round me carries me to our bed in the great, bare ice-cold room. Soon he is with me, and we lie speechless and trembling in each other's arms. I cannot stop crying. My body is torn with terrible sobs. I am engulfed in this despair like a drowning man by the sea. My mind is incapable of thought. Only now and again, as they say drowning people do, I have visions of things that have been – the room where my son was born; a day, years after, when we were together walking before breakfast by a stream with hands full of bluebells; and in the kitchen of our honeymoon cottage, and I happy in his pride of me. David did not speak except now and then to say some tender word or name, and hold me tight to him. 'I've always been able to warm you, haven't I? 'Yes, your lovely body never feels cold as mine does. How is it that I am so cold when my heart is so full of passion?' 'You must have Elizabeth to sleep with you while I am away. But you must not make my heart cold with your sadness, but keep it warm, for no one else but you has ever found my heart, and for you it was a poor thing after all.' 'No, no, no, your heart's love is all my life. I was nothing before you came, and would be nothing without your love.'

So we lay, all night, sometimes talking of our love and all that had been, and of the children, and what had been amiss and what right. We knew the best was that there had never been untruth between us. We knew all of each other, and it was right. So talking and crying and loving in each other's arms we fell asleep as the cold reflected light of the snow crept through the frost-covered windows.

David got up and made the fire and brought me some tea, and then got back into bed, and the children clambered in, too, and we sat in a row sipping our tea. I was not afraid of crying any more. My tears had been shed, my heart was empty, stricken with something that tears would not express or comfort. The gulf had been bridged. Each bore the other's suffering. We concealed nothing, for all was known between us. After breakfast, while he showed me where his account books were and what each was for, I listened calmly, and unbelievingly he kissed me when I said I, too, would keep accounts. 'And here are my poems. I've copied them all out in this book for you, and the last of all is for you. I wrote it last night, but don't read it now . . . It's still freezing. The ground is like iron, and more snow has fallen. The children will come to the station with me; and now I must be off.'

We were alone in my room. He took me in his arms, holding me tightly to him, his face white, his eyes full of a fear I had never seen before. My arms were round his neck. 'Beloved, I love you,' was all I could say. 'Jenny, Jenny, Jenny,' he said, 'remember that, whatever happens, all is well between us for ever and ever.' And hand in hand we went downstairs and out to the children, who were playing in the snow.

A thick mist hung everywhere, and there was no sound except, far away in the valley, a train shunting. I stood at the gate watching him go; he turned back to wave until the mist and the hill hid him. I heard his old call coming up to me: 'Coo-ee!' he called. 'Coo-ee!' I answered, keeping my voice strong to call again. Again through the muffled air came his 'Coo-ee'. And again went my answer like an echo. 'Coo-ee' went out of my lungs strong enough to pierce to him as he strode away from me. 'Coo-ee!' So faint now, it might be only my own call flung back from the thick air and muffling snow. I put my hands up to my mouth to make a trumpet, but no sound came. Panic seized me, and I ran through the mist and the snow to the top of the hill, and stood there a moment dumbly, with straining eyes and ears. There was nothing but the mist and the snow and the silence of death.

Then with leaden feet which stumbled in a sudden darkness that overwhelmed me I groped my way back to the empty house.

EDWARD THOMAS

'God Save England'

Edward Thomas, born in London of Welsh parents and educated at Lincoln College, Oxford, enlisted in the Artists' Rifles in July

1915. He volunteered for service overseas in 1916 and was killed during the first hour of the Battle of Arras in April 1917. In 1916 he met the American poet Robert Frost, who encouraged him to write poetry. His 142 poems were produced within two years.

This is no case of petty right or wrong
That politicians or philosophers
Can judge. I hate not Germans, nor grow hot
With love of Englishmen, to please newspapers.
Beside my hatred of the Kaiser is love true:–
A kind of god he is, banging a gong.
But I have not to choose between the two,
Or between justice and injustice. Dinned
With war and argument I read no more
Than in the storm smoking along the wind
Athwart the wood. Two witches' cauldrons roar.
From one the weather shall rise clear and gay;
Out of the other an England beautiful
And like her mother that died yesterday.
Little I know or care if, being dull,
I shall miss something that historians
Can rake out of the ashes when perchance
The phoenix broods serene above their ken.
But with the best and meanest Englishmen
I am one in crying, God save England, lest
We lost what never slaves and cattle blessed.
The ages made her that made us from the dust:
She is all we know and live by, and we trust
She is good and must endure, loving her so:
And as we love ourselves we hate her foe.

'DO YOUR BALLS HANG LOW?'

Variants of this marching song have been sung since the American Civil War. 'Do Your Ears Hang Low?' was a nursery rhyme;

Confederate soldiers would remove ears and testicles from the corpses of dead slaves, place them on a rope necklace which was worn as a trophy. Douglas Haig was not amused when he heard an officer singing the song.

Do your balls hang low?
Do they dangle to and fro?
Can I tie them in a knot?
Can you tie them in a bow?

Do they itch when it's hot?
Do you rest them in a pot?

Do you get them in a tangle?
Do you catch them in a mangle?
Do they swing in stormy weather?
Do they tickle with a feather?

Do they rattle when you walk?
Do they jingle when you talk?

Can you sling them on your shoulder
Like a lousy fucking soldier?
DO YOUR BALLS HANG LOW?

CONSCIENTIOUS OBJECTOR

Told to Beverley Nichols by Robert Mennell

As a conscientious objector, Robert Mennell, a Quaker, was sentenced to four periods of imprisonment during the war. The writer Beverley Nichols is best remembered as a columnist for the weekly magazine *Woman's Own* at a time when it sold in the millions.

"'It was right at the beginning," he said, "that I learnt that the only people from whom I was to expect sympathy were the soldiers, and not the civilians. When I was waiting in that first guard-room, sitting down rather dazed on the floor, five men were bustled into the room, and the door was slammed on them. I made myself as inconspicuous as possible, hoping that they would not notice me. They were all in a towering rage. Their language was incredible. I gathered that they were all soldiers who, for some reason or other, either for breach of discipline or overstaying leave, were under arrest. They cursed and stormed for some time. Finally, they noticed me in my corner. They stopped swearing for a moment, and one of them walked up to me.

'"What are you in here for, mate?"

'I thought it best to be as simple as possible, so I said: "Well, you see, I am a Quaker, and I refused to join the army, because I think that war is murder."

'The man took a step backwards. A terrible light came into his eyes. He raised his arm, which had a wound stripe on it. I thought that he was going to spring at me. The room was very silent.

'"Murder?"' he whispered, '"murder"? It's *bloody* murder!'

'And then we were friends. We had only a little while together, because the men were soon marched away, and I never saw them again. But as they went, they each came up to me, and shook me by the hand. "Stick to it, matey! Stick!" they said, one after another.'

HAROLD MACMILLAN

'More than a War – a Crusade'

Harold Macmillan (1894–1986) succeeded Anthony Eden as Prime Minister in 1957. He was the fourth Prime Minister who had served on the Western Front. Educated at Eton and Balliol College, Oxford, his studies were interrupted by the war. He went to France with the Grenadier Guards in August 1915. He was wounded three times, most seriously at the Somme when he was hit in his left thigh and ended the war on crutches. In this letter to his mother Nellie he describes the patriotism and idealism that inspired both him and his fellow officers.

May 13, Perhaps the most extraordinary thing about a modern battlefield is the desolation and emptiness of it all . . . one cannot emphasise too much. Nothing is to be seen of war or soldiers – only the split and shattered trees and the burst of an occasional shell reveal anything of the truth. One can look for miles and see no human being. But in those miles of country lurk (like moles or rats, it seems) thousands, even hundreds of thousands of men, planning against each other perpetually some new device of death. Never showing themselves, they launch at each other bullet, bomb, acrial torpedo and shell. And somewhere too (on the German side we know of their existence opposite us) are the little cylinders of gas, waiting only for the moment to spit forth their nauseous and destroying fumes. And yet the landscape shows nothing of all this – nothing but a few shattered trees and three or four lines of earth and sandbags, these and the ruins of towns and villages are the only signs of war anywhere visible. The glamour of red coats – the martial tunes of flag and drum – aide-de-camps scurrying hither and thither on splendid chargers – lances glittering and swords flashing – how different the old wars must have been!

The thrill of battle comes now only once or twice a twelvemonth. We need not so much the gallantry of our fathers; we need (and in our army at any rate I think you will find it) that indomitable and patient determination which has saved England over and over again. If anyone at home thinks or talks of peace, you can truthfully say that the army is weary enough of war but prepared to fight for another 50 years if necessary until the final object is attained . . . Many of us could never stand the strain and endure the horrors which we see every day, if we did not feel that this was more than a War – a Crusade. I never see a man killed but think of him as a martyr. All the men (tho' they could not express it in words) have the same conviction – that our cause is right and certain in the end to triumph. And because of this unexpressed and almost unconscious faith, our allied armies have a superiority in morale which will be (some day) the deciding factor.

JAMES WILLIAM GRAYSTONE

'Dear Old Pals'

James Graystone was twenty-two when, on 4 June, he wrote this account of the courage and compassion of his comrades in the 10th Battalion, the East Yorkshire Regiment. He was wounded in the spring of 1918 but survived the war and died in 1964.

Daylight showed us the damage that had been done during the night's inferno. It was absolutely awful – beyond description. The raiding party when they returned reported fearful carnage in the German lines, but whatever losses they have suffered, our own casualties have been appalling. Our front line trench is no more – just a mass of shell-holes and a pile of sandbags. We don't yet know anything definite but most of our men must be either wounded or buried alive. At dawn the cry went up for volunteers to hold the front line and to dig up the buried. There was an instant response and everybody ran like the wind to the line to do what he could to save life. The trenches simply ran with the blood of dead and wounded. Oh what a horrible sight! At 3 a.m. the wounded began to stream out in one long procession. They went by for hours – more than a hundred of them. Men with arms and legs splintered or blown off and big shrapnel holes in their heads and bodies, but one and all cheerful and smiling as they were brought up for treatment. Some are dying as they reach the doctor – with almost a smile on their lips to the last. What a grand lot our lads are! Not a murmur from one of them, though many are twisted with pain. They are joking with one another and with the doctor as he dresses their wounds. The list of dead is growing and growing. Already the bodies of twenty have been unearthed. The efforts of the diggers are being rewarded. Occasionally a man with a spark of life still in him is pulled out of the ground and his life saved. Poor old Lieut. Palmer – the most popular officer in the battalion – has been buried alive and suffocated. He was due for his captaincy today. Another officer – the youngest and newest arrived – Lieut. Spink, has been blown to pieces. His poor brother in our company is simply distracted. It is pitiful to see him.

Three other officers are severely wounded. One is expected to die at any moment for he is simply peppered with shrapnel. May God have mercy on those who caused this war: they will get none from us.

There are many stories of love to tell. The attached ser-geants praised our lads to the skies. They said that they had never been in a worse bombardment, even in those awful days at Ypres, and yet our lads never for a moment showed a sign of fear. They stood up on the platform and waited with set faces for their fate. Not a man left his post. There were no shirkers or cowards in the face of death. When one man fell his comrades closed and filled the gap. One man now dead stood up on the parapet and gave his pals the signal where each shell would fall. He died a hero's death.

At daylight the front line and the communication trenches leading to it were hardly recognisable. They were all smashed in, in some cases level with the ground, with dozens of dead, wounded and dying lying buried beneath. Some were never recovered and will be there till the end of the war.

One thing we have to praise the enemy for – a little incident which occurred in broad daylight. A wounded man was lying in great pain just in front of the German wires.

A Y & L [York and Lancaster Regiment] private insisted

on going out into no man's land to bring him in and he did so in spite of his captain's order to the contrary. Not a shot was fired as he brought the helpless man back to safety, when it was discovered that his wounds had been carefully dressed by the Germans. Our estimate of the enemy has gone up considerably in consequence.

All day long things have been very quiet – both sides are exhausted and are thankful for a rest. A sort of unofficial truce has been mutually arranged to get the wounded away and to bury the dead. This afternoon I saw the whole of the battalion's dead. The bodies were laid out along the trench side just as they fell. I shall never forget the sight as long as I live. Their hands held up in supplication and faces drawn in agony. It was hard to look on them – dear old pals – the best we ever had. May God grant that the scene never be repeated.

RAYMOND ASQUITH

An Accursed Place

The war touched families high and low. All four sons of Herbert Asquith, the Prime Minister, joined the Army in 1914. Raymond was an outstanding scholar: he swept the board at Oxford, according to Asquith's biographer, surpassing his father's record. He joined the Army, he said, rather than spend the rest of his life explaining why he did not. This letter was written to Lady Diana Manners.

23rd June . . . Another night I was in a much worse place than this – the most accursed unholy and abominable place I have ever seen, the ugliest filthiest most putrid and most desolate – a wood where all the trees had been cut off by the shells the week before, and nothing remained but black stumps of really the most obscene heights and thickness, craters swimming in blood and dirt, rotting and smelling bodies and rats like shadows, fattened for the market moving cunningly and liquorishly among them, limbs and bowels nestling in the hedges, and over all the most supernaturally shocking scent of death and corruption that ever breathed o'er Eden. The place simply stank of sin and all Floris could not have made it sweet . . . The only dug-out turned out to be a 'dirt trap' if not a death trap, awash with sewage, stale eyeballs, and other debris, so I spent 2 days on a stretcher in a shell hole in the gutter certainly, but looking all the while at the stars with which you have so richly studded my memory.

There is a great deal after all to be said for the existence of evil; it might almost be held to prove the existence of God. Who else could have thought of it? . . .

THE SOMME

The Battle of the Somme lasted officially from 1 July to 16 November. For Britain it was the biggest battle its army had ever fought – the 4th Army had 519,324 men. The aim was to divert the Germans from Verdun and to push the Germans back from the Channel ports, where they threatened Amiens and Paris.

EWART ALAN MACKINTOSH

'In Memoriam'

Ewart 'Tosh' Mackintosh was an officer in the Seaforth Highlanders. On 16 May he carried the wounded Private David Sutherland through a hundred yards of German trenches hotly pursued by Germans. But Sutherland died and his body was left behind. Mackintosh won the Military Cross. He wrote 'In Memoriam' in memory of Sutherland. In November 1917 he was killed, aged twenty-four.

So you were David's father
And he was your only son,
And the new-cut peats are rotting
And the work is left undone,
Because of an old man weeping,
Just an old man in pain,
For David, his son David,
That will not come again.

Oh, the letters he wrote you
And I can see them still,
Not a word of the fighting
But just the sheep on the hill
And how you should get the crops in
Ere the year got stormier,
And the Bosches have got his body,
And I was his officer.

You were only David's father,
But I had fifty sons
When we went up in the evening
Under the arch of the guns,
And when we came back at twilight –
O God! I heard them call
To me for help and pity
That could not help at all.

Oh, never will I forget you,
My men that trusted me,
More my sons than your fathers',
For they could only see
The helpless babies
And the young men in their pride.
They could not see you dying,
And hold you while you died.

Happy and young and gallant,
They saw their first-born go,
But not the strong limbs broken
And the beautiful men brought low,
The piteous writhing bodies,
They screamed 'Don't leave me, sir,'
For they were only your fathers
But I was your officer.

Thomas Kettle

No man's land

Thomas Kettle, who was born in 1850, was an Irish nationalist and one of the first prominent men to be identified with the Irish volunteers in November 1913. He was commissioned in the Dublin Fusiliers in 1914, used as an orator to encourage recruitment, but was in France in 1916, where he wrote an essay 'Silhouettes From the Front', in which he writes this description of no man's land:

In the trenches it is the day-by-dayness that tells and tries. It is always the same tone of duty: certain days in billets, certain days in reserve, certain days in the front trench . . . But this nibbling process works both ways. We nibble; they nibble. They are nibbled; we are nibbled. A few casualities every turn, another grating of the saw-teeth of death and disease, and before very long a strong unit is weak. And, of course, the nerve-strain is not slight. Everybody going up to the trenches from CO down to the last arrival in the last draft knows it to be moral certainty that there are two or three that will not march back. Everybody knows that it may be anybody. In the trenches death is random, illogical, devoid of principle. One is shot not on sight, but on blindness, out of sight . . . There is much to nibble the nerves . . .

Over there in front across no man's land there are shell-holes and unburied men. Strange things happen there.

Patrols and counterpatrols come and go. There are two sinister fences of barbed wire, on the barbs of which blood-stained strips of uniform and fragments more sinister have been known to hang uncollected for a long time. The air is shaken with diabolical reverberations; it is stabbed with malign illumination as the Very lights shoot up, broaden to a blaze, and go out. This contrast of night and light and gloom is trying to the eyes. The rifle-grenades and trench-mortars, flung at short range, that scream through the air are trying to the ears . . .

Ratavia, as one may designate it, resembles China in that there has never been a census of its population but that it approximates to the mathematical infinite. They are everywhere, large rats, small rats, bushy rats, shy rats and impudent, with their malign whiskers, their obscene eyes, loathsome all the way from over-lapping teeth to kangaroo tail. You see them on the parados and the shelter-roofs at night, slinking along on their pestiferous errands. You lie in your dug-out, famished, not for food (that goes without saying), but for sleep, and hear them scurrying up and down their shafts, nibbling at what they find, dragging scraps of old newspapers along, with intolerable cracklings, to bed themselves. They scurry across your blankets and your very face. Nothing suppresses their numbers. Not dogs smuggled in in breach of regulations. Not poison, which most certainly ought not to be used. Not the revolver-practice in which irritated subalterns have been known to indulge. Men die and rats increase.

SECOND LIEUTENANT JOHN SHERWIN ENGALL

My God, my Country, my King

The twenty-year-old writer of this letter, who had been at St Paul's School in London and was about to do 'my little bit in the cause of civilization', was killed within three days of arriving on the Somme, on the first day of the battle, 1 July. There were many such letters.

Friday 28th [30th] June, 1916
My dearest Mother and Dad,
I'm writing this letter the day before the most important moment in my life – a moment which I must admit I have never prayed for, like thousands of others have, but nevertheless a moment which now it has come, I would not back out of for all the money in the world. The day has almost dawned when I shall really do my little bit in the cause of civilization. To-morrow morning I shall take my men – men whom I have got to love, and who, I think, have got to love me – over the top to do our bit in the first attack in which the London Territorials have taken part as a whole unit. I'm sure you will be pleased to hear that I'm going over with the Westminsters. The old regiment has been given the most ticklish task in the whole of the Division; and I'm very proud of my section, because it is the only section in the whole of the Machine Gun Company that is going over the top; and my two particular guns have been given the two most advanced, and therefore most important, positions of all – an honour that is coveted by many. So you can see that I have cause to be proud, inasmuch as at the moment that counts I am the officer who is entrusted with the most difficult task.

I took my Communion yesterday with dozens of others who are going over to-morrow; and never have I attended a more impressive service. I placed my soul and body in God's keeping, and I am going into battle with His name on my lips, full of confidence and trusting implicitly in Him. I have a strong feeling that I shall come through safely; but nevertheless, should it be God's holy will to call me away, I am quite prepared to go; and, like dear Mr Le Patourel, I could not wish for a finer death; and you, dear Mother and Dad, will know that I died doing my duty to my God, my Country, and my King, I ask that you should look upon it as an honour that you have given a son for the sake of King and Country . . .

I wish I had time to write more, but time presses . . .

I fear I must close now. Au revoir, dearest Mother and Dad. Fondest love to all those I love so dearly, especially yourselves.

Your devoted and happy son, Jack.

'I Don't Want To Be A Soldier'

(Tune: 'Come, My Lad, and Be a Soldier')
Note the obvious rhyme 'whore' with 'war' in the second line.

I don't want to be a soldier,
I don't want to go to War.
I'd rather stay at home,
Around the streets to roam
And live on the earnings of a high-born lady.
I don't want a bayonet up my arse-hole,
I don't want my bollocks shot away,
I'd rather stay in England.
Merry, merry England
And fornicate my bleeding life away.

William Noel Hodgson

'Before Action'

William Noel Hodgson, a subaltern with the Devonshire Regiment, also died, aged twenty-three, on 1 July, two days after writing his last poem, 'Before Action'. He had been awarded the Military Cross during the Battle of Loos in 1915.

By all the glories of the day
And the cool evening's benison,
By the last sunset touch that lay
Upon the hills when day was done,
By beauty lavishly outpoured
And blessings carelessly received,
By all the days that I have lived
Make me a soldier, Lord.

By all of all man's hopes and fears,
And all the wonders poets sing,
The laughter of unclouded years,
And every sad and lovely thing;
By the romantic ages stored
With high endeavour that was his
By all his mad catastrophes
Make me a man, O Lord.

I, that on my familiar hill
Saw with uncomprehending eyes
A hundred of Thy sunsets spill
Their fresh and sanguine sacrifice,
Ere the sun swings his noonday sword
Must say good-bye to all of this:–
By all delights that I shall miss,
Help me to die, O Lord.

Captain Maurice Gamon

'Gaily and gladly they go'

A captain in the Lancashire Fusiliers and a keen Scout, Maurice Gamon wrote this letter to his '½ Miler' (obviously still a young boy at school at Wellington) on the eve of battle – and of his death. The poem 'For England' was written the previous Christmas.

Dear ½ Miler,

Ever since I returned to France I have been trying to find time to write to you to tell you that I know how disappointed you must have been when you could not come to stay at Wimbledon and Deakin came in your stead. And I wanted to tell you also that I was glad you were able to play the true Scout and put up with a bit of disappointment.

If we were always able to do as we like we should soon be most miserable people.

So good Scouts learn to bear their disappointments with a smile to do their duty whatever the cost.

Out here tomorrow, thousands and thousands of Englishmen will go out to suffer and die in the fight for England and her allies. You would love to be here to see how gaily and gladly they go – doing their bit to smash the tyrant foe.

You Scouts cannot help out here.

But you can help at home. And I hope that you and the other Wellingtons will always buck up and do your best to become brave Englishmen in the days ahead, fit and ready to take the place of those who fall today.

Nor is it necessary to go to war to serve England. War is only one of the ways in which England calls us to her service when need arises. A boy can serve England by being honest and brave at home, faithful in all he may have to do and above all clean in heart and mind.

So then I hope that you will peg away to become as efficient as you can, ready to do all that a Scout should do at a moment's notice, and above all faithful to the Scout Law.

Next time I am home I will be able to tell you some wonderful stories of these days. At the moment I may only tell you that our big guns have smashed the German trenches to pieces, their villages are in terrible ruins and their barbed wire is swept away.

So I hope Wellingtons will be ready to cheer when still better news comes through.

Meanwhile, like you, I too must be ready to meet disappointment, you know, and if I should not come home, why you fellows must push along and keep the Troop going and work all the harder to make up for my absence.

As Scouts we must never be downhearted nor despair of final victory. I believe at last England's day has come, and if the price of victory is leaving, why we must not be sad. And so I hope you Scouts won't despair if I go down in the fight, will you?

Now I must close.

I am trying to fit in with this letter a little five penny piece which I have carried for days intending to send it as a souvenir to you – something to remind you never to be downhearted and ready to smile at every disappointment.

Give my love to your comrade Wolf Cub Scouts. If God wills next year I'll hope to see you all run in the Relay Race – and to see you win!

Goodbye. Be good.

Your faithful friend Maurice Gamon, Capt.

'For England'
What can a Boy Scout do to-day
While England stands at bay?
He can be steadfast, straight and true
In all that he may say or do;
He can be loyal to God and king;
And sacrifice of self can bring
In tribute. He can lend a hand
Each day to someone in the land –
Always the friend of everyone,
Scorning reward for good turns done.
Like knights of old, so brave and true,
He can be gentle mannered too:
While for all living things around
He can let kindliness abound.

Prompt to obey at duty's call,
Cheery, no matter what befall;
Careful of all that he may spend,
Lest he on others should depend,
He can be pure in mind and heart,
That he may be ready to bear his part –
These are the things a Scout can do
To help while England battles through.
What can an Old Scout do one day
If England still should be at bay?
He can go forth, prepared to give
Himself, that England still may live!

THE TIMES, 19 AUGUST

'Gloriously British'

This letter from an officer at the front, published in *The Times* and describing an advanced dressing station, is indeed 'gloriously British':

A crowd of wounded men in London with their white bandages and blue uniforms has inspired pictures entitled 'Broken in the Wars', but until some genius arises who can produce on canvas the scene at an advance dressing station or field ambulance when an attack is in progress the people at home will have little idea of the true significance of the phrase.

A few hours before all this they swung past us with a smile on their faces and a song on their lips, their bodies the picture of life and energy, and their uniforms clean and smart; and now they have come out again with bodies maimed with shot and shell, and with their khaki stained with the mud and blood of battle.

Sad, pathetic, ghastly! Yes, it would be but for one thing and that something so gloriously British. All the horrors of the fight and the agony of the wounds have not broken their spirits, or taken the smile from their faces and the cheery words from their lips. They are magnificent, even more so in their weakness than in the strength in which they went out. The only time the smile leaves their faces is when they inquire anxiously whether their comrades are holding the ground and whether the regiment is upholding its proud traditions. It is just the same as their wounds are dressed. No complaints, no peevishness, no regrets. It strikes the onlooker as something more than human, and he feels that there is something almost divine in a race that can produce such men as these from factory and office, field and market-place.

The Royal Army Medical Corps is just as wonderful. All the livelong day these splendid men work on without rest or food, they have a smile and a cheery word for each, and they are as gentle, in spite of the rush, as the gentlest woman.

CECIL LEWIS

The Somme

Cecil Lewis, last met in London bidding his mother goodbye as he set off for France, is now flying over the battlefield:

July 1st, the zero day of the Somme offensive, dawned misty and still. Before it was light I was down in the sheds looking over my machine – an extra precaution, for I had been over it minutely the evening before. I was detailed for the first patrol, and soon we got the machine out and ran it up.

We were to watch the opening of the attack, co-ordinate the infantry flares (the job we had been rehearsing for months), and stay out over the lines for two and a half hours. Before we left, a second machine would overlap us, stay out its two and a half hours, and so continuous patrols would run throughout the day.

We climbed away on that cloudless summer morning towards the lines. There was a soft white haze over the ground that the sun's heat would quickly disperse. Soon we were in sight of the salient, and the devastating effect of the week's bombardment could be seen. Square miles of country were ripped and blasted to a pock-marked desolation. Trenches had been obliterated, flattened out, and still, as we watched, the gun fire continued, in a crescendo of intensity. Even in the air, at four thousand feet, above the roar of the engine, the drumming of firing and bursting shells throbbed in our ears.

'Keep clear of La Boisselle' were my orders. There was a small but heavily fortified salient there. It was to be blown up. Two huge mines, the largest ever laid, were to lift it sky-high at the moment the attack was launched. Weeks before, I had taken the officer in charge of the tunnelling up over the spot, and had heard stories of how the men worked down there in the darkness with pick and shovel, stopping at inter-vals to listen whether enemy miners were tunnelling under their galleries. But all was well, the mines were complete, wired, the troops had been retired clear of them, and the officer in charge was waiting, hand on switch, to set them off. Once they were fired, the infantry were to sweep through Boisselle and on up to the Bapaume road to Pozières their first day's objective.

Now the hurricane bombardment started. Half an hour to go! The whole salient, from Beaumont-Hamel down to the marshes of the Somme, covered to a depth of several hun-dred yards with the coverlet of white wool – smoking shell bursts! It was the greatest bombardment of the war, the greatest in the history of the world. The clock hands crept on, the thrumming of the shells took on a higher note. It was now a continuous vibration, as if Wotan, in some paroxysm of rage, were using the hollow world as a drum and under his beat the crust of it was shaking. Nothing could live under that rain of splintering steel. A whole nation was behind it. The earth had been harnessed, the coal and ore mined, the flaming metal run; the workshops had shaped it with care and precision; our womenkind had made fuses, prepared deadly explosives; our engineers had designed machines to fire the product with a maximum of effect; and finally, here, all these vast credits of labour and capital were being blown to smithereens. It was the most effective way of destroying wealth that man had yet devised; but as a means of extermination (roughly one man for every hundred shells), it was primitive and inefficient.

Now the watch in the cockpit, synchronized before leaving the ground, showed a minute to the hour. We were over Thiepval and turned south to watch the mines. As we sailed down above it all, came the final moment. Zero!

At Boisselle the earth heaved and flashed, a tremendous and magnificent column rose up into the sky. There was an ear-splitting roar, drowning all the guns, flinging the machine sideways in the repercussing air. The earthy column rose, higher and higher to almost four thousand feet. There it hung, or seemed to hang, for a moment in the air, like the silhouette of some great cypress tree, then fell away in a widening cone of dust and debris. A moment later came the second mine. Again the roar, the upflung machine, the strange gaunt silhouette invading the sky. Then the dust cleared and we saw the two white eyes of the craters. The barrage had lifted to the second-line trenches, the infantry were over the top, the attack had begun.

R. H. TAWNEY

The Attack

After the Great War R. H. Tawney (1880–1962) was to become one of England's most distinguished economic historians, president of the Workers' Educational Association, professor at London University and author of *Religion and the Rise of Capitalism*.

During the war he was a sergeant in the Manchester Regiment. He was severely wounded during the Battle of the Somme.

It was a glorious morning, and, as though there were some mysterious sympathy between the wonders of the ear and of the eye, the bewildering tumult seemed to grow more insistent with the growing brilliance of the atmosphere and the intenser blue of the July sky. The sound was different, not only in magnitude, but in quality, from anything known to me. It was not a succession of explosions or a continuous roar; I, at least, never heard either a gun or a bursting shell. It was not a noise; it was a symphony. It did not move; it hung over us. It was as though the air were full of a vast and agonised passion, bursting now into groans and sighs, now into shrill screams and pitiful whimpers, shuddering beneath terrible blows, torn by unearthly whips, vibrating with the solemn pulse of enormous wings. And the supernatural tumult did not pass in this direction or that. It did not begin, intensify, decline, and end. It was poised in the air, a stationary panorama of sound, a condition of the atmosphere, not the creation of man. It seemed that one had only to lift one's eyes to be appalled by the writhing of the tormented element above one, that a hand raised ever so little above the level of the trench would be sucked away into a whirlpool revolving with cruel and incredible velocity over infinite depths. And this feeling, while it filled one with awe, filled one also with triumphant exultation. The exultation of struggling against a storm in mountains, or watching the irresistible course of a swift and destructive river. Yet at the same time one was intent on practical details, wiping the trench dirt off the bolt of one's rifle, reminding the men of what each was to do, and when the message went round, 'five minutes to go', seeing that all bayonets were fixed. My captain, a brave man and a good officer, came along and borrowed a spare watch off me. It was the last time I saw him. At 7.30 we went up the ladders, doubled through the gaps in the wire and lay down, waiting for the line to form up on each side of us. When it was ready we went forward, not doubling, but at a walk. For we had nine hundred yards of rough ground to the trench which was our first objective, and about fifteen hundred to a further trench where we were to wait for orders. There was a bright light in the air, and the tufts of coarse grass were grey with dew.

I hadn't gone ten yards before I felt a load fall from me. There's a sentence at the end of *The Pilgrim's Progress* which has always struck me as one of the most awful things imagined by man: 'Then I saw that there was a way to Hell, even from the Gates of Heaven, as well as from the City of Destruction.' To have gone so far and be rejected at last! Yet undoubtedly man walks between precipices, and no one knows the rottenness in him till he cracks, and then it's too late. I had been worried by the thought: 'Suppose one should lose one's head and get other men cut up! Suppose one's legs should take fright and refuse to move!' Now I knew it was all right. I shouldn't be frightened and I shouldn't lose my head. Imagine the joy of that discovery! I felt quite happy and self-possessed. It wasn't courage. That, I imagine, is the quality of facing danger which one knows to be danger, of making one's spirit triumph over the bestial desire to live in this body. But I knew that I was in no danger. I knew I shouldn't be hurt; knew it positively, much more positively than I know most things I'm paid for knowing.

Well, we crossed three lines that had once been trenches, and tumbled into the fourth, our first objective. 'If it's all like this it's a cake-walk,' said a little man beside me, the kindest and bravest of friends, whom no weariness could discourage or danger daunt, a brick-layer by trade, but one who could turn his hand to anything, the man whom of all others I would choose to have beside me at a pinch;

but he's dead. While the men dug furiously to make a fire-step, I looked about me. On the parados lay a wounded man of another battalion, shot, to judge by the blood on his tunic, through the loins or stomach. I went to him, and he grunted, as if to say, 'I am in terrible pain; you must do something for me; you must do something for me.' I hate touching wounded men – moral cowardice, I suppose. One hurts them so much and there's so little to be done. I tried, without much success, to ease his equipment, and then thought of getting him into the trench. But it was crowded with men and there was no place to put him. So I left him. He grunted angrily, and looked at me with hatred as well as pain in his eyes. It was horrible. It was as though he cursed me for being alive and strong when he was in torture. I tried to forget him by snatching a spade from one of the men and working fiercely on the parapet. But one's mind wasn't in it; it was over 'there', there where 'they' were waiting for us. Far away, a thousand yards or so half-left, we could see tiny kilted figures running and leaping in front of a dazzlingly white Stonehenge, manikins moving jerkily on a bright green cloth. 'The Jocks bombing them out of Mametz,' said someone, whether rightly or not, I don't know. Then there was a sudden silence, and when I looked round I saw the men staring stupidly, like calves smelling blood, at two figures. One was doubled up over his stomach, hugging himself and frowning. The other was holding his hand out and looking at it with a puzzled expression. It was covered with blood – the fingers, I fancy, were blown off – and he seemed to be saying: 'Well, this is a funny kind of thing to have for a hand.' Both belonged to my platoon; but our orders not to be held up attending to the wounded were strict. So, I'm thankful to say, there was no question what to do for them It was time to make for our next objective, and we scrambled out of the trench.

I said it was time for us to advance again. In fact, it was, perhaps, a little more. By my watch we were three minutes over-due, not altogether a trifle. The artillery were to lift from the next trench at the hour fixed for us to go forward. Our delay meant that the Germans had a chance of reoccupying it, supposing them to have gone to earth under the bombardment. Anyway, when we'd topped a little fold in the ground, we walked straight into a zone of machine-gun fire. The whole line dropped like one man, some dead and wounded, the rest taking instinctively to such cover as the ground offered. To my immediate right three men lay in a shell-hole. With their heads and feet just showing, they looked like fish in a basket.

In crossing no-man's-land we must have lost many more men than I realised then. For the moment the sight of the Germans drove everything else out of my head. Most men, I suppose, have a palaeolithic savage somewhere in them, a beast that occasionally shouts to be given a chance of showing his joyful cunning in destruction. I have, anyway, and from the age of catapults to that of shot-guns always enjoyed aiming at anything that moved, though since manhood the pleasure has been sneaking and shamefaced. Now it was a duty to shoot, and there was an easy target. For the Germans were brave men, as brave as lions. Some of them actually knelt – one for a moment even stood – on the top of their parapet, to shoot, within not much more than a hundred yards of us. It was insane. It seemed one couldn't miss them. Every man I fired at dropped, except one. Him, the boldest of the lot, I missed more than once. I was puzzled and angry. Three hundred years ago I should have tried a silver bullet. Not that I wanted to hurt him or anyone else. It was missing I hated. That's the beastliest thing in war, the damnable frivolity. One's like a merry, mischievous ape tearing up the image of God. When I read now the babble of journalists about 'the sporting spirit of our soldiers', it makes me almost sick. God forgive us all! But then it was as I say.

ISAAC ROSENBERG

'Returning, We Hear the Larks'

Rosenberg was born into a working-class Jewish family in 1890. He attended the Slade School of Art with Stanley Spencer and Paul Nash and was taken up by Laurence Binyon and began to write poetry seriously. He enlisted in 1915 and served throughout as a private: he was killed after a night patrol on 1 April 1918.

Sombre the night is
And though we have our lives, we know
What sinister threat lurks there.

Dragging these anguished limbs, we only know
This poison-blasted track opens on our camp –
On a little safe sleep.

But hark! Joy – joy – strange joy.
Lo! Heights of night ringing with unseen larks.
Music showering on our upturned list'ning faces.

Death could drop from the dark
As easily as song –
But song only dropped,
Like a blind man's dreams on the sand
By dangerous tides,
Like a girl's dark hair for she dreams no ruin lies there,
Or kisses where a serpent hides.

SIDNEY ROGERSON

Goodwill Among Men

Sydney Rogerson, who was born in 1894 and educated at Sidney
Sussex College, Cambridge, was commissioned into the Prince of
Wales's Own (West Yorkshire) Regiment but did not go to France
until 20 July 1916. *Twelve Days* was his book about the last
spell of front-line duty performed by the 2nd Battalion, the West
Yorkshire Regiment, on the Somme.

At no other time in the war did I meet a better, keener,
or more reliable set of men than that mixed Yorkshire-
Northumbrian contingent in front of Le Transloy. With little
except cold bully to eat, with nowhere to sleep except the
open trench, they behaved for the three days as if the whole
affair were some tiresome form of entertainment which they
were compelled to sit through.

The pacifists may inveigh against war's hideousness,
leagues and societies may condemn it in vigorous resolutions
and solemnly declare that 'there must be no more war', yet the
fact remains that, terrifying as they sometimes, and uncom-
fortable as they often were, the war years will stand out in the
memories of vast numbers of those who fought as the happi-
est period of their lives. And the clue to this perhaps
astonishing fact is that though the war may have let loose the
worst it also brought out the finest qualities in men.

In spite of all differences in rank, we were comrades,
brothers, dwelling together in unity. We were privileged to see
in each other that inner, ennobled self which in the grim,
commercial struggle of peace-time is all too frequently atrophied for lack of opportunity of expression. We could note
the intense affection of soldiers for certain officers, their
absolute trust in them. We saw the love passing the love of
women of one 'pal' for his 'half-section'. We saw in his letters

home which came to us for censoring, the filial devotion of the 'toughest', drunkenest private for his aged mother back in the slums by the Tyne at North Shields. We saw the indomitable kindliness of the British character expressing itself towards the French children, the wretched mangy French dogs, and, yes, even to the German wounded and prisoners! The English soldier could not hate his enemies for long. Only a few days previously during the attack on Zenith Trench, when, with a third of the battalion killed or wounded, the shivering remainder stayed two days on the scene of the action, in rudimentary water-logged trenches under incessant rain and steady shell-fire: rations could not be got up, yet, wet, famished, and miserable as they were, the men insisted on sharing their infrequent mugs of tea with a wounded German, who, hit in the side, lay under a sopping oilskin in the trench. 'Here's a drop of tea for Fritz,' the men would say, as they propped up the captive and fed him as a nurse would feed a patient.

We were privileged, in short, to see a reign of goodwill among men, which the piping times of peace, with all their organised charity, their free meals, free hospitals, and Sunday sermons have never equalled. Despite all the propaganda for Christian fellowship and international peace, there is more animosity, uncharitableness, and lack of fellowship in one business office now than in a brigade of infantry in France then. Otherwise, we could never have stood the strain.

ANONYMOUS SOLDIER OF THE 1ST BORDER REGIMENT

'Can you pray?'

This powerful description of what happened when soldiers went over the top is quoted in Peter Barton's book *The Somme: A New Panoramic Perspective*:

We climbed out on ladders that had been set ready. All hell and its fury broke loose. My comrade just in front of me, the one who said he would be killed, had spoken only too true – dead with a bullet through the heart. We tried to make headway, but our men were mown down as if with a scythe. The earth suddenly seemed to open and hundreds of men were blown up into the air. Mines had been exploded; arms, legs and bodies were flying everywhere. I dropped into a shell-hole. Someone else jumped in against me. There we lay, unable to move, bullets cutting furrows along the rims above us. To crawl out would have been sudden death. Enemy shells, ploughing up no man's land covered us with lumps of soil. I heard my companion in the shell-hole saying, 'Oh dear, we are done!' I turned my head and asked, 'Can you pray?' The poor chap said he couldn't. I said, 'Well, I will, and you just lie still.' If ever man prayed hard, I did. I implored the Blessed Virgin Mary to save us, I prayed until I imagined I could see her.

Then I fell asleep. When I awoke I was still in the shell-hole still in the same position. My companion was lying there also asleep. All was strangely quiet. The stars were shining. It was night or early morning. I woke my companion. He gazed around. We could hardly believe we were still alive. I whispered to him to follow me and we would try to get back to our lines. We crept out of the shell-hole. The ground was littered with dead bodies, some lying one on top another. Very lights went up. A rifle cracked here and there. At last we hear the challenge, in a low voice, 'Halt! Who goes there?' 'Two of the Border Regiment.' 'Advance and be recognised.' We found our front line was occupied by a battalion of the Yorkshires. I asked where the 1st Borders were. The sentry looked at me, surprised. 'Most of them are lying out there' was the answer.

SECOND LIEUTENANT ERNEST ROUTLEY MC

'Think of your mother'

In this letter home, quoted in Peter Barton's book on the Somme, Routley pleads with his brother to stay in England rather than join the Army and be killed – as Ernest was on 7 October:

Dear Frank

Just received your letter. No words of mine can express my absolute amazement at the news. In spite of all warning you go and volunteer to come out to France of all places. I really can't make you out. If you only knew what you were asking for: you see you aren't a specialist in anything. You don't know Trench Mortars or Machine Guns. You are just an ordinary Tommy who can fire a rifle and perhaps throw a bomb. You don't know what you will be used for, do you? Well, I do. There have been thousands of casualties in the Push and some Regiments are hard put to it to make up their numbers, so they have asked for volunteers from Home Service Units, and you like a fool have volunteered. I really can't see why you can't take advice. Surely you must admit that I know more about it than you. I have been in the Push and have had 3 Bayonet Charges and by an extraordinary stroke of luck have come through, but I know full well my number will be up soon. One can't always escape.

You probably think it's a very fine thing to come out here and be killed. Well, just wait. It isn't being killed that worries you; it's the waiting for it. Just wait until you hear that you have got to attack, and then as you are waiting your turn to go over the top, you see your pals get cut down by machine gun fire, and then see if you think it's a glorious thing to die. It would be glorious if you could have a fair fight, but it's absolute murder here and you don't get a sporting chance. If only I could get home out of it, I would give up my M.C.

and commission and all I possess, but I can't, and I am doomed to stick it. But you aren't.

Another side is, how about those at home? Haven't you got the sense to see that Mother is nearly breaking her heart about me, because she realises one's life is not worth 2d out here, and yet in spite of this you go and volunteer and just double her grief. I don't know what will happen to her – I know her heart isn't strong and the shock of this may finish her. If so, I hold you responsible, I have been out here an officer and have done well but can't get leave in 8 months. Now what chance do you expect as a Tommy to come home. You really ought to think of others. What difference does it make to you? If you insist on going you will endorse every word of what I have said about things out here. An infantryman's job is to die – if you miss one show, then you are in for the next. The only chance you have is a 'blighty one', and even if you get that you will only remain in England until you are well, then you will come out again.

Why don't you profit by the experience of others? When I was at Shoreham, I was H[ome] Service and Physical Drill and Bayonet Fighting Instructor to the Brigade and could have remained such until the end of the war but like a fool I got fed up and volunteered to come out and now I can't get back. I wish I had never seen the Front here, I would risk being called a slacker – what does it matter. If you are in Khaki – isn't that enough? When the war is over, who will care? It is the H.S. people who will get on because all the others will be dead. You have no idea of what our casualties are and what they will be before it is over. Nobody has, until they have seen it all as I have.

Don't believe what wounded Tommies say about pic-nics [sic]. They were probably wounded by shrapnel before they went over and came out of it without seeing the show. Of course it's a picnic for them. You can draw whatever conclusions you like from my letter – all I ask is that you consider Mother. Isn't it better to have a few ignorant people say 'slacker' than to have your Father and sister and brothers all holding you responsible for your Mother's death.

Now if you knew T.M. and Mach. Gun, it wouldn't be so bad because these two branches have a good time and they never go over the top. I want you to think over this very seriously and if you possibly can get somebody to take your place – do so. I am going to try for a Special Leave to get home and see you and if necessary your C.O. as I don't want to hear that Mother has died suddenly from Heart Failure.

Please take this letter in the spirit it is meant. I appreciate your motives entirely as I had them myself. I know exactly how you felt as I felt the same way only I am paying for it now. If it only concerned you, I shouldn't mind because I should say, Well, if you won't take advice come out here yourself and try and see if I'm not right. But say for example you don't get hit, well I'm certain the extra anxiety will finish Mother and will turn Hilda grey.

I leave it to you now to make what alterations you can, and rely on me to back you up. I will put with Brigade my Applic[ation] for Special leave as soon as possible.

Believe me to be,
Your loving brother
Ernest.

J. R. ACKERLEY

'A bottle of whisky'

After failing his entrance examination for Cambridge, Joe Ackerley (1896 –1967) joined the 8th Battalion of the East Surrey Regiment and went to France in 1915. He described how he was wounded on 1 July in his autobiographical memoir *My Father and Myself*. He had returned to France by December but was taken prisoner in May 1917. He later became arts editor of *The Listener*, the weekly magazine of the BBC:

Sir Douglas Haig's masterly operation has often been described. This last, full-scale attack was prepared for by an incessant bombardment of the German lines, prolonged over many days and so heavy that, we were told, all resistance would be crushed, the enemy wire destroyed, their trenches flattened, and such Germans as survived reduced to a state of gibbering imbecility. It would be, for us, a walk-over. Very different was our reception. The air, when we at last went over the top in broad daylight, positively hummed, buzzed, and whined with what sounded like hordes of wasps and hornets but were, of course, bullets. Far from being crushed, the Germans were in full possession of senses better than our own; their smartest snipers and machine-gunners were coolly waiting for us. GHQ, as was afterwards realised, had handed the battle to them by snobbishly distinguishing us officers from the men, giving us revolvers instead of rifles and marking our rank plainly upon our cuffs. The 'gibbering imbeciles' confronting us were thus enabled to pick off the officers first, which they had been carefully instructed to do, leaving our army almost without leadership.

Many of the officers in my battalion were struck down the moment they emerged into view. My company commander was shot through the heart before he had advanced a step. Nevill, the battalion buffoon, who had a football for his men to dribble over to the 'flattened and deserted' German lines and was then going to finish off any 'gibbering imbecile' he might meet with the shock of his famous grin (he had loose dentures and could make a skull-like grimace when he smiled), was also instantly killed, and so was fat Bobby Soames, my best friend. I had spent the previous evening with him and he had said to me quietly, without emotion, 'I'm going to be killed tomorrow, I don't know how I know it but I do.' How far I myself got I don't remember; not more than a couple of hundred yards is my guess. I flew over the top like a greyhound and dashed forward through the wasps, bent double. Squeamish always about blood, mutilations and death, averting my gaze, so far as I could, from the litter of corpses left lying about whenever we marched up to the line through other regiments' battle-fields, never hurrying when word was passed down to me, as duty officer in the trenches, that someone had been killed or wounded, in the hope that, if I dawdled, the worst of the mess might be cleared up before I arrived, my special private terror was a bullet in the balls, which accounts psychologically, for it was, of course, unavailing physically, for the crouched up attitude in which I hurled myself at the enemy. The realisation that I was making an ass of myself soon dawned; looking back I saw that my platoon was still scrambling out of the trench, and had to wait until they caught up with me. My young Norfolk servant, Willimot, who then walked at my side, fell to the ground. 'I am paralysed, sir,' he whimpered, his face paper-white, his large blue ox-like eyes terrified. A bullet, perhaps aimed at me with my revolver and badges, had severed his spine. My platoon-sergeant, Griffin, lifted him into a shell-hole and left him there. Then I felt a smack on my left upper arm. Looking down I saw a hole in the sleeve and felt the trickling of blood. Then my cap flew off. I picked it up and put it on again; there was a hole in the crown. Then there was an explosion in my side, which sent me reeling to the ground. I lay there motionless. Griffin and one of the men picked me up and put me in a deep shell-hole. Griffin then tried to unbutton my tunic to examine and perhaps dress my wound. I was not unconscious, only dazed, and I had by now a notion of what had happened. It was another instance of the credulity of the time – my company commander's contribution – that we officers had been told to carry a bottle of whisky or rum in

our haversacks for the celebration of our victory after the
'walk-over'. Some missile had struck my bottle of whisky
and it had exploded. Of this I became dimly aware when
Sergeant Griffin moved me; I felt the crunch of broken glass
in the sack beneath my arm. What precisely had occurred I
did not know; besides the smarting that had now started in
my arm I had a sensation of smarting in my side, so I was
damaged there also, though by what or how much I could
not tell. What I do remember perfectly well is resisting
Griffin's attempts to examine me. I lay with my eyes closed
and my wounded arm clamped firmly to my wounded side
so that he could not explore beneath my tunic. I did not
want to know, and I did not want *him* to know, what had
happened to me. I did not feel ill, only frightened and dazed.
I could easily have got up, and if I could have got up I should
have got up. But I was down and down I stayed. Though my
thoughts did not formulate themselves so clearly or so
crudely at the time, I had a 'Blighty' one, that sort of wound
that all the soldiers sighed and sang for ('Take me back to
dear old Blighty'), and my platoon, in which I had taken
much pride, could now look after itself.

My injuries were indeed of a shamefully trivial nature; a
bullet had gone through the flesh of my upper arm, missing
the bone, and a piece of shrapnel or bottle glass (I can't
remember which) had lodged beneath the skin of my side
above the ribs. The explosion must therefore have been
fairly violent to have driven this object through my tunic and
shirt. I was welcomed home like a conquering hero and was
disinclined to exhibit my wounds when requested by sym-
pathetic admirers to do so, though not disinclined to give the
impression that the exploding bottle had entirely deprived
me of my senses. Yet so strange are we in our inconsistencies
that I was not happy in Blighty and, in a few months' time,
got myself sent back to France. I was at once promoted to
the rank of captain.

ACCRINGTON PALS

'There was nothing left for them to shoot at'

Lieutenant-Colonel A. W. Rickman, commanding the East
Lancashire Regiment's 11th Battalion (who became known as the
Accrington Pals), had devoted fifteen months to training his battalion. But by 7.50 a.m. on 1 July he knew the attack had failed
and he could only watch in despair the slaughter of his battalion.
The toll on that one day alone was 146 killed, 90 missing and 348
wounded. There were only 135 survivors. Some of them tell their
stories of the day in William Turner's book *Accrington Pals*:

> Pte Clarke:
> 'While we were walking in line, my section came to a shell-
> hole. We had to decide which way to go round. Some went
> to the left. I went to the right. A shell came over and I was
> thrown to the ground by the blast of the explosion. I picked
> myself up and realised I had a flesh wound in the leg. I
> looked around and to the left of me was nothing – not a
> man. For fifty yards on either side, no other man was going
> forward, only dead and wounded on the ground. I went
> forward about twenty yards and again was wounded, this
> time in the arm. The wound was quite bad. My hand
> dropped and was useless. I remember it felt cold. I thought
> 'I'm not going forward with this hand, I'd better get back
> and get a dressing on it.' Then another shell burst and
> knocked me over.
> 'I was still lying prone on the ground when a piece of
> shrapnel hit me behind the ear. I slipped into a shell-hole
> about 25 yards from the German front trench, wiped away
> the blood and pulled shrapnel out. Creeping forward I spot-
> ted some Germans. I fired just one shot. Then, Thud! I
> thought my head was blown in two, I was blinded with
> blood.'

Pte Kay had a similar experience:

'My job in the attack was to follow my No 1 on the Lewis gun team and supply him with the drums I carried round my neck. The Germans had their machine-guns on us as soon as we were over the parapet. We waited for our artillery to lift their fire from the German front to the second line. We got as far as their wire and I was wounded in the leg. My Corporal, Sam Smith, was killed outright. A piece of shrapnel went right through his entrenching tool. I dropped into a shell-hole with Pte Bill Bowers. We were no sooner in there than the Germans threw stick-grenades in at us. I caught a wound in the arm.'

L/Cpl. J. Snailham:

'Six men were killed in our section of the trench before the whistle blew to go. My best friend, Pte. James Leaver, was killed by my side as we struggled out of the firing-step towards the gap in our wire. We found our wire had not been cut for us to get through. We couldn't run because of the weight of our packs and men were going down like ninepins. By some miracle, I got to the German wire about ten yards in front of their trenches completely untouched. I then dropped to the ground. I looked round and saw not a soul moving, just dead and wounded. The Germans must have thought I was dead. Moments later a shell burst above me. I felt a pain and a piece of shrapnel was sticking out of my leg. It started bleeding. There was a German on top of the trench playing a machine-gun over my head. There was still nobody to be seen. Another shell burst and a piece of shrapnel went in my other leg. I couldn't move and I could feel blood running from me. I must have gone unconscious because the next thing I remember was the sun sinking down over the horizon.'

Pte Sayer:

'Suddenly a piece of shrapnel hit Joe Rountree on the leg. His clothing set alight, I knocked the shrapnel away and smothered the flames. I asked Pte. Pickering to go for the stretcher-bearers. I made Joe as comfortable as I could with splints made from box lids. He was in agonising pain, his leg smashed. A runner on his way to Brigade came into the dug-out. He obviously knew me but I didn't know him. 'Hallo Fred, how's things?' he said. I told him, 'It's a wasted effort to come here to issue bombs, nobody wants them.' He replied, 'Bugger t'bombs, everybody's gone – it's been a wash out.' He told me as much as he knew. As he left I gave him a postcard for my sister. She later got the postcard so I knew he had made it to Brigade. Sometime later the stretcher-bearers came for Joe.'

FRANK RICHARDS

The Spy

The German shells were uncannily accurate. Frank Richards explains why:

Just behind us on a ridge was a battery of small howitzer guns, and as we were watching them, guns, men and every-thing else vanished. The enemy shells were simply raining on that ridge. It was the most accurate shellfire I had seen, and Duffy who was standing by me said: 'If the Jerry gunners were only fifty yards away they couldn't drop their shells more accurately than what they are doing.' We both thought it very queer. About a couple of hours later two men of the Middlesex were on the scrounge in Bazentin Le Petit wood which was just in front of us, and happened to see a man dressed in grey disappear in a dug-out. They followed him but on reaching the bottom of the dug-out could see no one. They didn't have a candle and were striking matches to have a look around it. One of the men said that they must have been mis-taken, but the other was positive that someone had entered and told his pal to bring along an officer with a pocket torch whilst he kept watch. The man arrived back with an officer who examined the walls of the dug-out with his torch, and found a door in one of the walls that they hadn't spotted because it fitted very close and was covered with canvas, the same as the wall. He said in a loud voice: 'No, you made a mistake, there's nothing here;' and they went back out of the dug-out. When outside, the officer said quietly to the men: 'Did you see that door? There may be someone behind it. We might have been met by a stream of bullets as we opened it. Now if there is anybody behind it he'll think we've gone away. I want one of you men to stay at the entrance and the other to come very quietly with me back inside.' So one man waited outside and the other, with the officer, re-entered the dug-out. Soon the door was quietly opened and man appeared in the doorway. The officer flashed his torch on him and at the same moment fired his revolver. It was a German officer dressed in his own uniform and the bullet got him in the breast. Behind the door was a neat little dug-out with an underground cable running into it and also two trench telephones. He had been sending back the positions of every one of our batteries that he spotted, and no wonder the German shellfire had been so accurate. He wasn't dangerously wounded; the bullet had entered high up in his breast and he was walking assisted by two men as he passed us. He admitted to the Middlesex officer that he had volunteered to stay behind for this dangerous work, and he was proud he had served his country so well. I heard some officers remark that he was a very brave man. Two days later when digging a trench on the right front of Bazentin Le Petit we came across the cable which must have run right back to High Wood.

FREDERIC MANNING

'Kill the bastards'

Frederic Manning, who was in the King's Shropshire Light Infantry and served on the Somme in 1916, published a memoir entitled *Her Privates We*. The characters are fictitious – Private Bourne stands for Manning – but the events Manning describes in the book happened during the last six months of 1916.

Suddenly the Hun barrage fell: the air was split and seared with shells. Fritz had been ready for them all right, and had only waited until their intentions had been made quite clear. As they hurried, head downward, over their own front line, they met men, some broken and bleeding, but others whole and sound, breaking back in disorder. They jeered at them, and the others raved inarticulately, and disappeared into the fog again. Jakes and Sergeant Tozer held their own lot together, and carried them through this moment of demoralization: Jakes roared and bellowed at them, and they only turned bewildered faces to him as they pressed forward, struggling through the mud like flies through treacle. What was all the bloody fuss about? they asked themselves, turning their faces, wide-eyed, in all directions to search the baffling fog. It shook, and twitched, and whirled about them: there seemed to be a dancing flicker before their eyes as shell after shell exploded, clanging, and the flying fragments hissed and shrieked through the air. Bourne thought that every bloody gun in the German army was pointed at him. He avoided some shattered bodies of men too obviously dead for help. A man stumbled past him with an agonized and bleeding face. Then more men broke back in disorder, throwing them into some confusion, and they seemed to waver for a moment. One of the fugitives charged down on James, and that short but stocky fighter smashed the butt of his rifle into the man's jaw, and sent him sprawling. Bourne had a vision of Sergeant-Major Glasspool.

'You take your bloody orders from Fritz!' he shouted as a triumphant frenzy thrust him forward.

For a moment they might have broken and run themselves, and for a moment they might have fought men of their own

blood, but they struggled on as Sergeant Tozer yelled at them
to leave that bloody tripe alone and get on with it. Bourne,
floundering in the viscous mud, was at once the most abject
and the most exalted of God's creatures. The effort and rage
in him, the sense that others had left them to it, made him
pant and sob, but there was some strange intoxication of joy
in it, and again all his mind seemed focused into one hard,
bright point of action. The extremities of pain and pleasure
had met and coincided too.

He knew, they all did, that the barrage had moved too
quickly for them, but they knew nothing of what was happening about them. In any attack, even under favourable
conditions, the attackers are soon blinded; but here they had
lost touch almost from the start. They paused for a brief
moment, and Bourne saw that Mr Finch was with them, and
Shem was not. Minton told him Shem had been hit in the
foot. Bourne moved closer to Martlow. Their casualties, as far
as he could judge, had not been heavy. They got going again,
and, almost before they saw it, were on the wire. The stakes
had been uprooted, and it was smashed and tangled, but had
not been well cut. Jakes ran along it a little way, there was
some firing, and bombs were hurled at them from the almost
obliterated trench, and they answered by lobbing a few
bombs over, and then plunging desperately among the steel
briars, which tore at their puttees and trousers. The last strand
of it was cut or beaten down, some more bombs came at
them, and in the last infuriated rush Bourne was knocked off
his feet and went practically headlong into the trench; getting
up, another man jumped on his shoulders, and they both fell
together, yelling with rage at each other. They heard a few
squeals of agony, and he saw a dead German, still kicking his
heels on the broken boards of the trench at his feet. He yelled
for the man who had knocked him down to come on, and followed the others. The trench was almost obliterated: it was
nothing but a wreckage of boards and posts, piled confusedly

in what had become a broad channel for the oozing mud. They heard some more bombing a few bays farther on, and then were turned back. They met two prisoners, their hands up, and almost unable to stand from fear, while two of the men threatened them with a deliberate, slow cruelty.

'Give 'em a chance! Send 'em through their own bloody barrage!' Bourne shouted, and they were practically driven out of the trench and sent across no man's land.

On the other flank they found nothing; except for the handful of men they had encountered at first, the trench was empty. Where they had entered the trench, the three first lines converged rather closely, and they thought they were too far right. In spite of the party of Germans they had met, they assumed that the other waves of the assaulting troops were ahead of them, and decided to push on immediately, but with some misgivings. They were now about twenty-four men. In the light, the fog was coppery and charged with fumes. They heard in front of them the terrific battering of their own barrage and the drumming of the German guns. They had only moved a couple of yards from the trench, when there was a crackle of musketry. Martlow was perhaps a couple of yards in front of Bourne, when he swayed a little, his knees collapsed under him, and he pitched forward on to his face, his feet kicking and his whole body convulsive for a moment. Bourne flung himself down beside him, and putting his arms round his body, lifted him, calling.

'Kid! You're all right, kid? he cried eagerly.

He was all right. As Bourne lifted the limp body, the boy's hat came off, showing half the back of his skull shattered where the bullet had come through it; and a little blood welled on to Bourne's sleeve and knee of his trousers. He was all right; and Bourne let him settle to earth again, lifting himself up almost indifferently, unable to realize what had happened, filled with a kind of tenderness that ached in him, and yet extraordinarily still, extraordinarily cold. He had to hurry, or he would be alone in the fog. Again he heard some rifle-fire, some bombing, and stooping, he ran towards the sound, and was by Minton's side again, when three men ran towards them, holding their hands up and screaming; and he lifted his rifle to his shoulder and fired; and the ache in him became a consuming hate that filled him with exultant cruelty, and he fired again, and again. The last man was closest to him, but as drunk and staggering with terror. He had scarcely fallen, when Bourne came up to him and saw that his head was shattered, as he turned it over with his boot. Minton, looking at him with a curious anxiety, saw Bourne's teeth clenched and bared, the lips snarling back from them in exultation.

'Come on. Get into it,' Minton cried in his anxiety.

And Bourne struggled forward again, panting, and muttering in a suffocated voice.

'Kill the bastards! Kill the bloody —ing swine! Kill them!'

All the filth and ordure he had ever heard came from between his clenched teeth; but his speech was thick and difficult. In a scuffle immediately afterwards a Hun went for Minton, and Bourne got him with the bayonet, under the ribs near the liver, and then, unable to wrench the bayonet out again, pulled the trigger, and it came away easily enough.

'Kill the bastards!' he muttered thickly.

He ran against Sergeant Tozer in the trench.

'Steady, ol' son! Steady. 'ave you been 'it? You're all over blood.'

'They killed the kid,' said Bourne, speaking with sudden clearness, though his chest heaved enormously. 'They killed him. I'll kill every bastard I see.'

ROBERT SMYLIE

'My three kids'

Before the war Robert Smylie, a forty-two-year-old father of three children, was headmaster of Sudbury Grammar School. He was commissioned in the Royal Scots Fusiliers, served with the 1st Battalion in Flanders and arrived at the Somme on 8 July. He was killed leading his men to the slopes of Longueval Ridge. In November 1915 he wrote this poem to his children:

I am writing this tonight, My three kids
By a little candle-light, My three kids
And the candlestick's a tin
With some dry tobacco in
And so that's how I begin, To three kids

Now I wonder what you're at, My three kids
Moll and Bids and little Pat, My three kids
Why of course there's two asleep
But perhaps Moll's thinking deep
Watching little stars that peep, At my kids

Since I left you long ago, My three kids
There's a lot you'd like to know, My three kids
That has happened to your dad
In the varied luck he's had
In adventures good and bad, My three kids

I have soldiered in a trench, My three kids
Serving under Marshall French, My three kids
Once a shell dropped with a thud
Quite close, covered me with mud
And its lucky 'twas a dud, For my kids

And I've crossed the ground outside, My three kids,
It's at night that's chiefly tried, My three kids
And the bullets sang all round
Overhead, or struck the ground
But your daddy none has found, No my kids

I have mapped out trenches new, My three kids
And some German trenches too, My three kids
I have sprinted past a wood
Counting steps, for so I could
Judge the distance as I should, My three kids

I have placed our snipers where, My three kids
On the Germans they could stare, My three kids
And they killed their share of men
Quite a lot for snipers ten
From their little hidden den, My three kids

And I've slept in bed quite warm, My three kids
But I haven't taken harm, My three kids
When upon the ground I lay
Without even straw or hay
In the same clothes night and day, My three kids

When they sent us back to rest, My three kids
Then they seemed to think it best, My three kids
To send on your dad ahead
To discover where a bed
Could be found, or some old shed, My three kids

And new officers were trained. My three kids
And the men we've lately gained, My three kids
And while that work was in hand
I was second in command
Of B Coy and that was grand, My three kids

But it didn't last all through, My three kids
There was other work to do, My three kids
When they made me adjutant
I was busy as an ant
And it's not much catch, I grant, My three kids

I have ridden on a horse, My three kids
Captured from a German force, My three kids
And I've marched and crawled and run
Night and day in rain and sun
And shall do it till we've won, My three kids

And I'd rather be with you, My three kids
Yet you know I'm lucky too, My three kids
Lots of men, I used to know
Now are killed or wounded, though
I remain, and back I'll go, To my kids

And I hope you'll all keep well, My three kids
Just as sound as any bell, My three kids
And when this long war is done
We shall have some glorious fun
Moll and Bids and little Son, My three kids.

Captain H. F. Bursey

The Scream of the Shells

Captain Bursey, who was forty-six and serving with the 18th Divisional Ammunition Column, wrote this in his diary in June, noting that his mother had asked if he was in the firing line:

I have just been witnessing the battle. As far as the eye can reach the horizon is one mass of bursting shell. Great volumes of smoke rise to be replaced by another burst before it can clear away.

There does not seem to be an inch of ground free from the bursting shell. And the roar of the guns is terrific. They seem to say:

'We are the guns and your masters, saw ye our flashes?
Heard ye the scream of the shells in the night and our
shuddering crashes,

Saw ye our work by the roadside, the shrouded things lying,
Moaning to God that he made them, the maimed and dying.
Husbands or sons,
Fathers or lovers, we break them.
We are the guns.'

How truly that has been brought home to me this week.

SIEGFRIED SASSOON

'The General'

'Good-morning, good-morning!' the General said
When we met him last week on our way to the line.
Now the soldiers he smiled at are most of 'em dead,
And we're cursing his staff for incompetent swine.
'He's a cheery old card,' grunted Harry to Jack
As they slogged up to Arras with rifle and pack.

But he did for them both by his plan of attack.

MAJOR J. V. BATES

'Priceless heroism, ghastly sights'

Nearly six hundred letters written by Major Johnathan Bates
of the Royal Army Medical Corps are held in the Imperial
War Museum. Most are addressed to his fiancée Alice, variously addressed as 'Girlie', 'old Girl' or, as here, 'Darling old
Kid', whom he married in 1917. This letter was written on
25 July:

My Darling old Kid,
I hope my last two letters have arrived safely, telling you that
I'm safe and sound and hope to be with you for a whole
fortnight before very long. Very many thanks for your long
letter which has just arrived. Your letters really have been

splendid, old girl. When things looked their bleakest in Longueval an orderly would dash into my dugout dressing station with a breathless 'A letter for you, sir!' and there would be one of yours for me to read in the middle of all that hell.

Well, old girl, I would like to write and tell you all about it but it really is impossible. I just can't put on paper all I saw during those five days and nights but I will tell you all I remember when I get home. I have just written a longish letter to Rene with a few odd experiences of mine and I have asked her to send it on to Randwick so you ought to see it there.

It is just wonderful to think that I got through it all safely – and yet all the time I *knew* I would – you know why. But the number of narrow squeaks! My word, I can't remember them all. During that first morning after we attacked, I was in a trench when a high explosive shrapnel burst exactly over my head. My servant, a yard on one side of me, was wounded and my orderly, a yard the other side, was killed outright. I then jumped into a shell hole to attend to two fellows wounded. I went back to the trench 20 yards away for some gauze and while I was getting it an enormous shell landed right in the hole I had just left and blew the two wounded men to bits and killed my corporal who I had left there. These are just two examples and there is no need to exaggerate for the facts are thrilling enough. I then selected a house for my dressing station and while I was there the house next to it was blown to smithereens by one enormous shell and smothered me and the patients with brick dust so we looked like millers! And five minutes afterwards the house opposite caught fire and was burnt down and we had to clear out. Then on the last day I was completely surrounded by Germans, but they never spotted me as I was in a dugout (with 3 patients), and during the 7 hours bombardment before, a shell had blown in the entrance so it

'They marched until they dropped, and then somehow got up
and marched again.' *A French Highway*, by John Nash, 1918.
He was the younger brother of Paul Nash. (IWM)

Over the Top. 1st Artists' Rifles at Marcoing, 30 December 1917, by John Nash. (IWM)

'A thousand flashes, and a lurid light spread over the battlefield.' *A Howitzer Firing*, by Paul Nash, 1918. (IWM)

The Christmas truce, 1914. A German soldier opens the truce by approaching the British lines with a small Christmas tree. (Illustrated London News)

Sketches by Cyril Lomax, chaplain
to the 8th Durham Light Infantry.
(IWM)

'This is a dugout that we occupy
with great joy and contentment.'

'One of the first tanks.'

'Is this the way to P.C. Belfort?'
'What d'you take me for?
The Harbour Master?'

'You may see, looking at their faces between the vertical gleams of their bayonets, that they are simply men.' Canadian soldiers prepare to go over the top, 1 July 1916, Somme. (Getty Images)

A burial service on the Somme, September 1916. (IWM)

'Well, if you knows of a better 'ole, go to it': cartoon by Bruce Bairnsfather, Royal Warwickshire Regiment. (IWM)

We are Making a New World, by Paul Nash, 1918. (IWM)

'The ground was not mud, not sloppy mud, but an octopus of sucking clay.' A stretcher party, Passchendaele, August 1917. (Getty Images)

Paul Nash's *The Field of Passchendaele*, 1917–18. (IWM)

'This area ought to remain as it is. No road, no well, no settlement ought to be made there . . . Then there would be no more wars.' *Ruined Country*, by Paul Nash, 1918. (IWM)

The Menin Road, by Paul Nash, 1919. (IWM)

didn't look like a dugout at all – just a heap of ruins. Our fellows did a magnificent charge, cleared the village of enemy and I was just able to escape – but on hands and knees as the Hun by that time had got a machine gun in the church 100 yards away and had spotted us trying to get away! All three patients could walk and we got them away all right. But I could write pages and pages about just one day – how at one spot I chose for a dressing station the only red cross flag I could hang up was a piece of German white shirt with two pieces of bandages soaked in blood pinned across it – the whole tied on to a German bayonet on a rifle which I stuck in a tree outside.

But I must reserve the whole story for when I get home – one long tale of priceless heroism by our men and ghastly sights.

P.S. Have got 2 Boche bayonets and a Boche hat (officer's) to decorate our home with some day.

Anonymous

Cricket on the Somme

'Spider' Webb was a Cockney – from Stepney, I believe – who was with us on the Somme in 1916. He was a splendid cricketer.

We had had a very stiff time for six or seven hours and were resting during a lull in the firing. Then suddenly Jerry sent over five shells. After a pause another shell came over and burst near to 'Spider' and his two pals.

When the smoke cleared I went across to see what had happened.

'Spider's' two pals were beyond help. The Cockney was propping himself up with his elbows surveying the scene.

'What's happened, Webb?' I said. 'Blimey! What's happened?' was the reply. 'One over – two bowled' (and, looking down at his leg) – 'and I'm stumped.' Then he fainted.

HANDWRITTEN DIARY – 25 AUGUST 1916

'A mockery of history'

This extract from a German war diary held by Britain's National Archive describes life in a German trench under bombardment and shows that both sides suffered the same conditions:

Thiepval, Hill 141, represents a hell which no imagination can picture. Shelters are destroyed and uninhabitable, trenches no longer exist. One lies in shell holes, which change hourly, no every minute. The heaviest shells come whistling in, cover in the living and unearth the dead. All communication is above ground, for that reason our losses are stupendous. In two or three nights almost a company is wiped out. Wax yellow, without emotion and unconcerned the stream of wounded passes to the rear. Warm food is not to be thought of, one takes iron rations which the stomach can hardly digest. As for water, we only get a few bottles of mineral water, hand grenades, cartridges, light rockets take precedence.

Today we had a tremendously heavy bombardment enough to drive you mad, which surpassed anything I have ever previously experienced. Whether it is the report of the firing or the burst, our own or the enemy's artillery, who can say? Further our own artillery has always shown an inclination to shoot short. It is enough to make one despair.

Today our new Major was severely wounded. He came from the Great General Headquarters, was accustomed to Russian conditions and much too careless. Here we stand under the severest artillery fire the world has ever seen, so accurately directed by 29 captive balloons and about 30 airmen that they bring every shelter, every trench and junction under fire. As opposed to that we have six captive balloons which scarcely venture up a bare 600 metres for fear of the overpowering airmen. At the same time they are so far behind in orders to get out of range of the naval guns that our artillery can scarcely be said to have aerial observation at all, even though the infantry and artillery observers do their utmost. Yet that is an insufficient compensation.

How ironical is the sentence used in the English Communiqué of the 21st instant:–

'Today the German aviators showed a livelier activity. Some even dared to cross our lines.' The bitterness is that it is perfectly true. All these visible signs strengthen the British morale. Every piece of trench is to be taken. 38 cm shells have been falling all around for 14 days and nights. Every quarter of an hour the earth is turned over. If a fortnight does not suffice, then they take 4 weeks over it or 8 weeks as on Hill 141. They do not need to be sparing with ammunition, accordingly firing continues until the captive balloons and aviators report that all the garrison is buried. If they have got one piece, then they treat the next piece in the same manner. How many infantry have been buried is immaterial.

And that is what nations do who want to civilize Africa and Asia, it is enough to drive you silly. And we have to battle with these inwardly hollow Englishmen and only outwardly polished French, who stand miles below us in intellect. It is a mockery of history.

CHARLES CARRINGTON

'The sickly stench of corruption'

Charles Carrington (1897–1990) was commissioned to the Royal Warwickshire Regiment's (15th) Territorial Battalion and fought in Italy and France. His memoir *A Subaltern's War* was published in 1929 and revised as *Soldier from the Wars Returning* in 1964.

It was then, turning back, that I knew what the novelists mean by a 'stricken field'. The western and southern slopes of the village had been comparatively little shelled; that is, a little grass had still room to grow between the shell-holes. The slope was held by tangle after tangle of rusty barbed wire in irregular lines. But among the wire lay rows of khaki figures, as they had fallen to the machine-guns on the crest, thick as the sleepers in the Green Park on a summer Sunday evening. The simile leapt to my mind at once of flies on a fly paper. I did not know then that twice in the fortnight before our flank attack had a division been hurled at that wire-encircled hill, and twice had it withered away before the hidden machine-guns. The flies were buzzing obscenely over the damp earth; morbid scarlet poppies grew scantily along the white chalk mounds; the air was thick and heavy with rank pungent explosives and the sickly stench of corruption.

EDMUND BLUNDEN

The Scarlet Dawn

Edmund Blunden's *Undertones of War* sold out in a day when it was first published in 1928. Blunden (1896–1974) was eighteen when the war began; he joined the Royal Sussex Regiment in 1915 as a subaltern and was nicknamed 'Rabbit'. This extract describes a day on the Somme in September:

The British barrage struck. The air gushed in hot surges along that river valley, and uproar never imagined by me swung from ridge to ridge. The east was scarlet with dawn and the flickering gunflashes; I thanked God I was not in the assault, and joined the subdued carriers nervously lighting cigarettes in one of the cellars, sitting there on the steps, studying my watch. The ruins of Hamel were soon crashing chaotically with German shells, and jags of iron and broken wood and brick whizzed past the cellar mouth. When I gave the order to move, it was obeyed with no pretence of enthusiasm. I was forced to shout and swear, and the carrying party, some with shoulders hunched, as if in a snowstorm, dully picked up their bomb buckets and went ahead. The wreckage around seemed leaping with flame. Never had we smelt high explosive so thick and foul, and there was no distinguishing one shell-burst from another, save by the black or tawny smoke that suddenly shaped in the general miasma. We walked along the river road, passed the sandbag dressing-station that had been rigged up only a night or two earlier where the front line ('Shankill Terrace') crossed the road, and had already been battered in; we entered no man's land, past the trifling British wire on its knife-rests, but we could make very little sense of ourselves or the battle. There were wounded Black Watch trailing down the road. They had been wading the marshes of the Ancre, trying to take a machine-gun post called Summer House. A few yards ahead, on the rising ground, the German front line could not be clearly seen, the water-mist and the smoke veiling it; and this was lucky for the carrying party. Half-way between the trenches, I wished them good-luck, and pointing out the place where they should, according to plan, hand over the bombs, I left them in charge of their own officer, returning myself, as my orders were, to my colonel. I passed good men of ours, in our front line, staring like persons in a trance across no man's land, their powers of action apparently suspended.

'What's happening over there?' asked Harrison (Major) (the company commander) with a face all doubt and stress, when I crawled into the candled, overcrowded frowziness of Kentish Caves. I could not say, and sat down ineffectively on some baskets, in which were the signallers' sacred pigeons. 'What's happening the other side of the river?' All was in ominous discommunication. A runner called Gosden presently came in, with bleeding breast, bearing a message written an hour or more earlier. Unsted, my former companion and instructor in Festubert's cool wars, appeared,

his exemplary bearing for once disturbed; he spoke breath-
lessly and as in an agony. This did not promise well, and, as
the hours passed, all that could be made out was that our
attacking companies were 'hanging on', some of them in the
German third trench, where they could not at all be reached
by the others, dug in between the first and the second.
Lintott wrote message after message, trying to share information north, east and west. South was impossible; the
marsh separated us from that flank's attack. Harrison, the
sweat standing on his forehead, thought out what to do in
this deadlock, and repeatedly telephoned to the guns and the
general. Wounded men and messengers began to crowd the
scanty passages of the Caves, and curt roars of explosion
just outside announced that these dugouts, shared by ourselves and the Black Watch, were now to be dealt with.
Death soon arrived there, among the group at the clumsy
entrance. Harrison meanwhile called for his runner, fastened
the chin-strap of his steel helmet, and pushed his way out
into the top trenches to see what he could; returned
presently mopping his forehead, with that kind of severe
laugh which tells the tale of a man who has incredibly
escaped from the barrage. The day was hot outside, glaring
mercilessly upon the stropped, burned, choked chalk
trenches. I came in again to the squeaking field telephones
and obscure candlelight. Presently Harrison, a message in his
hand, said: 'Rabbit, they're short of ammunition. Get round
and collect all the fellows you can and take them over – and
stay over there and do what you can.' I felt my heart thud at
this; went out, naming my men among headquarters 'odds
and ends' whenever I could find them squatted under the
chalk-banks, noting with pleasure that my nearest dump
had not been blown up and would answer our requirements;
we served out bombs and ammunition, then I thrust my
head in again to report that I was starting, when he delayed,
and at length cancelled, the enterprise. The shells on our

breathless neighbourhood seemed to fall more thickly, and
the dreadful spirit of waste and impotence sank into us,
when a sudden telephone call from an artillery observer
warned us that there were Germans in our front trench. In
that case Kentish Caves was a death-trap, a hole in which
bombs would be bursting within a moment; yet here at last
was something definite, and we all seemed to come to life,
and prepared with our revolvers to try our luck.

The artillery observer must have made some mistake. Time
passed without bombs among us or other surprise, and the
collapse of the attack was wearily obvious. The bronze noon
was more quiet but not less deadly than the morning. I went
round the scarcely passable hillside trenches, but they were
amazingly lonely: suddenly a sergeant-major and half a dozen
men bounded superhumanly, gasping and excited, over the
parapets. They had been lying in no man's land, and at last
had decided to 'chance their arm' and dodge the machine-
guns which had been perseveringly trying to get them. They
drank pints of water, of which I had luckily a little store in a
dugout there, now wrecked and gaping. I left them sitting
wordless in that store. The singular part of the battle was that
no one, not even these, could say what had happened, or what
was happening. One vaguely understood that the waves had
found their manoeuvre in no man's land too complicated; that
the Germans' supposed derelict forward trench near the railway was joined by tunnels to their main defence, and enabled
them to come up behind our men's backs; that they had used
the bayonet where challenged, with the boldest readiness;
'used the whole dam' lot, minnies, snipers, rifle grenades,
artillery'; that machine-guns from the Thiepval ridge south of
the river were flaying all the crossings of no man's land. 'Don't
seem as if the 49th Div. got any farther.' But the general effect
was the disappearance of the attack into mystery.

Orders for the withdrawal were sent out to our little groups
in the German lines towards the end of the afternoon. How

the runners got there, they alone could explain, if any survived. The remaining few of the battalion in our own positions were collected in the trench along Hamel village street, and a sad gathering it was. Some who had been in the waves contrived to rejoin us now. How much more fortunate we seemed than those who were still in the German labyrinth awaiting the cover of darkness for their small chance of life! And yet, as we filed out, up Jacob's Ladder, we were warned by low-bursting shrapnel not to anticipate. Mesnil was its vile self, but we passed at length. Not much was said, then or afterwards, about those who would never again pass that hated target; among the killed were my old company commanders, Penruddock and Northcote (after a great display of coolness and endurance in the German third line) – laughing French, quiet Hood and a hundred more. The Cheshires took over the front line, which the enemy might at one moment have occupied without difficulty; but neither they nor our own patrols succeeded in bringing in more than two or three of the wounded; and, the weather turning damp, the Germans increased their difficulty in the darkness and distorted battlefield with a rain of gas shells.

Eric Lever Townsend

'We shall live for ever'

Eric Lever Townsend was a twenty-year-old second lieutenant in the 1/15th London Regiment. These are some of the paragraphs he wrote to his parents on 8 September:

> Dearest Mother and Father
> You are reading this letter because I have gone under.
>   Of course I know that you will be terribly cut up, and that it will be a long time before you get over it, but get over it you must. You must be imbued with the spirit of the Navy and the Army to 'carry on'.

You must console yourselves with the thought that I am happy, whereas if I had lived – who knows?

Remember the saying attributed to Solon, 'Call no man happy till he is dead'. Thanks to your self-sacrificing love and devotion I have had a happy time all my life. Death will have delivered me from experiencing unhappiness.

It has always seemed to me a very pitiful thing what little difference the disappearance of a man makes to any institution, even though he may have played a very important role. A moment's regret, a moment's pause for readjustment, and another man steps forward to carry on, and the machine clanks on with scarce a check. The death of a leader of the nation is less even than seven days' wonder. To a very small number is it given to live in history; their number is scarcely one in ten millions. To the rest it is only granted to live in their united achievements.

PHILIP CHRISTISON

'The red caps must go!'

Philip Christison (1893–1993) was commissioned into the Queen's Own Cameron Highlanders and won the Military Cross at the Battle of Loos, where he was wounded. After recuperating in England he left to return to the front on 8 September. He rose to become a general in the Second World War where he deputised both for General Sir William Slim and Admiral Mountbatten.

On arrival at the Re-inforcement Camp at Etaples I was assigned, pending posting orders, to instruct, or rather supervise instruction, at the notorious 'Bull Ring', a large, sandy hollow where elderly NCOs tried to provide instruction for a mixture of recruits and hardened veterans. Although there had been discontent over the type of training and lack of recreation, little had been done to ameliorate conditions, and when the Military Service Act men came out and conscripts for the first time and veterans, many of whom had been two or even three times at the front, were mixed together to do out-of-date exercises and monotonous drill, discontent boiled over. The chief grouses were the monotony of the training, the restrictions on recreation and amusement and the bullying by the 'Red Caps', the military police. What I saw of it, the training was indeed monotonous; and it was out-of-date and badly organised. Squads were marched out to a huge, sandy area known as 'The Bull Ring', and there for 6 hours a day, they sweated away at arms drill or made short rushes in the open. The same Officers seldom took the same men and the permanent staff was inefficient, and naturally bored stiff. No attempt was made to bring new reinforcements up to date in tactics and weaponry. There was a Base Commandant, Major General Thomson – and staff; an assistant Provost Marshal with a large detachment of Military Police, many of them bullies of a bad type, several were peacetime prison warders and lunatic asylum attendants.

In Calais and Etaples sub-depots were numbered or lettered and had a Lt. Colonel in charge. Men often spent up to 2 months in these depots, while Officers seldom stayed more than a week or 10 days during which they were used as instructors and even on occasions paraded under a 'dug-out' who had never been to the front. The results were, of course, farcical and ended in trouble. Recreation grounds were hopelessly inadequate and men naturally turned to the town. Inevitably there were instances of drunkenness and disorder, but on a minor scale. After one incident in Calais, when an estaminet window was smashed, the Base Commandant placed the town out of bounds. Next morning, men had refused to go on parade. No arrests were made. That evening large numbers poured into the town. The MPs tried to clear the troops out and one opened fire with his pistol, whereupon the mob rushed the police and beat them up, killing three. They then proceeded to the 'red light' area and broke up some cafes. Examples were made of a few of the ringleaders, but the restrictions were removed. News of this event, grossly exaggerated of course, reached Etaples and some troops who were refused wine after hours in a café broke the glass surround. General Thomson then committed the same error as his colleague had done in Calais; he put Etaples out of bounds.

The news spread and the men got together, including a large number of NCOs, and decided they also would not go on parade till the restrictions were lifted. That evening some men tried to cross the bridge over the railway into town but were turned back by a force of Military Police. That night the cry went up 'The red-caps must go!!!' A large mob surrounded the MPs' hut near the bridge, set it on fire, and next morning the charred remains of 11 MPs were found in the wreckage. Very few troops paraded next day, and at 17.00 hours a mob of over 15,000 men marched down to the bridge headed by a big Sergeant in the Gordons. I took him for a heavyweight athlete of Highland Games. As we watched, they were met on the bridge by a duty platoon under an Officer who drew his pistol and said he would order fire to be opened if they did not disperse. After some argument, the big Sergeant made a grab and, twisting it out of the Officer's hand, chucked it over the bridge and the mob surged on brushing aside the platoon which took no action. The behaviour of the troops that night in the town was exemplary and there was no trouble of any kind; every man was back in camp by tattoo. Next day the men went on parade but again at 17.00 hours made for the town. When they reached the bridge they were met by a young Officer commanding the duty platoon of New Zealand troops. His orders were not to get closely involved but to stand behind the platoon and order fire to be opened, if necessary, to stop the mob crossing the bridge. As the mob arrived, led again by the Gordon Sergeant, he dismissed the platoon and stood alone on the bridge, revolver in hand. As the big Sergeant approached, he called out, 'My orders were to hold the bridge and order my men to fire if you came on. Had I done this, there would have been a bloody mess, so I've sent the men away. Now you play the game too. If you must go into town, find another way. I'm going to shoot the first man that comes on this bridge.' The mob hesitated, then a few pulled back the big Sergeant and they cheered the Officer for a stout-hearted sportsman, and melted away, a few making for the town by a long and tedious detour to the next bridge, but the majority returning to camp. Next day all troops paraded and said they hoped by last night's gesture that their grievances would be put right. Twenty-one men were arrested and court-martialled, and some – I believe those concerned in the MPs' murder, and the big Sergeant – were shot. During these days neither the Base Commandment nor any member of his staff, nor any of the senior commanders in the depot made any appearance, either to take control or hear the men's grievances; while, in their absence, the larger number of reinforcement Officers in the camp (of whom I was one) looked on – in sympathy.

PHILIP GIBBS

The Arrival of the Tank

The fifteenth of September 1916 was the day that tanks proved their value as instruments of war. Philip Gibbs, the Western Front correspondent of the *Morning Post*, reported on the new and mysterious weapon:

They 'went over' at dawn yesterday filled with the spirit of victory, and it was half the battle won.

Many of them went over, too, in the greatest good-humour, laughing as they ran. Like children whose fancy has been inflamed by some new toy, they were enormously cheered by a new weapon which was to be tried with them for the first time – 'The heavily armoured car' mentioned already in the official bulletin.

That description is a dull one compared with all the rich and rare qualities which belong to these extraordinary vehicles. The secret of them was kept for months jealously and nobly. It was only a few days ago that it was whispered to me.

'Like prehistoric monsters. You know, the old "Ichtyosaurus",' said the officer.

I told him he was pulling my leg.

'But it's a fact, man!'

He breathed hard, and laughed in a queer way at some enormous comicality.

'They eat up houses and put the refuse under their bellies. Walk right over 'em!'

I knew this man was a truthful and simple soul, and yet could not believe.

'They knock down trees like matchsticks,' he said, staring at me with shining eyes. 'They go clean through wood!'

'And anything else?' I asked enjoying what I thought was a new sense of humour.

'Everything else,' he said earnestly. 'They take ditches like kangaroos. They simply love shell craters! Laugh at 'em!'

It appeared, also, that they were proof against rifle bullets, machine-gun bullets, bombs, shell-splinters. Just shrugged their shoulders and passed on. Nothing but a direct hit from a fair-sized shell could do them any harm.

'But what's the name of these mythical monsters?' I asked, not believing a word of it.

He said 'Hush!'

Other people said 'Hush! . . . Hush!' when the subject was alluded to in a remote way. And since then I have heard that one name for them is the 'Hush-hush'. But their real name is Tanks.

For they are real, and I have seen them, and walked round them, and got inside their bodies, and looked at their mysterious organs, and watched their monstrous movements.

I came across a herd of them in a field, and, like the countryman who first saw a giraffe, said 'Hell! . . . I don't believe it.' Then I sat down on the grass and laughed until the tears came into my eyes. (In war one has a funny sense of humour.) For they were monstrously comical, like toads of vast size emerging from the primeval slime in the twilight of the world's dawn.

The skipper of one of them introduced me to them.

'I felt awfully bucked,' said the young officer (who is about five feet high), 'when my beauty ate up her first house. But I was sorry for the house, which was quite a good one.'

'And how about trees?' I asked.

'They simply love trees,' he answered.

When our soldiers first saw these strange creatures lolloping along the roads and over old battlefields, taking trenches on the way, they shouted and cheered wildly, and laughed for a day afterwards. And yesterday the troops got out of their trenches laughing and shouting and cheering again because the Tanks had gone on ahead, and were scaring the Germans dreadfully, while they moved over the enemy's trenches and poured out fire on every side.

Over our own trenches in the twilight of the dawn one of those motor-monsters had lurched up, and now it came crawling forward to the rescue, cheered by the assaulting troops, who called out words of encouragement to it and laughed, so that some men were laughing even when bullets caught them in the throat.

'Crème de Menthe' was the name of this particular creature, and it waddled forward right over the old German trenches, and went forward very steadily towards the sugar factory.

There was a second of silence from the enemy there.

Then, suddenly, their machine-gun fire burst out in nervous spasms and splashed the sides of 'Crème de Menthe'.

But the tank did not mind. The bullets fell from its sides, harmlessly. It advanced upon a broken wall, leaned up against it heavily until it fell with a crash of bricks, and then rose on to the bricks and passed over them, and walked straight into the midst of the factory ruins.

From its sides came flashes of fire and a hose of bullets, and then it trampled around over machine-gun emplace-ments, 'having a grand time', as one of the men said with enthusiasm.

It crushed the machine-guns under its heavy ribs, and killed machine-gun teams with a deadly fire. The infantry followed in and took the place after this good help, and then advanced again round the flanks of the monster.

Before the dawn, two of them had come up out of the darkness and lumbered over our front line trenches looking towards the enemy as though hungry for breakfast. Afterwards they came across no man's land like enormous toads with pains in their stomachs, and nosed at Martinpuich before testing the strength of its broken barns and bricks.

The men cheered them wildly, waving their helmets and dancing round them. One company needed cheering up, for they had lost two of their officers the night before in a patrol adventure, and it was the sergeants who led them over.

Twenty minutes afterwards, the first waves were inside the first trench of Martinpuich, and in advance of them waddled a monster.

The men were held up for some time by the same machine-gun fire which has killed so many of our men, but the monsters went on along, and had astounding adventures.

They went straight through the shells of broken barns and houses, straddled on top of German dug-outs, and fired enfilading shots down German trenches.

From one dug-out came a German colonel with a white,

frightened face, who held his hands very high in front of the tank, shouting 'Kamerad! Kamerad!'

'Well, come inside then,' said a voice in the body of the beast, and a human hand came forth from a hole opening suddenly and grabbed the German officer.

For the rest of the day, the tank led that unfortunate man about on the strangest journey the world has ever seen.

Another tank was confronted with one hundred Germans, who shouted 'Mercy! Mercy!' and at the head of this procession led them back as prisoners to our lines. Yet another tank went off to the right of Martinpuich, and was so fresh and high-spirited that it went far into the enemy's lines, as though on the way to Berlin.

BATTERY SERGEANT-MAJOR DOUGLAS PEGLER

The Tanks

Sergeant-Major Douglas Pegler was wounded in the battle but in his diary offered his thoughtful reflections on the 'land crabs':

I have forgotten the 'land crabs', the great armoured cars that took part in the battle of the 15th – some are lying on their backs mangled masses of twisted and broken iron, others are back in their repairing yards, all are more or less crocked but Gad the execution they did was awful. It struck me as I saw them from the corner of Leuze Wood, how symbolic of all war they were. Then one saw them creeping along at about four miles an hour, taking all obstacles as they came, sputtering death with all their guns, enfilading each trench as it came to it – and crushing beneath them our own dead and dying as they passed. I saw one body on a concrete parapet over which one had passed. This body was just a splash of blood and clothing about two feet wide and perhaps an inch thick, an hour before this thing had been a thinking, breathing man, with life before him and loved ones awaiting him at home, probably somewhere in Scotland, for he was a kiltie.

Nothing stops these cars, trees bend and break, boulders are pressed into the earth. One had been hit by a large shell and the petrol tanks pierced, she lay on her side in flames, a picture of hopelessness but every gun on the uppermost side still working with dogged determination. The firing gradually slackened and she lay silent, the gallant little crew burned to death each man at his gun.

RUDYARD KIPLING

My Boy Jack

The British writer Rudyard Kipling (1865–1936), who won the Nobel Prize for Literature in 1907, is most famous for his *Barrack-Room Ballads*, 'If', the *Just So Stories* and the two *Jungle Books*. When his son John applied to join the Irish Guards he was rejected because of poor eyesight but Kipling used his influence to get him a commission. He went missing during the Battle of Loos in September 1915. Kipling wrote this poem in 1916.

> *'Have you news of my boy Jack?'*
> *Not this tide*
> *'When d'you think that he'll come back?'*
> *Not with this wind blowing, and this tide.*
>
> *'Has any one else had word of him?'*
> *Not this tide*
> *For what is sunk will hardly swim,*
> *Not with this wind blowing, and this tide.*
>
> *'Oh, dear, what comfort can I find?'*
> *None this tide,*
> *Nor any tide*

Except he did not shame his kind –
Not even with that wind blowing, and that tide.

Then hold your head up all the more
This tide,
And every tide
Because he was the son you bore,
And gave to that wind blowing and that tide!

ERICH MARIA REMARQUE

On Leave

Erich Maria Remarque did not take part in the fighting on the frontline, but was wounded by shrapnel while carrying a wounded comrade out of action. His novel *All Quiet on the Western Front* (*Im Westen nichts Neues*) was probably read by more Britons than any other book on the Great War. It was published in England in March 1929 and reprinted fifteen times in the next four months, selling 133,000 copies. This extract is about the awkwardnesses that occur on visits from the battlefront to mother:

'Sit here beside me,' says my mother.

She looks at me. Her hands are white and sickly and frail compared with mine. We say very little, and I am thankful that she asks nothing. What ought I to say? Everything I could have wished for has happened. I have come out of it safely and sit here beside her. And in the kitchen stands my sister making the evening bread and singing.

'Dear boy,' says my mother softly.

We were never very demonstrative in our family; poor folk who toil and are full of cares are not so. It is not their way to protest what they already know. When my mother says to me 'dear boy', it means much more than when another uses it. I know well enough that the jar of whortle-berries is the only one they have had for months, and that she has kept it for me; and the somewhat stale cakes that she gives me too.

It is the last evening at home. Everyone is silent. I go to bed early, I seize the pillow, press it against myself and bury my head in it. Who knows if I will ever lie in a feather bed again?

Late in the night my mother comes into my room. She thinks I am asleep, and I pretend to be so. To talk, to stay awake with one another, it is too hard.

She sits long into the night although she is in pain and often writhes. At last I can bear it no longer, and pretend I have just wakened up.

'Go and sleep, mother, you will catch cold here.'

'I can sleep enough later,' she says.

I sit up. 'I don't go straight back to the front, mother. I have to do four weeks at the training camp. I may come over from there one Sunday, perhaps.'

She is silent. Then she asks gently: 'Are you very much afraid?'

'No, mother.'

'I would like to tell you to be on your guard against the women out in France. They are no good.'

Ah! Mother, Mother. You still think I am a child – why can I not put my head in your lap and weep? Why have I always to be strong and self-controlled? I would like to weep and be comforted, too, indeed I am little more than a child; in the wardrobe still hang my short, boy's trousers – it is such a little time ago, why is it over?

'Where we are there aren't any women, mother,' I say as calmly as I can.

'And be very careful at the front, Paul.'

Ah, Mother, Mother! Why do I not take you in my arms and die with you. What poor wretches we are!

'Yes, mother, I will.'

'I will pray for you every day, Paul.'

Ah! Mother, Mother! Let us rise up and go out, back through the years, where the burden of all this misery lies on us no more, back to you and me alone, Mother!

'Perhaps you can get a job that is not so dangerous.'

'Yes, mother, perhaps I can get into the cook-house, that can easily be done.'

'You do it then, and if the others say anything –'

'That won't worry me, mother –'

She sighs. Her face is a white gleam in the darkness.

'Now you must go to sleep, mother.'

She does not reply. I get up and wrap my cover round her shoulders.

She supports herself on my arm, she is in pain.

And so I take her to her room. I stay with her a little while.

'And you must get well again, mother, before I come back.'

'Yes, yes, my child.'

'You ought not to send your things to me, mother. We have plenty to eat out there. You can make much better use of them here.'

How destitute she lies there in her bed, she, that loves me more than all the world. As I am about to leave, she says hastily: 'I have two pairs of under-pants for you. They are all wool. They will keep you warm. You must not forget to put them in your pack.'

Ah! Mother! I know what these underpants have cost you in waiting, and walking, and begging! Ah! Mother, Mother! How can it be that I must part from you? Who else is there that has any claim on me but you. Here I sit and there you are lying, and we have so much to say, that we could never say it.

'Good-night, mother.'

'Good-night, my child.'

The room is dark. I hear my mother's breathing, and the

ticking of the clock. Outside the window the wind blows and the chestnut trees rustle.

On the landing I stumble over my pack which lies there already made up, because I have to leave early in the morning.

I bite into my pillow. I grasp the iron rods of my bed with my fists. I ought never to have come here. Out there I was indifferent and often hopeless; – I will never be able to be so again. I was a soldier, and now I am nothing but an agony for myself, for my mother, for everything that is so comfortless and without end.

I ought never to have come on leave.

WINSTON CHURCHILL

True Glory

The campaign of 1916 on the Western Front was from beginning to end a welter of slaughter, which after the issue was determined left the British and French armies weaker in relation to the Germans than when it opened, while the actual battlefronts were not appreciably altered, and except for the relief of Verdun, which relieved the Germans no less than the French, no strategic advantage of any kind had been gained. The German unwisdom in attacking Verdun was more than cancelled in French casualties, and almost cancelled in the general strategic sphere by the heroic prodigality of the French defence. The loss in prestige which the Germans sustained through their failure to take Verdun was to be more than counterbalanced by their success in another theatre while all the time they kept their battlefront unbroken on the Somme.

But this sombre verdict, which it seems probable posterity will endorse in still more searching terms, in no way diminishes the true glory of the British Army. A young army, but the finest we have ever marshalled; improvised at the sound of the cannonade, every man a volunteer inspired not only by love of country but by a widespread conviction that human freedom was challenged by military and Imperial tyranny, they grudged no sacrifice however unfruitful and shrank from no ordeal however destructive. Struggling forward through the mire and filth of the trenches, across the corpse-strewn crater fields, amid the flaring, crashing, blasting barrages and murderous machine-gun fire, conscious of their race, proud of their cause, they seized the most formidable soldiery in Europe by the throat, slew them and hurled them unceasingly backward. If two lives or ten lives were required by their commanders to kill one German, no word of complaint ever rose from the fighting troops. No attack however forlorn, however fatal, found them without ardour. No slaughter however desolating prevented them from returning to the charge. No physical conditions however severe deprived their commanders of their obedience and loyalty. Martyrs not less than soldiers, they fulfilled the high purpose of duty with which they were imbued. The battlefields of the Somme were the graveyards of Kitchener's Army. The flower of that generous manhood which quitted peaceful civilian life in every kind of workaday occupation, which came at the call of Britain, and as we may still hope, at the call of humanity, and came from the most remote parts of her Empire, was shorn away for ever in 1916. Unconquerable except by death, which they have conquered, they have set up a monument of native virtue which will command the wonder, the reverence and the gratitude of our island people as long as we endure as a nation among men.

GUY CHAPMAN

'A good morning's work'

Guy Chapman, who was born in 1889, became a lawyer after leaving Oxford. He joined the Royal Fusiliers as a junior officer

in 1914 and arrived in France in August 1915. Although he suffered badly from a mustard-gas attack, he survived the war and
became Professor of Modern History at Leeds University. This is
an extract from his book *A Passionate Prodigality*:

The failure of the Somme had bred in the infantry a wry
distrust of the staff; and there was fierce resentment when
brass-hats descended from their impersonal isolation to
strafe platoon and company commanders for alleged short-
comings in the line. The Old Army could not grasp that the
New Army cared nothing for soldiering as a trade; thought
of it only as a job to be done, and the more expeditiously
the better. The man in the line wanted practical help; but in
its place he too often received theory based on a type of
warfare which had passed away with the Old Army before
the end of 1914. He resented the staff's well-meant but frequently out-of-date admonitions. It made him mad

To see him shine so brisk and smell so sweet
And talk so like a waiting gentlewoman
Of guns and drums and wounds . . .

Such bald unjointed chat produced some true Hotspur ani-
madversions. 'If that perky swashbuckler shows his nose in
my trench again . . .,' an infuriated company commander
would rage. Meanwhile the rouser of this bile would be
equably pursuing his way back to his château and his lunch,
conscious of a good morning's work.

I was very aware of both sides when I was commandeered
by one of my superiors to assist in a jaunt round the line.
The red and white brassard of Corps staffs, the undeniable
elegance of the wearer, his specially padded and exceptionally clean tin hat, his glowing boots, his thick manly stick,
made one think of dowagers slumming. Further, out of long
absence from the focal point of war, he was often extremely

sensitive to the ordinary noises of the line, the crack of a bullet and the purr of a Minnie. I felt painfully embarrassed as my senior crept gingerly along the duckboards, cringing slightly behind the sandbags, under the solemn gaze of half a dozen old sweats, unconcernedly cleaning rifles, cooking, shaving, or writing letters, smoking their pipes, and altogether at ease in this cushy sector. I was therefore delighted when, one grey afternoon, the GSO 3 and I were penned up in a famous sap-head while Fritz conscientiously lobbed some twenty little pineapples at the trench end. This unseasonable pleasure was further heightened when, as we hurried back, a 5.9 whooped over and crashed into some ruins a hundred yards away, and my companion, throwing dignity to the winds, took to his heels and galloped with the grotesque gait of a terrified foal through the water dismally covering the duckboards. It required considerable persistence to clean himself to a seemly state before he reached the car.

1917

On 1 February Germany resumed unrestricted submarine warfare and two days later the United States severed diplomatic relations with Germany (by the end of January the U-boat campaign had forced the introduction of rationing in Britain).

On the Western Front, meanwhile, on 4 February the Germans withdrew about twenty miles to the heavily fortified 'Hindenburg Line', which they had fully occupied by mid-March. As U-boats began to sink neutral but mostly American shipping the United States drew ever closer to declaring war against Germany. Woodrow Wilson, the President, announced the arming of US merchant shipping on 12 March and his war cabinet voted unanimously for war on 20 March. The United States finally declared war on 6 April and in July General John J. Pershing, commander of the American Expeditionary Force, asked for an army of a million men. In his speech to Congress, Wilson said that the Americans were fighting for the rights of nations great and small and the privilege of men everywhere to choose their way of life and of obedience. 'The world must be made safe for democracy. Its peace must be planted upon the tested foundations of political liberty.'

The French had replaced General Joffre with General Nivelle, who prepared to attack the Germans in the southern Aisne while the British attacked at Arras and Vimy Ridge. When the so-called 'Nivelle offensive' began on 9 April the British triumphed at Arras and the Canadians captured Vimy Ridge, but the impetus petered out and the Germans were able to reinforce their positions. The Battle of Arras went on until May, when there had been 150,000 British casualties for no real gain of ground – as well as 100,000 German casualties. The French were soundly defeated, with 29,000 soldiers killed, and Nivelle was replaced by Pétain.

There were now 'strikes' or 'mutinies' involving almost half the French Army, with the French troops saying they would not return to the trenches. Pétain succeeded in restoring order but only after 3427 courts-martial, at which 554 men were condemned to death. Forty-nine were eventually shot. Hundreds were sentenced to life imprisonment. The French Army did not attack on the Western Front from June 1917 until July 1918.

On 31 July, to relieve the pressure on the French as they wrestled with the 'mutinies', Sir Douglas Haig launched the Battle of Passchendaele (officially the Third Battle of Ypres). His aim was to push the Germans out of northern France and Belgium and to capture their submarine bases. Passchendaele has joined the Somme as a battle connoting slaughter and futility and which again raised doubts about Haig's command. Lloyd George was certainly disillusioned and starved Haig of reinforcements.

As at the Somme, there was a massive bombardment before the attack but rain fell and the ground became a quagmire. The British troops were bogged down in no man's land and became an easy target for the Germans. The Passchendaele ridge was eventually taken but when Haig finally called off the attack the British forces had advanced only five miles.

The growing disillusion among the younger officers found its voice when the poet Siegfried Sassoon, who had won the Military Cross for conspicuous bravery, wrote the most famous protest of the war in 'A Soldier's Declaration', made, he said, as an act of 'wilful defiance' of military authority and 'acting on behalf of soldiers'. Thanks to an intervention from another poet and fellow officer, Robert Graves, who had been serving in the same regiment, Sassoon was treated as a psychiatric patient at Craiglockhart Hospital (Sassoon, the hospital and W. H. R. Rivers, the Army psychologist, are the subjects of Pat Barker's novel *Regeneration*, which was also made into a film). Sassoon later returned to the front.

In November there was at least one reason for the British Army to celebrate when the Tank Corps at last demonstrated the power of their new weapon of war. In an attack on the Hindenburg Line, on a front of 13,000 yards, the infantry were able to advance 10,000 yards in ten hours, meanwhile taking 8000 prisoners at a cost of 1500 British casualties (compared with 300,000 at Passchendaele for a similar advance). Bells were rung in all churches in England.

On the home front, in recognition of how the war had changed the situation of women, Parliament made history by voting for women's suffrage at the end of the war. Women volunteers were also now in uniform in three new services – the Women's Royal Naval Service, known as the 'Wrens', the Women's Auxiliary Army Corps and the Women's Royal Air Force. Horse racing was suspended, as were county cricket, the university boat race, the Henley and Cowes regattas and the FA Cup final. In London there was air-raid shelter for about a million people. Coal was rationed. In July King George V proclaimed that the House of Saxe-Coburg-Gotha would henceforth be known as the House of Windsor. He renounced all German titles for himself and other descendants of Queen Victoria.

After the Russian Revolution Tsar Nicholas II abdicated in March and was later assassinated. Lenin arrived in Russia in April and a Communist government under Lenin took office on 7 November. Shortly afterwards Russia opened peace negotiations with Germany.

WILFRED OWEN

'Seventh hell'

For most critics Wilfred Owen (1893–1918) was the greatest poet of the First World War. He was exceptionally close to his mother and this letter was written during his first experience of the trenches in the middle of January 1917.

To Susan Owen
Tues: 16 January 1917
My own sweet Mother,
I am sorry you have had about 5 days letterless. I hope you had my two letters 'posted' since you wrote your last, which I received tonight. I am bitterly disappointed that I never got one of yours.

I can see no excuse for deceiving you about these last 4 days. I have suffered seventh hell.

I have not been at the front.

I have been in front of it.

I held an advanced post, that is, a 'dug-out' in the middle of no man's land.

We had a march of 3 miles over shelled road then nearly 3 along a flooded trench. After that we came to where the trenches had been blown flat out and had to go over the top. It was of course dark, too dark, and the ground was not mud, not sloppy mud, but an octopus of sucking clay, 3, 4 and 5 feet deep, relieved only by craters full of water. Men have been known to drown in them. Many stuck in the mud and only got on by leaving their waders, equipment, and in some cases their clothes.

High explosives were dropping all around about, and machine guns spluttered every few minutes. But it was so dark that even the German flares did not reveal us.

Three quarters dead, I mean each of us ¾ dead, we reached the dug-out, and relieved the wretches therein. I then had to go forth and find another dug-out for a still more advanced post where I left 18 bombers. I was responsible for other posts on the left but there was a junior officer in charge.

My dug-out held 25 men tight packed. Water filled it to a depth of 1 or 2 feet, leaving say 4 feet of air.

One entrance had been blown in and blocked.

So far, the other remained.

The Germans knew we were staying there and decided we shouldn't.

Those fifty hours were the agony of my happy life.

Every ten minutes on Sunday afternoon seemed an hour.

I nearly broke down and let myself drown in the water that was now slowly rising over my knees.

Towards 6 o'clock, when, I suppose, you would be going to church, the shelling grew less intense and less accurate: so that I was mercifully helped to do my duty and crawl, wade, climb and flounder over no man's land to visit my other post. It took me half an hour to move about 150 yards.

I was chiefly annoyed by our own machine guns from behind. The seeng-seeng-seeng of the bullets reminded me of Mary's canary. On the whole I can support the canary better.

In the Platoon on my left the sentries over the dug-out were blown to nothing. One of these poor fellows was my first servant whom I rejected. If had kept him he would have lived, for servants don't do sentry duty. I kept my own sentries half way down the stairs during the most terrific bombardment. In spite of this one lad was blown down and, I am afraid, blinded.

This was my only casualty.

The officer of the left platoon has come out completely prostrated and is in hospital.

I am now as well, I suppose, as ever.

I allow myself to tell you all these things because *I am never going back to this awful post*. It is the worst the Manchesters have ever held; and we are going back for a rest.

I hear that the officer who relieved me left his 3 Lewis guns behind when he came out. (He had only 24 hours in). He will be court-martialled.

ARTHUR GUY EMPEY

'Crucifixion'

After the sinking of the *Lusitania* Arthur Guy Empey (1883–1963), a recruiting sergeant with the New York National Guard, travelled to England and enlisted in the Royal Fusiliers. After he was invalided out of the Army he wrote about his experiences in *Over the Top*, published in 1917, which sold more than a million copies in America and was used as a propaganda weapon. Many things puzzled him about the British, including the strict military discipline:

> In the British Army discipline is very strict. One has to be very careful in order to stay on the narrow path of government virtue.
>
> There are about seven million ways of breaking the King's Regulations; to keep one you have to break another.
>
> The worst punishment is death by a firing squad or 'up against the wall' as Tommy calls it. This is for desertion, cowardice, mutiny, giving information to the enemy, destroying or wilfully wasting ammunition, looting, rape, robbing the dead, forcing a safeguard, striking a superior etc.
>
> Then comes the punishment of sixty-four days in the front-line trench without relief. During this time you have to engage in all raids, working parties in no man's land, and every hazardous undertaking that comes along. If you live through the sixty-four days you are indeed lucky.
>
> This punishment is awarded where there is a doubt as to

the wilful guilt of a man who has committed an offence punishable by death.

Then comes the famous Field Punishment No. 1. Tommy has nicknamed it 'crucifixion.' It means that a man is spread eagled on a limber wheel, two hours a day for twenty-one days. During this time he only gets water, bully beef, and biscuits for his chow. You get 'crucified' for repeated minor offences.

Next in order is Field Punishment No. 2.

This is confinement in the 'Clink,' without blankets, getting water, bully beef, and biscuits for rations and doing all the dirty work that can be found. This may be for twenty-four hours or twenty days, according to the gravity of the offence.

Then comes 'Pack Drill' or Defaulters' Parade. This consists of drilling, mostly at the double, for two hours with full equipment. Tommy hates this, because it is hard work. Sometimes he fills his pack with straw to lighten it, and sometimes he gets caught. If he gets caught, he grouses at everything in general for twenty-one days, from the vantage point of a limber wheel.

MARCHING SONG

America's decision to enter the war introduced good marching songs to the repertoire of soldiers in France, among which was:

Way down in Tennessee,
That's where I long to be.
Right at my mother's knee,
She thinks the world of me.
All I can think of tonight
Is the fields of snowy white.
Banjos ringing,
Darkies singing,
All the world seems bright.

The roses round the door
Make me love mother more.
I'll see my sweetheart Flo,
And friends I used to know.
They'll be right there to meet me,
Just imagine how they'll greet me,
When I get back,
When I get back,
To my home in Tennessee.

MAJOR ERIC FISHER WOOD

The Unknown Hero

Eric Fisher Wood was an American major who served in the British Army. This touching story is taken from his *The Notebook of an Intelligence Officer*:

March 17, 1917. On return from Bapaume, we pass through the little hamlet of Tilloy. It has been entirely wrecked by the artillery fire of the Germans, who are still shelling it in a desultory way – a big shell falling here and there every minute or two.

In all the village neither wall, nor fence, nor tree still stands. Its site is to-day merely a stretch of muddy ground, strewn with bits of brick and splinters of wood. As one skirts the crater-lips and clambers over debris, in what was once its main street, one can look straight out in all directions across an open country.

I come upon a spot where, not more than a quarter of an hour before, a shell, passing by the charmed cradle, had burst upon the road to kill a British soldier boy.

I pause for a moment to puzzle out the sequence of events. An infantry pack stands in the highway. Against the pack leans a rifle, whose speckless, shining barrel bears sterling testimony to the soldierly qualities of its late owner. Upon the hard and pitted surface of the highway, beside the pack and rifle, lies a great pool of lifeblood, still fresh and bright scarlet in colour.

Across the gutter, at a distance of four or five paces from where I stand, is a shallow new-made grave. The lumps of fresh earth upon its surface have not yet commenced to dry and crumble into grains, while on it the plain print of a hand the mark of a final spade-pat still show distinct and unobliterated. The shallow upstanding mound even seems to silhouette the body beneath. A broken fragment of a board, blown from the mantelpiece of a once peaceful home-hearth, has been hurriedly whittled into some semblance of a rude headboard; rough characters are printed upon it in pencil. I cross the ditch and stoop to read:

Here lies an
UNKNOWN HERO
Of The
Australian Corps

One can visualize the puzzled face of the rough soldier-sexton as he wrote 'here lies' and then paused for one perplexed moment in unprofane profanity – to seek for some proof of identity which had so evidently been lacking – before adding the epitaph 'An Unknown Hero.'

As I start on my way again, I ponder upon the strange paradoxes and curious combinations which this great war has brought about. Here am I, from one far-off country, rendering silent homage to the unknown dead young soldier, who had come from a land still farther away. I feel an earnest gratitude to the other passing soldier who, not satisfied to cover the shattered body with a blanket of mother-earth, had in rude epitaph recorded his own tribute to one, who had just rendered up his life for our common cause.

The three of us had never stood face to face, nor heard the

voice, nor known the name one of the other, yet were comrades, one in sympathy and one in aim.

The dead boy is a type of the ten million soldiers of
Democracy who have so completely consecrated themselves
to the great cause that, in order best to serve that cause,
they gladly sacrifice, for the time being, the very personal liberty for which they are fighting. They cheerfully submerge
their ego, in order that the German system of the permanent
subordination of the individual may not be forcibly
extended over all nations, and that the Liberty won through
long ages of struggle against Tyranny might not altogether
perish from the earth.

The Unknown Hero, resting beside the uptorn road of
the shattered village, had voyaged ten thousand miles from
his homeland to do his bit in this present struggle, to safe-
guard the democratic ideals of his own race against the
democracy-destroying and liberty-suppressing system of that
other race, now known as the enemy. With ten million
others, moved by similar ideals, he had been content to
become so completely a mere anonymous cog in the great
military machine, that when a chance shell finally struck
him down, he was so hurriedly buried by a fellow cog that
his body was laid at rest, his blanket of earth thrown over
him, and his nameless epitaph inscribed before his life-blood
had time to congeal upon the frozen winter road of that
obscure French village.

RICHARD ALDINGTON

'Soliloquy'

Although he is best known now for his novel *Death of a Hero* (an
extract from which is on pages 67–8), Richard Aldington was also
a poet who mixed with Ford Madox Ford, T. S. Eliot, Ezra Pound
and W. B. Yeats. Aldington joined the Army in 1917 and went to
France in 1917.

SOLILOQUY I

No, I'm not afraid of death
(Not very much afraid, that is)
Either for others or myself;
Can watch them coming from the line
On the wheeled silent stretchers
And not shrink,
But munch my sandwich stoically
And make a joke when 'it' has passed.

But – the way they wobble! –
God! that makes one sick.
Dead men should be so still, austere,
And beautiful,
Not wobbling carrion roped upon a cart . . .

Well, thank God for rum.

SOLILOQUY II

I was wrong, quite wrong;
The dead men are not always carrion.
After the advance,
As we went through the shattered trenches
Which the enemy had left,
We found, lying upon the fire-step,
A dead English soldier,
His head bloodily bandaged
And his closed left hand touching the earth,

More beautiful than one can tell,
More subtly coloured than a perfect Goya,
And more austere and lovely in repose
Than Angelo's hand could ever carve in stone.

JOHN MASEFIELD

'Dirty wanton devilry'

John Masefield (1878–1967), who was to become Poet Laureate in 1930, wrote this letter to his wife after the Germans retired 20–30 miles to the Hindenburg Line, leaving the Allies the shelled area of the Somme battlefield and laying waste the country they left behind.

21 March: You would have thought that the enemy would have learned a little, and been perhaps humble, and eager to win the sympathy of neutrals now, as a brave people about to endure disaster; but all through this retreat he has been repeating Belgium. He has systematically destroyed what he could not carry away. Everything easily moveable has been pillaged and sent back to their dirty nest the Vaterland, and everything not easily moveable has been fouled and broken. Bureaus, mirrors, tables, sofas, have been smashed with axes, fruit trees have been cut, lopped or ringed. Beds have been used as latrines, so have baths and basins, and the officers who used them thus have left their cards on the mess. Houses, churches, cottages, farms, barns and calvaries have been burnt, blown up, pulled down or gutted. Every dirty wanton devilry of rape, defilement and degradation has been committed on the inhabitants. In Péronne, the books of the library were taken down, defiled with human excrement, and then put back upon the shelves. In the same town a poor cat was found crucified by these devils, and they had put a cap on its head and a cigar in its mouth. I can understand mental degenerates doing these things, but not men. They are not the acts of men. They are not the acts of beasts. They are not civilised human beings. They will bloodily suffer for what they have done during this retreat.

ROBERT FITZGERALD

'Trenches were wiped out of existence'

Robert Fitzgerald was at Gresham's School at Holt in Norfolk when war broke out. He sent this account of the successful attacks on Vimy Ridge to the *Gresham*, the school magazine:

> The preliminary bombardment started four days before the actual show, a steady shelling all day and night. We did not hear much of this as we were billeted in some gigantic caves capable of holding 6000 men. Well, we were in the caves until 9 o'clock on Sunday night. That night we all moved up to the assembly trenches, and there we had a cold and dreary vigil until half-past five on Monday morning, the 9th. We only suffered one casualty in these 'jumping off' trenches, in spite of short bursts of shelling from his 'whizzbang' batteries.
>
> At three o'clock it began to rain pretty heavily, which made things most unpleasant; at five o'clock we all partook of our last meal before going over, and my Company Commander and myself consumed two hard-boiled eggs in stony silence. At 5.30 a.m. the Canadians went over the top in front of Vimy Ridge, preceded by an intense barrage from our Field Guns and also a liquid fire attack, the most wonderful sight you can possibly imagine.
>
> From where we were in our trenches we could see the Vimy Ridge quite plainly, and, on the stroke of 5.30, two mines went up, which was the signal for our guns to open fire and at the same time let off liquid fire. The Bosche at once sent up every conceivable coloured rocket and alarm signals, green stars, red rockets, lovely golden rain star shells, in fact an exact imitation of a Brock's firework display. This attack took place two hours before ours, which started at 7.34 a.m. The idea was to make him think that

our attack was only going to be a faint one, and not on a big scale, and also to deceive him into thinking that our attack would not come off the same day as the Vimy Ridge show.

At 7.34 a.m. we went over behind our barrage followed by four tanks. For the first two hundred yards the going was uphill and by the time we reached the summit of the Ridge there was not an ounce of wind left in any of the men to do the remaining three hundred yards, and we were also rather disorganised. On coming in sight of the Bosche we were met by machine gun fire and a certain amount of rifle fire, but not much shelling. At one moment things looked rather black, as we came up to our barrage too soon and were compelled to halt for a couple of minutes, during which time we took cover as best we could in shell holes, from which we had a good deal of trouble in getting the men out as soon as the barrage lifted, but we managed to reach our objective, where the Bosche was very ready to give himself up.

The trenches were wiped out of existence, and not a trace of wire, which bears testimony to the marvellous shooting of the Artillery. They came streaming out of their dug-outs by the hundreds, miserable wretches, having been down there without food for the previous two days; in fact an officer came out of a dug-out after we had been there for a couple of hours, calmly smoking a cigar, and was very much astonished to find British Tommies in possession of his sector of the trench. This same officer, seeing an officer in our Company walking towards him, shot him point blank, killing him instantly, and then had the cheek to hold up his hands in surrender. He did not hold them up for long though, being shot dead by the officer's servant. I have related this small incident just to show the true character of the Bosche officers. They are simply out to kill, and when they have done that, they are satisfied.

PAUL MAZE

Hospital Ward

The artist Paul Maze (1887–1979), who was of Anglo-French parentage, served with both the French and British armies during the war. His book *A Frenchman in Khaki* describes his experiences. He taught Winston Churchill drawing and painting and the two men became firm friends.

The sun is out and there is an increasing glow inside the ward as the tent turns yellow and dries. But the dampness of the heat turns it into a hothouse. This change has brought a sensation of new life even into this ward where death is lurking round so many beds. All the men in the ward with the exception of myself are bad cases. They have been here some days and I have watched them with the eye of a man who observes but cannot feel – I can feel no more . . . there is now a routine as each case in the ward is dealt with. I see how nervous they become, those whom the nurses must prepare for the surgeon's visit. They have a horror of the pain which daily they have to endure as a long, sharp needle is inserted in their back and the fluid inside their lungs has to be drawn out by an instrument like a bicycle pump. They sit up one after another for their turn, supported by a nurse, and give that hopeless howl of a weak man who can resist no more. Some have to be anaesthetized to have their wounds dressed . . . there is a man with gangrene who has to be carried out every second day to have a bit more of his leg off. One boy has both his legs cut off and the nurses watch over him constantly – he smells terribly of decomposition, poor fellow, and infects the ward. I notice the nurse put a screen round his bed and attend him as if she were making him comfortable. I have not understood that he has died until I see a stretcher slip out of the side door, a blanket covering his pitiably short body . . . there comes a diversion. One young fellow, a very bad case, shouts, 'Nursie darling, don't leave me.' Throughout his delirium he makes love to her. She responds sweetly. He is so lively that I cannot believe that death is near him but he is shot in the head and there is no hope, so the nurse tells me. She has to leave him for a minute, an orderly watching him from the door. Several times he has attempted to get up. This time the orderly is too far off to catch him before he has nipped out of bed and slipped through an open flap of the tent where for a few seconds he sprawls and shouts, making diabolical gesticulations among the ropes and pegs. Like a truant child, he is carried gently back and with one last shout that rings in my ears for days afterwards, he dies. Every day there seems to be a critical period for bad cases to survive. Just as shipwrecked people clinging to the raft let go one after another, so sometimes a wounded man will die although his condition shows an improvement as if he were too tired to make the slight greater voluntary effort required. A charming fellow in the bed next to mine seemed so much better. As he woke from his sleep so the doctor on duty, the Harrow school doctor, was waiting by his bed with a letter for him. 'Would you like me to read it to you?' I remember how gentle the voice sounded which read aloud to the young man the words of his mother who, with little bits of home news, tried to hide her anxiety. I saw the letter lying between two white hands as the doctor walked away to the other side of the ward – then suddenly two arms went up despairingly like a drowning man unable to shout for help. He never uttered a sound. His white face moved once or twice on the pillow and within a few minutes he was dressed for the last time and carried out.

'We Don't Want to Lose You'

(Words and music by Paul A. Rubens)

We've watched you playing cricket
And every kind of game

At football golf and polo,
You men have made your name,
But now your country calls you
To play your part in war,
And no matter what befalls you
We shall love you all the more,
So, come and join the forces
As your fathers did before.

Chorus:
Oh! We don't want to lose you
But we think you ought to go
For your King and Country
Both need you so;
We shall want you and miss you
But with all our might and main
We shall cheer you, thank you, kiss you
When you come back again.

We want you from all quarters
So, help us South and North
We want you in your thousands,
From Falmouth to the Forth,
You'll never find us fail you
When you are in distress,
So, answer when we hail you,
And let your word be 'Yes'
And so your name, in years to come
Each mother's son shall bless.

Chorus:
Oh! We don't want to lose you (etc.)

PAUL NASH

'A bitter truth'

Paul Nash (1889–1946), who was educated in London at St Paul's School and the Slade School of Art, enlisted in the Artists' Rifles in 1914 and served on the Western Front. He became one of the finest painters of the war. No one in England knew what the scene of the war was like, he wrote. They could not imagine the daily and nightly background of the fighters. 'If I can, I will show them.' He wrote this letter in April:

> I have just returned, last night, from a visit to Brigade Headquarters up the line, and I shall not forget it as long as I live. I have seen the most frightful nightmare of a country more conceived by Dante or Poe than by nature, unspeakable, utterly indescribable. In the fifteen drawings I have made I may give you some vague idea of its horror, but only being in it and of it can ever make you sensible of its dreadful nature and of what our men in France have to face. We all have a vague notion of the terrors of a battle, and can conjure up with the aid of some of the more inspired war correspondents and the pictures in the *Daily Mirror* some vision of a battle-field; but no pen or drawing can convey this country – the normal setting of the battles taking place day and night, month after month. Evil and the incarnate fiend alone can be master of this war and no glimmer of God's Lord is seen anywhere. Sunset and sunrise are blasphemous, they are mockeries to man, only the black rain out of the bruised and swollen clouds all through the bitter black of night is fit atmosphere in such a land. The rain drives on, the stinking mud becomes more evilly yellow, the shell holes fill up with green-white water, the roads and tracks are covered in inches of slime, the black dying trees ooze and sweat and the shells never cease. They alone plunge overhead, tearing away the

rotting tree stumps, breaking the plank roads, striking down horses and mules, annihilating, maiming, maddening, they plunge into the grave which is this land; one huge grave, and cast up on it the poor dead. It is unspeakable, godless, hopeless. I am no longer an artist interested and curious, I am a messenger who will bring back word from the men who are fighting to those who want the war to go on for ever. Feeble, inarticulate, will be my message, but it will have a bitter truth, and may it burn their lousy souls.

CECIL LEWIS

Tumult in the Skies

Another account – on the occasion of a night patrol – from Cecil Lewis's *Sagittarius Rising*. Lewis survived the war and was variously a Hollywood writer who won a joint Oscar in 1938 for his work on *Pygmalion* and co-founder of the BBC.

The squadron sets out eleven strong on the evening patrol. Eleven chocolate-coloured, lean noisy bullets, lifting, swaying, turning, rising into formation – two fours and a three – circling and climbing away steadily towards the lines. They are off to deal with Richthofen and his circus of Red Albatrosses.

The May evening is heavy with threatening masses of cumulus cloud, majestic skyscapes, solid-looking as snow mountains, fraught with caves and valleys, rifts and ravines – strange and secret pathways in the chartless continents of the sky. Below, the land becomes an ordnance map, dim green and yellow, and across it go the Lines, drawn anyhow, as a child might scrawl with a double pencil. The grim dividing Lines! From the air robbed of all significance.

Steadily the body of scouts rises higher and higher, threading its way between the cloud precipices. Sometimes, below, the streets of a village, the corner of a wood, a few dark figures moving, glides into view like a slide into a lantern and then is hidden again.

But the fighting pilot's eyes are not on the ground, but roving endlessly through the lower and higher reaches of the sky, peering anxiously through fur-goggles to spot those black slow-moving specks against land or cloud which mean full throttle, tense muscles, held breath, and the headlong plunge with screaming wires – a Hun in the sights, and the tracers flashing.

A red light curls up from the leader's cockpit and falls away. Action! He alters direction slightly, and the patrol, shifting throttles and rudder, keep close like a pack of hounds on the scent. He has seen, and they see soon, six scouts three thousand feet below. Black crosses! It seems interminable till the eleven come within diving distance. The pilots nurse their engines, hard-mined and set, test their guns and watch their indicators. At last the leader sways side-ways, as a signal that each should take his man, and suddenly drops.

Machines fall scattering, the earth races up, the enemy patrol, startled, wheels and breaks. Each his man! The chocolate thunderbolts take sights, steady their screaming planes, and fire. A burst, fifty rounds – it is over. They have overshot, and the enemy, hit or missed, is lost for the moment. The pilot steadies his stampeding mount, pulls her out with a firm hand, twisting his head right and left, trying to follow his man, to sight another, to back up a friend in danger, to note another in flames.

But the squadron plunging into action had not seen, far off, approaching from the east, the rescue flight of Red Albatrosses patrolling above the body of machines on which they had dived, to guard their tails and second them in the battle. These, seeing the maze of wheeling machines, plunge down to join them. The British scouts, engaging and disen-gaging like flies circling at midday in a summer room, soon find the newcomers upon them. Then, as if attracted by some mysterious power as vultures will draw to a corpse in the desert, other bodies of machines swoop down from the peaks of the cloud mountains. More enemy scouts, and, by good fortune, a flight of Naval Triplanes.

But, nevertheless, the enemy, double in number, greater in power and fighting with skill and courage, gradually overpower the British, whose machines scatter, driven down beneath the scarlet German fighters.

It would be impossible to describe the action of such a battle. A pilot, in the second between his own engagements, might see a Hun diving vertically, a British SE5 on his tail, on the tail of the SE another Hun, and above him again another British scout. These four, plunging headlong at two hundred miles an hour, guns crackling, tracers screaming, suddenly break up. The lowest Hun plunges flaming to his death, if death has not taken him already. His victor seems to stagger, suddenly pulls out in a great leap, as a trout leaps on the end of a line, and then, turning over on his belly, swoops and spins in a dizzy falling spiral with the earth to end it. The third German zooms veering, and the last of that meteoric quartet follows bursting . . . But such a glimpse, lasting perhaps ten seconds, is broken by the sharp rattle of another attack. Two machines approach head-on at breakneck speed, firing at each other, tracers whistling through each other's planes, each slipping sideways on his rudder to trick the other's gun fire. Who will hold longest? Two hundred yards, a hundred, fifty, and then, neither hit, with one accord they fling their machines sideways, bank and circle, each striving to bring his gun on to the other's tail, each glaring through goggle eyes calculating, straining, wheeling, grim, bent only on death or dying.

But, from above, this strange tormented circling is seen by another Hun. He drops. His gun speaks. The British machine, distracted by the sudden unseen enemy, pulls up, takes a burst through the engine, tank and body, and falls bottom uppermost down through the clouds and the deep unending desolation of the twilight sky.

The game of noughts and crosses, starting at fifteen thousand feet above the clouds, drops in altitude engagement by engagement. Friends and foes are scattered. A last SE, pressed by two Huns, plunges and wheels, gun-jammed, like a snipe over marshes, darts lower, finds refuge in the ground mist, and disappears.

Now lowering clouds darken the evening. Below flashes of gun fire stab the veil of the gathering dusk. The fight is over! The battlefield shows no sign. In the pellucid sky, serene cloud mountains mass and move unceasingly. Here where guns rattled and death plucked the spirits of the valiant, this thing is now as if it had never been! The sky is busy with night, passive, superb, unheeding.

Of the eleven scouts that went out that evening, the 7th of May, only five of us returned to the aerodrome.

WOODROW WILSON

'The world must be made safe for democracy'

When the First World War broke out US President Woodrow Wilson issued a proclamation of neutrality. But neutrality was impossible for a nation so powerful, especially after the sinking of the *Lusitania*. One month after his second inaugural address, Wilson went before a joint session of Congress on 2 April to ask for a declaration that a state of war existed between Germany and the United States – and got what he wanted by a nearly unanimous vote on 6 April, Good Friday:

We are accepting this challenge of hostile purpose because we know that in such a government, following such methods, we can never have a friend; and that in the presence of its organized power, always lying in wait to accomplish we know not what purpose, there can be no assured security for the democratic governments of the world. We are now about to accept the gage of battle with this natural foe to liberty and shall, if necessary, spend the whole force of the nation to check and nullify its pretensions and its power. We are glad, now that we see the facts with no veil of false pretence about them, to fight thus for the ultimate peace of the world and for the liberation of its peoples, the German peoples included: for the rights of nations great and small and the privilege of men everywhere to choose their way of life and of obedience. The world must be made safe for democracy. Its peace must be planted upon the tested foundations of political liberty. We have no selfish ends to serve. We desire no conquest, no dominion. We seek no indemnities for ourselves, no material compensation for the sacrifices we shall freely make. We are but one of the champions of the rights of mankind. We shall be satisfied when those rights have been made as secure as the faith and the freedom of nations can make them.

Just because we fight without rancor and without selfish object, seeking nothing for ourselves but what we shall wish to share with all free peoples, we shall, I feel confident, conduct our operation as belligerents without passion and ourselves observe with proud punctilio the principles of right and of fair play we profess to be fighting for . . .

It will be all the easier for us to conduct ourselves as belligerents in a high spirit of right and fairness because we act without animus not in enmity toward a people or with the desire to bring any injury or disadvantage upon them, but only in armed opposition to an irresponsible government which has thrown aside all consideration of humanity and of right and is running amuck. We are, let me say again, the sincere friends of the German people, and shall desire nothing so much as the early re-establishment of intimate relations of mutual advantage between us – however hard it may be for them, for the time being, to believe that this is spoken from our hearts. We have borne with their present government through all these bitter months because of that friendship – exercising a patience and forbearance which would otherwise have been impossible. We shall, happily, still have an opportunity to prove that friendship in our daily attitude and actions toward the millions of men and women of German birth and native sympathy who live amongst us and share our life, and we shall be proud to prove it toward all who are in fact loyal to their neighbors and to the government in the hour of test. They are, most of them, as true and loyal Americans as if they had never known any other fealty or allegiance. They will be prompt to stand with us in rebuking and restraining the few who may be of a different mind and purpose. If there should be disloyalty, it will be dealt with a firm hand of stern repression; but, if it lifts its head at all, it will lift it only here and there and without countenance except from a lawless and malignant few.

It is a distressing and oppressive duty, gentlemen of the Congress, which I have performed in thus addressing you. There are, it may be, many months of fiery trial and sacrifice ahead of us. It is a fearful thing to lead this great peaceful people into war, into the most terrible and disastrous of all wars, civilization itself seeming to be in the balance. But the right is more precious than peace, and we shall fight for the things which we have always carried nearest our hearts – for democracy, for the right of those who submit to authority to have a voice in their own governments, for the dominion of right by such a concert of free peoples as shall bring peace and safety to all nations and make the world itself at last free. To such a task we can dedicate our lives and our fortunes, everything that we are and everything that we have, with the pride of those who know that the day has come when America is privileged to spend her blood and her might for the principles that gave her birth and happiness and the peace which she has treasured. God helping her, she can do no other.

Major Johnathan Bates

'Out for a picnic'

Ten months after we met him on the Somme, Major Bates is in action, as he reports in another letter to his girlfriend, Alice:

Monday, 9th April 1917
6.30 p.m.
My Darling old Girl
The most wonderful day – marvellous and I scarcely know how to start.

We did a very big attack this morning as you will have seen from the papers, and it was a tremendous success. Of course, we have been preparing this for a long time but I didn't say anything in case you should worry. Well, here's your old Johnathan sitting in a dugout that the Boche occupied this morning – got through without a scratch and thank God for it. The noise of our guns and the general row was absolute Hell, but thank heavens, I've got used to it by now and it hasn't upset me one little bit. I'm absolutely as right as rain. I should like to tell you all about it and I'll try to do so briefly.

At 5.30 a.m. this morning our guns opened a terrific bombardment and our fellows walked over the Boche lines. Well, in short, in 2 hours we had reached our objective (over a mile from the start) and had killed or captured every Boche in the way. We reckon that our battalion took 150 prisoners alone. They were simply streaming back and put up *no* fight whatever. 'Kamerad, kamerad,' every time.

Well, I followed the battalion over and after going about half a mile managed to find the Boche dressing station – a fine big dugout. The two Boche doctors had just been taken prisoner and I found 7 Boche wounded inside in the pitch dark! I said 'Est-ce que quelqu'un qui parle français?' and one man said 'Oui'. So I said in a ferocious voice 'Donnez-moi des bougies' whereupon every man produced a few candles. So we soon got a light. The place was in a fearful mess but all the Boches had been dressed by their own doctor. So we set to work, cleaned it out and shifted all the Boches up to our end to make room for our boys. Then I left this place in charge of my corporal and set out with my servant to go up to our objective, a railway cutting. The Boche was shelling with gas shells which was annoying as we had to wear our gas helmets for ½ hour. Well, we reached the railway cutting successfully and found not a single wounded man on the way up there nor in the cutting itself. Our boys were lighting fires and making their breakfast there and smoking Boche cigars as if they were out for a picnic! The weather was glorious.

The large number of prisoners made the evacuation of wounded easy. I had every prisoner taken by the battalion sent to my dressing station and put them on to a stretcher to carry it down. I really think I have dressed more Boches today than our own boys.

We had 4 tanks. One stuck but the other 3 were a grand success. I walked up behind one of them for a long way.

The whole thing was an absolute picnic. Another division has gone right through us and is now chasing the Boche. We have advanced about 3 miles today here and our guns are already blazing away from ground captured this morning. Wonderful.

I suppose we will have a rest and refit and then join in the chase again. Mind you, the Boche had been in this position for about 2 years and it was a veritable fortress we have captured. And our losses are very light indeed. The Colonel is delighted as in fact are all of us.

That, in a few words, is what has happened today and it is delightful to write it all down.

I hope you get this in good time, Girlie, as you will see in the papers all about it. Well, if all the strafes were as successful as this, I wouldn't mind one once a month!

PRIVATE E. N. GLADDEN

'Pillars of fire'

The Battle of Messines, where a ridge 150 feet high ran to the south of the Ypres Salient, won the Salient for the British. Nineteen deep mines packed with a million pounds of explosive had been laid by 6 June. At 3.10 a.m. on 7 June they were all set off simultaneously. Private E. N. Gladden, a Northumberland Fusilier, describes the explosion:

June 7: The trench was newly dug somewhere on the hill and nowhere more than 4.5 feet deep. We looked like getting a thrashing when the show commenced.

The attack was to be preceded by the explosion of the mine. There in the bowels of the earth after many months of preparation, tunnelling, and counter-tunnelling by the enemy, an unprecedented amount of explosive had been buried and the effects of the detonation of such an immense charge were uncertain.

We might all be involved. In any case our trenches might close in, and to evade that possibility, we were ordered to lay out on top for the event.

The night was clear; the guns were silent. Ever and anon an enemy Very light went up from his line and spread a lurid glare over the scene. Those hours of waiting were hardly bearable. At last the first streaks of dawn showed in the sky, and whispered orders sent us to our positions a few yards in front of the trench.

The last few minutes dragged with relentless slowness; each second seemed an hour, each minute an eternity. The greyness of a new day now suffused the sky. I felt a tremor of fear run through my body; the silence of the grave seemed to enfold the whole world.

With a sharp report an enemy rocket began to mount

towards the heavens. A voice behind cried 'Now!' It was the hour, and that last enemy light never burst upon the day. The ground began to rock and I felt my body carried up and down as by the waves of the sea.

In front the earth opened and a large black mass was carried to the sky on pillars of fire, and there seemed to remain suspended for some seconds while the awful red glare lit up the surrounding desolation. No sound came. I had been expecting a noise from the mine so tremendous as to be unbearable.

For a brief space all was silent, as though we had been too close to hear and the sound had leapt over us like some immense wave. A line of men rose from the ground a few yards in front and advanced towards the upheaval, their helmets silhouetted and bayonets glinting in the redness of that unearthly dawn. I saw no more.

We hurled ourselves back to the trench. And then there was a tremendous roar and a tearing across the skies above us, as the barrage commenced with unerring accuracy.

It was as though a door had been suddenly flung open. The skies behind our lines were lit by the flashes of many thousand guns, and above the booming din of the artillery came the rasping rattle of the Vickers guns pouring a continuous stream of lead over into the enemy's lines.

Never before, surely, had there been such a bombardment, and I shuddered for those unfortunates caught in that storm of death. Yet the German gunners were not slow to answer their S.O.S. call, for before I had crossed the few yards back to the trench their shells were already bursting around. I saw the trench before me and in my excitement I slipped upon the edge and fell head foremost amidst a rain of loose earth.

My helmet slipped off and I was just able to drag out my Lewis gun buckets before a stream of humanity striving to reach the deeper parts of the trench carried me before it.

I had lost my steel helmet and could think of little else during the whole bombardment. The shells lashed the ground with fury. Each piece of flying shrapnel seemed to be searching for my unprotected head and as I pushed it into the parapet the loose grains of earth matted my hair and trickled into the collar of my tunic. The rest of the section crouched near.

Our corporal, regular soldier and veteran of the First Battle of Ypres, sat crouched in the corner, his knees almost to his chin, and, except for an occasional blasphemy or laconic 'The next one'll get us', he remained motionless. My pal leaned against the parapet, his eyes closed as though death had already come to him, and a little further along another youngster cried audibly.

From right and left came cries of pain and the stretcher bearers, risking all in their devotion, pushed backwards and forwards to dress the wounded.

Our casualties were heavy, but fortunately the enemy batteries were disorganized and the shooting somewhat haphazard, otherwise few of us would have escaped that morning. News came back of the success of the first advance with comparatively light casualties, and, after a lull, our guns increased again to tremendous fury while the attack was further developed.

FRANK RICHARDS

Siegfried Sassoon

Frank Richards describes a bombing attack led with conspicuous bravery by 2nd Lieutenant Siegfried Sassoon, known to his men as 'Mad Jack':

During the operations Mr Sassoon was shot through the top of the shoulder. Late in the day I was conversing with an old soldier and one of the few survivors of old B Company who had taken part in the bombing raid. He said, 'God strike me pink, Dick, it would have done your eyes good to have seen young Sassoon in that bombing stunt. It was a bloody treat to see the way he took the lead. He was the best officer I have seen in the line or out since Mr Fletcher, and it's wicked how the good officers get killed or wounded and the rotten ones are still left crawling about. If he don't get the Victoria Cross for this stunt I'm a bloody Dutchman; he thoroughly earned it this morning.' This was the universal opinion of everyone who had taken part in the stunt, but the only decoration Mr Sassoon received was a decorated shoulder where the bullet went through. He hadn't been long with the Battalion, but long enough to win the respect of every man that knew him.

SIEGFRIED SASSOON

'A soldier's declaration'

Siegfried Sassoon made the most famous protest of the First World War when he signed his soldier's declaration which Bertrand Russell and John Middleton Murry, the writer and critic, had helped him to draft. The second and fourth paragraphs most clearly represent Sassoon's own view.

July 6: I am making this statement as an act of willful defiance of military authority, because I believe the war is being deliberately prolonged by those who have the power to end it.

I am a soldier, convinced that I am acting on behalf of soldiers. I believe that this war, upon which I entered as a war of defence and liberation, has now become a war of aggression and conquest. I believe that the purposes for which I and my fellow soldiers entered upon this war should have been so clearly stated as to have made it impossible to change them, and that, had this been done, the objects which actuated us would now be attainable by negotiation.

I have seen and endured the suffering of the troops, and I can no longer be a party to prolong these sufferings for ends which I believe to be evil and unjust.

I am not protesting against the conduct of the war, but against the political errors and insincerities for which the fighting men are being sacrificed.

On behalf of those who are suffering now I make this protest against the deception which is being practiced on them; also I believe that I may help to destroy the callous complacence with which the majority of those at home regard the continuance of agonies which they do not share, and which they have not sufficient imagination to realize.

SIEGFRIED SASSOON

'Base Details'

Sassoon's poem was written in March before his declaration but indicates the anger within him that helped to provoke it:

> If I were fierce, and bald, and short of breath,
> I'd live with scarlet Majors at the Base,
> And speed glum heroes up the line to death.
> You'd see me with my puffy petulant face,
> Guzzling and gulping in the best hotel,
> Reading the Roll of Honour. 'Poor young chap,'
> I'd say – 'I used to know his father well;
> Yes, we've lost heavily in this last scrap.'
> And when the war is done and youth stone dead,
> I'd toddle safely home and die – in bed.

LIEUTENANT HARRY SACKVILLE LAWSON

Playing the Game

Harry Sackville Lawson, educated at Haileybury and Peterhouse, Cambridge, was headmaster of Buxton College in Derbyshire. But in July 1917 he was with the Royal Field Artillery in a dugout in France, writing to the sound of guns a message to his 'dear boys' at the school as he handed over the headmastership to his successor. This letter about 'playing the game' speaks for the English upper class of its era. Lawson was killed in action, aged forty-one, in February 1918.

My Dear Boys

I've got one thing in particular to say to you all – just the main thing we've talked about together in its different bearings in the past – just the one important thing which keeps life sweet and clean and gives us peace of mind. It's a Christian teaching, and it's a British thing. It's what the Bible teaches – it's what the Christian martyrs suffered in persecution for. It soon found root in England and began not only to fill the land, but also to spread abroad and become the heritage of the Empire. It's the story of the crusaders, of the Reformation, of the downfall of the power of Spain, of our colonisation, of the destruction of Napoleon's might, of the abolition of slavery, and of the coming awakening of Germany. The thing is: Playing the game for the game's sake.

Now I've had many opportunities in years gone by of having a talk with you about this, and I've always found that we've got a clear starting-off point. For whether I have been talking to a boy alone, or to a class in its class-room, or to the school met together in the New Hall, I have found opinion quite clear and quite decided as to what the game is and what the game is not. We've had a sure foundation. And the difficulty for us all consists, not in knowing what the game is, but in trying to live up to the standard of life which our knowledge of the game puts before us. Don't think that I am referring to the breaking of school rules. I am not. School rules don't live for ever, and, further, school rules suffer change. I am referring to deeper things than these, to rules which do live for ever and which do not suffer change. I am thinking of high honesty of purpose and of the word duty.

I am going to tell you a story of something that happened at the College in days, I think, not within the memory of any of you. I pick this story because it illustrates well what I have said about school rule and deeper rule.

On a certain whole school day afternoon in the Lent Term some years ago, the Vth Form made a raid upon the IVth Form. The IVth Form barricaded themselves very securely in their own class-room by piling up desks and furniture against both doors. The raid was still in progress when I came along at half-past three to take the IVth in English. I passed through the IIIrd, where there were evident symptoms of excitement, and came to the door of the IVth. The door wouldn't open. But my voice acting as a kind of 'Sesame', the barricade was quickly removed and I entered. The class-room was pandemonium, desks littering the place in wild confusion, and in particular concentrated against the door opposite to that through which I had entered. I held a court of enquiry – pronounced judgment – went to the study for my cane and dealt with the IVth Form ringleaders on the spot. This, mind you, for a breach of school rule. Desks are not designed to be used for splinter-proof dug-outs. Now the enquiry showed clearly that though the IVth were guilty, they were not nearly so guilty as the Vth. So peace once more reigning in the IVth, I went along to the

New Hall to have a talk with the Vth. I told them what had happened – what punishment had been meted out to the IVth, and I said, 'You've got the IVth into a row and you are the guiltier party of the two. I have caned the principal culprits in the IVth, and I shall be in the study at five o'clock and shall be glad to cane there those of you who feel you ought to turn up.'

At five o'clock seven of them arrived and received their caning. Before they left I said to them, 'I am very proud of you chaps, and I've got to thank you for the first caning I've ever enjoyed giving.'

They felt they ought to turn up. They did turn up. I need say no more . . .

H. S. Lawson,
2nd Lieutenant, R.F.A., and
Headmaster of Buxton College.

JULIAN BICKERSTETH

'Safe in the arms of Jesus'

Canon Samuel Bickersteth of Leeds had six sons, four of whom served on the Western Front. Julian, the third brother, was chaplain of Melbourne Grammar School when war broke out and returned from Australia to England to become an army chaplain. In this letter home he describes assisting a soldier condemned to death and with only twelve hours left to live:

> There were not a few who said he was mad, or at least that there was something wrong with his brain, but our doctor had been unable to certify that he was in any way not responsible for his actions, and certainly he was quite intelligent in a good many ways. He could read and write well.
>
> He sat down heavily on a chair. The room was furnished with a small round table, three chairs, and a wire bed raised

six inches from the ground. I took a chair and sat next to him. 'I am going to stay with you and do anything I can for you. If you'd like to talk, we will, but if you would rather not, we'll sit quiet.' Two fully-armed sentries with fixed bayonets stand one by the door and the other by the window. The room is only nine feet by ten feet. Anything in the nature of a private talk seems likely to be difficult. An appeal that the sentries might be removed is not accepted. There are no bars to the window and the prisoner might seek to make an end of himself. So I sit on silently. Suddenly I hear great heaving sobs, and the prisoner breaks down and cries. In a second I lean over close to him, as he hides his face in his hands, and in a low voice I talk to him. He seems still a little doubtful about his fate, and I have to explain to him what is going to happen tomorrow morning. I tell him about Morris and of how many splendid men have 'passed on'; what fine company he will find on the other side.

After a time he quietens down and his tea comes up – two large pieces of bread and butter, a mess tin half-full of tea and some jam in a tin. One of the sentries lends me his clasp knife so that I may put jam on his bread, for the prisoner of course is not allowed to handle a knife. After his tea is over, I hand him a pipe and tobacco. These comforts, strictly forbidden to all prisoners, are not withheld now. He loved a pipe – and soon he is contentedly puffing away.

Time goes on. I know that he must sleep, if possible, during the hours of darkness, so my time is short. How can I reach his soul? I get out my Bible and read to him something from the Gospel. It leaves him unmoved. He is obviously uninterested and my attempt to talk a little about what I have read leaves him cold. Where is my point of contact? I make him move his chair as far away from the sentry as possible, and speaking in a very low voice close to him, I am not overheard; but of what to speak? There is no point of contact through his home, which means nothing to him.

I get out an Army Prayer Book, which contains at the end about 130 hymns, and handing him the book, ask him to read through the part at the end so that I can find a hymn he knows, I can read it to him. He hits 'Rock of Ages' and asks, not if I will read to him, but if we can sing it. The idea of our solemnly singing hymns together while the two sentries eye us coldly from the other side of the room seems to me so incongruous that I put him off with the promise of a hymn to be sung before he goes to sleep, but he is not satisfied and he returns to the suggestion again. This time I had enough sense, thank goodness, to seize on 'the straw'; and we sat there and sang hymns together – for three hours or more.

The curious thing about this extraordinary man is that he takes command of the proceedings. He chooses the hymns. He will not sing any one over twice. He starts the hymn on the right note, he knows the tunes and pitches them all perfectly. Music has evidently not been denied him. The words mean nothing to him, or else he is so little gifted with imagination that the pathos of such lines as 'Hold Thou Thy Cross before my closing eyes' and many similar lines, which in my view of the morrow should cut deep, leave the prisoner unmoved.

Oh how we sang! – hymn after hymn. He knew more tunes than I did. After half an hour away for some dinner, I returned to the little room and in the rapidly fading light went on with the hymn-singing. I brought him a YMCA hymn book which contained several hymns not in the other. He was delighted, and we sang 'Throw out the life-line', 'What a friend we have in Jesus' and others. When 10.30 p.m. came I was anxious to see the prisoner sleeping for his own sake, though I was willing to go on singing hymns if he wanted to. His stock, however, was nearly exhausted, as he would never sing the same hymn twice over. So we agreed to close the singing, but he would sing one of the hymns he had already sung, a second time as a last effort. So he chose 'God be with us until we meet again'. He sang it utterly unmoved. While I was ruminating over how to make use of the hymns for getting a little further in he said, 'We haven't finished yet; we must have God Save the King, and then and there we rose to our feet, and the two Military Police, who had replaced the ordinary guards and had been accommodated with two chairs, had to get up and stand rigidly to attention while the prisoner and I sang lustily three verses of the National Anthem. A few seconds later the prisoner was asleep.

I felt that the hymns, even if the words had not meant much to him, had been a prayer, or rather many prayers, and seeing him inclined to sleep, I did not try to get his attention to pray with him more. I have never spent a stranger evening.

I think it was a distinct effort on his part to give religion full play. To him, hymn singing meant religion. Probably no other aspect or side of religion had ever touched him, and now that he was 'up against it' he found real consolation in singing hymns learnt in childhood – he had been to Sunday school up to twelve or thirteen. Anyhow, that was the point of contact I had been seeking for.

All night I sat by his side. One sentry played Patience, the other read a book. Once or twice the prisoner woke up, but he soon slept again. At 3.00 a.m. I watched the first beginnings of dawn through the window. At 3.30 a.m. I heard the tramp, tramp of the firing party marching down the road. A few minutes later, the Sergeant-Major brought me a cup of tea and I had a whispered consultation with him as to how long I could let the prisoner sleep. A minute or two later I was called down to the APM, and he gave me some rum to give the prisoner if he wanted it. It was a dark morning, so he did not want the prisoner awakened for another ten minutes. I went up again, and at the right time awakened him. While his breakfast was being brought up, we knelt together in prayer. I commended him to God and we said together the Lord's Prayer, which he knew quite well and was proud of knowing. Then he sat down and ate a really good breakfast – bread and butter, ham and tea.

When he had finished, it was just four o'clock and I poured into his empty mug a tablespoonful of rum, but when he had tasted it, he wouldn't drink any of it. 'Is it time to go?', he said. 'Yes, it is time. I will stay close to you.' Down the narrow stairs we went, and through the silent streets of the village our weird little procession tramped. First, a burly military policeman, then the prisoner, unbound, and myself, followed close on our heels by two more policemen, the APM, the doctor and one other officer. We had about 300 yards to go to a deserted and ruined house just outside the village. I held the prisoner's arm tight for sympathy's sake. Reaching the house, the police immediately hand-cuffed the man and the doctor blindfolded him. He was breathing heavily and his heart going very quickly, but outwardly he was unmoved. I said a short prayer and led him the ten or twelve paces out into the yard, where he was at once bound to a stake. I whispered in his ear, 'Safe in the arms of Jesus', and he repeated quite clearly, 'Safe in the arms of Jesus.' The APM motioned me away. In three or four seconds the Firing Party had done their work. Poor lads – I was sorry for them. They felt it a good deal, and I followed them out of the yard at once and spoke to them and handed them cigarettes.

Another chaplain arrived (I had arranged this earlier) and he and I took the body in a motor ambulance to the nearest cemetery where I had a burial party waiting, and we gave his body Christian Burial.

I went back to the Transport Lines and tried to get some sleep.

LIEUTENANT HENRY PAUL MAINWARING JONES

War – The Big Thing

The theme of 'playing the game' is again seen in this letter to his brother from Tank Corps Subaltern Henry Jones, educated at Balliol College, Oxford, who was killed at the age of twenty-one four days later:

July 27: Have you ever reflected on the fact that, despite the horrors of the war, it is at least a big thing? I mean to say that in it one is brought face to face with realities. The follies, selfishness, luxury and general pettiness of the vile commercial sort of existence led by nine-tenths of the people of the world in peacetime are replaced in war by a savagery that is at least more honest and outspoken. Look at it this way: in peacetime one just lives one's own little life, engaged in trivialities; worrying about one's own comfort, about money matters, and all that sort of thing – just living for one's own self. What a sordid life it is! In war, on the other hand, even if you do get killed you only anticipate the inevitable by a few years in any case, and you have the satisfaction of knowing that you have 'pegged out' in the attempt to help your country. You have, in fact, realised an ideal, which, as far as I can see, you very rarely do in ordinary life. The reason is that ordinary life runs on a commercial and selfish basis; if you want to 'get on', as the saying is, you can't keep your hands clean.

Personally, I often rejoice that the War has come my way. It has made me realise what a petty thing life is. I think that the War has given to everyone a chance to 'get out of himself', as I might say. Of course, the other side of the picture is bound to occur to the imagination. But there! I have never been one to take the more melancholy point of view when there's a silver lining in the cloud.

Certainly, speaking for myself, I can say that I have never in all my life experienced such a wild exhilaration as on the commencement of a big stunt, like the last April one for example. The excitement for the last half-hour or so before it is like nothing on earth. The only thing that compares with it are the few minutes before the start of a big school match. Well, cheer-oh!

PASSCHENDAELE

The Third Battle of Ypres began on 31 July and ended in the ruins of Passchendaele in November. According to Lyn Macdonald, the defence of the Ypres Salient since 1914 had cost 430,000 British and Allied casualties, killed, wounded and missing – and probably as many Germans. Estimates of the number killed during the Battle of Passchendaele range from 36,000 to 150,000. Nobody knows the precise number.

Macdonald's books on the Great War tell the story through the words of the soldiers who fought in the trenches. One of her many books is *They Called It Passchendaele*, from which the following four vignettes are taken.

> Sergeant John Carmichael, of the 9th Battalion, North Staffordshire Regiment:
> 'We were on Hill 60, digging a communication trench, and I was detailed off with a party of men to get it done quick. I was supervising the job. We had men working in the trench and men working outside of it as well. One of the chaps was deepening the trench when his spade struck an unexploded grenade, just lodged there in the side of the trench, and it started to fizz. I was an instructor in bombing, so, knowing a bit about explosives, I knew that there would be seven seconds before it went off unless I did

something. I couldn't throw it out, because there were men working outside the trench as well as the blokes in it. So I shouted at them to get clear and I had some idea of smothering it, to get the thing covered, keep it down until they were out of range. All I had was my steel helmet. So I took if off my head, put it over the grenade as it was fizzing away, and I stood on it. It was the only way to do it. There was no thought of bravery or anything like that. I was there with the men to do the job, and that's what mattered.

'Well, it *did* go off. They tell me it blew me right out of the trench, but I don't remember that. The next thing I remember is being carried away. That's how I got this thing . . . ['this thing' was the Victoria Cross]'

Lt A. Angel, of the 214th Battalion, Royal Fusiliers:
'Most of my boys were young Londoners, just eighteen or nineteen, and a lot of them were going into a fight for the first time. Regularly during the night I crawled round to check on my scattered sections, having a word here and there and trying to keep their spirits up. The stench was horrible, for the bodies were not corpses in the normal sense. With all the shell-fire and bombardments they'd been continually disturbed, and the whole place was a mess of filth and slime and bones and decomposing bits of flesh. Everyone was on edge and as I crawled up to one shell-hole I could hear a boy sobbing and crying. He was crying for his mother. It was pathetic really, he just kept saying over and over again. "Oh Mum! Oh Mum!" Nothing would make him shut up, and while it wasn't likely that the Germans could hear, it was quite obvious that when there were lulls in the shell-fire the men in shell-holes on either side would hear this lad and possibly be affected. Depression, even panic, can spread quite easily in a situation like that. So I crawled into the shell-hole and asked

Corporal Merton what was going on. He said, "It's his first time in the line, sir. I can't keep him quiet, and he's making the other lads jittery." Well, the other boys in the shell-hole obviously *were* jittery and, as one of them put it more succinctly, "fed up with his bleedin' noise". Then they all joined in, "Send him down the line and home to Mum" – "Give him a clout and knock him out" – "Tell him to put a sock in it, sir."

'I tried to reason with the boy, but the more I talked to him the more distraught he became, until he was almost screaming. "I can't stay here! Let me go! I want my Mum!" So I switched my tactics, called him a coward, threatened him with court-martial, and when *that* didn't work I simply pulled him towards me and slapped his face as hard as I could, several times. It had an extraordinary effect. There was absolute silence in the shell-hole and then the corporal, who was a much older man, said, "I think I can manage him now, sir.' Well, he took that boy in his arms, just as if he was a small child, and when I crawled back a little later to see if all was well, they were both lying there asleep and the corporal still had his arms round the boy – mud, accoutrements and all. At zero hour they went over together.'

Lt J. Annan, of the 1st/9th Battalion, Royal Scots:
'As we were struggling up to it one of the boys got hit with a huge shell fragment. It sliced him straight in two. He dropped his rifle and bayonet and threw his arms up in the air, and the top part of his torso fell back on to the ground. The unbelievable thing was that the legs and the kilt went on running, just like a chicken with its head chopped off! One of my boys – I think it was his special pal – went rushing after him. He had some mad idea of picking up the upper part of the torso and chasing the legs to join him up. I shouted him back and he was wild with me because he

wanted to help his pal. He couldn't realise that he was beyond help.'

W. Lockey, No. 71938, 1st Btn., Notts and Derbyshire Regiment (The Sherwood Foresters):
'It was a terrible sight, really awe-inspiring, to see the barrage playing on the German front lines before we went over. It was an inferno. Just a solid line of fire and sparks and rockets lighting up the sky. When the barrage began to lift we went over like one man towards what had once been the German front line. It didn't exist. There was not a bit of wire, hardly a trench left, that hadn't been blown to smithereens by our barrage. We were moving uphill over the Hooge Ridge to skirt the Bellewarde Lake, and then we were supposed to cross the Bellewarde Ridge and make for Westhoek, which was our objective.

'We weren't so much running forward as scrambling on over fallen trees and shell-holes, and although our own barrage was going in front of us the German field artillery was firing back, so there were shells exploding all around. The chap on my right had his head blown off, as neat as if it had been done with a chopper. I saw his trunk stumbling on for two or three paces and then collapsing in a heap. My pal, Tom Altham, went down too, badly wounded, and Sergeant-Major Dunn got a shell all to himself. The noise and the din were unbelievable, but apart from the shelling and a bit of machine-gun fire we met very little opposition until we were going up the Bellewarde Ridge. Then a fellow on my left was hit in the leg by a bullet that had come from the rear. When we turned round we saw two Germans with their heads sticking out of a hole, up went our rifles, but, to our amazement, the Jerries didn't stand their ground. They threw down their arms and ran towards our lines with their hands up.

'On the top of the ridge we came to a big dug-out, deep in the earth. Some of the boys shouted down, but there was no reply. Just to make sure, they chucked a Mills bomb down and the Jerries replied to *that* all right! Out they came, those of them that could still move, and there were about forty filing out one after the other with their hands up. We left an escort with them and pushed on. In fact, we pushed on so fast that we reached our first objective about half an hour before the scheduled time and even went past it. Our officers had to signal us back because we were getting into our own gunfire, which was supposed to be falling in front of us in this creeping barrage. Now we were deeper into the German lines, even beyond their second line, so there were bits of trenches and dug-outs, not too badly shattered. We got into a bit of a trench that we'd just cleared of Jerries and saw the smoke and explosions.

'On the ground all around us it was simply carnage. Bits of bodies and knocked-out guns lying all over the place and in front of us were the bodies of about thirty German soldiers, all tossed about anyhow, who had probably been caught in the barrage of our guns as they tried to get away. There were some chaps in our lot who would do anything for souvenirs, so while we were waiting for the barrage to lift, they got out of the trench and started searching these bodies for anything they could get. They were after watches and buttons and things like that, and they'd go through their pockets as well for wallets and money, cigars, even photographs. Anything they could say they took off a German.

'Well, these chaps were turning over the bodies, rifling them, not bothering about taking cover, when all of a sudden a shell came over. There was this tremendous explosion and the whole earth in front of us went up. We ducked down in the trench with mud and earth and debris showering down on top of us. When we got up, and looked at where our chaps had been, they'd got the full force of the explosion and there they were, lying there – dead Tommies and bits of Tommies lying all tangled up with the dead

Germans. A couple survived, badly wounded, so someone crawled forward and pulled them back to wait for the stretcher-bearers.'

A. M. Burrage

'A tornado of shells'

Alfred McLelland Burrage (1889–1956) used a pseudonym – Ex-Private X – when he published *War is War* from which this description of Passchendaele is taken, in 1930. He was a writer throughout his life, mainly of short fiction for magazines. He joined the Artists' Rifles (28th Battalion, London Regiment) in 1917:

> Everything at Passchendaele was unique. The arrangement of our equipments – 'battle order' it used to be called – was all different from that of former and future occasions. We had to go over with our packs on. This was because we had to carry with us three days' rations, it being impossible for supplies to be sent up. We wore our entrenching tools in front instead of behind, to protect a part of the anatomy which it would be indelicate to mention. When we attacked every man carried a spade stuck down his back between his pack and equipment, so that he could consolidate any position in which he happened to find himself. Moreover, each of us carried a hundred and eighty rounds of extra ammunition hung round our necks and I – being a rifle-grenadier – had to carry twelve grenades in an extra haversack, perforated at the bottom to allow the rods to stick through.
>
> A Mills grenade, if I remember rightly weighs about five pounds, three hundred cartridges weigh a bit, and there was one's rifle and the usual accoutrements, so obviously one was not quite a feather-weight. Yet, burdened like pack-horses, we were expected to fight for our lives with the bayonet if the occasion arose. No wonder that Haig afterwards said that no

troops in the whole history of war had ever fought under such conditions; and the square-headed Hindenburg smugly observed that 'the British broke its teeth on Passchendaele Ridge'. It may be added that we had to wade through mud of various depths and of consistencies varied between that of raw Bovril and weak cocoa.

We are to go over from tapes laid by the Engineers. The whole thing must be done with mathematical precision, for we are to follow a creeping barrage which is to play for four minutes only a hundred yards in front of the first 'ripple' of our first 'wave'. I am in the second 'ripple' fifty yards behind the first. The first 'ripple' is to start in artillery formation – sections in single file at a given distance apart – changing to extended order after having covered two hundred yards. It is of the utmost importance that we should keep as close as possible to our own barrage and even risk becoming casualties from it. Well, if we know our own gunners we haven't much doubt about the risk!

At midnight we move up to the tapes amid heavy shell-fire. Each section digs for itself a little pit in which to crouch. It is called intensive digging. Each man in turn digs like fury until he is fagged out and flops, the others meanwhile lying on their bellies and waiting their turn to seize the spade. In this way quite a big hole, like a small section of a trench, can be dug in a very few minutes.

All the while shells are screaming over our heads, throwing up great geysers of mud all around us and further mutilating the ruined landscape. Our better 'ole is about big enough to accommodate us when there is a cry for help. The section which includes Dave Barney, has been buried by a shell. Dave has given up stretcher-bearing for the time being and is a rifleman or bomber – I forget which. We dig them out again, swear at them heartily, and get back to our own slot in the ground. Ten minutes later they are all blown up and buried again, with worse results than before. Dave is the only one of them left alive, and he is entirely unscathed but badly shaken and inclined to think that war is an over-rated pastime. I want some rest, and beg him not to make a hobby of getting himself buried. One could always say light-hearted and stupid things even when one was frightened to death.

I salute the artillery. At ten minutes to six, hundreds, per-haps thousands, of guns behind us went off like one gun. All the inhabitants of hell seemed to have been let loose and to be screaming and raving in the sky overhead. The darkness just in front of us was rent and sundered. Blinding flashes in a long and accurate line blazed and vanished, and blazed and vanished, while the guns which had at first roared in unison now drummed and bellowed and thumped and crashed in their own time. Their din was half drowned by the variegated noises of the exploding shells. No maniac ever dreamed anything like it.

Matters didn't improve. The German was not asleep, and within a minute his own barrage had multiplied the inferno by two, while machine-guns broke out with the rattling of a thousand typewriters. I stood dazed by the din and didn't notice that our own barrage had lifted until somebody shouted: 'Come on!'

I must say, without meaning to praise myself, that it was a good show. Nobody hesitated or looked back. I was simply a sheep and I went with the flock. We moved forward as if we were on the parade-ground.

But it didn't last long. With shell-holes and impassable morasses we had to pick our way. It was no use looking for 'dressing' to the section on the left or right, which was either in the same predicament or had already been blotted out. Led by Edmonds my section made a detour, turning a little to the left and heading for some higher and drier ground. Unfortunately most of the battalion were compelled to do this.

We had already seen what had happened to the first 'ripple'. They had all made for that spot of higher and drier ground, and the Germans, having retired over it, knew exactly what must happen, and the sky rained shells upon it. Shrapnel was bursting not much more than face high, and the liquid mud from ground shells was going up in clouds and coming down in rain.

The first 'ripple' was blotted out. The dead and wounded were piled on each other's backs, and the second wave, coming up behind and being compelled to cluster like a flock of sheep, were knocked over in their tracks and lay in heaving mounds. The wounded tried to mark their places, so as to be found by stretcher-bearers, by sticking their bayonets into the ground, thus leaving their rifles upright with the butts pointing at the sky. There was a forest of rifles until they were uprooted by shell-bursts or knocked down by bullets like so many skittles.

The wounded who couldn't crawl into the dubious shelter of shell holes were all doomed. They had to lie where they were until a stray bullet found them or they were blown to pieces. Their heartrending cries pierced the incessant din of explosions. The stretcher-bearers, such as still survived, could do nothing as yet.

How my section had so far remained intact is a mystery which I shall never solve in this world. After a minute or two of stupor we discovered that we were all as thickly coated with mud from the shell-bursts as the icing on a Christmas cake. Our rifles were all clogged, and directly we tried to clean them more mud descended. If the Germans had counter-attacked we had nothing but our bayonets. In the whole battalion only one Lewis gun was got into action, and I don't think that more than half a dozen men in the three attacking companies were able to use their rifles during the first few hours.

We saw Germans rise out of the ground, and bolt like

rabbits, and we had to let them bolt. They had been able to keep their rifles covered and clean, but we had bayonets on ours. Moreover their artillery knew just where we were, and our own gunners were now firing speculatively. We were getting the shells and the rain of mud and the German wasn't. Good soldier that he was, he soon took advantage of this, and we began to suffer from the most hellish sniping.

The mud which was our enemy was also our friend. But for the mud none of us could have survived. A shell burrowed some way before it exploded and that considerably decreased its killing power.

There was still a tornado of shells raging around us, and one must have landed in the same shell-hole with me. I didn't hear it come, and I didn't hear it burst, but I suddenly found myself in the air, all arms and legs. It seemed to me that I rose to about the height of St Paul's Cathedral, but probably I only went up about a couple of feet. The experience was not in the least rough, and I can't understand why it disturbed me so little. I think that by this time I was so mentally numb that even fear was atrophied. It was like being lifted by an unexpected wave when one is swimming in the sea. I landed on all fours in a shell-hole which Edmonds had told me to leave, sprawling across the backs of the rest of the section.

'And now,' I said firmly, 'I'm going to stop.'

Edmonds didn't demur, and I asked him what about some rum. The Nonconformist conscience prevailed, and he said that we might need it presently. Merciful heavens! didn't I need it now? We lit cigarettes and I began trying to think. I wondered if I could smile, and still having control of my face muscles, found that I could.

Nothing had stood up and lived on the space of ground between ourselves and the pill-box a hundred and fifty yards away. I saw a stretcher-bearer, his face a mask of blood, bending over a living corpse. He shouted to some-body and beckoned, and on the instant he crumpled and fell and went to meet his God. To do the enemy justice, I don't suppose for one moment that he was recognised as a stretcher-bearer.

Another man, obviously off his head, wandered aim-lessly for perhaps ninety seconds. Then his tin hat was tossed into the air like a spun coin, and down he went. You could always tell when a man was shot dead. A wounded man always tried to break his own fall. A dead man gener-ally fell forward, his balance tending in that direction, and he bent simultaneously at the knees, waist, neck and ankles.

Several of our men, most of whom had first been wounded, were drowned in the mud and water. One very religious lad with pale blue watery eyes died the most appalling death. He was shot through the lower entrails, tumbled into the water of a deep shell-hole, and drowned by inches while the coldness of the water added further torture to his wound. Thank God I didn't see him. But our C of E chaplain – who went over the top with us, the fine chap! – was killed while trying to haul him out.

I don't subscribe to the creed of the Church of England. The cognoscenti of my Church – when they can be got to speak frankly – are dubious about the post-mortem fate of heretics and less than dubious about the fate of heretic clergy. But I am very sure, if I am to believe in anything at all, that our dear Padre is in one of the Many Mansions. I like to think of him feasting with Nelson and Drake, Philip Sidney, Richard of the Lion Heart, Grenville, Wolfe, and Don Johne of Austria. And perhaps when these have dallied a little over their wine they go to join the ladies – such ladies as Joan of Arc, Grace Darling, Florence Nightingale, and Edith Cavell. *Requiescat* – but he needs no prayer from a bad soldier and a worse sinner.

Edwin Vaughan

'Sobbing moans of agony'

Edwin Vaughan (1897–1931) left the Jesuit College of St Ignatius
in Stamford Hill, London, in 1915 to join the Artists' Rifles, was
commissioned into the Royal Warwickshire Regiment in 1916
and sailed to France in 1917. His diary for 27 August describes
one of the small battles of the Passchendaele Campaign – at
Langemarck, where the advance was held up by impassable
ground and heavy German fire. Vaughan was the last officer left
in his company, which captured the pillbox called Springfield.

Up the road we staggered, shells bursting around us. A man
stopped dead in front of me, and exasperated I cursed him
and butted him with my knee. Very gently he said, 'I'm
blind, Sir', and turned to show me his eyes and nose torn
away by a piece of shell. 'Oh God! I'm sorry, sonny,' I said.
'Keep going on the hard part,' and left him staggering back
in his darkness. At the Triangle the shelling was lighter and
the rifle fire far above our heads. Around us were numerous
dead, and in shell-holes where they had crawled to safety
were wounded men. Many others, too weak to move, were
lying where they had fallen and they cheered us faintly as we
passed: 'Go on boys! Give 'em hell!' Several wounded men
of the 8th Worcesters and 7th Warwicks jumped out of their
shell-holes and joined us.

   A tank had churned its way slowly behind Springfield and
opened fire; a moment later I looked and nothing remained
of it but a crumpled heap of iron. It had been hit by a large
shell. It was now almost dark and there was no firing from
the enemy; ploughing across the final stretch of mud, I saw
grenades bursting around the pillbox and a party of British
rushed in from the other side. As we all closed in, the Boche
garrison ran out with their hands up; in the confused party

I recognized Reynolds of the 7th Battalion, who had been working forward all the afternoon. We sent the 16 prisoners back across the open but they had only gone a hundred yards when a German machine gun mowed them down.

Reynolds and I held a rapid conference and decided that the cemetery and Spot Farm were far too strongly held for us to attack, especially as it was then quite dark; so we formed a line with my party on the left in touch with the Worcesters, who had advanced some 300 yards further than we, and Reynolds formed a flank guard back to the line where our attack had broken. I entered Springfield, which was to be my HQ.

It was a strongly-built pillbox, almost undamaged; the three defence walls were about ten feet thick, each with a machine gun position, while the fourth wall, which faced our new line, had one small doorway – about three feet square. Crawling through this I found the interior in a horrible condition; water in which floated indescribable filth reached our knees; two dead Boche sprawled face downwards and another lay across a wire bed. Everywhere was dirt and rubbish and the stench was nauseating.

Now with a shrieking and crashing, shells began to descend upon us from our own guns, while simultaneously German guns began to shell their own lines. In my haversack all this time I had been carrying a treasure which I now produced – a box of 100 Abdulla Egyptians. I had just opened the box when there was a rattle of rifles outside and a voice yelled 'Germans coming over, Sir!' Cigarettes went flying into the water as I hurled myself through the doorway and ran forward into the darkness where my men were firing. I almost ran into a group of Germans and at once shouted 'Ceasefire!' for they were unarmed and were 'doing Kamerad'.

The poor devils were terrified; suspicious of a ruse I stared into the darkness while I motioned them back against the wall with my revolver. They thought I was going to shoot them and one little fellow fell on his knees babbling about his wife and 'Zwei kindern'. Going forward I found that several of the party were dead and another died as I dragged him in. The prisoners clustered around me, bedraggled and heartbroken, telling me of the terrible time they had been having, 'Nichts essen, Nichts trinken', always shells, shells, shells . . . I could not spare a man to take them back, so I put them into shell holes with my men who made a great fuss of them, sharing their scanty rations with them.

Re-entering the pillbox I found the Boche officer quite talkative. He told me how he had kept his garrison fighting on, and would never have allowed them to surrender. He had seen us advancing and was getting his guns on to us when a shell from the tank behind had come through the doorway, killed two men and blown his leg off. His voice trailed away and he relapsed into a stupor. So I went out again into the open and walked along our line; a few heavies were still pounding about us, but a more terrible sound now reached my ears.

From the darkness on all sides came the groans and wails of wounded men; faint, long, sobbing moans of agony, and despairing shrieks. It was too horribly obvious that dozens of men with serious wounds must have crawled for safety into new shell holes, and now the water was rising about them and, powerless to move, they were slowly drowning. Horrible visions came to me with those cries, of Woods and Kent, Edge and Taylor, lying maimed out there trusting that their pals would find them, and now dying terribly, alone amongst the dead in the inky darkness. And we could do nothing to help them; Dunham was crying quietly beside me, and all the men were affected by the piteous cries.

The cries of the wounded had much diminished now, and as we staggered down the road, the reason was only too apparent, for the water was right over the tops of the shell holes . . . I hardly recognised the headquarters pillbox, for it had been hit by shell after shell and its entrance was a long mound of bodies. Crowds of soldiers had run there for cover and had been wiped out by shrapnel. I had to climb over them to enter HQ and as I did so a hand stretched out and clung to my equipment. Horrified I dragged a living man from amongst the corpses.

Next morning, when I awoke to take a muster parade, my worst fears were realised. Standing near the cookers were four small groups of bedraggled, unshaven men from whom the quartermaster sergeants were gathering information concerning any of their pals they had seen killed or wounded. It was a terrible list . . . out of our happy little band of 90 men, only 15 remained.

HARRY PATCH

Born on 17 June 1898, Harry Patch is, at the time of writing, the last surviving Tommy of the Great War.

I can still see the bewilderment and fear on the men's faces as we went over the top. We crawled, because if you stood up you'd be killed.

All over the battlefield the wounded were lying there, English and German, all crying for help. But we weren't like the Good Samaritan in the Bible, we were the robbers who passed by and left them. You couldn't stop to help them. I came across a Cornishman who was ripped from shoulder to waist with shrapnel, his stomach on the ground beside him. A bullet wound is clean – shrapnel tears you all to pieces. As I got to him he said, 'Shoot me.' Before I could draw my revolver, he died. I was with him for the last 60 seconds of his life. He gasped one word – 'Mother'. That one word has run through my brain for 88 years. I will never forget it. I think it is the most sacred word in the English language. It wasn't a cry of distress or pain – it was one of surprise and joy. I learned later that his mother was already dead, so he felt he was going to join her.

LIEUTENANT MELVILLE HASTINGS, 32ND BATTALION, CANADIAN EXPEDITIONARY FORCE

Honour

It is not to be wondered at that many a Fritz, who has lived amongst us for years, bears us far from bitter feelings. When a very green soldier, I was sent out at Armentières to cover a party engaged in cutting down a patch of seeding chicory a few yards in front of our own wire. Being ordered to advance a hundred yards Fritzwards, I had paced but eighty odd, when, to my astonishment, I found myself securely entangled in the wire of what was evidently an unlocated listening post. My rifle, wrenched from my hands, evidently collided with a screw stake, and a flare shot up *instanter*. Not fifteen yards away, sticking out from a hole sunk into the turf, were a rifle and the head and shoulders of a man. Of course I 'froze' stiff. Seeing, however, no movement of the rifle, I began to think – though such seemed impossible – that I was undis-covered. It was impossible. He had seen me plainly. Perhaps he was a sportsman, and scorned to wing a defenceless man. He laughed heartily, called out 'Hallo Johnny Bull, you silly old —,' and sank into the earth. Yours truly likewised, plus rifle, but minus half a yard of tunic, and nearly a pair of pants. A very similar experience befell my friend a Captain of Canadian Infantry. Scouting alone in no man's land – a most unwise proceeding, by the way – he walked on to the levelled rifle of a sniper. Halting the Captain, the sniper ordered him to hands up and step back five paces. In the couple of min-utes of conversation that ensued it appeared that my friend was in the hands of a Saxon, an Oxford graduate, and a man who – despite repeated requests not to be used on the

British Front – had been sent against us. My friend was right-abouted and ordered to count fifty. At fifty-one he found himself alone and free. On the Roll of Honour of Oxford University is the name of a German who fell in defence of his fatherland. I have often wondered whether this hero and my friend's captor are different men, or just one and the same.

STODDARD KING

'The Long, Long Trail'

Stoddard King wrote the words of this sentimental anthem in 1915. It was very popular among the 'doughboys', the American soldiers departing for France. The song was recorded by the celebrated Irish-born American tenor John McCormack in June 1917. Yale-educated King served with the 3rd Washington Infantry of the National Guard.

> *Nights are growing very lonely, days are very long;*
> *I'm a-growing weary only list'ning for your song.*
> *Old remembrances are thronging thro' my memory*
> *Thronging till it seems, the world is full of dreams*
> *Just to call you back to me.*
>
> *Chorus:*
> *There's a long, long trail a-winding*
> *Into the land of my dreams,*
> *Where the nightingales are singing*
> *And a white moon beams:*
> *There's a long, long night of waiting*
> *Until my dreams all come true;*
> *Till the day when I'll be going down*
> *That long, long trail with you.*
>
> *All night long I hear you calling,*
> *Calling sweet and low;*

Seem to hear your footsteps falling ev'rywhere I go.
Tho' the road between us stretches many a weary mile,
Somehow I forget that you're not with me yet
When I think I see you smile.

Chorus:
There's a long, long trail a-winding (etc.)

GUY CHAPMAN

'Those are your orders'

Guy Chapman served as a junior officer with the Royal Fusiliers. After the war as Professor of Modern History at Leeds University he became a noted anthologist of the Great War. He describes the reaction of a staff officer to a major's appeal for common humanity:

On the day before the next attack, I was collared by one of the General staff to bear him company to the front line brigade headquarters. It was a fine morning; and the Boche was using it. We ducked and fled through a covey of whizz-bangs which suddenly cracked about us, and took refuge in what must have been the Hell bunker of the Arras links. At one point we dropped into a tiny dugout, where my companion was to give the final instructions to the commanding officers of one of the assault brigades. One major, one captain and two second lieutenants listened with gloomy faces to his unemotional lecture. Just as we were leaving, the major, a plump little man, whose eyes belied his fierce moustache, looked up and stammered through trembling lips: 'Look here, you don't expect us to do this? You know we've hardly got an officer left. Two battalions are commanded by junior officers; and the men – what there are left – are badly shaken.' There was a moment's pause. My companion viewed the pleader coldly. 'Those are your orders,' he said in a harsh voice. 'Obey them.'

PRIVATE WILLIE ROBINS

'A lot of mugs with titles'

Any man can do what Haig is doing with the number of men at his disposal, complains Private Robins from the trenches of the South African Infantry Brigade:

> The British high command badly wants reorganizing. They are nothing but a lot of mugs with titles, money and whisky, but no brains. Some of them have never been so well off in their lives before. Goodness knows what they are going to do after the war. Just the bulldog pluck and perseverance of the ordinary British Tommy is keeping the British Army where it is and of course the Red Tabs take the credit and the poor old British Tommy is taking his life in his hand and going through hell every day while those rotters sit 20 miles behind the line and sip their whisky and take all the credit and congratulations and CBs and KCMGS etc. It is a mere game of ping pong and the Infantryman of today is nothing but sure cannon fodder. There are thousands of lives being thrown away every day that Britain can ill afford and I am convinced that so surely as Britain has been guilty of so many muddles so surely has she been guilty of many lost opportunities of bringing this war to an end.

GENERAL BORDEAUX

For the American Fallen

General Bordeaux, Commander of the French 18th Division, delivered this eulogy in November in front of the flag-draped coffins of three of the first Americans to be killed: Private Tom Enright of Pittsburgh, Corporal James Bethel Gresham of Henderson, Kentucky, and Private Merle Hay of Glidden, Iowa. They were buried in wooden coffins, an honour in times of scarcity, and guns were fired as they were lowered into shallow graves.

In the name of the 18th Division, in the name of the French Army, and in the name of France I bid farewell to Private Enright, Corporal Gresham and Private Hay of the American Army.

Of their own free will they had left a prosperous and happy country to come over here. They knew war was continuing in Europe, they knew that the forces fighting for honor, love of justice and civilization were still checked by the long prepared forces serving the powers of brutal domination, oppression and barbarity. They knew that efforts were still necessary. They wished to give us their generous hearts and they have not forgotten old historical memories while others forget more recent ones.

They ignored nothing of the circumstances, and nothing had been concealed from them – neither the length and hardships of war, nor the violence of battle, nor the dreadfulness of new weapons, nor the perfidy of the foe. Nothing stopped them. They accepted the hard and strenuous life; they crossed the ocean at great peril; they took their places on the front by our side, and they have fallen facing the foe in a hard and desperate hand-to-hand fight. Honor to them. Their families, friends and fellow citizens will be proud when they learn of their deaths.

Men! These graves the first to be dug in our national soil, and but a short distance from the enemy, are as a mark of the mighty land we and our Allies firmly cling to in the common task, confirming the will of the people and the army of the United States to fight with us to the finish, ready to sacrifice as long as is necessary until we find victory for the most noble of causes, that of the liberty of nations, the weak as well as the mighty.

Thus the death of this humble corporal and these privates

appeals to us forever. We will inscribe on their tombs, 'Here lie the first soldiers of the United States to fall on the fields of France for justice and liberty!' The passer-by will stop and uncover his head. Travellers and men of heart will go out of their way to come here to pay their respective tributes.

Private Enright, Corporal Gresham, Private Hay! In the name of France, I thank you. God receive your souls. Farewell!

RUDOLF BINDING

'My fellows are in tears'

As Rudolf Binding reports in his diary, the suffering of the German soldiers during the battle for Passchendaele was as acute as that of the Allied troops:

West Flanders, November 14, 1917: It is appalling up at the Front. I have just come back from a visit to our best regiment, which is holding a position I know well to the north of Passchendaele and has had heavy losses in the very first days. It is right in the mud, without any protection, without a single decent dug-out, for in this rapid withdrawal there is no time to dig. How many of those fellows who a fortnight ago were cheerfully celebrating the glorious record of their regiment will never laugh again; even the others who can laugh again do not laugh for long. 'My fellows are in tears,' reports one battalion-commander in despair, whose whole battalion lay covered by a regular blanket of English shells. Many of the men can hardly speak. You see wild eyes gazing out of faces which are no longer human. They have a craving after brandy which can hardly be satisfied, and which shows how badly they yearn to lose the faculty for feeling. Men drink it who have never touched it before as though by instinct. Although nothing very much in the way of bombardment was being vouchsafed us, I found myself practically the only one going towards the Front;

I saw nothing but men coming back. Only field-kitchens and stretcher-bearers – that is to say, people whose nerves are fed from the rear – were making their way forwards. Scores of men were streaming to the rear, one by one but without stopping, all in need of rest; not malingerers – no doubt merely men who need one day or two to come to themselves again. It is a perfectly honourable demand to make, but while the company-commanders are forced to send first one and then another, and then a third to the rear because they are no use in the line, the battalion-commander or the regimental-commander is always calling out for more men to defend a position which is in danger, or to meet an expected attack.

One sees much magnificent conduct calmly and coolly shown in the middle of much which is less admirable and weaker. That type of man makes allowances for the others by increasing his own efforts. A battalion-commander, Freiherr von G., stuck to his battalion for two days with a splinter of shell in his lung. He remained simply as an example; he knew it; and such examples have an effect. One cannot say that the *morale* is low or weak. The regiments simply show a sort of staggering and faltering, as people do who have made unheard-of efforts.

Francis Meynell

'Starving at the Ritz'

The *Daily Herald* splashed this report across the front page on 20 November as part of its campaign against the inequality of sacrifice on the home front between the rich and the poor. The writer, who was not then identified, was Francis Meynell. The words 'No Tea', 'No Sugar', 'No Margarine', 'No Butter' had become quite familiar to the soldiers' wives and children, said the *Herald*.

20th November: A *Herald* representative dined at the Ritz on 20 November. His job was to see for himself, and for the readers of this paper, how the patriotic rich had 'tightened their belts', how thin the fare had become, how the grim tragedy of the war had affected the proudest heritage of our race – or, as the proverb says, an 'Englishman's kitchen is his castle'.

The menu tells a story, but not the full story. Those of our readers whose hearts go out in sympathy to the Fat Man on account of these deplorably short commons will be relieved to hear that it is possible to supplement the menu almost at will. The *Herald* representative, having heard some nonsense about the shortage of milk, is now able to reassure the world living east of — that the whole thing is a myth – invented no doubt by the crafty Germans or the pacifist Bolos. For we demanded whipped cream to add to our soup – and a bowl was produced; a cream sauce was served with the fish; cream flowed plentifully over the *macédoine de fruits*, and a jug of cream came with our coffee. Moreover, that providence which puts us all in our places has made wheat to grow accordingly. The *Herald* representative managed to eat four rolls himself – and there would have been no difficulty in obtaining more if he could have swallowed more.

The first course was *hors d'oeuvres* – little dishes of sardines, shelled shrimps, eggs mayonnaise, olives, etc. – *a sufficient meal by itself*. The second, a rich soup, for which he ordered – and obtained – the bowl of cream – *almost a meal by itself*. The third course was a generous helping of exquisitely cooked sole, lobster and white wine joining with the cream for its dressing – *an ample meal by itself*. The fourth course was chicken, cooked to a turn. Half a fowl (less its leg, which is, as everyone knows, quite impossible to eat) is served for two persons – *a substantial meal by itself*. To test whether another course of meat would be served and whether one might go outside the narrow limits of the menu, bacon with tomatoes was then ordered. The choice may sound a little odd. Its aesthetic justification, our readers need not be reminded, is as a jerk, a strong division, a contrast between the delicately cooked chicken of the previous course and the charm of the sweet to follow.

Moreover, in other places is there not supposed to be a shortage of bacon? Clearly a mistake. The *Herald* representative had three rashers and three tomatoes to his share – again, *a meal in itself*. Then the *macédoine de fruits*. One did not need sugar, for the Muscat grapes and the Maraschino were effective, if a trifle expensive, substitutes. Here, too, the cream flowed. Coffee, cream and liqueur rounded off a dinner which, with the cheaper champagne (only 14s. a bottle, against the average £1. 1s.), fed two people quite respectably for £3 – and paid the tip into the bargain.

These notes will, we hope, put an end to the miserable suspicions entertained by the lower orders that the rich are better off than themselves in wartime. The war, we know, has levelled everyone. If prices are high and food is short down your way, why not 'pig it' in the Ritz?

As we were bowed out of the door we saw, under the arches at the front of the hotel, three old women huddled up in their rags for the night.

B. D. PARKIN

'I wanted to hide myself from it all'

Second Lieutenant B. D. Parkin, serving with the 2/4th Battalion, the Duke of Wellington Regiment, was an 'Officer just out' from England when the Battle of Cambrai started. He wrote a frank and rare account of the fear he experienced when 'theory' became the stark reality of war on the Western Front.

Punctually to the tick Hell was let loose. All my theoretical battle collapsed in a moment of time. All my indifference or curiosity or newness or inexperience or whatever you may call it disappeared in a flash. The reality came as a thunderbolt, as something from which I have never been prepared. From that moment I was no longer an 'Officer just out' – I was a poor specimen of humanity possessed with something indescribable. I wanted to find a hole in the earth – to go down and down to hide myself from it all. I couldn't hold my water. I just simply grovelled full length at the bottom of the trench trying to dig my ginger nails into the earth at the side. Oh God! Give me courage! I thought of my wife and boy, my parents, and that haunting picture of a dying warrior they possess. Oh smash that picture from my mind! Stop these guns or let me get out of it! No! it's impossible. I'm in in and I shall never get out! I don't know how long I lay there but I felt and knew that the others were lying flat too at the bottom of the trench. Once I caught the face of Graham. He had his teeth and lips snarling like a terrible vicious dog. And then Birdsall crawled to me and touched me and said, 'Are you hurt, sir?' How strange they all looked – yellow and grey and drawn, for shells were bursting all around us. This time they were not over there – somewhere else – they were not theoretical. Here they were – just here. God! That was pretty near. The trench is blown in.

A tree on the roadside by the trench had a direct hit and crashed with that noise only associated with cracking trees. And then the debris of earth and stones fell over us mingled with the smell of explosives – that never-to-be-forgotten smell. Something dropped on my leg a little bit sharper than a stone. I picked it up and immediately dropped it. It was hot. My puttee was torn and my leg hurt me. Then another burst which smothered us with horrid black smoke and black dust. One general staff officer had said, had said, 'You may be caught in the enemy's counter barrage', but at the time, this had meant nothing but a theoretical barrage. *Now* I knew what a barrage was, but afterwards I learned that really this particular barrage was a weak one. But *then* I didn't think so. And really, if I had known – if, if someone had told me – I need not have flopped down as I did at Zero, for it was the instantaneous outburst from those hundreds of guns of ours wheel to wheel in front of Harincourt Wood and from there southwards.

And it was more than I could stand! The desire for cover need not have happened until the counter barrage arrived. When it did, it was different from anything I had imagined. Another hit on the road, 2 yards from us. We were in the trench and only got the debris, but a couples of mules with the one driver went up into the air – a direct hit. Someone moved them later and buried the man. He was unseeable. They cut off the limbs of the mules and buried the entrails, leaving the limbs to be collected later. And then our calico received some direct hits in the mess of earth and hole – no airman could possibly see calico. Graham ran for all he was worth and did what he could and then dropped into the trench. And I am ashamed to relate that from Zero until the enemy's barrage weakened or until perhaps I got more accustomed to it, I never once gave a thought to the boys who were to attack, or even to the job of picking up aeroplane messages. I cannot remember when my senses returned and when that unholy fear departed. But they did go and I pulled myself together.

F. MITCHELL

Triumph of the Tanks

Mitchell was attached to the 21st Division in France from 1915 to 1917 and was then a lieutenant in the 1st Battalion, the Tank Corps. In *Tank Warfare* Mitchell wrote this vivid account of the day when the Corps demonstrated the power of its new weapon:

On the evening of the 19th November, Brigadier-General H. J. Elles, the commander of this battle fleet of land ships, issued his famous order:

Special Order, No. 6

'1. To-morrow the Tank Corps will have the chance for which it has been waiting for many months, to operate on good going in the van of the battle.

'2. All that hard work and ingenuity can achieve has been done in the way of preparation.

'3. It remains for unit commanders and for tank crews to complete the work by judgment and pluck in the battle itself.

'4. In the light of past experience I leave the good name of the corps with great confidence in your hands.

'5. I propose leading the attack of the Centre Division.

'(Signed) Hugh Elles,

'B.-G. Commanding Tank Corps.

'November 19, 1917.'

The last paragraph filled everybody with astonishment and pride. The fleet was going into battle led by the commander in person in his flagship, the *Hilda*. Every crew felt that the eye of the chief would be watching them, and they swore not to betray his trust.

Throughout the whole of the war, on no matter what front, no general in command of any large body of troops ever led his troops in action. A general's place during a modern battle is well in the rear.

General Elles was the one outstanding exception, but then he was a young man under forty, in charge of a young corps engaged in an entirely new form of warfare. His task was not to follow precedents but to create them. He fully realised too that his fleet of land ships, designed and brought into being by naval men, should go into action in naval fashion. An admiral always leads his battle squadrons into action and shares the same dangers as every sailor. General Elles went one better: he ran up the Tank Corps flag on his landship, and proposed to lead the very centre and spearhead of the attack. This flag, which was designed at Cassel in August, 1917, was of three colours – brown, red and green.

Brown represented the earth or mud; red, fire, or the fighting spirit; green the fields, or 'good going.' These colours symbolised the ambition of the Tank Corps, which was to fight its way through mud and blood to the green fields and open country beyond.

By flying the flag the general would inevitably attract attention to his tank and be in the very forefront of danger, but when great issues are at stake to take great risks is the prerogative of a great leader, and the brave flapping of that lonely flag was, that day, easily worth another hundred tanks to the enheartened Tank Corps.

At 4.30 a.m. on 20th November, the enemy suddenly came to life, and there was an ominous burst of shelling and trench-mortar fire. Had the Germans discovered our plans? Was everything doomed to failure at the eleventh hour? The tanks, thickly wrapped in mist and darkness, held their breath and waited anxiously. In half an hour the shelling died down and a strained silence took its place.

By 6 a.m. all the tanks were ready in front of our trenches in one long line stretching for six miles. The leading tanks were 150 yards ahead of the rest, and behind, at the gaps in our own wire, the infantry stood silently waiting. There was a thick mist, and it was cold. Rum was served to the tank crews.

Sunrise was at 7.30 a.m. At ten minutes past six the tanks began to move forward in the semi-darkness, the infantry following quietly in single file. Ten minutes later a thousand guns opened out and a fierce barrage of high explosive and smoke shells descended like a hurricane on the German outpost line, 200 yards in front of the advancing tanks. Overhead squadrons of bombers boomed past, dropping their deadly eggs on German Headquarters and gun positions. Above the roaring of their engines and the thunder of the bombardment the tank crew could hear the rending and snapping of the barbed wire as their machines trampled a way through.

The amazed Germans were completely overwhelmed. As scores of these monsters loomed up out of the mist, with their weird humps on their backs, the defenders of the line fled in panic, throwing away their arms and equipment as they ran. The great fascines were released and cast into the bottom of the trench. The snouts of the tanks stretched out and out over the wide trenches until the point of balance was reached, then dipped down and down until they seemed to be standing on their heads. Then, when they touched the far side, up and up they reared until their tails rested on the fascines, and their tracks being able to get a firm grip, their huge bodies clambered back on to the level again.

Thus was the famous Hindenburg Line, the much boomed bulwark of the German Army, crossed as easily as a boy jumps over a small stream.

By 4 p.m. on the 20th November, the battle from the Tank Corps' point of view was won and finished. On a front of 13,000 yards the infantry had been enabled to advance 10,000 yards in ten hours. Eight thousand prisoners and 100 guns were captured, in addition to numerous stores, canteens, field post offices, hospitals and even cinemas.

The British casualties had not been more than 1,500.

At the Third Battle of Ypres a similar advance took three months, and cost nearly 400,000 casualties.

The Tank Corps, numbering a little over 4,000 men, had that day changed the face of warfare.

The tactics outlined by the far-seeing Colonel Swinton in February, 1916, seven months before the first tank went into action, had at last triumphed. If only the Higher Command had carried out his ideas earlier, what lives would have been saved, what victories would have been gained.

The amazing victory roused England to great enthusiasm. Bells were rung in all churches. Little knowing what disasters were ahead, people talked of the end being in sight; they were mistaken, and yet their instinct was right, for that day the eyes of the generals had been suddenly opened, and a weapon placed in their hesitating hands which was destined to cleave the way to victory.

DRIVER A. BACON

The Most Glorious Day for the Tank

Another soldier driving a tank in the Battle of Cambrai was Driver A. Bacon, a 1st Driver in the 5th Battalion of the Tank Brigade. This description of his experience appears in the memoirs of Lt. Col. Archie Browne at the Imperial War Museum.

At six-twenty a.m. the British artillery opened fire all along the six mile front, and the massed tanks crept over the front line towards the cascade of white shell-bursts that smothered the German trenches.

My tank was operating with others on the left flank near the Canal du Nord with the 62nd (West Riding) Division. We crawled on in front of the infantry and demolished the barbed wire entanglements and came under enemy machine-gun fire which did little harm.

We reached the German front line and the first thing I noticed as I raised the nose of my tank to cross over the trench was several grey-clad enemy lying right in my path, and just as the tank gave her downward lurch one of them turned and looked up in a despairing effort to avoid the monster. I am afraid there were many that day who suffered a similar fate.

The enemy artillery shelling gradually increased but owing to the rapid rate of our advance the shells were dropping in No Man's Land and their front line long after we left that behind. We bounded merrily away up the hill past Yorkshire Bank and Wigan Copse, but then ran into some pretty stiff cross-fire from enemy machine-gun nests. The infantry meantime were mopping up behind us and had taken a large number of prisoners.

The enemy defence was now stiffening and a barrage of high explosives and machine-gun barrage was being put down in front of us. We were now approaching the famous Hindenburg Line – this support line was reported to be impregnable and 'untakeable'.

A pitched battle soon raged between the Hindenburg Line of concrete and steel, and the mobile steel line of our tanks. We fought our way to the belt of wire, and then allowed the tanks on our right and left to come up into alignment. Then we opened our throttles to the fullest extent and plunged through the barbed wire. Our tracks flattened out a clear pathway for the infantry to advance, and as we emerged from the wire we ran into a hailstorm of flying bullets and shrapnel and as we reached the enemy main trench we found it was a colossal depth and we had to use our fascine, which we dropped into the depth below, to get us across it.

The enemy had by now disappeared and we were left in the undisputed possession of the Hindenburg Line. Once over this line the tanks were able to take advantage of the widening front, and we, therefore, ceased to concern ourselves with the activities of the tanks to the right and left of us but just determined to go right ahead and do all the damage we could. On our way we helped the infantry to overcome some strong points holding up their advance.

The attack was succeeding beyond our wildest dreams and it is difficult to convey the exhilaration that possessed us as we roamed about unchecked in this verdant country behind the German lines. By four-twenty p.m., when dusk began to fall, we had skirted the important village of Anneaux and were well out of the Bapaume–Cambrai national road. By five p.m. it was really dark and by this time we had reached a point just north west of Bourlon Wood – an advance of over five miles on the day. The infantry had now commenced 'digging in' on their objectives, and our tanks were ordered back to our rallying point which we reached at seven-thirty and then went into billets.

Thus ended the most glorious day in the history of the Tank Corps.

B. D. PARKIN

'Peace and content'

In a previous article, Second Lieutenant Parkin described his fear when he experienced battle for the first time. The battalion carried on fighting into December, when it was finally relieved. Parkin describes the intensity of his relief at leaving the front line, as it was experienced by the soldier who survived.

Although we passed the terrible sights of the results of the German shelling – although dead men fearfully disfigured were on the route – nothing was said. We passed with a reverent look and a prayer of gratitude and a desire to run away like Hell. And so by the middle of the morning we reached another railhead.

And there to our heart's delight was a long train with an engine, into which we mounted with alacrity, trying to hurry up and get away. The train took us via Bapaume, by the junction near Achiet-le-Petit, Achiet-le-Grand – and on towards Arras. It crawled, of course – we didn't enter Arras but swung round on to the St. Pol–Arras Railway – and it was dark before we reached our destination.

Back again to the station at which I had arrived on 10 November, and now it was 4 December. What a lot had happened between these two dates. It seemed ages. It was actually 24 days. We de-trained in the dark. How peaceful everything was! We could hear the guns booming, but they were a long long way off. We could see their flashes, but they were over the eastern horizon.

Then we formed up and marched again – a weary march but a thoughtful one. There was no singing, just peace and content. We arrived at the village in the pitch dark and of course saw nothing. With difficulty we saw our platoons into their billets – which were barns – and then we of 'A' company dossed down on the floor of an upstairs room in some house near the centre of the village. Birdsall opened my valise and when once I was inside I was lost to the world, sleeping a more peaceful sleep than I had known for over a month. No guns disturbed the peacefulness of that sleep, no crashes, no fear.

And now I cannot do better than quote from the letter I wrote home the next morning:

'On Tuesday afternoon and all Tuesday night we had to endure some more of the Boche's wrath, but now Ah! Luxury! Happiness! Rest! Glorious! I woke up from a beautiful night's rest this morning to the sound of the cocks crowing, children playing, clock striking, dogs barking. What joy! What peace! It's more than I can say. A cat sits by me while I scribble this. I have just been buying eggs, vegetables, bread. Ah! Luxury! I won't tell how we've existed for the last fortnight – that is, what remains of us. I am so thankful we are here. The guns can still be heard, but a long way off. Oh! Joy! I am so glad – you don't know.

'I wanted to give you a taste of my joy and peace. The cocks crowing delight me after the time we've had.'

1918

As the war settled into its fourth year, Woodrow Wilson, the American President, issued his fourteen-point plan for peace in January, but his terms suited neither the Germans nor the French nor the English. Soviet Russia, however, concluded peace negotiations with the Germans at Brest-Litovsk in March, although fighting in Russia stopped in February.

With peace declared in the east, General Ludendorff moved a million men and three thousand guns to the Western Front where he now had 3.5 million soldiers. Against a background of unrest in Germany, the crumbling of Austria-Hungary and Turkey, and American troops soon to arrive in France, he now sought a decisive victory in the west and launched his spring offensive. After a massive bombardment, on 21 March he attacked the British with three armies and advanced forty miles on a front of forty miles. Within six days the British lost 150,000 men, 90,000 as prisoners. It was this attack which prompted Sir Douglas Haig's famous 'With our backs to the wall' order of the day declaring that every position must be defended to the last man. On 29 March, however, the Germans were repulsed at Arras. With French support the British had held up the greatest offensive ever launched.

Ludendorff's next attack, in Flanders, was resisted and he

then attacked the French on the Aisne and reached the Marne, forty miles from Paris. But the Americans, arriving at the rate of 250,000 a month, helped to stop the Germans crossing the river. On 18 July Marshal Foch, now commander-in-chief of the Allied armies, attacked the Germans and forced them to abandon the Marne Salient. The tide was turning against the Germans.

The eighth of August was described by Ludendorff as the 'black day' for the German Army that put the decline of its fighting powers beyond all doubt. The Army, he said, had ceased to be a perfect fighting instrument. As the historian Barrie Pitt has written, the most significant event of 1918 did not occur on the battlefield but in Ludendorff's office, when he read the reports of the fighting and began to believe that his army was breaking up from within.

It was on that black day that Allied troops, supported by more than 500 tanks, 2000 guns and 1900 aircraft, smashed the German lines near Amiens and achieved for Douglas Haig his greatest triumph. By the end of August the Germans had been forced back to the Hindenburg Line from which they had launched Ludendorff's offensive in March. They had suffered 800,000 casualties. The British stormed the German line at the end of September and the German retreat began. Between 8 August and 11 November, the Allied armies took 188,700 prisoners and 2840 guns. The French, American and Belgian forces took another 196,000 prisoners and 3775 guns. Germany started suing for peace in October and Ludendorff resigned on 27 October.

The war ended when the armistice was signed in November. Fighting ended at the eleventh hour of the eleventh day of the eleventh month. Ninety years later Armistice Day is still commemorated in cities, towns and villages throughout Britain, France, Germany, Australia, New Zealand and Canada, and millions of poppies are worn in remembrance of the millions who died.

On the home front the Royal Air Force came into existence on 1 April. Under the Military Service Act, every man between eighteen and fifty was enlisted for the period of the war. Compulsory rationing of food was introduced in July and in November women became eligible for Parliament but could not vote until they were thirty.

Three consequences of the war were that the Ottoman and Habsburg empires came to an end and that Russia had become a communist state. There were others equally profound – though not the subject of this book – which led twenty-one years later to the Second World War. There were also big changes in England. At the beginning of this anthology, I quoted A. J. P. Taylor's account of English society in 1914. The war had brought great changes:

The mass of the people became, for the first time, active citizens. Their lives were shaped by orders from above; they were required to serve the state instead of pursuing exclusively their own affairs. Five million men entered the armed forces, many of them (though a minority) under compulsion. The Englishman's food was limited, and its quality changed, by government order. His freedom of movement was restricted; his conditions of work prescribed. Some industries were reduced or closed, others artificially fostered. The publication of news was fettered. Street lights were dimmed. The sacred freedom of drinking was tampered with; licensed hours were cut down, and the beer watered by order. The very time on the clocks was changed. From 1916 onwards, every Englishman got up an hour earlier in summer than he would otherwise have done, thanks to an act of parliament. The state established a hold over its citizens which, though relaxed in peacetime, was never to be removed and which the Second World War was again to increase. The history of the English state and the English people merged for the first time.

THE KING'S PROCLAMATION

Forms of Prayer and Thanksgiving to Almighty God
To be used on The Feast of the Epiphany
Sunday, Sixth of January, 1918
Being the day appointed for Intercession on Behalf of the
Nation and Empire
in this Time of War.
Issued under the Authority of the Archbishops of Canterbury
and York.

In the Order of Holy Communion after the Creed at least once in the day, and at Morning or Evening Prayer, or before the Forms of Prayer hereinafter set forth, the Minister shall read the King's Proclamation, saying as follows:

Brethren, I bid you hear the words of His Majesty the king appointing this day to be set aside as a Day of Prayer and Thanksgiving in all the Churches throughout his Dominions.

To My People: The world-wide struggle for the triumph of right and liberty is entering upon its last and most difficult phase. The enemy is striving by desperate assault and subtle intrigue to perpetuate the wrongs already committed and stem the tide of a free civilization. We have yet to complete the great task to which, more than three years ago, we dedicated ourselves.

At such time I would call upon you to devote a special day to prayer that we may have the clear-sightedness and strength necessary to the victory of our cause. This victory will be gained only if we steadfastly remember the responsibility which rests upon us, and in a spirit of reverent obedience ask the blessing of Almighty God upon our endeavours. With hearts grateful for the Divine guidance which has led us so far towards our goal, let us seek to be enlightened in our understanding and fortified in our courage in facing the sacrifices we may yet have to make before our work is done.

I therefore hereby appoint January 6th – the first Sunday of the year – to be set aside as a special day of prayer and thanksgiving in all the Churches throughout my dominions, and require that this Proclamation be read at the services held on that day.

George R.I.

HERBERT READ

'A piteous band of men'

Herbert Read (1893–1968) rose to the rank of captain in the Green Howards during the Great War and won both the Military Cross and the Distinguished Service Order. After the war he became a distinguished art historian, critic and poet. This extract from Read's *In Retreat*, published in 1919, gives a particularly vivid description of the Battle of St Quentin in March, which began with the most concentrated artillery bombardment the world had ever known.

Shortly after midday, the enemy came in direct contact with the inner ring of the redoubt.

We fired like maniacs. Every round of ammunition had been distributed. The Lewis-guns jammed; rifle-bolts grew stiff and unworkable with the expansion of heat.

In the lull before noon, the colonel and I had left the dug-out, in which we were beginning to feel like rats in a trap, and had found an old gun-pit about two hundred and fifty yards farther back, and here we established our headquarters. An extraordinary thing happened. The gun-pit was dug out of the bank on the roadside. About two o'clock one of our guns, evidently assuming that Roupy had been evacuated, began to pound the road between Roupy and Fluquières. One of these shells landed clean on the road edge of out pit. We were all hurled to the ground by the explosion, but, on recovering ourselves, found only one casualty: the colonel had received a nasty gash in the forearm. We then went two hundred to three hundred yards across the open, away from the road, and found a smaller overgrown pit. The colonel refused to regard his wound as serious; but he soon began to feel dizzy, and was compelled to go back to the dressing-station. I was then left in charge of the battalion.

It was now about 2.30. The attack still persisted in a guerrilla fashion. But the enemy was massing troops in the trenches already taken. At 4 p.m. the intensity of the attack deepened suddenly. A new intention had come into the enemy's mind; he was directing his attack on the flanks of our position in an effort to close round us like pincers. On the left he made use of cover offered by the ruined village, and eventually brought machine-guns to bear against us from our left rear. On the right he made use of the trenches evacuated by the Inniskillings.

In the height of this attack, while my heart was heavy with anxiety, I received a message from the brigade. Surely reinforcements were coming to our aid? Or was I at length given permission to withdraw? Neither: it was a rhetorical appeal to hold on to the last man. I rather bitterly resolved to obey the command.

Another hour passed. The enemy pressed on relentlessly with a determined, insidious energy, reckless of cost. Our position was now appallingly precarious. I therefore resolved to act independently, and do as perhaps I should have done hours earlier. I ordered B. to organise a withdrawal. This message despatched, I lay on my belly in the grass and watched through my field-glasses every minute trickling of the enemy's progress. Gradually they made way round the rim of the redoubt, bombing along the traverses. And now we only held it as lips might touch the rim of a saucer. I could see the heads of my men, very dense and in a little space. And on either side, incredibly active, gathered the grey helmets of the Boches. It was like a long bowstring along the horizon, and our diminished forces the arrow to be shot into a void. A great many hostile machine-guns had now been brought up, and the plain was sprayed with hissing bullets. They impinged and spluttered about the little pit in which I crouched.

I waited anxiously for B. to take the open. I saw men crawl out of the trenches, and lie flat on the parados, still firing at the enemy. There, after a little while, the arrow was launched. I saw a piteous band of men rise from the ground, and run rapidly towards me. A great shout went up from the Germans: a cry of mingled triumph and horror. 'Halt Eenglisch!' they cried, and for a moment were too amazed to fire; as though aghast at the folly of men who could plunge into such a storm of death. But the first silent gasp of horror expended, then broke the crackling storm. I don't remember in the whole war an intenser taste of hell. My men came along spreading rapidly to a line of some two hundred yards length, but bunched here and there. On the left, by the main road, the enemy rushed out to cut them off. Bayonets clashed there. Along the line men were falling swiftly as the bullets hit them. Each second they fell, now one crumpling up, now two or three at once. I saw men stop to pick up their wounded mates, and as they carried them along, themselves get hit and fall with their inert burdens. Now they were near me, so I rushed out of my pit and ran with them to the line of trenches some three hundred yards behind.

It seemed to take a long time to race across those few hundred yards. My heart beat nervously, and I felt infinitely weary. The bullets hissed about me, and I thought: then this is the moment of death. But I had no emotions. I remembered having read how in battle men are hit, and never feel the hurt till later, and I wondered if I had been hit. Then I reached the line. I stood petrified, enormously aghast. The trench had not been dug, and no reinforcements occupied it. It was as we had passed it on the morning of the 21st, the sods dug off the surface, leaving an immaculately patterned 'mock' trench. A hundred yards on the right a machine-gun corps had taken up a position, and was already covering our retreat. I looked about me wildly, running along the line and signalling to the men to drop as they reached the slender parapet of sods. But the whole basis of my previous tactics had been destroyed. I should never have ordered my men to cross that plain of death, but for the expectation that we were falling back to reinforce a new line. We found an empty mockery, and I was in despair. But I must steady the line. On the actual plain the men obeyed my signals, and crouched in the shallow trench. But even as they crouched, the bullets struck them. On the road, the straight white road leading to the western safety zone, there was something like a stampede. S. and the sergeant major went and held it with pointed revolvers. But it was all useless – hopeless. On the right, I saw the enemy creeping round. They would soon enfilade us, and then our shallow defence would be a death-trap. I accordingly gave the signal to withdraw, bidding the two Lewis-guns to cover us as long as possible. Once more we rose and scattered in retreat. It would be about seven hundred yards to the next trenches – the village line round Fluquières, and this we covered fairly well, sections occasionally halting to give covering fire. The enemy had not yet ventured from the redoubt, and our distance apart was now great enough to make his fire of little effect. And I think as we moved up the slope towards the village we must have been in 'dead' ground, so far as the enemy advancing on the right was concerned.

Ernst Jünger

Storm of Steel

Jünger, born in 1895, fought in the German Army throughout the conflict. Here he describes the Great Battle of March 1918, when, as Basil Liddell Hart wrote, four thousand German guns 'heralded the breaking of a storm which, in grandeur of scale, of awe and of destruction, surpassed any other in the war':

> I looked left and right. The moment before the engagement was an unforgettable picture. In shell craters against the enemy line, which was still being forked over and over by the fire-storm, lay the battalions of attackers, clumped together by company. At the sight of the dammed-up masses of men, the breakthrough appeared certain to me. But did we have the strength and the stamina to splinter also the enemy reserves and rend them apart? I was confident. The decisive battle, the last charge, was here. Here the fates of nations would be decided, what was at stake was the future of the world. I sensed the weight of the hour, and I think everyone felt the individual in them dissolved, and fear depart.
>
> The great moment was at hand. The wave of fire had trundled up to the first lines. We attacked.
>
> Our rage broke like a storm. Thousands must have fallen already. That was clear; and even though the shelling continued, it felt quiet, as though it had lost its imperative thrust.
>
> No man's land was packed tight with attackers, advancing singly, in little groups or great masses towards the curtain of fire. They didn't run or even take cover if the vast plume of an explosion rose between them. Ponderous, but unstoppable, they advanced on the enemy lines. It was as though nothing could hurt them any more.
>
> In the midst of these masses that had risen up, one was still alone; the units were all mixed up. I had lost my men from sight; they had disappeared like a wave in the crashing surf. All I had with me were my Vinke and a one-year volunteer by the name of Haake. In my right hand, I gripped my pistol, in my left, a bamboo riding-crop. Even though I was feeling hot, I was still wearing my long coat, and, as per

regulations, gloves. As we advanced, we were in the grip of a berserk rage. The overwhelming desire to kill lent wings to my stride. Rage squeezed bitter tears from my eyes.

The immense desire to destroy that overhung the battle-field precipitated a red mist in our brains. We called out sobbing and stammering fragments of sentences to one another, and an impartial observer might have concluded that we were all ecstatically happy.

The shredded wire entanglements provided no obstacle at all, and we cleared the first trench, barely recognizable as such, in a single bound. The wave of attackers danced like a row of ghosts through the white seething mists of the flat-tened dip. There was no one here to oppose us.

Then I saw my first enemy. A figure in brown uniform, wounded apparently, crouched twenty paces away in the middle of the battered path, with his hands propped on the ground. I turned a corner, and we caught sight of each other. I saw him jump as I approached, and stare at me with gaping eyes, while I, with my face behind my pistol, stalked up to him slowly and coldly. A bloody scene with no witnesses was about to happen. It was a relief to me, finally, to have the foe in front of me and within reach. I set the mouth of the pistol at the man's temple – he was too frightened to move – while my other fist grabbed hold of his tunic, feeling medals and badges of rank. An officer; he must have held some command post in these trenches. With a plaintive sound, he reached into his pocket, not to pull out a weapon, but a photograph which he held up to me. I saw him on it, surrounded by numerous family, all standing on a terrace.

It was a plea from another world. Later, I thought it was blind chance that I let him go and plunged onward. That one man of all often appeared in my dreams. I hope that meant he got to see his homeland again.

Our attention now shifted to that obstacle, which loomed up in front of us like a menacing wall. The scarred field that

separated us from it was still held by hundreds of scattered
British. Some were trying to scramble back, others were
already engaged in hand-to-hand fighting with our forward
troops.

Amid such scenes, we had come up to the embankment,
barely realising it. It was still spewing fire like a great
machine. Here my recollection begins again, with the registration of an extremely advantageous position. We hadn't
been hit, and now that we were right up against it, the
embankment changed from being an obstacle to being cover
for us. As though waking from a deep dream, I saw German
steel helmets approaching through the craters. They seemed
to sprout from the fire-harrowed soil like some iron harvest. At the same time, I noticed that right by my foot there
was the barrel of a heavy machine-gun, stuck through a
dugout window covered over with sacking. The noise was
such that it was only the vibration of the barrel that told us
that it was firing. The defender was only an arm's length
away from us then. It was that degree of proximity that
kept us safe. And that spelled his doom. Hot haze rose from
the weapon. It must have hit a great many men, and it was
still mowing [sic]. The barrel moved little; its fire was aimed.

I fixed the hot, shaking piece of steel that was sowing
death, and that I could almost brush with my foot. Then I
shot through the sacking. A man who turned up next to me
ripped it clean away, and dropped a hand-grenade in the
hole. A shock and the issue of a whitish cloud told the rest of
the story. The means were rough, but satisfactory. The
muzzle no longer moved, the weapon had stopped firing. We
ran along the embankment to treat the next holes in similar
fashion, and so we must have broken a few vertebrae out of
the spine of the defence. I raised my hand to let my troops,
whose shots were ringing round our ears, know who we
were and what we were about. They waved happily back.
Then we and a hundred others scaled the embankment. For

the first time in the war, I saw masses of men collide. The British were defending a couple of terraced trenches the other side of the embankment. Shots were exchanged at point-blank range, hand-grenades looped down.

I leaped into the nearest trench; plunging round the traverse, I ran into an English officer in an open jacket and loose tie; I grabbed him and hurled him against a pile of sandbags. An old white-haired major behind me shouted: 'Kill the swine!'

There was no point. I turned to the lower trench, which was seething with British soldiers. It was like a shipwreck. A few tossed duck's eggs, others fired Colt revolvers, most were trying to run. We had the upper hand now. I kept firing off my pistol as in a dream, although I was out of ammunition long ago. A man next to me lobbed hand-grenades at the British as they ran. A steel helmet took off into the air like a spinning plate.

It was all over in a minute. The British leaped out of their trenches, and fled away across the field. From up on the embankment, a wild pursuing fire set in. They were brought down in full flight, and, within seconds, the ground was littered with corpses. That was the disadvantage of the embankment.

Our success had a magical effect. There was no question of leadership, or even of separate units, but there was only one direction: forwards! Every man ran forward for himself.

MICHAEL MACDONAGH

'A kind of pulsation'

The thunder of the big guns across the Channel in France could even be heard in suburban London:

March 27: Having to-day off, and the weather being lovely, I had a walk through Richmond Park and over Wimbledon

Common. I sat down to rest in the sunshine on the high ground of the Royal Wimbledon Golf Course called Caesar's Camp – it is really Saxon – which commands a fine view of Surrey to the Downs. Here, I thought to myself, is a retreat – remote, silent, beautiful, joyous – from thoughts of the slaughter of war. But not for long did this mood prevail. I soon became conscious of a curious atmospheric sensation – a kind of pulsation in regular beats. There was not the faintest breeze. The air was as still as the air could be. Yet there were persistent tremors or throbs, which, as I concentrated my mind upon them, affected me physically like a succession of thuds – silent but very perceptible to my sense of feeling.

What was it? It was the guns – the terrible cannonade of the great Battle in France which was shaking the earth literally, and indeed the whole world metaphorically. Not for long was I able to stand the sinister sensation. It affected my nerves. I got up and hastened away.

'THEY DIDN'T BELIEVE ME'

(Music: Jerome Kern; words: M. E. Rourke)

The American composer Jerome Kern wrote this song for the 1914 musical *The Girl from Utah*. American soldiers at the front in France added their own parody (which decades later became one of the most moving moments of the musical and later film *Oh! What A Lovely War*).

The original song:

And when I told them
How beautiful you are
They didn't believe me!
They didn't believe me!
Your lips, your eyes, your cheeks, your hair
Are in a class beyond compare
You're the loveliest girl that one could see!

And when I tell them
And I'm certainly going to tell them,
That I'm the man whose wife one day you'll be,
They'll never believe me,
They'll never believe me,
That from this great big world you've chosen me!

The parody is particularly powerful:

And when they asked us
How dangerous it was.
Oh! We'll never tell them,
No, we'll never tell them.
We spent our pay in some café,
And fought wild women night and day,
T'was the cushiest job we ever had.

And when they ask us,
And they're certainly going to ask us.
The reason why we didn't win the
Croix de Guerre.
Oh! We'll never tell them,
No! we'll never tell them,
There was a front but damned if we knew where.

CHARLES CARRINGTON

'Clear-eyed young men'

A check on young male conscripts in 1916 revealed that 41 per cent were given the lowest health classification of C3; only 33 per cent were classified A1. State-educated children, fed on bread and margarine, tea and condensed milk, were five inches shorter than their public-school officers. The Army fattened them up (too often for slaughter). Charles Carrington served on both the Western and Italian fronts, and this report by an officer was quoted in his *Soldier from the Wars Returning*:

> The skinny, sallow, shambling, frightened victims of our industrial system, suffering from the effect of wartime shortages, who were given into our hands, were unrecognisable after six months of good food, fresh air, and physical training. They looked twice the size and, as we weighed and measured them, I am able to say that they put on an average of one inch in height and one stone in weight during their time with us. One boy's mother wrote to me complaining that her Johnny was half-starved in the Army and what was I doing about it. I was able to convince her that Johnny had put on two stone of weight and two inches of height, and had never had so good an appetite before. Beyond statistical measurement was their change in character, to ruddy, handsome, clear-eyed young men with square shoulders who stood up straight and were afraid of no one, not even the sergeant-major. 'The effect on me,' I wrote in a letter, 'is to make me a violent socialist when I see how underdeveloped industrialism has kept them, and a Prussian militarist when I see what soldiering makes of them.' Then I added, rather inconsequently, in a phrase that dates: 'I shall never think of the lower classes again in the same way after the war.' An odd forecast but true; I never have.

RUDOLF BINDING

'Nothing like it on earth'

At the age of forty-six, Rudolf Binding served with one of the Jungdeutschland divisions in October 1914, and in August 1916 was appointed ADC on the staff of one of the new German division then being formed. This extract is from his book *Fatalist at War*:

Beaucourt, April 4, 1918: The hardships are very great. One does not think about them, because it is natural that they should exist and that they should be insignificant compared with the greatness of the issue – if, indeed, wars are to be considered great things. The private who lies day and night in the mud in the open, waiting for a shell or an air-bomb to blow him to bits, is worse off than I am, but I can only speak for myself.

Imagine a series of stinking rooms which yesterday or the day before were a château. The wind and rain come in at the windows, in which fragments of glass tinkle at every shell-burst. The walls tremble all day and all night. When the heavy shells are seeking out their mark by degrees and draw nearer the men run to the cellar. There is no room there for us officers and we go on working. Stretcher-cases get smothered there in the darkness of the night by others who are trying to get shelter. The place stinks of blood, sweat, urine, excrement, iodoform, and wet clothes. Down below in the passages they peel potatoes, but nobody thinks of throwing away the peel; one puts down the wounded on top of it. The house rings day and night with cries of pain, but with craven and selfish demands as well. The numbers of dead on the lawn of the park steadily increase, while the scum of the army stand round and stare at them with revolting curiosity. In the corner there is a man digging graves without ceasing.

A single shell lays out ten horses at once under the trees. They are not removed; they would be just as much in the way anywhere else. No sooner have thirty wounded been evacuated than there are fifty more in their place. The hospital in the church has had 631 entries in one day and there is one surgeon. Of course, there are other hospitals just as full. All rations and ammunition have to be brought up from Péronne, twenty miles away. All wounded, damaged guns, and transport trains have to be sent back there or even farther. We have had no fresh meat for a week; only one or two chickens serve to supply the illusion that chicken-broth was invented to stay one's hunger in war-time. The wells have been exhausted or defiled through the carelessness of the men. One or two sheep and cattle which might have been some use had they been properly slaughtered get butchered anyhow as if there were thousands of them. It is impossible to keep a room or any sort of shelter or bed-place clean because there is no water, no brooms, nor even the most primitive utensil available. Chairs and cupboards are broken up to light fires; we have no other fuel, and when this is used up there is nothing left. By the light of a guttering tallow candle two officers are writing reports and orders which will settle the fate of thousands of others, possibly our own. My bed is as hard as a board; when I get up from it I feel more of a wreck than when I lay down, but by changing position I try to pretend that I am getting rest.

Our division has not struck it lucky. It is ours which has had the heavy fighting on the heights on the north of Moreuil, which are mentioned in the reports. We can make no progress here. Even the fresh divisions do no better. The slippery ground is against us; for every step forward one slides back two, and the ground rises all the way.

I suppose the march and the fighting through the devastated zone were really harder work, but we were fresher then and we had a retreating enemy in front of us. I can still find no word nor image to express the awfulness of that waste. There is nothing like it on earth, nor can be. A desert is always a desert; but a desert which tells you all the time that it used not to be a desert is appalling. That is the tale which is told by the dumb, black stumps of the shattered trees which still stick up where there used to be villages. They were completely flayed by the splinters of the bursting shells, and they stand there like corpses upright. Not a blade of green anywhere round. The layer of soil which once covered the loose chalk is now buried underneath it. Thousands of shells have brought the stones to the surface and smothered the earth with its own entrails. There are miles upon miles of flat, empty, broken, and tumbled stone-quarry, utterly purposeless and useless in the middle of which stand groups of these blackened stumps of dead trees, poisoned oases, killed for ever.

This area ought to remain as it is. No road, no well, no settlement ought to be made there, and every ruler, leading statesmen, or president of a republic ought to be brought to see it, instead of swearing an oath on the Constitution, henceforth and for ever. Then there would be no more wars.

FIELD MARSHAL DOUGLAS HAIG

'With our backs to the wall'

Haig issued this famous order of the day after the Germans had engulfed twenty-four miles of the front during General Ludendorff's successful spring campaign in Flanders. But Ludendorff was to be the eventual loser:

To all ranks of the British Army in France and Flanders:

Three weeks ago to-day the enemy began his terrific attacks against us on a fifty-mile front. His objects are to separate us from the French, to take the Channel Ports and destroy the British Army.

In spite of throwing already 106 Divisions into the battle and enduring the most reckless sacrifice of human life, he has as yet made little progress towards his goals.

We owe this to the determined fighting and self-sacrifice of our troops. Words fail me to express the admiration which I feel for the splendid resistance offered by all ranks of our Army under the most trying circumstances.

Many amongst us now are tired. To those I would say that Victory will belong to the side which holds out the longest. The French Army is moving rapidly and in great force to our support

There is no course open to us but to fight it out. Every position must be held to the last man: there must be no retirement. With our backs to the wall and believing in the justice of our cause each one of us must fight on to the end. The safety of our homes and the Freedom of mankind alike depend upon the conduct of each one of us at this critical moment.

D. Haig, F.M.
Commander-in-Chief
British Armies in France.
General Headquarters
Thursday, April 11th, 1918.

Geoffrey Kennedy

'Sorrowing'

Geoffrey Kennedy, an Anglican chaplain at the front, was nicknamed Woodbine Willy because he gave Woodbine cigarettes to wounded and dying soldiers. He won the Military Cross in 1917, wrote two books of poems about his experiences and died in 1929.

There's a soul in the Eternal,
Standing stiff before the King.
There's a little English maiden
Sorrowing.
There's a proud and tearless woman,
Seeing pictures in the fire.
There's a broken battered body
On the wire.

MANCHESTER GUARDIAN

'Like Armageddon'

Three days after Haig's order of the day, this vivid report in the *Manchester Guardian* of 15 April suggested that the German advance was lunging forward:

> I wish I could make the people at home see this battle as it really is. Looking out over the Flanders plain from the low hills that mark the high tide of the struggle – hills that seem to rock under the thunder of the guns – you have at your feet a scene such as might be painted by an imaginative artist seeking to over-emphasise the impressiveness of war. It is a spectacle that fills every onlooker with awe; the grandeur of it touches even the tired brain of the fighting man when he is able to rest above the tumult of the plain; and the thought voiced by a staff officer as he swept the smoke-ridden horizon has come unconsciously to the lips of others. 'Yes,' he said, lowering his glasses, 'it looks like Armageddon.'
>
> Beyond everything you are beaten down by the number and the weight of guns. The land is sown with guns – red-hot guns – and they have turned it into a furnace. There it is, the battlefield we have dreamed about for a generation, thrown across forty miles of ruined farms and flaming villages, streaked and blotched with greasy smoke (and yesterday overlaid with heavier fog), its atmosphere heavy with that acrid scent of shell – a battlefield as flat as a table, creased by canals and shallow streams, with lines of khaki melting into sluggish fog and tiny tongues of red darting in every direction. It is all there, even to the general on his horse beside a tree, moving battalions with curt word and impassive face.
>
> The wounded staggering drunkenly up a country land in stained bandages, the cross-roads dressing-station where a

surgeon in shirt-sleeves stands at the head of a file of men like a ticket-taker at a theatre, the flash of bayonets in the mellow sunshine, the rattle of laden limbers going up and the ambulances crawling back, the dusty orderlies arriving with breathless messages in a stable yard where officers stand around a kitchen table, all fit naturally into the picture.

All around you is movement, swift or slow, but always methodical: a feeling of tension, but no confusion. The men are tired. You can see fatigue written on the faces of the staff officers as they pore over their scarred maps in a wayside building or under trees. When shells find them they move again, yet never lose grip of the threads that bind them to the front. Motorcyclists, hooded and masked, crouching over the handle bars, flash into the smoke with their despatches, weaving their way along a ranged highway unmindful of the shrapnel in their wake. Signallers, most imperturbable of men go up and down the front, trailing a new wire, mending broken ones. Their blue-and-white arm-bands are on every side – a badge of courage not always remembered by the public when they praise the fighting men. The fields are full of wagons and tethered horses. Little fires dot farms, where weary soldiers are cooking their first hot meal in rest.

Yet all you see clearly hardly touches the fringe of the panorama of this battle. The great agony is hidden yonder in the thick fog beyond the guns that overrun the naked countryside. Only the airmen dropping down through the bombardment can penetrate the heavy veil and see the German army lunging forward, its tentacles striking at Bailleul, at St. Venant, its massive body spread across the plain to the citadel of Lille. They follow the convulsive movements of the locked front lines and the fresh waves of grey flowing across the marshes, bunching together at a canal bridge to spread again on the other side or pausing at a ditch, for all the world like ants halted on a garden path. They are an army of roadmakers behind the storm troops, the roads from Lille choked with wagons and howitzers drawn by tractors and bridging trains crawling across the plain, the ant-like legions trying to turn Armentières into a storehouse under a storm of shell, piling ammunition, working furiously on a broken railway, carrying forward baulks of timber and iron girders to be thrown astride the River Lys if our guns go further back.

Nor is the battlefield at night a sight ever to be forgotten. The burning barns or cottages set alight by German shells, the flashes of guns and bursting shell under the clear starlit sky give one a sharp realisation of the grimmest side of war.

Floyd Gibbons

Death of the Red Knight

The German airman Baron Manfred von Richthofen in his red triplane was the greatest flying ace of the Great War. He had shot down eighty enemy planes when he was killed. This account of his final flight, his death and funeral in a book by the Special Correspondent of the *Chicago Tribune* captures the sense of chivalry and honour among the pilots who fought with such cavalier spirit on both sides of the war:

Trouble lit on young Mr May immediately. It came out of the sky from above and behind. It came with terrific speed in the form of an all-red Fokker triplane.

In the single cockpit sat a young man who, during three years of war, had earned the title of death's ablest ambassador. It was his proud boast that any flyer that got below and in front of him was a 'goner'. That was the way he had killed one of England's greatest aces. That was the way he had shot down eighty planes: that was the way he had sent scores of men to death.

Richthofen was flying on May's tail. He had selected him for his next victim. It will never be known whether the

Flying Uhlan recognized his selected prey as a beginner or not, but that is beside the case. In his string of victories, amateur victims counted just as much as a fallen master of the air. In the business of war one destroys as one can.

The nose of the all-red Fokker was within thirty yards of the fleeing Camel. May, looking over his shoulder, saw the approach of death. He saw the openwork air-cooling casings of the two Spandau barrels pointing down on him from above. Between the butt-ends of the machine-guns, the top of a leather helmeted head was just visible, down as far as a pair of dark glass goggles. This he could see through the blur of the invisible propeller. The eyes of Germany's deadliest marksman in the air peered through the glasses.

The open cockpit of May's Camel comes within the wire-crossed circle of Richthofen's sights. The pressure of a steady finger on the trigger – two jets of lead – short burst – spout from the gun barrels. Bullets snap through the air close by May's ears. Splinters fly from the struts before him.

He is defenceless from the rear. He can only shoot forward. Richthofen keeps behind him. The young Australian resorts to every stunt he knows to get out of that deadly line of fire. He darts to one side – darts back – goes into a zig-zag course, but his pursuer seems able to foresee his every manoeuvre. Richthofen keeps the nose of the red Fokker trained on the body of the fuselage. The short bursts continue to rip out from the Spandaus.

May pulls on the stick – kicks over the rudder – pulls up hard – loops – side-slips, and turns in the opposite direction. He comes out of the evolution only to find the sputtering red-nosed Fokker still bearing down on him.

The speed of the pair is terrific. They are going down the wind with full motors and depressed planes. May is flying for life against an agent of death who has seldom failed before.

Roy Brown, from the height of 1,000 feet, has seen the frantic efforts of his fledgling to extricate himself from the talons of the pursuing eagle. He noses the Camel down again at full speed towards the whirling duellists, who are now not more than two hundred feet off the ground.

Directly in front and beneath the pair are the trench positions and gun pits of the Thirty-third Australian Field Battery of the Fifth Division. They are sited near the crest of the ridge, and the waiting gunners watch with bated breath the two whirling, twisting forms of Richthofen and his harassed quarry.

May, still zig-zagging, makes for the crest of the ridge in a last desperate effort to land before those two streams of lead reach him. One bullet has already traversed his right arm. The pain is forgotten in the excitement of the moment.

The Australian gunners see that the leading machine is British and that the one behind it is an all-red Fokker.

The machine-gunner on the nearer flank of the battery aims forward and upward at the writhing oncoming pair, but so close is Richthofen upon May's tail that the gunner dare not fire. The two planes are almost in line. Another Lewis gunner beyond the ridge sprays a stream of lead upward. His range is 100 yards. He sees splinters flying from the woodwork of the German plane.

But Brown has arrived at the end of his dive. He comes out of it slightly above and to the right of the darting Fokker. His last drum of ammunition is in place. His sights come to bear on the red machine. He presses the trigger, and the ready Vickers speak in deadly unison.

He watches the tracer-bullets going to the red triplane from the right side. They hit the tail first. A slight pull on the stick – a fractional elevation of the Camel's nose, and the Canadian's line of fire starts to tuck a seam up the body of the Fokker.

Richthofen, with his spurting Spandaus still trained on May, is unaware of this new attack from the rear.

Brown sees his tracers penetrate the side of the Fokker cockpit.

The Fokker wavers in mid-air – falters – glides earthward.
The Red Knight of Germany goes down.

Mellersh, from the Australian line beyond which he has
landed, has witnessed the escape of May, and now he hears
the roar of Brown's motor as it swoops overhead less than a
hundred feet off the ground.

The red Fokker hits the uneven ground, but rolls on an
even keel. It loses one undercarriage wheel and comes to a
stop right side up in a shell-hole not fifty yards from where
Mellersh is standing. It is on the outskirts of the ruined village of Sailly-le-Sec, not far from Corbie.

The German pilot is sitting bolt upright in his seat,
strapped to the back. His hands still hold the control stick
between his knees. There is blood on that part of the face
which shows below the strapped helmet and the broken goggles. Blood is coming from the mouth, and the lower jaw
sags. The man is dead.

The form is unstrapped from the seat and laid on the ground.
From the pockets of the unknown are removed a gold watch
and some papers carrying the name and rank of the bearer.

'My God, it's Richthofen!' exclaims Mellersh.

'They got the bloody baron!' an Australian in the group
shouts over to the next trench. Men crawl forward to take a
look at the body of the terror of the air.

Under Mellersh's instruction the body is carried with awed
reverence to the nearest underground shelter, where a medical
officer unfastens the bloodstained leather jacket and opens
the red-wet blue silk pyjama coat found underneath. There is
a bullet-hole in both the right and the left breast.

Richthofen's body lay in state in one of the English tent
hangars at Bertangles the following day. All English airmen
who could be present viewed the remains and paid their
respects in silent admiration for a brave foe.

Richthofen was buried with full military honours on the
afternoon of the day after his death. From the tent hangar, a

plain black-stained wooden box, containing the remains, were carried on the shoulders of six fighting pilots of the Royal Air Force, who acted as pall-bearers.

The coffin was placed in an open Army tender and covered with floral tributes that came from all neighbouring air squadrons. Preceded by a guard of Australian infantrymen, who carried their rifles reversed, the cortège proceeded slowly down the road beside the aerodrome. To the left of the road, the hum and roar of motors told of the arrival and departure of fighting planes to and from the front. The war continued as usual, but the busy war traffic on the road slowed up for once to the pace of a solemn funeral.

The procession arrived at the cemetery on the outskirts of Bertangles. There, at the foot of a tall poplar tree, an open grave awaited. The black box was placed beside the grave while the pall-bearers stood bareheaded at the foot. At one side were stationed two files of Anzacs, standing rigidly with bowed heads and the muzzles of their rifles grounded. French children and old civilians beyond the years of military service attended, while Australians from the ranks ranged themselves behind the hedge fence on the road.

From the east, the rumble of the guns, continues, as the English chaplain in white surplice repeats the words of the burial service of the Church of England.

The coffin is gently lowered into the grave by the pall-bearers. The quiet is broken by a sharp order from an officer. The double rank of Australians snaps to attention. Another order, and they raise their rifles. Three volleys – a parting salute – are fired over the remains of a respected fallen foe. The grave is filled.

On the following day, a British pilot flew low over Richthofen's old aerodrome at Cappy. He threw down a metal container attached to a streamer. It fell not far from the hangars in front of which the German ace had stopped to pet the puppy mascot three days before.

The container bore a photograph of the funeral party firing its parting salute over the grave in Bertangles cemetery, and the following message:

To the German Flying Corps

Rittmeister Baron Manfred von Richthofen was killed in aerial combat on 21 April 1918. He was buried with full military honours.

From the British Royal Air Force

JOHN WILLIAMS

Rationing

The war was now in its fourth year and there were serious shortages of food on the home front:

At the end of January Londoners found themselves subjected to two meatless days a week. But this just touched the fringe of the food emergency. There was now only one recourse: compulsory rationing of all main foodstuffs. One item – sugar – was already just rationed, after prolonged scarcity. [Robert Graves, married in January, had to save a month's sugar, along with butter, for his three-tiered wedding cake. Even then the cake had a plaster case of imitation icing.] The general order came a month later, applying to London and the Home Counties; and a further order, early in April, brought in the rest of the country. Rationing covered butcher's meat and bacon, butter, margarine and lard. Two cards were issued to every registered consumer, one for meat and bacon, the other for fats. They contained detachable coupons allowing for a weekly 15 ounces of meat, 5 ounces of bacon, and 4 ounces of fats, which could be used either for household purchases or meals in restaurants and cafés. The April rationing order came in none too soon, for by then meat was so scarce that some butchers were open for only one hour a day. Hoarding attracted a £100 fine. In the

London area the benefits of rationing – improving, as it did, food distribution in relation to known local demands – were immediately apparent. Queues almost disappeared. The final rationing step came in July, when the existing cards were withdrawn and national ration books distributed, containing coupons for all previously rationed foods. With milk restricted under a separate scheme, the only items remaining unrationed were tea, cheese and bread.

Under the urgency of the war-effort, many ordinary refinements of life had vanished for the duration. In March lighting was banned in entertainment places and restaurants after 10.30 p.m. Along with the stringencies, there was a strong anti-waste drive. Waste paper collections in April reached 3,000 tons. Meanwhile food production was proceeding vigorously. At the start of April the king directed that the flowerbeds around the Queen Victoria Memorial outside Buckingham Palace were to be planted with vegetables instead of the customary scarlet geraniums. And this Eastertide saw extensive vegetable growing in the Royal Parks, Kew Gardens having two hundred acres under cultivation. On the suburban commons allotmenteers were out in force, furthering the movement that in the last months had taken in 3,000 additional acres.

MICHAEL MACDONAGH

The Government is ruling almost by dictatorship, Michael MacDonagh complains, as rationing applies throughout Britain:

July 15: This is Thursday. Since Monday the compulsory rationing of food has been nationalised, in the sense of being applied to the whole country. The rationing-cards hitherto in use are withdrawn, and national ration-books issued, each containing separate coupons of different colours for the rationed foods, which are sugar, butter, margarine, lard, butchers' meat and bacon. Tea and cheese are not rationed, but authority is given to local food committees to ration them in their areas should supplies fall short. There is no rationing of potatoes or other vegetables. Nor is bread rationed. I have already recorded that in order to enable the four-pound loaf to be sold to consumers at ninepence the millers and bakers have been subsidised by the State to the amount of £40,000,000 a year. So considerable has been the increase in the consumption of bread that, according to the latest returns, the subsidy is approaching the sum of £60,000,000! Thus do the Government ensure for us our daily bread.

Well, each and every individual must now have a ration book, if he wants to make sure from day to day of getting a good meal. Forty millions of books for adults have been issued (there are separate books for children), and it is essential that each must contain the holder's name and address and the name of the local food committee by which it has been issued. The appropriate coupon is cut out by the grocer, butcher or provision dealer when the holder buys his ration.

The coupons are used also in hotels and eating-houses. I had a cup of tea to-day at one of Lyons's shops and from their menu-card copied the following particulars:

'Half a coupon is required for one sausage; half veal and ham pie; or egg and bacon.

'A whole coupon is required for two sausages; plate of cold ham or tongue; or stewed steak and carrots.'

No meal was served until the coupon or the half-coupon was given to the waitress. Some had to go without a meal. The excuse that the ration-book had been left with the grocer or butcher or at home, and would be surely brought to-morrow, was not accepted. On the other hand, when the coupon was forthcoming the money was not required until the meal was eaten. Payment is of lesser importance than coupons!

We are now living under a Government that rules practically by dictatorship. It compels the citizens to join the Army and fight the Germans; it restricts the citizens to the kind and quantity of food they are to eat – not to speak of the other numerous bans imposed upon our movements by the Defence of the Realm regulations.

Are we not to be pitied!

EVADNE PRICE

'Forgive me, Mother'

The parents of the young women – 'England's Splendid Daughters' – who worked at the French front as ambulance drivers had no idea of the horror they experienced nor any wish to know. One of these young women was Winifred Constance Young, who kept a diary which was used by Evadne Price (1886–1985) when she wrote *Not So Quiet* under the pseudonym Helen Zenna Smith in 1930. It was intended to be a parody of Erich Maria Remarque's *All Quiet on the Western Front*, but became a memorial to the dead, a pacifist denunciation of the futility of war, based on Winifred Young's experiences in 1918 – which a mother simply could not comprehend.

Oh, come with me, Mother and Mrs Evans-Mawnington. Let me show you the exhibits straight from the battlefield. This will be something original to tell your committees, while they knit their endless miles of khaki scarves . . . something to spout from the platform at your recruiting meetings. Come with me. Stand just there.

Here we have the convoy gliding into the station now, slowly, so slowly. In a minute it will disgorge its sorry cargo. My ambulance doors are open, waiting to receive. See, the train has stopped. Through the occasionally drawn blinds you will observe the trays slotted into the sides of the train. Look closely, Mother and Mrs Evans-Mawnington, and you shall see what you shall see. Those trays each contain something that was once a whole man . . . the heroes who have done their bit for king and country . . . the heroes who marched blithely through the streets of London town singing 'Tipperary', while you cheered and waved your flags hysterically. They are not singing now, you will observe. Shut your ears, Mother and Mrs Evans-Mawnington, lest their groans and heart-rending cries linger as long in your memory as in the memory of the daughter you sent out to help win the war.

See the stretcher-bearers lifting the trays one by one, slotting them deftly into my ambulance. Out of the way, quickly, Mother and Mrs Evans-Mawnington – lift your silken skirts aside . . . a man is spewing blood, the moving has upset him, finished him . . . He will die on the way to hospital if he doesn't die before the ambulance is loaded. I know . . . All this is old history to me. Sorry this has happened. It isn't pretty to see a hero spewing up his life's blood in public, is it? Much more romantic to see him in the picture papers being awarded the VC, even if he is minus a limb or two. A most unfortunate occurrence!

That man strapped down? That raving, blaspheming creature screaming filthy words you don't know the meaning of . . . words your daughter uses in everyday conversation, a habit she has contracted from vulgar contact of this kind. Oh, merely gone mad, Mother and Mrs Evans-Mawnington. He may have seen a headless body running on and on, with blood spurting from the trunk. The crackle of the frost-stiff dead men packing the duck-boards watertight may have gradually undermined his reason. There are many things the sitters tell me on our long night rides that could have done this.

No, not shell-shock. The shell-shock cases take it more quietly as a rule, unless they are suddenly startled. Let me find you an example. Ah, the man they are bringing out now. The one staring straight ahead at nothing . . . twitching, twitching, twitching, each limb working in a different direction, like a Jumping Jack worked by a jerking string. Look at him, both of you. Bloody awful, isn't it, Mother and Mrs Evans-Mawnington? That's shell-shock. If you dropped your handbag on the platform, he would start to rave as madly as the other. What? You won't try the experiment? You can't watch him? Why not? *Why not?* I have to, every night. Why the hell can't you do it for once? Damn your eyes.

Forgive me, Mother and Mrs Evans-Mawnington. That was not the kind of language a nicely-brought-up young lady from Wimbledon Common uses. I forget myself. We will begin again.

See the man they are fitting into the bottom slot. He is coughing badly. No, no pneumonia. Not tuberculosis. Nothing so picturesque. Gently, gently, stretcher-bearers . . . he is about done. He is coughing up clots of pinky-green filth. Only his lungs, Mother and Mrs Evans-Mawnington. He is coughing well tonight. That is gas. You've heard of gas, haven't you? It burns and shrivels the lungs to . . . to the mess you see on the ambulance floor there. He's about the age of Bertie, Mother. Not unlike Bertie, either with his gentle brown eyes and fair curly hair. Bertie would look up pleadingly like that in between coughing up his lungs . . . The son you have so generously given to the war. The son you are so eager to send out to the trenches before Roy Evans-Mawnington, in case Mrs Evans-Mawnington scores over you at the next recruiting meeting. 'I have given my only son.'

Cough, cough, little fair-haired boy. Perhaps somewhere your mother is thinking of you . . . boasting of the life she has so nobly given . . . the life you thought was your own, but which is hers to squander as she thinks fit. 'My boy is not a slacker, thank God.' Cough away, little boy, cough away. What does it matter, providing your mother doesn't have to face the shame of her son's cowardice?

FLOYD GIBBONS

'The glory of American arms'

Until he was wounded in this engagement, Floyd Gibbons reported on the American Expeditionary Force for the *Chicago Tribune*. His account of the death of the German fighter pilot von Richthofen appears on pages 366–71. At the climax of Germany's triumphant advances in the spring of 1918, according to Gibbons, the American soldier stepped into the breach to save the democracy of the world.

It was at five o'clock on the bright afternoon of June 6th that the United States Marines began to carve their way into history in the battle of the Bois de Belleau. Major General Harbord, former Chief of Staff to General Pershing, was in command of the Marine brigade. Orders were received for a general advance on the brigade front. The main objectives were the eastern edge of the Bois de Belleau and towns of Bussiares, Torcy and Bouresches.

Owing to the difficulty of liaison in the thickets of the wood, and because of the almost impossible task of directing it in conjunction with the advancing lines, the artillery preparation for the attack was necessarily brief. At five o'clock to the dot the Marines moved out from the woods in perfect order, and started across the wheat fields in four long waves. It was a beautiful sight, these men of ours going across those flat fields toward the tree clusters beyond from which the Germans poured a murderous machine gun fire.

The woods were impregnated with nests of machine guns, but our advance proved irresistible. Many of our men fell, but those that survived pushed on through the woods, bayoneting right and left and firing as they charged. So sweeping was the advance that in some places small isolated units of our men found themselves with Germans both before and behind them.

The enemy put up a stubborn resistance on the left, and it was not until later in the evening that this part of the line reached the northeast edge of the woods, after it had completely surrounded a most populous machine gun nest which was located on a rocky hill. During the fighting Colonel Catlin was wounded and Captain Laspierre, the French liaison officer, was gassed, two casualties which represented a distinct blow to the brigade, but did not hinder its further progress.

On the right Lieutenant Robertson, with twenty survivors out of his entire platoon, emerged from the terrific enemy barrage and took the town of Bouresches at the point of the bayonet. Captain Duncan, receiving word that one Marine company, with a determination to engage the enemy in hand-to-hand combat, had gone two hundred yards in advance, raced forward on the double quick with the 96th Marine Company, and was met by a terrific machine gun barrage from both sides of Bouresches.

Lieutenant Robertson, looking back, saw Duncan and the rest of his company going down like flies as they charged through the barrage. He saw Lieutenant Bowling get up from the ground, his face white with pain, and go stumbling ahead with a bullet in his shoulder. Duncan, carrying a stick and with his pipe in his mouth, was mowed down in the rain of lead. Robertson saw Dental Surgeon Osborne pick Duncan up. With the aid of a Hospital Corps man, they had just gained the shelter of some trees when a shell wiped all three of them out.

In the street fighting that ensued in Bouresches, Lieutenant Robertson's orderly, Private Dunlavy, who was later killed in the defence of the town, captured one of the enemy's own machine guns and turned it against them.

In the dense woods the Germans showed their mastery of

machine gun manipulation and the method of infiltration by which they would place strong units in our rear and pour in a deadly fire. Many of these guns were located on rocky ridges, from which they could fire to all points. These Marines worked with reckless courage against heavy odds, and the Germans exacted a heavy toll for every machine gun that was captured or disabled, but in spite of losses the Marine advance continued. Lieutenant Overton, command- ing the 76th Company, made a brilliant charge against a strong German position at the top of a rocky hill. He and his men captured all of the guns and all of their crews. Overton was hit later when the Germans retaliated by a concentra- tion of fire against the captured position for forty-eight hours.

Lieutenant Robertson, according to the report brought back by a regimental runner, was last seen flat on a rock not twenty yards away from one enemy gun, at which he kept shooting with an automatic in each hand. He was hit three times before he consented to let his men carry him to the rear.

'There was not an officer left in the 82nd Company.' According to a letter by Major Frank E. Evans, Adjutant of the Sixth, 'Major Sibley and his Adjutant reorganised them under close fire and led them in a charge that put one par- ticular machine gun nest out of business at the most critical time in all the fighting. I heard later that at that stage some- one said: "Major Sibley ordered that" – and another man said: "Where in hell is Sibley?" Sibley was twenty yards away at that time and hush went down the line when they saw him step out to lead the charge.

'And when the word got around that dead-tired, crippled outfit that "the Old Man" was on the line, all hell could not have stopped that rush.'

In such fashion did the Marines go through the Bois de Belleau. Their losses were heavy, but they did the work. The sacrifice was necessary. Paris was in danger. The Marines constituted the thin line between the enemy and Paris. The Marines not only held that line – they pushed it forward.

The fighting was terrific. In one battalion alone the casualties numbered sixty-four per cent officers and sixty-four per cent men. Several companies came out of the fighting under command of their first sergeants, all of the officers having been killed or wounded.

I witnessed some of that fighting. I was with the Marines at the opening of the battle. I never saw men charge to their death with finer spirit . . . The bravery of that Marine brigade in the Bois de Belleau fight will ever remain a bright chapter in the records of the American Army. For the performance of deeds of exceptional valour, more than a hundred Marines were awarded Distinguished Service Crosses. General Pershing, in recognition of the conduct of the Second Division, issued the following order:

'It is with inexpressible pride and satisfaction that your commander recounts your glorious deeds on the field of battle. In the early days of June on a front of twenty kilometres, after night marches and with only reserve rations which you carried, you stood like a wall against the enemy advance on Paris. For this timely action you have received the thanks of the French people whose homes you saved and the generous praise of your comrades in arms.

'Since the organisation of our sector, in the face of strong opposition, you have advanced your lines two kilometres on a front of eight kilometres. You have engaged and defeated with great loss three German divisions and have occupied important strong points – Belleau Wood, Bouresches, and Vaux. You have taken about 1,400 prisoners, many machine guns, and much other material. The complete success of the infantry was made possible by the splendid co-operation of the artillery, by the aid and assistance of the engineer and signal troops, by the diligent and watchful care of the medical and supply services, and by the unceasing work of the well-organised staff. All elements of the division have worked together as a well-trained machine.

'Amid the dangers and trials of battle, every officer and every man has done well his part. Let the stirring deeds, hardships and sacrifices of the past month remain forever a bright spot in our history. Let the sacred memory of our fallen comrades spur us on to renewed effort and to the glory of American arms.'

Vera Brittain

The Death of a Brother, 15 June 1918

Two years earlier Vera Brittain had learned of the death of her fiancé Roland Leighton. Now it was the turn of Roland's great friend Edward, Vera's brother:

I had just announced to my father, as we sat over tea in the dining room, that I really must do up Edward's papers and take them to the post office before it closed for the weekend, when there came the sudden loud clattering at the front-door knocker that always meant a telegram.

For a moment I thought that my legs would not carry me, but they behaved quite normally as I got up and went to the door. I knew what was in the telegram – I had known for a week – but because the persistent hopefulness of the human heart refused to allow intuitive certainty to persuade the reason of that which it knows, I opened and read it in a tearing anguish of suspense.

'Regret to inform you Captain E. H. Brittain M.C. killed in action Italy June 15th.'

'No answer,' I told the boy mechanically, and handed the telegram to my father, who had followed me into the hall. As we went back into the dining room I saw, as though I had never seen them before, the bowl of blue delphiniums on the table; their intense colour, vivid, ethereal, seemed too radiant for earthly flowers.

Long after the family had gone to bed and the world had grown silent, I crept into the dining room to be alone with Edward's portrait. Carefully closing the door, I turned on the light and looked at the pale, pictured face, so dignified, so steadfast, so tragically mature. He had been through so much – far, far more than those beloved friends who had died at an earlier stage of the interminable War, leaving him alone to mourn their loss. Fate might have allowed him the little, sorry compensation of survival, the chance to make his lovely music in honour of their memory. It seemed indeed the last irony that he should have been killed by the countrymen of Fritz Kreisler, the violinist whom of all others he had most greatly admired.

And suddenly, as I remembered all the dear afternoons and evenings when I had followed him on the piano as he played his violin, the sad, searching eyes of the portrait were more than I could bear, and falling on my knees before it I began to cry, 'Edward! Oh, Edward!' in dazed repetition, as though my persistent crying and calling would somehow bring him back.

Captain M. S. Esler

Prisoner of War

Captain Esler, of the Royal Army Medical Corps, was captured in 1918 and became a prisoner of war at a camp at Stralsund on Germany's Baltic coast. It was a much better life than being in the trenches:

What a different and more happy sight met our eyes in our new camp on our little prison island. There were newly erected huts each hut holding eight men to a room and twelve rooms to each hut. There were two small rooms with stoves where all 96 cooked their meals. The cooking came later when we had something to cook. There was a recreation hall and, also, playing fields and we had the sea to look at and the fishing boats going out each morning and coming back each night. We would be allowed to fish from the shore if we could get tackle. There were blankets and, I think sheets on the beds which was a pleasant change from the louse infected straw at Baden. There was a great uplift of spirits at the change for the better. Later, of course, freedom of movement outside the camp, or rather lack of it, began to weary us.

Before being admitted to this Elysium we went to the showers for the very necessary process of de-lousing. All our clothing was taken away to be baked, we got a top and bottom shave and a shower so that we emerged as hairless as the day that we were born. We could hardly recognise each other. It was wonderful to be louse free after three months, no more scratching and irritation of the skin at nights. At last we were able to write a card to our people to say that we were prisoners of war and to give the address of our camp. Our relations had heard nothing about us since we were reported missing three months previously and there was much relief on the home front.

A week after we had settled in and the people at home and the War Office had heard that we were prisoners the food parcels started arriving. The first one came from that wonderful institution 'The British Red Cross'. I forget the exact contents but I remember the first things that we dealt with, a loaf of white bread, a packet of tea, condensed milk, sugar and cigarettes. Then Aladdin's cave was opened gold, emeralds and pearls of great price were discovered but that was nothing compared to our first parcel. Pearls of great price are not edible.

We hacked a slice of bread from our loaf and brewed a cup of strong tea with plenty of sugar. We ate the bread dry, we did not want to spoil its flavour. Never can I remember enjoying a meal so much. After the meal we lay on our beds and each lit a cigarette and smoked in complete silence. The magic of the moment was too great to have our concentration disturbed. Even the greatest gourmet cannot savour the delight of eating unless they have, first, experienced a period of enforced starvation.

After this private parcels began coming in for all of us. From starvation we reached completion during the next few weeks. In our room we pooled our parcels and the menu was decided upon for the following day. We were soon having three course lunches and four course dinners. The situation became quite ridiculous, because, at the same time, the sentries and guards outside our huts at night consisted of older soldiers who were not fit for duty at the front and they were starving as we had been. We used to pass bits of bread, legs of chicken, fruit and all sorts of things out to them, and those were most gratefully received. I had never heard of prisoners feeding their jailers before.

I was asked whether I would like to play hockey. I said that I had never played but would try anything once. I was not very good and was never asked again! There were no tennis courts and no horses, so my exercise consisted of walking around the perimeters of the barbed wire and I always made a point of walking two miles in the morning and two miles in the evening.

When we got our parcels we got packs of playing cards, and what a godsend that was. We had four keen bridge players in our room and every evening we played the same four from 8 to 11 p.m. What a wonderful game that is, I am so sorry that the younger generation have not the time to take it up, for it seems to be dying out altogether.

As far as I can remember, I think there were on our camp about six hundred officers. They were represented by all the different trades and professions in civilian life. There were

doctors, there were actors, artists, business men, school teachers and university professors. Classes were therefore arranged,
and students who had left their studies to join the army were
able to take up working for their degrees in any subject under
the tuition of eminent tutors. Also we were able to get a show
together for entertainment run by men who had been top
actors and entertainers in civilian life. These were always
enjoyed by the German staff who attended.

SIEGFRIED SASSOON

'Can I forget? . . .'

Can I forget the voice of one who cried
For me to save him, save him, as he died? . . .

Can I forget the face of one whose eyes
Could trust me in his utmost agonies? . . .

I will remember you; and from your wrongs
Shall rise the power and poignance of my songs:
And this shall comfort me until the end,
That I have been your captain and your friend.

August 10, 1918

ERNEST THURTLE MP

Shootings at Dawn

After the war, when he was wounded in the throat, Ernest Thurtle
became an MP in 1923 and campaigned for the abolition of the
death penalty for military crimes. His pamphlet 'Shootings at
Dawn and the Army Death Penalty at Work' drew on letters written by soldiers who had witnessed firing squads during the First
World War. The military death penalty was abolished in 1930.

'I quite agree with you that the Death Penalty should be abolished. It cost me one of my best pals during the War. His name was Private "W", B Coy., 2nd Battalion S.W.B., 87th Brigade, 29th Division. He deserted twice or three times, but he was not a coward, as a braver man never went on active Service. He told me that the reason of his conduct in that way was that he was the sole support of a widowed mother, and that the Government only paid her an allowance of 5s. 6d. a week. He said he would never soldier until they gave her more, which was not done, according to his own words to me. The last time he deserted was at the beginning of July, 1918. He was arrested at St. Omer early in August, 1918, was court-martialled and sentenced to death, the sentence being confirmed by Sir Douglas Haig. The execution was carried out at dawn on August 10, 1918, between the town of Hazebrouck and the village of Bore, by men from his own Company, and he was buried in Bore Cemetery.'

'"Come out, you" ordered the corporal of the guard to me, I crawled forth, it was snowing heavily. "Stand there!" he said, pushing me between two sentries. "Quick march" and away we went, not as I dreaded, to my first taste of "pack drill" but out and up the long street to an R.E. dump. There the police corporal handed in a "chit", whereupon three posts, three ropes and a spade were given me to carry back. Our return journey took us past the guard room, up a short hill until we reached a secluded spot surrounded by trees. Certain measurements were made in the snow, after which I was ordered to dig three holes at stipulated distances apart. I began to wonder . . . Could it be . . .? No, perhaps spies . . . perhaps oh, perhaps only my fancy . . . The next scene a piercingly cold dawn; a crowd of brass hats, the medical officer, and three firing parties. Three stakes a few yards apart and a ring of sentries around the woodland to keep the curious away. A motor ambulance arrives conveying the doomed men. Manacled and blindfolded they are helped out and tied up to the stakes. Over each man's heart is placed an envelope. The officer in charge holds his stick aloft and as it falls thirty-six bullets usher the souls of three of Kitchener's men to the great unknown. As a military prisoner I helped clear the traces of that triple murder. I took the posts down. I helped carry those bodies towards their last resting place; I collected all the blood-soaked straw and burnt it. Acting upon police instructions I took all their belongings from the dead men's tunics (discarded before being shot). A few letters, a pipe, some fags, a photo. I could tell you of the silence of the military police after reading one letter from a little girl to "Dear Daddy", of the blood-stained snow that horrified the French peasants, of the chaplain's confession that braver men he had never met than those three men he prayed with just before the fatal dawn . . . I could take you to the graves of the murdered.'

JOHN TERRAINE

The Beginning of the End

The military historian John Terraine sets the scene for Haig's greatest triumph on 8 August, which was described by Ludendorff as the blackest day of the German Army in the history of the war:

The Battle of Amiens was one of the great surprises of the War – a military classic. Zero hour for Rawlinson's Fourth Army was 4.20 a.m.; for the French First Army on his right it was three-quarters of an hour later. The preparations had been carried out with meticulous secrecy; they involved the assembly of over 500 tanks – the largest concentration yet achieved – on the British front; Rawlinson also deployed over 2,000 guns, 684 of them heavies; the Allies between them massed 1,900 aircraft for the occasion. An outstanding achievement of surprise was the concealment of the whole Cavalry Corps – a dangerously conspicuous unit. But the peak of all was the secret transfer of the four divisions of the Canadian Corps, nearly 100,000 strong, from the Ypres front, their insertion behind the right wing of the Australian Corps, and unsuspected entry into the battle. The skills required for such arrangements were great; their smooth completion was a due reward for the slow, arduous process of professionalisation which the British Army had been undergoing in the midst of war. Not since the compact, Regular Expeditionary Force of 1914 had quietly mobilised, embarked and deployed at Mons, had such cool efficiency been seen.

On August 8th Nature favoured the Allies, as she had favoured the Germans on March 21st: a thick mist covered the battlefield, neutralising the effect of the defending machine guns. Tanks and infantry loomed upon the Germans suddenly out of this mist, over-running their defences. By 1.30 p.m. the day's main fighting was over. By then the Canadians had advanced 8 miles; they took over 5,000 prisoners and 161 guns. The Australians were on all their objectives, except on their extreme left; they took nearly 8,000 prisoners and 173 guns. The total German losses for the day were about 27,000. Their Official Monograph states:

'As the sun set on the battlefield on 8 August the greatest defeat which the German Army had suffered since the beginning of the war was an accomplished fact.'

BARRIE PITT

The Black Day of the German Army

Winston Churchill chose the day after the opening of the Amiens battle to visit his old friend Henry Rawlinson, who commanded the 4th Army on the Somme and broke the German Hindenburg

Line at Amiens. As he passed streams of German prisoners, he noted a significant change of attitude among the German soldiers.

'No one who has been a prisoner of war himself,' [Churchill] wrote, 'can be indifferent to the lot of the soldier whom the fortunes of war condemn to this plight. The woe-begone expression of the officers contrasted sharply with the almost cheerful countenances of the rank and file.'

There were, of course, many more rank and file than officers, and troops glad to fall into enemy hands belong to a losing army. This was a point which was already impressing itself deeply into Ludendorff's mind as he read, with growing horror, of various events which had taken place during that epochal first day of the Amiens battle. It was not so much the loss of territory, of material, or even of men, which worried him; the Allies had lost far more in all these categories every day for over a week during the March retreat, but they had not lost the war. It was an entirely different type of loss which spelt out to him the presage of doom. It was the loss of spirit.

According to reports which reached him, six German divisions had collapsed that day in scenes unprecedented in German military legend. Companies had surrendered to single tanks, platoons to single infantrymen, and on one occasion retreating troops had hurled abuse at a division going forward resolutely to buttress the sagging line, accusing them of blacklegging and of 'toadying to the Junkers'. These were, indeed, ominous happenings, and they sounded in Ludendorff's already melancholy mind uncommonly like the first warning notes of disaster.

'August 8th was the Black Day of the German Army . . .' he wrote afterwards. 'It put the decline of our fighting powers beyond all doubt. The Army had ceased to be a perfect fighting instrument.'

There is a wealth of significance in that last sentence. To a Commander capable of believing that any Army could be a 'perfect instrument' – composed as it is of frail humanity – the first signs of serious infirmity in his own, will come as a considerable shock: and possibly owing to the narrowness of Ludendorff's knowledge and experience, he lacked mental resilience. That the German Army had suffered a defeat and that some of its elements had failed to uphold its highest military traditions were undoubtedly facts of high importance: but their effect upon Ludendorff was infinitely more so.

This was crisis.

The most significant event of 1918 did not occur on the field of battle. It occurred in Ludendorff's office – for as he read the reports of the fighting of 8 August he began to believe that his Army was breaking up from within.

And history is made in men's minds.

H. J. C. MARSHALL

Tomb of the German Empire

Captain Marshall was adjutant to the 46th Division, Territorial Force, in September when its soldiers attacked three strongly defended lines of German trenches, crossed the St Quentin Canal and broke through the Hindenburg Line in one of the decisive battles of the war. It was that evening Ludendorff first made peace overtures. Between 24 September and 11 November the 46th Division took 8000 prisoners and 120 guns at the cost of 800 casualties.

The fateful morning dawned, cold and misty, but with a promise of sun later. At 5.50 a.m. (zero hour) a cyclone of shells descended upon the German lines, under cover of which our men dashed on the nearest trenches where 1,000 Germans were found dead, mostly from the fire of the 800 machine guns, which had been arranged to rake these trenches immediately the attack commenced. Our men, by hook or by crook, got across the Canal. From every gun position sprang continuous streams of fire, while a perfect tornado of sound rent the air.

The Bridge at Riqueval, which the Germans were too late to destroy, proved of the greatest use in getting our artillery forward, while the Royal Engineers built two other bridges, suitable for field artillery, on the concrete dams across the Canal bed.

Prior to the attack we had provided the Battalion Commanders with 10,000 three-inch squares of tin, cut from biscuit boxes. These were issued to the men, who were told to flash them about when one of our aeroplanes was overhead. This enabled the aeroplanes to judge the strength of our troops in any part of the battlefield, and to note the positions in which they had established themselves, and to report to the G.O.C. It also enabled the aeroplanes to drop boxes of ammunition where they were useful.

The arrival of the aeroplanes with news of the fight was a very pretty sight. A large circle had been marked out on the ground in white canvas, and the observer from each plane had to drop his message in or near this circle. He signalled by a maroon that he was dropping a message, and then threw it downwards; a long trail of ribbons marked its flight through the air, and smoke rose from where it had dropped. Many messages actually fell inside the circle.

Suddenly the mist rose, and the sun of our 'Austerlitz' appeared, strong and refulgent. Over the brow of the rise opposite to us came a great grey column. Never had we seen such a thing; we counted the files; there were nearly 1,000 prisoners in the column. Half an hour later a similar column appeared, and then another and another – we had broken the Hindenburg Line, and 4,200 prisoners, 70 cannon and more than 1,000 machine guns were the trophies of the fight gathered by our single Division.

The huge dugout, or system of dugouts and tunnels, which ran from Bellenglise to a point near Magny-la-Fosse, was found to contain nearly 2,000 nerve-shattered men who surrendered in haste, the more especially as all exits were stopped by squads of bombers, and my old friend Captain Teeton and his men had dragged a German howitzer to the Magny end of the tunnel, and were cheerfully firing it down the opening. The shell bursts in the narrow tunnel cannot have been very comforting to our Bosche friends.

The tunnel was fitted up with a complete electric light system, and provided with a very fine Field Hospital, with its equipment, staff of surgeons, etc. Lt. Read, the Divisional Intelligence Officer, informed me of this, stating that the Electrical Staff had been taken prisoners. I asked him where they were and was told that they were on the way to the nearest Prisoners' Camp. On this I suggested that he should try to get hold of them again, as if the tunnel, which we, naturally, were making use of, was mined, the men would be sure to know it.

Within a few hours he had retrieved them, and on being put to run their engine again, they made haste to point out the change-over switch by which it had been arranged that the mines should be fired automatically on the re-starting of the engine. The positions of the charges were also pointed out with alacrity.

It was into these tunnels that King George descended. I saw the tunnels again six months later. Streamers of the dry-rot fungus descended from roof to floor, in six-foot pendants. The timber supports appeared to be in imminent danger of collapse, and the weird aspect of the caverns, viewed by a flickering candle, made me chary of venturing very far in their dismal recesses. The very airs which came from them, dank and tainted by the fungus breath, seemed fitting to this tomb in which were interred the hopes of the German World Empire.

MAJOR DENIS REITZ

Blasting through the Hindenburg Line

Major Denis Reitz was second-in-command of the 1st Royal Scots Fusiliers when they attacked the German Hindenburg Line on 27 September 1918. This account appears in the memoirs of Lt. Col. Archie Browne held at the Imperial War Museum.

At twenty minutes past five the British barrage came down on the German line with a tremendous roar, and our battalion stood ready with bayonets fixed to vault the parapet at the given word to advance. At zero plus ten minutes the barrage moved forward and the signal was given for us to go; the men swarmed over the parapet straight for the German line.

Almost at once the German S.O.S. barrage came down upon us as we scrambled and stumbled over the wire, screwstakes and shell craters that obstructed every yard of the way. I have a confused memory of shells spurting and flashing, of men going down in great numbers, and then the Germans rising from behind their breastworks to meet the attackers, and then the Scots Fusiliers clubbing and bayoneting among them.

The enemy artillery then ceased firing to protect their next line of defence and our men quickly rushed across No Man's Land and dropped down into the great Hindenburg Line. They rounded up prisoners in the trench and flushed out those who were in the dug outs by throwing down Mills grenades in to the shaft openings.

The trench we captured was six feet wide by eight feet deep, and every few yards along the parapet stood a machine gun, and in addition there were many trench mortars and anti-tank rifles.

The trench was full of dead and wounded Germans and

beside almost every machine gun lay its crew, smitten down by the hurricane of artillery barrage.

By this time the British guns had lifted their range on to the next enemy trench, some four hundred yards in front, and the advance continued to the next objective, with the 2nd Royal Scots leap-frogging through us. In our advance the 1st Royal Scots had suffered many casualties, and in one small area I counted over one hundred officers and men lying in all manner of attitudes; some were still hugging their rifles, others horribly torn by shells, and others in shell holes as if they had crawled there to die.

Meanwhile the main battle raged unabated. Overhead wheeled squadrons of aeroplanes, and a steady flow of infantry battalions was hurrying past us to continue the advance beyond the rise, from which came the sound of heavy rifle and machine-gun fire and the bursting of shells. To our right towards Flesquieres a dozen or more tanks were going into action. The British batteries were also coming forward to take up fresh positions nearer to the enemy.

Ahead was the Canal du Nord, which was bridged by the engineers immediately the German barrage had lifted that morning, and in a very short time guns, ammunition limbers and ambulances were pouring on to the ground which scarcely an hour earlier had been held by the enemy.

By about eight p.m. practically every British battery had moved up and along the lip of the Hindenburg Line the guns stood in an unbroken line firing as fast as they could load. By now many walking wounded were coming back from the forward battle line and they told us things were going well. Large numbers of German prisoners were also coming back.

The battle situation towards Bourlon Wood was satisfactory with the English slowly advancing in open country. The British shell-fire was no longer a barrage and the shrapnel was taking a heavy toll among the enemy on the rise. About four miles ahead stood Cambrai and the Germans were fighting a desperate rear-guard action with machine guns from the outskirts of the town.

Away to the left, however, the British advance was being held up before the village of Graincourt, and the German garrison was inflicting heavy punishment on the British troops, whose dead lay thick before the ruins. The Guards Brigade was then called forward to attack the village and under the fire of several batteries they were able to capture Graincourt and batches of enemy prisoners.

The British had by now bitten three miles into the German defences since dawn, and by doing so had reached the final objective of the battle plan at practically every point.

Cambrai, now fiercely burning, and the Bourlon Wood were now at least in the hands of the British. On this day the British had blasted their way through the Hindenburg Line into the open country beyond, and from there onward the evil of the old trench warfare was a thing of the past, and a new phase had begun.

SECOND LIEUTENANT HENRY LAMONT SIMPSON

My Fellow Men

Henry Lamont Simpson was commissioned in the 1st Battalion, the Lancashire Fusiliers, in June 1917 and was at Ypres in August. He wrote this letter to his English master at Carlisle Grammar School. He was killed, aged twenty-one, on 29 August. He also left behind the brief poem that follows the letter.

The more I see of men, the more I love them ... A common song (even now and then a dirty song) can make one glad and sad beyond words, because one has heard men singing it times out of number. In all seriousness, the cheap popular songs of the last few years can move me infinitely more than the divinest music, because of the men

I have heard sing them. This is not merely a sentimental lingering over dead friendships and individual passions – that element is very small. The main thing is a love for, a passionate faith in, my fellow men . . . I believe with all my heart that man is, in the main, a loveable, and, at bottom, a good creature. (Curse the word good! but you know what I mean – worthy, sterling, right, true, real.) He sings dirty songs and swears, and is altogether a sensual drunken brute at times; but get to know him, start by loving him, believe in him through thick and thin, and you will not go unrewarded.

If it should chance that I be cleansed and crowned
With sacrifice and agony and blood,
And reach the quiet haven of Death's arms,
Nobly companioned of that brotherhood
Of common men who died and laughed the while,
And so made shine a flame that cannot die,
But flares a glorious beacon down the years –
If it should happen thus, some one may come
And, pouring over dusty lists, may light
Upon my long-forgotten name and, musing,
May say a little sadly – even now
Almost forgetting why he should be sad –
May say, 'And he died young', and then forget . . .

CHRISTOPHER STONE

'Wanton outrages'

Three years on from the letter to his wife Alyce describing his life in the trenches, Christopher Stone, now on the staff of the 99th Infantry Brigade and working with Major-General Sir Cecil Pereira, familiarly known as 'Pinto', describes the Germans' tactics as they retreated before the British.

11th October,

I have had a most interesting day because this morning I went with Pinto to villages where I had only seen on the map before, and then we motored back through the big town (presumably Cambrai). Our first effort to enter was baffled by a railway bridge which had been blown up (or down) across the road but we eventually found a way and picked it very carefully through the suburbs to the heart of the city where the great square stands gaunt and smoking with every single house round it gutted and destroyed. Of course most of the houses in the town have been touched by shellfire or bombs or just wanton Boche destruction; but the square is a most damning witness of vandalism. The shell of the very fine Hotel de Ville stands with gaping windows, and outside it is a piano with a chair – just a black cottage piano. No-one dared to touch it yet because of course it's a booby trap and contains a bomb. We wanted to find a prisoner and make him play it. I was more impressed today than I have ever been by the conviction that real vengeance must be wreaked on Germany, and that her towns must actually and methodically be destroyed in retaliation for these utterly use-less and wanton outrages on the property of harmless French people. No military purpose whatever has been served by the damage that has been done.

WILFRED OWEN

'Anthem for Doomed Youth'

Wilfred Owen's last letter to his mother was written on 31 October from a smoky cellar, surrounded by his comrades, offi-cers and men. 'It is a great life,' he wrote. 'I am more oblivious than alas! yourself, dear Mother, of the ghastly glimmering of the guns outside, and the hollow crashing of the shells. There is no danger down here, or if any, it will be well over before you read these lines.'

But there was danger above. Owen was killed on 4 November, after being awarded the Military Cross for 'conspicuous gallantry' the previous month for capturing an enemy machine gun and taking prisoners. The family received the news on Armistice Day.

What passing-bells for these who die as cattle?
– Only the monstrous anger of the guns.
Only the stuttering rifles' rapid rattle
Can patter out their hasty orisons.
No mockeries now for them; no prayers nor bells;
Nor any voice of mourning save the choirs, –
The shrill, demented choirs of wailing shells;
And bugles calling for them from sad shires.

What candles may be held to speed them all?
Not in the hands of boys but in their eyes
Shall shine the holy glimmers of goodbyes.
The pallor of girls' brows shall be their pall;
Their flowers the tenderness of patient minds,
And each slow dusk a drawing-down of blinds.

Herbert Read

As It Was in the Beginning

Herbert Read (1893–1968) served with the Yorkshire Regiment in France and Belgium throughout the war. After the war he became one of Britain's most distinguished critics and poets.

In the early days of November, 1918, the Allied Forces had for some days been advancing in pursuit of the retreating German Army. The advance was being carried out according to a schedule. Each Division was given a line to which it must attain before nightfall; and this meant that each battalion in a division had to reach a certain point by a certain time. The schedule was in general being well adhered to, but the opposition encountered varied considerably at different points.

On November 10th, a certain English battalion had been continuously harassed by machine-gun fire, and late in the afternoon was still far from its objective. Advancing under cover, it reached the edge of a plantation from which stretched a wide open space of cultivated land, with a village in front about 500 yards away. The officer in charge of the scouts was sent ahead with a corporal and two men to reconnoitre, and this little party reached the outskirts of the village without observing any signs of occupation. At the entrance of the village, propped against a tree, they found a German officer, wounded severely in the thigh. He was quite conscious and looked up calmly as Lieut. S— approached him. He spoke English, and when questioned, intimated that the village had been evacuated by the Germans two hours ago.

Thereupon Lieut. S— signalled back to the battalion, who then advanced along the road in marching formation. It was nearly dusk when they reached the small *place* in front of the church, and there they were halted. Immediately from several points, but chiefly from the tower of the church, a number of machine-guns opened fire on the massed men. A wild cry went up, and the men fled in rage and terror to the shelter of the houses, leaving a hundred of their companions and five officers dead or dying on the pavement. In the houses and the church they routed out the ambushed Germans and mercilessly bayoneted them.

The corporal who had been with Lieut. S— ran to the entrance of the village, to settle with the wounded officer who had betrayed them. The German seemed to be expecting him; his face did not flinch as the bayonet descended.

When the wounded had been attended to, and the dead gathered together, the remaining men retired to the schoolhouse to rest for the night. The officers then went to the château of the village, and there in a gardener's cottage, searching for fuel, the corporal already mentioned found the naked body of a young girl. Both legs were severed, and one severed arm was found in another room. The body itself was covered with bayonet wounds. When the discovery was reported to Lieut. S—, he went to verify the strange crime, but there was nothing to be done: he was, moreover, sick and tired. He found a bed in another cottage near the château, where some old peasants were still cowering behind a screen. He fell into a deep sleep, and did not wake until the next morning, the 11th of November, 1918.

Armistice: 11/11/18

The Armistice came into effect on the eleventh hour of the eleventh day of the eleventh month. It was a momentous time at home and on the front. Soldiers, journalists, a politician and a woman diarist recall the experiences of the day:

Burgon Bickersteth

Burgon was the fourth of Samuel Bickersteth's six sons. He served in the Royal Dragoons. In the Second World War he was director of Army Education.

> The column halted. The head of it was actually in the centre of Leuze. The news spread like wildfire. We went into a house which we made our temporary HQ, and sent out copies of the message to all concerned. The chief thing was to get the news to the advance regiments and to the patrols. This was eventually done, though it was 1.30 p.m. before the message reached one of the patrols who were nearly in Enghien being fired at from some woods near Bassilly. It was 10.30 by the time the messages were sent

out, and we had half-an-hour to arrange a little ceremony.

Drawn up in the square was an infantry battalion with its band. They were at once asked to take part and to supply the music. Representatives from all our regiments and various units were summoned, and just before 11 o'clock struck, we were all drawn up; mounted men formed three sides of a square and the infantry the fourth. The General and his Staff were mounted and by his side stood the Major. The civilians crowded round and every window had its onlookers. As the hour struck, the trumpeters played 'Cease Fire' and then the band crashed out 'God Save the King'. The infantry presented arms, and every cavalryman sat on his horse at attention, the officer saluting. Then followed the *Marseillaise* and after that the Belgian National Anthem. There was a great deal of cheering and waving of flags and handkerchiefs. The General then dismounted. The Mayor, an old man with a grey beard, made a speech about '*nos vaillants defenseurs*' and the '*prouesse incroyable des troupes alliées*'; and then the General and he wrung each other's hands amid the greatest enthusiasm. The ceremony ended, and the infantry marched off through a lane of mounted men, the cavalry giving cheer after cheer for the infantry. We then formed the column again and moved off to the eastern side of Leuze.

Philip Gibbs

Our troops knew early this morning that the Armistice had been signed. I stopped on my way to Mons outside brigade headquarters, and an officer said 'Hostilities will cease at eleven o'clock.' Then he added, as all men add in their hearts, 'Thank God for that!' All the way to Mons there were columns of troops on the march, and their bands played ahead of them, and almost every man had a flag on his rifle, the red, white and blue of France, the red, yellow and black of Belgium. They wore flowers in their caps and in their tunics, red and white chrysanthemums given them by crowds of people who cheered them on their way, people who in many of these villages had been only one day liberated from the German yoke. Our men marched singing, with a smiling light in their eyes. They had done their job, and it was finished with the greatest victory in the world.

C. E. MONTAGUE

Finally – last happy thrill of the war – the first stroke of eleven o'clock, on the morning of Armistice Day, on the town clock of Mons, only captured that morning; Belgian civilians and British soldiers crowding together into the square, shaking each other's hands and singing each other's national anthems; a little toy-like peal of bells in the church contriving to tinkle out 'Tipperary' for our welcome, while our airmen, released from their labours, tumbled and romped overhead like boys turning cartwheels with ecstasy.

WINSTON CHURCHILL

'The hour of deliverance'

I stood at the window of my room looking up Northumberland Avenue towards Trafalgar Square waiting for Big Ben to tell that the War was over. My mind strayed back across the scarring years to the scene and emotions of the night at the Admiralty when I listened for these same chimes in order to give the signal of war against Germany to our Fleets and squadrons across the world. And now all was over! The unarmed and untrained island nation, who with no defence but its Navy had faced unquestioningly the strongest manifestation of military power in human record, had completed its task. Our country had emerged from the ordeal alive and safe, its vast possessions intact, its war effort still waxing, its institutions unshaken, its people and Empire united as never before. Victory had come after all the hazards and heartbreaks in an absolute and unlimited form. All the Kings and Emperors with whom we had warred were in flight or exile. All their Armies and Fleets were destroyed or subdued. In this Britain had borne a notable part, and done her best from first to last.

And then suddenly the first stroke of the chime. I looked again at the broad street beneath me. It was deserted. From the portals of one of the large hotels absorbed by Government Departments darted the slight figure of a girl clerk, distractedly gesticulating while another stroke resounded. Then from all sides men and women came scurrying into the street. Streams of people poured out of all the buildings. The bells of London began to clash. Northumberland Avenue was now crowded with people in hundreds, nay, thousands, rushing hither and thither in a frantic manner, shouting and screaming with joy. I could see that Trafalgar Square was already swarming. Around me in our very headquarters in the Hotel Metropole, disorder had broken out. Doors banged. Feet clattered down corridors. Everyone rose from the desk and cast aside pen and paper. All bounds were broken. The tumult grew. It grew like a gale, but from all sides simultaneously. The street was now a seething mass of humanity. Flags appeared as if by magic. Streams of men and women flowed from the Embankment. They mingled with torrents pouring down the Strand on their way to acclaim the King. Almost before the last stroke of the clock had died away, the strict, war-straitened, regulated streets of London had become a triumphant pandemonium. At any rate it was clear that no more work would be done that day. Yes, the chains which had held the world were broken. Links of imperative need, links of discipline, links of brute force, links of self-sacrifice, links of terror, links of honour which had held our nation, nay, the greater part of mankind, to grinding toil, to a compulsive cause – every one had snapped upon a few strokes of the clock. Safety, freedom, peace, home, the dear one back at the fireside – all after fifty-two months of gaunt distortion. After fifty-two months of making burdens grievous to be borne and binding them on men's backs, at last, all at once, suddenly and everywhere the burdens were cast down. At least so for the moment it seemed.

My wife arrived, and we decided to go and offer our congratulations to the Prime Minister, on whom the central impact of the home struggle had fallen, in his hour of recompense. But no sooner had we entered our car than twenty people mounted upon it, and in the midst of a wildly cheering multitude we were impelled slowly forward through Whitehall. We had driven together the opposite way along the same road on the afternoon of the ultimatum. There had been the same crowd and almost the same enthusiasm. It was with feelings which do not lend themselves to words that I heard the cheers of the brave people who had borne so much and given all, who had never wavered, who had never lost faith in their country or its destiny, and who could be indulgent to the faults of their servants when the hour of deliverance had come.

MICHAEL MACDONAGH

'An enormous family party'

MacDonagh was there to record the joy of those on the Home Front.

In Trafalgar Square munition girls who, at the sound of the maroons, had left the factories in their working garb of blue, black or scarlet caps and overalls, were romping with soldiers. 'Have we won the War?' they shouted, and answered back, 'Yes, we have won the War!' I stood for a while in the Square looking on in amazement at the fantastic tricks which were being played before high heaven by the excited, noisy and jostling masses of people. A rollicking band of young subalterns came along blowing police whistles and dancing round a big teddy-bear on wheels decorated with Union Jacks. A group of American soldiers had evidently made a raid on a Lyons or ABC teashop, for they were provided with waitresses' trays, which they beat like tambourines, keeping time to the singing of 'Yankee Doodle'. Taxi cabs crawled by, each with a Dominion soldier and a girl sprawling on the roof. The girls were obtained by a form of the primitive system of capture. At least I saw one Dominion soldier, who had been sitting alone on a cab, drop to the ground, seize a girl from the pavement, swing her over his shoulders and climbing to his perch again drive off with a triumphant shout. The girl submitted to her captor with little squeals of delight, mixed only slightly, I thought, with apprehension.

But surely the most unexpected and queerest incident of the day was that supplied by a body of men wearing silk hats and frock coats, who marched in fours up Northumberland Avenue from the Embankment headed by a 'band' whose instruments consisted of tin-kettles containing stones, and the music produced being an infernal rattle. These men – one can hardly believe it – were members of the Stock Exchange, the most cautious and crafty of beings. Could they have stood on the pavement in their normality and seen themselves and their antics as they marched in the middle of the road, they would have said, 'What silly asses!' or at the most have looked on with slightly contemptuous amusement. But then, no one is normal to-day. Everyone is thrown off their bearings. Nothing is taken seriously. It is a day of 'Laughter holding both his sides'.

We are, in truth, an enormous family party, engaged in what may be called a stupendous house-warming – the re-opening and occupation of a new London, inaugurating an era of peace and security, after years of care and worry; and, like the social function of infinitely less degree with which I have compared it, everyone taking part is, as befits the unparalleled occasion, in high spirits of the most extravagantly irresponsible kind – utterly forgetful of self-propriety, pretentiousness, absorbed in the desire to contribute something to the Pandean frolic.

ROBERT GRAVES

'Armistice Day, 1918'

Robert Graves was in North Wales on Armistice night. In *Goodbye to All That*, he wrote that the news sent him out walking alone along the dyke above the marshes of Rhuddlan – an ancient battlefield, the Flodden of Wales – cursing and sobbing and thinking of the dead.

What's all this hubbub and yelling,
Commotion and scamper of feet,
With ear-splitting clatter of kettles and cans,
Wild laughter down Mafeking Street?

O, those are the kids whom we fought for
(You might think they'd been scoffing our rum)
With flags that they waved when we marched off to war
In rapture of bugle and drum.

Now they'll hang Kaiser Bill from a lamp-post,
Von Tirpitz they'll hang from a tree . . .
We've been promised a 'Land Fit for Heroes' –
What heroes we heroes must be!

And the guns that we took from the Fritzes,
That we paid for with rivers of blood,
Look, they're hauling them down to Old Battersea
Bridge
Where they'll topple them, souse, in the mud!

But there's old me and women in corners
With tears falling fast on their cheeks,
There's the armless and legless and sightless –
It's seldom that one of them speaks.

And there's flappers gone drunk and indecent
Their skirts kilted up to the thigh,
The constables lifting no hand in reproof
And the chaplain averting his eye . . .

When the days of rejoicing are over,
When the flags are stowed safely away,
They will dream of another wild 'War to End Wars'
And another wild Armistice day.

But the boys who were killed in the trenches
Who fought with no rags and no rant
We left them stretched out on their pallets of mud
Low down with the worm and the ant.

CAROLINE PLAYNE

'Mafficking joyousness'

Playne was a pacifist activist in London who kept a diary throughout the war.

Starting from Hampstead to go by omnibus to Chancery Lane that morning, I noticed how everything appeared to be proceeding as 'for the duration' of the war, till we were near Mornington Crescent Tube Station. Suddenly maroons went off, a startling explosion just above us. An air-raid, another air-raid! A woman ran out of a house and gazed anxiously at the sky. But before one could recollect that it might mean the Armistice, people were pouring out of buildings, streaming into the streets. The war was ended. Tools must have been downed in no time. Crowds grew bigger every minute.

There was great liveliness, calls, cries, whistles and hooters sounding, noise and crowds grew as we proceeded. Chancery Lane was very lively. Going out for lunch about one o'clock, great excitement prevailed, happy daylight mafficking produced most unusual sights. Every vehicle going along the Strand was being boarded by people, most of whom waved flags. Boys and girls flung themselves on anywhere and clung as best they might. One scene was more unusual than others. At the corner of Chancery Lane a stout policeman on point duty was surrounded by girls all clamouring to dance with him. The London bobby rose to the occasion – without a word he took on one after another for a turn round on the narrow pavement as they stood, whilst his countenance remained absolutely impassive. Custom and convention melted away as if a new world had indeed dawned. Officers and privates mixed in equal comradeship. Private drilled officers, munitionettes commanded platoons made up of both. The spirit of militarism was turned into comedy.

Never in history perhaps have such great multitudes experienced such restoration of joyousness in the twinkling of an eye.

This great spontaneous joy of relief helps us to fathom the long-endured, agonizing strain, rarely acknowledged, usually hidden away and overlaid with wartime's preoccupations, exactions and hazardous undertakings. We were freed, the burden was rolled away, the demon of ardour no longer drove us.

The transition from war to peace conditions began forthwith. Recruiting was stopped, call-up notices were cancelled. Bells might be rung and public clocks might chime again at night. The light in the tower of the Houses of Parliament and other lights reappeared on the first evening. Just as hearts had sunk when the extinction of lights brought home the incredible certainty that Britain was at war, so now, seeing the lights shine out, men dared believe that the great war was indeed over.

There was every right to be thankful, and to join in the shouting on the great day, November 11, 1918. Thousands went into the churches, the Baltic Exchange sang the Doxology and the Stock Exchange the hymn *O God, our help in ages past.*

People flocked through the doors of St Paul's until the building was filled from end to end. It was manifest that hearts overflowed with gratitude. 'In the Abbey the crowd seemed swept away as on a vast stream of thankfulness.' The hearts of civilians and soldiers overflowed with gratitude and joy during the brief but most memorable service.

Outside, especially in Trafalgar Square, mafficking joyousness continued for some days.

The bells are ringing

At last with the Armistice, the church bells were ringing for the soldiers and their sweethearts at home:

The bells are ringing
For me and my girl.
The birds are singing
For me and my girl.
Everybody is knowing,
Everybody is going,
Every Susie and Sal.

The Parson's waiting
For me and my girl.
They're congregating
For me and my girl.
And some day we'll build a little home
For two or three or four or more,
In Love Land
For me and my girl.

SIR DOUGLAS HAIG

Was there ever such an insult?

David Lloyd George, the Prime Minister, and Sir Douglas Haig, his commander-in-chief, manoeuvred against each other constantly: Lloyd George was not an admirer of Haig nor his tactics. After the armistice, as Haig recorded in his diary, the Prime Minister, had his revenge:

> A telephone message was received from my ADC [aide-de-camp] on duty at Beaurepaire Château stating that Brooke (Private Secretary of CIGS [Chief of the Imperial General Staff] War Office) had telephoned at request of CIGS (who was in Downing Street with the Cabinet) to give me a message from the prime minister to the effect that he wished me to come to London tomorrow (Sunday) to take part in a ceremonial drive through the streets with Marshal Foch, M. Clemenceau, M. Orlando (prime minister of Italy) and a number of other French and Italian officers. The special train would leave Dover at 12 noon.
>
> Later I heard that I was to be in the fifth carriage along with General Henry Wilson. I felt that this was more of an insult than I could put up with, even from the prime minister.
>
> For the past three years I have effaced myself, because I felt that, to win the war, it was essential that the British and French Armies should get on well together. And in consequence I have patiently submitted to Lloyd George's conceit and swagger, combined with much boasting as to 'what *he* had accomplished, thanks to his *foresight* in appointing Foch as C in C of the Allied Forces, to his having sent armies to Egypt, Palestine, Mesopotamia, Salonika, etc. etc.' The real truth, which history will show,

is that the British Army has won the war in France in spite of LG and I have no intention of taking part in any triumphal ride with Foch, or with any pack of foreigners, through the streets of London, mainly in order to add to LG's importance and help him in his election campaign. So I had a message to the following effect sent by telephone to the War Office.

First, that I could not come to London tomorrow to take part in any ceremonial procession unless I was ordered to do so by the Army Council (tomorrow is a *Sunday*).

Second, was I wanted for any discussion by the War Cabinet or merely for a ceremonial pageant?

General Lawrence telephoned to the War Office on my behalf and later in the afternoon he stated that he had spoken with General Harrington who fully realised my views on the matter, and that this question was closed so far as the War Office and I were concerned.

Meantime, Lord Stamfordham (who is at Buckingham Palace) took it upon himself, on hearing of the proposed ceremony, to telephone to GHQ to beg me *not* to come to England tomorrow, as he felt sure that the King would be much displeased that any reception of the kind should be held during his absence.

Evidently this pageant of Lloyd George's is causing a great stir all round. Further details of the proposed 'triumphal progress' show that the procession is to go to the French Embassy at Albert Gate for a reception to which I am not invited. A motor car, however, is to be in waiting for me there, to take me 'wherever I like!'

Was there ever such an insult prepared for the welcome of a General on his return after successfully commanding an Army in the field during four long years of war? Yet this is the view of the Prime Minister of England of what is fitting.

RICHARD GIRLING

For Whom the Bell Tolls

There were few homes in the land, high or low, that were not affected in some way by the Great War as it took its toll of fathers and brothers, sons and nephews. Many of the men who died had only just left school.

Gresham's, in the north Norfolk town of Holt, was a small public school of 287 boys. By the end of the war 101 of them had died in the war. In this report Richard Girling, a writer for the *Sunday Times Magazine*, tells the poignant story of the school's last cricket match before the war:

> George Howson, the headmaster of Gresham's School, was buried on 11 January 1919. There was a psalm, two hymns and Chopin's funeral march played lightly on the organ. After a short ceremony, almost puritanical in its simplicity, they lowered him into a brick-lined grave against the sunlit south wall of the school chapel.
>
> He had no bullet in his head; no shrapnel in his side. His lungs had not been seared by chlorine gas, or his body flayed by wire. And yet, as his friend Edith Hamilton phrased it in a letter to the school magazine, 'The war killed him as straightly and as surely as if he had fallen at the front. He spent himself in grief.'
>
> Although Howson had no sons of his own, the scale of his loss was unimaginable even to a generation inured to pain. In the summer of 1914, he'd had just 287 on roll. One hundred and one times since then he had heard the worst. One hundred and one times he had grieved, once for every 12 days of war. Pupils and old boys, soldiers, sailors, flyers, officers and men – he had shaped their talents, understood their needs, forgiven their weaknesses. He had exchanged letters with them at the front, had welcomed them back,

five or six at a time, to the School House during their leave and given his counsel, just as he had done when he was *in loco parentis*. Their deaths had hit him, 101 times over, as hard as they had hit their families. 'I can't sleep in my comfortable bed,' he had said. 'I feel it ought to be a trench.'

Like all schools, Gresham's mirrored the philosophy and personality of its headmaster – which in Howson's case meant a rare combination of educational progressiveness and lantern-jawed moral conservatism. His progressiveness showed itself in a cutting-edge emphasis on science and technology; his conservatism in a behavioural code that owed more to the physical terrors of Robert Baden-Powell than to the hearty, playing-field ethic of Dr Arnold. The congregation at his memorial service, three weeks after the funeral, heard a eulogy from the Bishop of Thetford that rang with Victorian sanctimony. 'He understood what a riot of lust could be in a boy's life, the ruin it brought, and he took care that no boy under his care was left in a false paradise. He was in daily touch with the infinite.'

Unlike Arnold, the Duke of Wellington or Baron Pierre de Coubertin (who founded the modern Olympics), Howson saw no link between character and athleticism. He suffered games to be played but, in fear of moral contamination, forbade contacts with other schools. Gresham's rugby, hockey and cricket teams therefore had to be content with fixtures against sides raised by their housemasters, old boys or members of the Norfolk gentry. Thus it was, on Saturday, July 18, 1914, that the cricket team filed from the pavilion to face the Old Boys. The school had been having a wretched season – poor catching, the want of a fast bowler and careless leg-side batting were blamed – and so it was on this balmy, shirtsleeve afternoon. The Old Boys declared at 232 for 5, then dismissed the school for 202. The result was of scant interest, certainly to Howson, yet the game's scorecard, with its indelible reek of youth and expectation, would become one of the school's most powerful totems of loss.

Gresham's School v. Old Boys
Played on July 18th
Gresham's School

J H C Wooldridge, c Wright, b Barker	11
R A Fitzgerald, b Barker	8
D W Jaques, run out	28
J Jefferson, c Hill, b Barker	18
C R H Farmer, b Wright	0
C A H Hill, b Barker	49
J A Nicholson, c Newsum, b Cadge	23
C N Newsum, c Newsum, b Cadge	4
A H Graves, hit wkt, b Rouse	0
J F Laverack, c Newsum, b Cadge	9
C H Stevens, hit wkt, b Rouse	3
C D Wells, not out	36
Extras	13
Total	202

Old Boys

H W Partridge, c Nicholson, b Farmer	14
R H Partridge, b Farmer	52
B J Cadge, c Steven, b Hill	46
H N Newsum, c Fitzgerald, b Farmer	40
A G Wright, b Farmer	28
M C Hill, not out	11
L F St J Davies, not out	25
W J Spurrell)	
M E B Crosse)	
C N Barker) did not bat	
F V Jacques)	
C V Rouse)	
Extras	16
Total (for 5 wkts)	232

War was declared 17 days later. By the armistice on November 11, 1918, no fewer than 11 of the 24 players would be dead, along with 89 of their erstwhile classmates and one teacher. Cuthbert Hill, the schools top scorer with 49, was drowned at Jutland. The man who bowled him out, Noel Barker, took a direct hit from an artillery shell. Cuthbert's older brother, Mark (11 not-out for the Old Boys), died on the Somme. The school's No 3 bat, David Jacques (run out for 28), was shot through the head by a sniper. Its No 8, Clement Newsum, caught for four by his brother, Henry, was killed by shellfire in 1917. In all, six members of the school team and five of the Old Boys would not live to see the consecration of the new school chapel, the bare ribs of which were rising out of muddy ground to the east.

Gresham's casualty list, though grievous, was no worse than that of any other school; the sacrifice of its boys no greater. Eton, for example, which had just over 1,000 on roll in the summer of 1914, lost 1,157; Marlborough lost 746 and Wellington 707.

Perhaps the most poignant of the school's relics is a wall chart kept by Dallas Wynne Willson, head of Gresham's tiny junior school, on which he marked the deaths of all the boys he had taught – and which he hung in the school dining room. The only pictures he had were old school photographs, from which he cut and pasted their 13-year-old faces – a lost generation of beardless little boys. Their names, in alphabetical order along with the others, are read out each year when the third-form history sets are taken on field trips to the battlefields of Ypres and the Somme.

SIR HENRY RAWLINSON

Show the world

As a career soldier Henry Rawlinson (1864–1925) had already served in the Sudan Campaign of 1898 with Lord Kitchener and the Second Boer War (1899–1901) when the First World War broke out. He was Lieutenant General of the Fourth Army at the Somme – a disaster – but was again commanding the Fourth Army when it broke through the German line in 1918. On the day of armistice, when he was made a peer, he wrote this missive to his men:

To All Ranks of The Fourth Army.

The Fourth Army has been ordered to form part of the Army of Occupation on the Rhine in accordance with the terms of the Armistice. The march to the Rhine will shortly commence, and, although carried out with the usual military precautions, will be undertaken generally as a peace march.

The British Army through over four years of almost continuous and bitter fighting has proved that it has lost none of that fighting spirit and dogged determination which has characterised British Armies in the past, and has won a place in history of which every soldier of the British Empire has just reason to be proud. It has maintained the highest standard of discipline both in advance and retreat. It has proved that British discipline, based on mutual confidence between officers and men, can stand the hard test of war far better than Prussian discipline based on fear of punishment.

This is not all. The British Army has, during the last four years on foreign soil, by its behaviour in billets, by its courtesy to women, by its ever ready help to the old and weak, and by its kindness to children, earned a reputation in France that no army serving in a foreign land torn by the horrors of war, has ever gained before.

Till you reach the frontier of Germany you will be marching through a country that has suffered grievously from the depredations and exactions of a brutal enemy. Do all that lies in your power by courtesy and consideration to mitigate the hardships of these poor people who will welcome you as deliverers and as friends. I would further ask you when you

cross the German frontier to show the world that British soldiers, unlike those of Germany, do not wage war against
women and children and against the old and weak.

The Allied Governments have guaranteed that private
property will be respected by the Army of Occupation, and
I rely on you to see that this engagement is carried out in the
spirit as well as in the letter.

In conclusion I ask you one and all, men from all parts of
the British Empire, to ensure that the fair name of the British
Army, enhanced by your exertions in long years of trial and
hardship, shall be fully maintained during the less exacting
months that lie before you.

I ask you to show the world that, as in war, so in peace,
British discipline is the highest form of discipline, based on
loyalty to our King, respect for authority, care for the well-
being of subordinated, courtesy and consideration for
non-combatants, and a true soldierly bearing in carrying out
whatever duty we may be called upon to perform.

AFTERMATH

Although there were problems over the length of time it took for men to be demobilised after the war – there were mutinies at Calais and Folkestone and Rhyl (where several men were killed) and an occupation of Horse Guards Parade in London by three thousand men – the great majority of men had been discharged by the summer of 1919. But some, particularly the literati, felt a sense of anti-climax captured in the following pages by the disenchantment of the *Manchester Guardian* journalist C. E. Montague. For some, represented here by the poet Ivor Gurney, the soldiers F. J. Brabyn and Frank Richards and others, there was a sense of anger and bitterness at the 'lead-swingers' who had remained in England while they were on the Western Front and who now had the best jobs or who exploited the welfare system to the disadvantage of the men who had answered the call. Still others felt the sense of pride in their war expressed by Charles Carrington and which was symbolised in Westminster Abbey by the tomb of the unknown soldier.

ANONYMOUS

'Any Soldier To His Son'

In this poem written after the war, the anonymous author tells his son about his experiences of the war; at first light-hearted, the poem becomes darker towards the end. It was contributed to firstworldwar.com by Alick Lavers.

What did I do, sonny, in the Great World War?
Well, I learned to peel potatoes and to scrub the barrack
*   floor.*
I learned to push a barrow and I learned to swing a pick,
I learned to turn my toes out, and to make my eyeballs
*   click.*
I learned the road to Folkestone, and I watched the
*   English shore,*
Go down behind the skyline, as I thought, for evermore.
And the Blighty boats went by us and the harbour hove in
*   sight,*
And they landed us and sorted us and marched us 'by the
*   right'.*
'Quick march!' across the cobbles, by the kids who rang
*   along*
Singing 'Appoo?' 'Spearmant' 'Shokolah?' throught dingy
*   old Boulogne;*
By the widows and the nurses and the niggers and Chinese,
And the gangs of smiling Fritzes, as saucy as you please.

I learned to ride as soldiers ride from Etaps to the Line,
For days and nights in cattle trucks, packed in like droves
*   of swine.*
I learned to curl and kip it on a foot of muddy floor,
And to envy cows and horses that have beds of beaucoup
*   straw.*
I learned to wash in shell holes and to shave myself in tea,
While the fragments of a mirror did a balance on my knee.
I learned to dodge the whizz-bangs and the flying lumps of
*   lead,*
And to keep a foot of earth between the sniper and my
*   head.*
I learned to keep my haversack well filled with buckshee
*   food,*
To take the Army issue and to pinch what else I could.

I learned to cook Maconochie with candle-ends and string,
With 'four-by-two' and sardine-oil and any God-dam
    thing.
I learned to use my bayonet according as you please
For a breadknife or a chopper or a prong for toasting
    cheese.
I learned 'a first field dressing' to serve my mate and me
As a dish-rag and a face-rag and a strainer for our tea.
I learned to gather souvenirs that home I hoped to send,
And hump them round for months and months and dump
    them in the end.
I learned to hunt for vermin in the lining of my shirt,
To crack them with my finger-nail and feel the beggars
    spirt;
I learned to catch and crack them by the dozen and the
    score
And to hunt my shirt tomorrow and to find as many more.

I learned to sleep by snatches on the firestep of a trench,
And to eat my breakfast mixed with mud and Fritz's heavy
    stench.
I learned to pray for Blighty ones and lie and squirm with
    fear,
When Jerry started strafing and the Blighty ones were near.
I learned to write home cheerful with my heart a lump of
    lead
With the thought of you and mother, when she heard that
    I was dead.
And the only thing like pleasure over there I ever knew,
Was to hear my pal come shouting, 'There's a parcel, mate,
    for you.'

So much for what I did do – now for what I have not
    done:
Well, I never kissed a French girl and I never killed a Hun,

I never missed an issue of tobacco, pay, or rum,
I never made a friend and yet I never lacked a chum.
I never borrowed money, and I never lent – but once
(I can learn some sorts of lessons though I may be borne a
  dunce).
I never used to grumble after breakfast in the Line
That the eggs were cooked too lightly or the bacon cut too
  fine.
I never told a sergeant just exactly what I thought,
I never did a pack-drill, for I never quite got caught.
I never punched a Red-Cap's nose (be prudent like your
  Dad),
But I'd like as many sovereigns as the times I've wished I
  had.
I never stopped a whizz-bang, though I've stopped a lot of
  mud,
But the one that Fritz sent over with my name on was a
  dud.
I never played the hero or walked about on top,
I kept inside my funk hole when the shells began to drop.
Well, Tommy Jones's father must be made of different
  stuff:
I never asked for trouble – the issue was enough.

So I learned to live and lump it in the lovely land of war,
Where the face of nature seems a monstrous septic sore,
Where the bowels of earth hang open, like the guts of
  something slain,
And the rot and wreck of everything are churned and
  churned again;
Where all is done in darkness and where all is still in day,
Where living men are buried and the dead unburied lay;
Where men inhabit holes like rats, and only rats live there;
Where cottage stood and castle once in days before La
  Guerre;

Where endless files of soldiers thread the everlasting way,
By endless miles of duckboards, through endless walls of
    clay;
Where life is one hard labour, and a soldiers gets his rest
When they leave him in the daisies with a puncture in his
    chest;
Where still the lark in summer pours her warble from the
    skies,
And underneath, unheeding, lie the blank upstaring eyes.

And I read the Blighty papers, where the warriors of the
    pen
Tell of 'Christmas in the trenches' and 'The Spirit of our
    men';
And I saved the choicest morsels and I read them to my
    chum,
And he muttered, as he cracked a louse and wiped it off his
    thumb:
'May a thousand chats from Belgium crawl under their fin-
    gers as they write;
May they dream they're not exempted till they faint with
    mortal fright;
May the fattest rats in Dickebusch race over them in bed;
May the lies they've written choke them like a gas cloud
    till they're dead;
May the horror and the torture and the things they never
    tell
(For they only write to order) be reserved for them in Hell!'

You'd like to be a soldier and go to France some day?
By all the dead in Delville Wood, by all the nights I lay
Between our lines and Fritz's before they brought me in;
By this old wood-and-leather stump, that once was flesh
    and skin;
By all the lads who crossed with me but never crossed again,

By all the prayers their mothers and their sweethearts
  prayed in vain,
Before the things that were that day should ever more
  befall
May God in common pity destroy us one and all!

JOHN S. ARKWRIGHT

'O Valiant Hearts'

John Stanhope Arkwright (1872–1954) wrote the words of this
stirring hymn during the war. Sung to the music of Gustav Holst,
it has become a staple of services of remembrance:

O valiant hearts who to your glory came
Through dust of conflict and through battle flame;
Tranquil you lie, your knightly virtue proved
Your memory hallowed in the land you loved.

Proudly you gathered, rank on rank, to war
As who had heard God's message from afar;
All you had hoped for, all you had, you gave,
To save mankind – yourselves you scorned to save.

Splendid you passed, the great surrender made;
Into light that nevermore shall fade;
Deep your contentment in that blest abode,
Who wait the last clear trumpet call of God.

Long years ago, as earth lay dark and still,
Rose a loud cry upon a lonely hill,
While in the frailty of our human clay,
Christ, our Redeemer, passed the self same way.

Still stands His Cross from that dread hour to this,
Like some bright star above the dark abyss;

Still, through the veil, the Victor's pitying eyes
Look down to bless our lesser Calvaries.

These were His servants, in His steps they trod,
Following through death the martyred Son of God:
Victor, He rose; victorious too shall rise
They who have drunk His cup of sacrifice.

O risen Lord, O Shepherd of our dead,
Whose Cross has bought them and Whose staff has led,
In glorious hope their proud and sorrowing land
Commits her children to Thy gracious hand.

F. P. CROZIER

Jilted

According to the popular song, '*Après la guerre fini, soldat anglais parti, Mademoiselle can go to hell après la guerre fini*'. As F. P. Crozier recounts, mademoiselles were indeed sent to hell.

Arriving at our hotel at Boulogne to spend the night, while at coffee in the lounge, after dinner, my eyes fall on Margot – the pretty waitress who had waited on the thousands of British officers during the past four years and nine months. She is crying. She is very upset. We call her over. She is very reticent, – but at last, breaking down completely, she unburdens her heart. Her trouble is simple. She has loved and been loved by many British officers during the hectic days – we guessed as much. Money has come easily. Excitement triumphed over remorse. She kept going while she supported an aged mother. Then she really fell in love with a good-looking young British officer, the son of a noble house, who – having slept with her on many occasions – promised to marry her. He had just jilted her. Hence the tears, the remorse, the utter disillusionment. The glamour, excitement and prosperity of war have disappeared – only utter disappointment remains for this poor girl.

Next morning as we enter the lounge after breakfast there is no Margot. She has joined the millions of other war victims. Demented, prostrate with anguish, frightened of the future, alone, forgotten, ignored, and perhaps wounded in pride – with British officers leaving France daily in large numbers, and her real lover ignoring her frantic appeals – she blew her brains out with a German pistol once given her by a colonel. 'I told you Boulogne has its war tragedies as well as the battlefields,' remarked my companion.

And then I pass out of the Great War and as I stand on the leave boat for the last time, looking at Boulogne, I say to a companion who is beside me, 'It may be for ever, in so far as this uniform is concerned, but there is a scar – unseen to any – slashed across my soul which will be with me to the end.' Am I the only man, at this moment, who feels this?

C. E. MONTAGUE

Fooled

Sir Douglas Haig came to Cologne when we had been there a few days. On the grandiose bridge over the Rhine he made a short speech to a few of us. Most of it sounded as if the thing were a job he had got to get through with, and did not much care for. Perhaps the speech, like those of other great men who wisely hate making speeches, had been written for him by somebody else. But once he looked up from the paper and put in some words which I felt sure were his own; 'I only hope that, now we have won, we shall not lose our heads, as the Germans did after 1870. It has brought them to this.' He looked at the gigantic mounted statue of the Kaiser overhead, a thing crying out in its pride for fire from heaven to fall and consume it, and at the homely squat British sentry moving below on his post. I think the speech was reported. But none of our foremen at home took any notice of it at all. They knew a trick worth two of Haig's. They were as moonstruck as any victorious Prussian.

So we had failed – had won the fight and lost the prize; the garland of the war was withered before it was gained. The lost years, the broken youth, the dead friends, the women's over-shadowed lives at home, the agony and bloody sweat – all had gone to darken the stains which most of us had thought to scour out of the world that our children would live in. Many men felt, and said to each other, that they had been fooled. They had believed that their country was backing them. They had thought, as they marched into Germany, 'Now we shall show old Fritz how you treat a man when you've thrashed him.' They would let him into the English secret, the tip that the power and glory are not to the bully. As some of them looked at the melancholy performance which followed, our press and our politicians parading at Paris in moral *Pickelhauben* and doing the Prussianist goose-step by way of *pas de triomphe*, they could not but say in dismay to them-selves: 'This is our doing. We cannot wish the war unwon, and yet – if we had shirked, poor old England, for all we know, might not have come to this pass. So we come home draggle-tailed, sick of the mess that we were unwittingly help-ing to make when we tried to do well.'

F. J. BRABYN

A Land Fit for Heroes?

F. J. Brabyn enlisted as a gunner and fought on the Somme and at Passchendaele. He became an army chaplain in the Second World War. He tells his story of disillusion after the First World War through the character of 'Ted', who was demobilised in February 1919. In his file at the Imperial War Museum (87/59/1) he tells his story:

The men who fought the most terrible war in history, whether on land, on the sea or in the air, and who survived the conflict, were, for the most part, in for a great disillusionment. Ted had no real grounds in these categories – apart from three years in action. His turn for demobilization came in February 1919. But what were his prospects? His one desire was to get back to his studies – so rudely interrupted by the war. School pals of his, who stayed on in the Dockyard, continued their studies and qualified themselves to occupy positions of responsibility under the Government. Some had got degrees – chiefly from London University – but poor Ted, and many like him who joined the army, found that they had backed a loser in this respect and would have to start again from scratch. There were very few educational grants available and so it meant beginning all over again almost. 'What gratitude!' they thought. Many gave up the unequal struggle: some made the best of it and began to slog: Ted was one of them. By the aid of private tuition and night classes at the local Technical Institute, he sat for and passed an examination for Admiralty Draughtsmen. He competed against many others who had not joined the army. He despaired of success. He even wrote to the Admiralty to enquire if some concession could be granted to the few ex-servicemen sitting the examination, but with no success. 'A land fit for heroes,' he thought. Fortunately for him he passed but he had to endure the smirks of those non-ex-servicemen higher up the pass list, and, of course, face the prospect of slower promotion. Ironically, some words of a wartime song came to his mind: 'We'll hug you, kiss you and love you, when you come back again.'

For relaxation he attempted to play tennis and to swim. Here he found his right shoulder – damaged on the Somme in 1916 – a handicap, even though the assessment of the Pensions Board of his disablement was only 'six to fourteen percent and of indeterminate duration'. He became embittered with life mainly because of the way the ex-servicemen were treated. Groups of them could be seen begging in the streets of our towns and cities. A soldier, who had lost his leg in the war, earned a few coppers by prancing about on his one leg in front of football crowds. When the body of the Unknown Soldier, which was to be buried in Westminster Abbey, passed slowly through the local station only Ted and about six or so others, lined the platform to pay their respects and this out of a local population of about 100,000. Ted, with four and a half years' war service behind him, including over three in action, his two wounds, to say nothing of lost opportunities, could be forgiven for feeling that the ex-servicemen had had a raw deal. He was still only 21 years of age in 1919.

FRANK RICHARDS

The Lead-swingers

In the village where I was living the majority of men receiving disability pensions in that year, 1923, were men who had never left the British Isles or who had served at the Bases and never seen the sky over the firing line. Some of them in this year of 1932 are now drawing life pensions and larger ones than the men who were wounded or disabled in action. One man who did two months on the Salisbury Plain is still drawing a pension, another who did six months somewhere else in England is still drawing a pension and doing work besides that would kill a buck nigger. Another actually went as far as Ireland and endured terrible hardships in a cookhouse. He is still drawing a pension.

I expect it is the same in every town and village throughout the British Isles. These men are greatly admired and are often spoken of as the men who worked their knobs during the War. Yet if the whole of the British Army had been like them during the War there would have been no pensions and not much England.

An old regular soldier had to complete twenty-one years' service with the Colours and if he was a private at the end of that period was entitled to a life service pension of one shilling a day; which has now been increased to two shillings a day. During the War if an old regular soldier was invalided out of the service his Reserve service would count as Colour service, and if he had over eleven years' service was entitled to a life service pension of one halfpenny a day for every year or part of a year served. If a man was invalided out, say, with sixteen years and one month's service, he would receive eightpence-halfpenny a day.

Living not far from me is an old artilleryman who had served abroad in his pre-War days, where he had his fair share of fever. He was a reservist when the War broke out and after serving in France for three years was wounded and gassed and finally invalided out of the service with a disability pension. He was receiving this pension for some time and was then given his final award. He still suffers with his health and simply receives his service pension of roughly five shillings a week. He is what the papers call one of the Old Contemptibles, and indeed no man has been treated with greater contempt than what he has.

This is a funny world and I have come to the conclusion that lead-swingers and dodgers get on best in it. Since 1921 I have had a pretty tough time and have had long periods of unemployment and I expect there are thousands of old soldiers like me who are worse off than I am. I was standing one day by a group of ex-Service men who had been lead-swingers and dodgers throughout the War and they were discussing the distribution of some work. One of them said that it was about time they had a say in the matter: they had done their bit during the War and it was only fair that the men who had served their country should have a greater share of the work than the men who had never left their own homes. This particular man had contracted several dangerous complaints through shaking the Crown and Anchor dice down at the Base.

It is Armistice day to-day and the ex-Service men are on parade wearing their War medals. The men who served at the Bases and a hundred miles behind the front line are wearing their medals more proudly than the men who served in the firing line. There is no distinction between the War medals. In former wars, for each engagement a man took part in he was awarded a bar, and a pukka old soldier would be very nearly ashamed to wear a war medal that did not have a bar attached. They were known as bare-arsed medals. The thought has often struck me during these parades how vain we all are, and how much preferable the old Red Indians were. In their belts they wore the scalps of their enemies that they had slain in action as proof of their soldiering: but we just wear war medals, and there are some on parade to-day wearing war-medals on their breasts as if to say that they have been in action – but the only action they were ever in was with some of the charming damsels in the Red Lamps behind the Front and down at the Bases where they served. The Red Indians were vain but they were honest.

W. F. WEST

'I thought of my country first'

Private West was taken prisoner on 23 August 1914, and was held in several German prison camps. He worked under duress in salt mines for eighteen months, suffered a nervous breakdown, was repatriated in December 1918, and sent to a mental hospital. He was discharged in June 1919. On 22 May 1920 he wrote this note on his inability to find work.

Since my Discharge I am finding it impossible to get any Work owing to my Complaint. They dont seem to want anything to do with anyone who served in the War. This is my experience up to Date, and when I think of all I and Hundred & Thousands of other men sufferd it makes me say to myself was it worth it, the Terrible Treatment I Personally Went through simply because I was patriotic. I realize now when it is too Late. What punishment I could have *escaped* by doing what the Germans wanted me to do. But I thought of my country first, now only a Year or so after the War, it seems we have already been forgotten. I hope that the Following Years will be much Better and that we all will be able to live & work peacefully which is all we want I am certain. Enough *work Etc* to help us forget our past Experiences and To make the future safe for all Time but up to writing To *Date* 22nd May 1920 it seems impossible to get any Work as I like Hundreds of others were Regular Soldiers before the War and we have no Trades. I have *already* come across *fellows* who has had & still got their Jobs all during th War. I cannot understand why they never went out to France Etc, because they were as fit as I was of that I am certain they still have their Jobs, but us with no Trades Etc, do not seem to be wanted at all.

Ivor Gurney

'Strange Hells'

Although he studied at the Royal College of Music and worked with such composers as Charles Stanford, Ralph Vaughan Williams and Herbert Howells, Ivor Gurney (1890–1937) is now remembered as one of the great war poets. He served with the Gloucestershire Regiment as a private and was wounded and then gassed in 1917, after which he published two volumes of poetry. He suffered a breakdown in 1918, was eventually declared insane and died in a mental hospital.

> *There are strange Hells within the minds War made*
> *Not so often, not so humiliatingly afraid*

As one would have expected – the racket and fear guns
  made.

One Hell the Gloucester soldiers they quite put out;
Their first bombardment, when in combined black shout
Of fury, guns aligned, they ducked low their heads
And sang with diaphragms fixed beyond all dreads,
That tin and stretched-wire tinkle, that blither of tune;
'Apres la guerre fini' till Hell all had come down,
Twelve-inch, six-inch, and eighteen pounders hammering
Hell's thunders.

Where are they now on State-doles, or showing shop pat-
  terns
Or walking town to town sore in borrowed tatterns
Or begged. Some civic routine one never learns.
The heart burns – but has to keep out of face how heart
  burns.

LYN MACDONALD

The histories of the war by the remarkable Lyn Macdonald are based on her interviews with soldiers who survived and their relatives. These interviews by her tell part of the story of what happened to some of the 'heroes' who returned home from the front.

Rifleman Fred White, 10th Battalion, King's Royal Rifle Corps
Us fellows, it took us years to get over it. Years! Long after when you were working, married, had kids, you'd be lying in bed with your wife and you'd see it all before you. Couldn't sleep. Couldn't lie still. Many's and many's the time I've got up and tramped the streets till it came daylight. Walking, walking – anything to get away from your thoughts. And

many's the time I've met other fellows that were out there doing exactly the same thing. That went on for years, that did.

Mrs I. McNicol
My husband only got home after the end of the war and he was so ill. Malaria. He was in the Scottish Horse and he'd been in Gallipoli and Egypt. I hadn't seen him for four years. My little girl was three and a bit and he'd never seen her. He came home straight off a hospital ship and he was so weary and unwell he went straight to bed. I said to Connie, 'Go in and see your Daddy.' She was very shy of him, but she went and stood at the bedroom door. I said, 'Well, say something to Daddy.' She said, 'My Mummy's made scones for you.' He just looked at her. He was too ill, too tired to speak. We lived with my family for a while. We'd had a war wedding before he left, so we didn't have a house of our own. After a few months we were given a railway carriage to live in. That was the Home for Heroes. It was the best they could do. So we started our married life in a converted railway carriage.

Trooper Sydney Chaplin, 1st Northamptonshire Yeomanry
In 1916 I went into Corbie with a limber and two horses and I saw an officer sitting very uncomfortably on a horse. The animal was throwing its head up, and dancing around. The officer called to me and said, 'Is anything wrong? This horse is usually very quiet to ride.' I told him to dismount and the first thing I found the bit had been pulled up tight in the horse's mouth and the curb chain was also too tight. So I slacked the curb and dropped the bit and by then the horse was quite docile. He thanked me and we had a talk. Then he said, 'I would like to be able to have a drink with you, but that's against orders.' So he handed me a ten-franc note and said, 'Drink my health,' and shook hands.

In 1923, I was still without regular work (just odd jobs when I could get them) when I was told that the Corps of

Commissionaires were interviewing ex-Servicemen in London. So I managed to scrape enough to pay for a return ticket to London and enough to pay for expenses. I was interviewed by a Major who took my particulars, checked my discharge papers, then informed me that owing to the amount of applications it would be a very long while before they could offer me a post. So that was it.

I had a walk round and eventually sat on a seat on the Embankment. I must have dozed off, because it was dark when I woke up, so I decided to stay put until the morning. I woke as the dawn was breaking, and what a sight it was. All the seats were full of old soldiers in all sorts of dress – mostly khaki – and a lot more were lying on the steps, some wrapped up in old newspapers. Men who had fought in the trenches, now unwanted and left to starve, were all huddled together. I was on the end of a seat, so I eased my fingers into my pocket to get a cigarette, as I did not want to wake the chap who was leaning against me, then I managed to light up. 'That smells good,' said the voice of the man I thought was asleep. I recognised him at once. I handed him a cigarette and said, 'Would you like a light, Major?' 'Good Lord! You, Corporal!' We stood up and looked at each other. 'Well, what about a spot of tea?' I said. He just spread out his hands and said, 'I am flat broke.' So I took him to a coffee stall and we had a mug of tea and two slices of bread and dripping each. The Major told me he had been caught out by one of the many crooks who were battening on to old soldiers. These offered shares in a business, producing false books, and when the money had been paid over they just disappeared. All his money had gone. However, he was to see one of his old junior officers that day and he was hoping to get a break. After an argument, I persuaded him to accept a few cigarettes and a shilling to carry him over.

I spent the day looking for work, but there were no vacancies anywhere. Finally I went to a cinema for a rest in the threepenny seats. It was dark when I came out and started to walk to St Pancras Station for the night train. As I was passing a shop doorway, I heard someone crying. I stopped and looked in and saw a man wearing an Army greatcoat with a turban on his head and a tray suspended from his neck with lucky charms on it. Another, unwanted after three years in the trenches. He and his wife were penniless when some crook offered him a chance to earn money easy if he could find five shillings. His wife pawned her wedding ring to get it, and in return he got a tray, a turban and a dozen or so lucky charms to sell at sixpence each. What a hope! Now after a day without anything to eat or drink he was broken-hearted at the thought of going home to his wife without a penny. He was an ex-Company Sergeant-Major. I sorted my cash out (one shilling and tenpence), gave him the bob and a fag. Then I carried on to the station, spent my tenpence at the coffee stall and got the train home.

It didn't last forever, but it lasted long enough. By 1930 I was happily married and in regular employment. One day I was returning from London to the Midlands by train. We pulled into Luton Station and stopped alongside a stationary train heading for London and in the first class compartment opposite I saw a well-dressed man smoking a cigar and reading a newspaper. Suddenly he looked up, the next moment down came both windows, and we clasped hands. It was the Major. He said, 'Corporal, you brought me luck. I found friends and a position that day I met you, and I have never looked back. And you?' 'Fine,' I said. At that moment his train moved out. We waved. I never knew his name.

Miss Kathleen Gibb

I was engaged to a dear boy who joined up when he was eighteen and came through (as we thought at the time) without a scratch. He used to tell me about his life in the trenches (Passchendaele, the Somme, Mons). Some time after, my fiancé was taken ill, recovered, but the illness recurred and was diagnosed as consumption, or tuberculosis. Then the doctors realised it was caused through being gassed twice during the conflict, it had eaten away one lung and was affecting the other. At that time there was no cure for TB. He died after four years, just faded away. I was broken-hearted. He had no war pension as it was too late to apply. When I think I could have been a happy grandmother today if it hadn't been for that terrible war.

CHARLES DOUIE

'Bewilderment'

Charles Douie wrote a vivid account of Passchendaele which appears in this anthology. Several years later he wrote this reflection on the bewilderment of many soldiers when they returned home, and it was published in his book *The Weary Road* in 1929. After the war he went to Oxford and then in 1927 became Secretary of University College London. In 1939 he joined the Ministry of Information.

On Armistice Day the sense of relief was great, but it was accompanied by feelings of bewilderment. For years one set purpose had dominated our lives; that purpose was now fulfilled, and for the moment there was nothing to take its place. For years our lives had been forfeit. We had watched our generation die, not one by one, but in hundreds, throughout four years. Our sorrows had come, not as single spies, but in battalions. So far as we had chosen, or dared, to reflect on the matter, we had known that the hour must come when, in the parlance of the trenches, 'our number was up.' Death had been our companion so long that we felt almost at a loss when he left us, and Life took his place.

Our new companion, however welcome, clearly made demands on us to which we were not used. We had to think ahead – a long way ahead. We had to adjust our sense of values, so as to pay adequate regard to the virtues held in honour by a community at peace, which are not the virtues most needed in time of war. Many who had gained a certain satisfaction from the sense that they were wanted in the hour of the country's need found that they were not wanted in the hour of her prosperity; others who had carried the heavy responsibilities of command discovered that henceforward they were to be denied any responsibility. These discoveries were far from welcome. During the war we had comforted ourselves on many occasions by the thought that things are never quite so bad as they seem. Peace, long deferred, was now to teach us the lesson that they are never quite so good.

Moreover we had time at last to realise how great had been our losses. Day by day the casualty lists had told their tale, but in the preoccupations of the hour their significance had not always been brought home to us. Returning home, we were to hear the full tale. Rugby was no doubt typical of most of the public schools. The school numbered usually between 550 and 560. The number serving in the war was over 3,000, and of these 675 are dead. My own generation probably suffered most. Of the 56 men in my house when I entered it in 1910 no less than 23 lost their lives . . .

Figures are rarely eloquent, but these figures may serve to tell the tale of the losses of my generation; they may illustrate how empty the world seemed to many of us on our return. Throughout our childhood we had looked forward to the great adventure of life . . . but always in those dreams the adventure had been shared with our friends. The great game was unthinkable without the companions of our smaller enterprises. But in its place we were given a greater adventure.

Looking back I sometimes think that the shadow of things to come was not wholly absent from our lives. Was Sir James

Barrie thinking of the menace of war when he wrote Peter Pan? Did no feeling of apprehension darken the mind of any mother in that audience which first heard 'My sons shall die like English gentlemen'; did no foreboding enter into the exultation with which those sons first heard youth's defiance of death – 'To die would be an awfully big adventure'?

The adventure of life paled into insignificance before the greater adventure which had been ours. Life, indeed, could no longer be an adventure in the absence of those friends who might have given zest to it. We were indeed rather weary of adventure, and we were conscious of proving a great disappointment to many earnest people who were anxious to recruit us on our return for a variety of crusades. As 1919 wore on I was surprised, in common with many others who fought in the war, at the hatred and bitterness preached and practised by many who had never borne arms, and I was much distressed by the drifting apart into two opposing camps of those who had fought as comrades in the war. The industrial troubles of late 1919 must have depressed me considerably, as some rough notes written at the time, couched in the language of exaggeration, show:–

'Everywhere we watch the triumph of the old regime and concurrently the inevitable growth of anarchy. And we who fought for a dream of a new world are weary and impotent. We have lost our leaders. We are but a remnant. Our hearts are in the past.'

The notes are headed by two lines of John Masefield:

And all their passionate hearts are dust,
And dust the great idea that burned.

My gloomy forebodings proved wrong in the event in this, though not in other countries. That they proved wrong, and that our land has been mercifully free from violence, I attribute in a great measure to the determination of those who fought in the war never to engage in civil strife against their late comrades. The advocates of violent courses, on each side, have been drawn almost exclusively from the ranks of those who took no combatant part in the Great War.

CHARLOTTE MEW

'The Cenotaph'

Although her poetry is little known today, Charlotte Mew, who was born in 1869, was admired by Siegfried Sassoon and Ezra Pound, as well as Virginia Woolf and Thomas Hardy, both of whom considered her the best woman poet of her time. She writes not of the national Cenotaph – a war memorial – but of the memorials that were being erected in villages, towns and cities throughout the country after the ending of the war and where so many Remembrance Day services are still held today. Mew, whose family had a history of mental illness, committed suicide in 1928.

Not yet will those measureless fields be green again
Where only yesterday the wild sweet blood of wonderful
*   youth was shed;*
There is a grave whose earth must hold too long, too deep
*   a stain,*
Though for ever over it we may speak as proudly as we
*   may tread.*
But here, where the watchers by lonely hearths from the
*   thrust of an inward sword have more*
slowly bled,
We shall build the Cenotaph: Victory, winged, with Peace,
*   winged too, at the column's head.*
And over the stairway, at the foot—oh! here, leave
*   desolate, passionate hands to spread*
Violets, roses, and laurel, with the small, sweet, tinkling
*   country things*

Speaking so wistfully of other Springs,
From the little gardens of little places where son or sweet-
heart was born and bred.
In splendid sleep, with a thousand brothers
To lovers—to mothers
Here, too, lies he:
Under the purple, the green, the red,
It is all young life: it must break some women's hearts to
see
Such a brave, gay coverlet to such a bed!
Only, when all is done and said,
God is not mocked and neither are the dead
For this will stand in our Marketplace—
Who'll sell, who'll buy
(Will you or I
Lie each to each with the better grace)?
While looking into every busy whore's and huckster's face
As they drive their bargains, is the Face
Of God: and some young, piteous, murdered face.

CHARLES CARRINGTON

Esprit de Corps

Middle-aged men, strenuously as they attempt to deny it, are united by a secret bond and separated by a mental barrier from their fellows who were too old or too young to fight in the Great War. Particularly the generation of young men who were soldiers before their characters had been formed, who were under twenty-five in 1914, is conscious of the distinction, for the war made them what they are. Generally speaking, this secret army presents to the world a front of silence and bitterness. Loath to speak of their experience, if they speak, it is with a sort of rough cynicism which it has become fashionable to describe as disillusion, disenchantment. A legend has grown up, propagated not by soldiers but by journalists, that these men who went gaily to fight in the mood of Rupert Brooke and Julian Grenfell, lost their faith amid the horrors of the trenches and returned in a mood of anger and despair. To calculate the effect of mental and bodily suffering, not on a man but on a whole generation of men, may seem an impossible task, but it can at least be affirmed that the legend of disenchantment is false.

It is based first on the belief that soldiers in the trenches endured such things as men have never known, that passing through the fire they were destroyed or purified in some strange way, a belief that will not bear a moment's examination. Any broad view of human life squares with the homely saying of Mercy in the 'Pilgrim's Progress': 'Well, you know your sore and I know mine; and, good friend, we shall all have enough evil before we come at our journey's end.' A rash man only would affirm that the scars of war are more terrible than any others of the 'thousand natural shocks that flesh is heir to'. What is remarkable about war is that its blows fall not on individuals but on groups. Outrageous fortune who strikes one man with the pangs of despised love, another with the oppressor's wrong, dealing such blows that only the sufferer can tell their weight, showers on the heads of multitudes in war, danger and discomfort which all her victims must bear. The deeper a spiritual experience goes the more difficult it is to communicate its meaning to another person. Those who have not known passionate love or passionate religion are generally unable to appreciate them and sometimes doubt their existence; but lovers or religious mystics feel for one another. They have an inner life in common. In the same way, though in a lesser degree, soldiers who have fought side by side are conscious of being initiated: they are 'illuminati'. It is important, too, to remember that not only unpleasant emotions have thus been shared. If we have known fear and discomfort we have also felt courage and comfort well up in our hearts, springing from the crowd-emotion of our company, for even Active Service brings moments of intense happiness. Mr. Sassoon caught and fixed such a glowing instant in his poem about the soldiers singing on the march.

'Everyone's voice was suddenly lifted;
And beauty came like the setting sun:
My heart was shaken with tears; and horror
Drifted away . . . O but everyone
Was a bird; and the song was wordless; the singing will
Never be done.'

Further, it is not honest to deny the existence of happiness which was actually derived from the war. First, the horrors and the discomforts, indescribable as they are, were not continuous. The unluckiest soldiers, whose leave was always stopped, who never had a 'blighty' wound, still spent only a comparatively few days in the face of the enemy, and of these only a few were of the most horrible kind. Their intensity, when they came, sharpened the senses and made the intervals correspondingly delightful. If no man now under thirty can guess the meaning of twenty-four hours' bombardment, nor has he any notion of the joy of ninety-six hours' rest. Who has never been drenched and frozen in Flanders mud, has never dreamed of the pleasure derivable from dry blankets on a stone floor. Secondly, it must be remembered that men like adventures. Anyone who has ever been through a street accident, anyone who has climbed a mountain, knows that. It is one of the strange attributes of the mind that we like things which make our flesh creep, and no one was very long at the front without sometimes feeling a thrill of excitement which quite banished the dragging fears of anticipation. Quite late in the war I have seen a man go to spend the afternoon in a trench under heavy shell-fire because he was bored with sitting in a safe dugout.

Thirdly, there was comradeship, richer, stronger in war than we have ever known since.

'From quiet homes, and first beginning,
Out to the undiscovered ends,
There's nothing worth the wear of winning,
But laughter and the love of friends.'

ANONYMOUS, 1920, WESTMINSTER ABBEY

Beneath this stone rests the body of a British warrior, unknown by name or rank, brought from France to lie among the most illustrious of the land and buried here on Armistice Day, 11 Nov: 1920, in the presence of His Majesty King George V, his Ministers of State, the Chiefs of his Forces, and a vast concourse of the nation . . . They buried him among the kings because he had done good toward God and toward his house.

MANCHESTER GUARDIAN

The man who won the war

The two-minute silence at 11 a.m. on 11 November, the eleventh month, was observed first at the Cenotaph in London in 1920 after which the body of the unknown soldier was lowered into its grave in Westminster Abbey. King George V was the chief mourner. Francis Perrot reported the occasion for the *Manchester Guardian*.

A warrior of the Great War known unto God: This was written on a wreath of laurel picked in the gardens of Ypres that was laid on the coffin in Westminster Abbey to-day. In the quiet, quiet spaces, in the exquisite ritual in between the flights of holy song, the prayers, the quiet speech by the graveside, one had time to let the mind busy itself with thoughts of what manner of man he was. Known to God, yes, and though his name will never be learned, known surely to us all by long intimacy in the years of war. Whatever is forgotten and unknown, the soldier as we knew him will never be, and this man stands for the type for ever. Such a man, one liked to think, as those honest-faced Guardsmen waiting there by the pillar to let the coffin down, an ordinary man, full of weakness, as we all are, but going through with the job as a plain matter of duty. The man who won the War.

They have given him for burial place the fittest that could be found. He lies apart from the great-named, the people of real or imagined importance in their day, right in the middle of the nave. The nave from ancient times was the people's part of a great church. This was a man of the people, and his stone will be trodden by everyone's feet. It is the true centre of the Abbey.

Sunlight came through the painted armour of a medieval warrior greeting a fellow-soldier with uplifted spear in a window over the grave. It made a bright patch on the yellowish columns and lit grotesquely the pompous effigies of eighteenth-century nobodies by the wall. A soft bell tolling in the misty height was the only sound for a long time.

A thousand bereaved women were sitting waiting, their mourning lightened by the flowers and wreaths on their knees. About a hundred V.C.s came in and formed an avenue from the choir gate – the Unknown's guard of honour. The heroes were ranged without distinction of rank. A naval commander, stiff with gold braid, would be next to an A.B., and among the soldiers you saw a famous officer like Freyberg shoulder to shoulder with an ex-private in civilian clothes. It was a little democracy of valour. Fourteen wives and mothers who received the V.C. for their dead men folk had places of honour.

Looking up this avenue there was a vague glimpse of distant richness, of colour and golden lights about the high altar, and down the long church poured elegiac music from a soldiers' band – soft fluty music that wandered to and fro like the pulses of thought. Quietness was the note of all.

After a long time the choir, a procession of floating white and scarlet, moved up the nave into the choir, the Dean, solemn, and erect in his stiff mourning cope, walking last. They were singing the hymn:

O valiant hearts who to your victory came
Through dust of conflict and through battle flame

with that unearthly wistfulness of cathedral choristers. The sound diminished and became a faint bell-like resonance in the distance. Then from the remote altar came a murmur of words. The precentor was intoning the Lord's Prayer.

Silence. The bell tolled eleven, one heavy stroke after another, and at once all of us in the church became part of the multitude outside in the same mood. Out there in the street some loud word of command followed the last stroke. All sound ceased in a strange intensity of stillness. For two minutes it lasted, so that a creaking chair or a cough jarred intolerably. The cathedral seemed to breathe as in sleep.

The singers broke the silence at last, breathing out like a sigh the opening of the Contakion of the faithful departed:

'Give rest, O Christ, to Thy servants with Thy saints where sorrow and pain are no more, neither sighing, but life everlasting.

'Thou only art immortal, the Creator and Maker of man, and we are mortal, formed of the earth, and unto earth we shall return.'

Although the body had not yet come this seemed the most beautiful moment of the service, the purest in emotion, the most favourable to memory and aspiration.

The service was interrupted for a time while the clergy and the choir went to the north transept to usher the Warrior into his resting-place. As they went gusts of diminishing song floated back to us. The door opened, and there was a rush of sound from the outside, where the King was waiting. The guns were firing the Field-Marshal's salute for the unknown, like nineteen soft bangs on a big drum.

At the end of this we heard, still from the outside, a band rolling out the Chopin march, the weeping ghost of a tune. Drums rolled, trumpets shrilled.

The bells pealed louder; as the procession turned and advanced through the choir towards us the funeral march swelled potently. The choristers led the way, pacing very slowly behind the golden cross, singing with many pauses the 'I am the Resurrection and the Life.'

Down the lane of khaki and naval blue and hospital blue – what thoughts of War days that unfamiliar colour gave – the Guardsmen carried the coffin. On it lay the man's steel helmet and laurel wreath. The soldiers set it down over the grave.

The King stood at the foot facing west. The Dean with the Archbishop, and the clergy clustered behind them, were at the head of the coffin, facing the mourner for a nation.

The customary ritual of burial took only a few more minutes: the Twenty-third Psalm, the recital of the chapter that tells of those who have come through 'the great tribulation,' and as we were singing 'Lead, kindly Light' the Guardsmen lowered the soldier into the grave – with the words 'The night is gone' he disappeared.

The Dean handed the King a silver shell in which was

soil brought from France. The King cast it upon the coffin. Last of all, in the secular key of warning, Kipling's cry against 'the frantic boast, the foolish word' rang through the church.

From the east came a reiterated roll of drums, then the clear call of the reveille – a cheerful challenge carrying us on to the life that must be lived in action. The King's wreath lay at the head of the grave. It was over.

The King and his following went out at the west door, that yawned now to let the chilly mist of the London day and the noises of the street in upon that warm-coloured splendour, that calm of recollection. The Unknown Warrior lay there wrapped in his purple. There was a pause, and the cathedral bells alone rang silverly high in the air. Soon the throng of dignitaries, statesmen, soldiers, and sailors who had followed the king went by, casting each a look into the grave as they passed.

Then the congregation moved and became a crowd pressing with one impulse towards the coffin. The V.C.s broke the solemn ranks and became just comrades looking their last on a comrade. The bandsmen, varying their instruments, came along sheepishly and gazed.

Then the women left their seats and began that long file past of the bereaved that was to last all through the day. West End and East End, all was one in this democracy of memory. The rich woman and the poor – for all the open grave meant exactly the same thing. A woman plucked a white chrysanthemum from a bunch she carried and threw it in the tomb. This example was quickly followed, and soon the purple carpet was thickly scattered with flowers white and red.

The drums and trumpets give you music,
But my heart, O my Warrior, my Comrade,
My heart gives you love.

RUDYARD KIPLING

Because our fathers lied

Rudyard Kipling was still mourning his son John, who went missing at the Battle of Loos in 1915 at the age of nineteen, when he wrote this poem in 1919. The last two lines are still frequently quoted.

A son
My son was killed while laughing at some jest. I would
I knew
What it was, and it might serve me in a time when jests are
few.

An Only Son
I have slain none except my Mother. She
(Blessing her slayer) died of grief for me

The Coward
I could not look on Death, which being known
Men led me to him, blindfold and alone

Two Canadian Memorials:
We giving all gained all.
Neither lament us nor praise.
Only in all things recall,
It is Fear, not Death that slays

From little towns in a far land we came,
To save our honour and a world aflame.
By little towns in a far land we sleep;
And trust that world we won for you to keep!

R.A.F. (Aged Eighteen)
Laughing through clouds, his milk-teeth still unshed,

Cities and men he smote from overhead
His deaths delivered, he returned to play
Childlike, with childish things now put away.

The Sleepy Sentinel
Faithless the watch that I kept: now I have none to keep.
I was slain because I slept: now I am slain I sleep.
Let no man reproach me again, whatever watch is unkept –
I sleep because I am slain. They slew me because I slept.

Batteries out of Ammunition
If any mourn us in the workshop, say
We died because the shift kept holiday.

Common form
If any question why we died,
Tell them, because our fathers lied.

ACKNOWLEDGEMENTS

My greatest debt is to Anne Manson, who typed the manuscript with unfailing good cheer and offered many helpful comments and criticisms. A lot of the reading was done at the French farmhouse of my friends Barry Turner and Mary Fulton. There has been support and encouragement from my agent, Hilary Rubinstein, and Stephen Guise (who had the idea for the anthology) and Ursula Mackenzie, Iain Hunt and Suzanne Fowler at Little, Brown. I acknowledge with gratitude the advice and wisdom of Roy Suddaby, keeper of archives at the Imperial War Museum.

Above all my wife, Maureen Waller, has lived with this book and its effect on our lives for nearly three years and it could not have been completed without her unstinting support and encouragement.

Others who have assisted are: Max Arthur, Sue Smart and Liz Larby of Gresham's School, Holt, Nova Jane Heath, Mrs C. M. Lucy, keeper of archives at Dulwich College, Richard Girling, Ian Park, Rae Shirvington, the magnificent London Library and the equally magnificent Google and Abebooks.com.

Other Great War anthologies are noted in the Bibliography, but I salute the work of Guy Chapman, George Panichas, Anne Powell, Andrew Motion, Max Arthur and Lyn Macdonald, Jon Silkin, John Brophy, Laurence Binyon and Philipp Witkop.

I also acknowledge: Simon Chater (grandson Alfred Chater); Emma Golding (Imperial War Museum); The Reverend Philip Graystone (son of James William Graystone); Sir Edward Hulse

(Captain Sir Edward Hamilton Westrow Hulse); Professor Richard Pankhurst, Institute of Ethiopian Studies, Addis Ababa, Ethiopia, has given permission for the use of extracts from the writings of his mother, Sylvia Pankhurst; Mrs Joan Plumley (Captain H. Bursey); Ronald John Shephard and Bruce Rossor (nephew of Lieutenant Ernest Shephard); Professor John Stallworthy (Wilfred Owen, joint copyright holder); Catherine Trippett (Permissions Department, Random House); Jonathan Wright (Pen-and-Sword, Bickersteth Diaries); David Leighton (nephew of Roland Leighton) and Bernard Wynick (Isaac Rosenberg).

I am also grateful for permission to reproduce extracts from the following: *Because He Bore My Name*, W. W. Gibson, Macmillan, London, Copyright © Wilfred Wilson Gibson, 1915; *Twelve Days on the Somme*, Sidney Rogerson, and *Sagittarius Rising*, Cecil Lewis, reproduced with the kind permission of Greenhill Books; *For the Fallen*, Laurence Binyon, Pollinger Ltd, September 1914, courtesy of the Society of Authors, the Literary Representative of the Estate of Laurence Binyon; *Gallipoli* by Alan Moorehead, by permission of Pollinger Ltd and the proprietor; *Outline, an autobiography and other writings* by Paul Nash, Tate Enterprises Ltd; *World Without End*, Helen Thomas, 1931, *Goodbye to All That*, Robert Graves, 1929, and *Collected Poems*, Ivor Gurney, Carcanet Press Limited; *Impacts of War* by John Terraine (Copyright © Estate of John Terraine, 1971) by permission of PFD (http://www.pfd.co.uk) on behalf of the Estate of John Terraine; the German War Diary, courtesy of the National Archives (UK), document reference (CAB 45/166); extract from Ernest Routley file (GS 1389), taken from *The Somme, a new panoramic perspective*, by Peter Barton, the Liddle Collection at the University of Leeds; '*Stand To*', *A Diary of the Trenches, 1915–1918* by Capt F. C. Hitchcock and *Weary Road, The Reactions of a Subaltern of Infantry* by Charles Douie, Naval and Military Press Ltd, http://www.naval-military-press.com; *Julian Grenfell: His Life and the Times of his Death* by Nicholas Mosley (Copyright © Nicholas Mosley 1976) by permission of PFD (www.pfd.co.uk) on behalf of Nicholas Mosley; *The Donkeys*, by

All attempts at tracing the copyright holders of *1914* by James Cameron, *War is War* by Alfred McLelland and *Vain Glory* by Guy Chapman (Orionbooks.co.uk), were unsuccessful. All attempts at tracing the copyright holder of *The Retreat from Mons,* by Bernard John Denore, and *How Easy to Scorn* by W. Walker from *Everyman at War*, Purdom, C. B. (ed.), J. M. Dent, 1930, Orion Publishing, were also unsuccessful. Every effort has been made to trace copyright holders and the author and the Imperial War Museum would be grateful for any information which might help to trace those whose identities or addresses are not currently known.

BIBLIOGRAPHY

Adam, George, *Behind the Scenes at the Front*, Chatto & Windus, 1915

Adcock, Arthur St John, *For Remembrance: Soldier Poets Who Have Fallen in the War*, Hodder, 1918

Aldington, Richard, *Death of a Hero*, Chatto & Windus, 1929; unexpurgated edn, Hogarth Press, 1984

Babington, Anthony, *For the Sake of Example: Capital Courts Martial, 1914–1920*, Leo Cooper, 1983

Bairnsfather, Bruce, *Bullets and Billets*, Grant Richards, 1916

Barton, Peter, *The Somme: A New Panoramic Perspective*, Constable, 2006

Bickersteth, John (ed.), *The Bickersteth Diaries 1914–1918*, Leo Cooper, 1995

Binding, Rudolf, *A Fatalist at War*, Allen & Unwin, 1929

Bishop, Alan, and Bostridge, Mark, *Letters from a Lost Generation*, Little, Brown, 1998

Blythe, Ronald, *Akenfield*, Allen Lane, 1969

Bloem, Walter, *The Advance from Mons*, Peter Davies, 1919

Blunden, Edmund, *Undertones of War*, Penguin, 1937

Brittain, Vera, *Testament of Youth: War Diary 1913–1917*, ed. Alan Bishop, Virago, 1978

Brophy, John (ed.), *The Soldier's War*, Dent, 1929

Brophy, John, and Partridge, Eric, *The Long Trail,* Deutsch, 1965

Brown, Malcolm, *The IWM Book of the Somme*, Sidgwick, 1996

Brown, Malcolm, *The IWM Book of the First World War*, Sidgwick, 1996

Brown, Malcolm, and Seaton, Shirley, *Christmas Truce*, Leo Cooper/Secker and Warburg, 1975

Cameron, James, *1914*, Cassell, 1969

Carrington, C. E., *A Subaltern's War*, Peter Davies, 1929

Chapman, Guy, *A Passionate Prodigality*, Nicholson and Watson, 1933

Chapman, Guy (ed.), *Vain Glory*, Cassell, 1937

Churchill, Winston S., *The World Crisis 1911–1918*, Vol. 2, Odhams, 1929

Clark, Alan, *The Donkeys*, Hutchinson, 1961

Crozier, F. P., *A Brass Hat in No Man's Land*, Cape, 1930

Denore, Bernard John, 'The Retreat From Mons' from *Everyman at War*, ed. C. B. Purdom, J. M. Dent, 1930

Eden, Anthony, *Another World*, Allen Lane, 1976

Ellis, John, *Eye-Deep in Hell*, Croom Helm, 1976

Empey, Arthur Guy, *Over the Top*, Puttnams, 1917

Eyre, Giles E. M., *Somme Harvest*, Naval and Military Press, 2001

Feilding, Rowland, *War Letters to a Wife*, Medici Society, 1929

Fisher, T., *Sixty American Opinions on the War*, Unwin, 1915

Fisher Wood, Eric, *The Notebook of an Intelligence Officer*, Century, 1915

Fussell, Paul, *The Great War and Modern Memory*, OUP, 1975

Gibbons, Floyd, *Red Knight of Germany*, Cassell, 1930

Gibbs, Sir Philip, *The War Dispatches*, Gibbs and Phillips at Times Press, 1964

Gladden, E. N., 'Memoirs and Diaries: At Messines Ridge in 1917', from *Everyman at War*, ed. C. B. Purdom, J. M. Dent, 1930

Glover, Jonathan, and Silkin, Jon (eds), *The Penguin Book of First World War Prose*, Viking, 1990

Graves, Robert, *Goodbye to All That*, Cape, 1929; Penguin, 1960

Graves, Richard Perceval, *Robert Graves, The Assault Heroic, 1895–1926*, Weidenfeld & Nicolson, 1986

Harris, Ruth Elwin, *Billie, The Nevill Letters, 1914–1916*, Julia MacRae, 1991

Hart-Davis, Rupert (ed.), *Siegfried Sassoon Diaries, 1915–1918*, Faber, 1983

Hay, Ian, *The First Hundred Thousand and K1, The June Sub, being the unofficial Chronicle of Unit 9 'K(1)'*, Blackwood, 1915

Hiscock, Eric, *The Bells of Hell Go Ting-A-Ling-A-Ling*, Arlington, 1976

Hitchcock, Captain F. C., 'Stand To', *A Diary of the Trenches, 1915–1918*, Naval & Military Press, 2001

Horne, Alistair, *The Price of Glory, Verdun 1916*, Macmillan, 1962

Horne, Alistair, *Macmillan 1894–1956*, Vol. I, Macmillan, 1988

Housman, Laurence (ed.), *War Letters of Fallen Englishmen*, Gollancz, 1930

Howard, Philip, *We Thundered Out, 200 Years of* The Times, *1785–1985*, Times Books, 1985

Jünger, Ernst, *Storm of Steel* (trans. Michael Hofmann) (first pub. in German 1920), Penguin, 2004

Keegan, John, *The First World War*, Hutchinson, 1998

Lewis, Cecil, *Sagittarius Rising*, Peter Davies, 1966 (first pub. 1936), Greenhill Books, 2006

Macdonald, Lyn, *They Called It Passchendaele*, Michael Joseph, 1978

Macdonald, Lyn, *Voices and Images of the Great War*, Michael Joseph, 1988

MacDonagh, Michael, *In London During the Great War*, Ebury, 2002

Macmillan, Harold, letter to his mother, taken from Peter Vansittart, *Voices from the Great War*, Jonathan Cape, 1981

Manning, Frederic, *Her Privates We*, Peter Davies, 1930, Pan, 1967

Manser, Christian (ed.), *Portrait of England*, Penguin, 1942

Masefield, John, *Letters from the Front, 1915–1917*, ed. Peter Vansittart, Constable, 1984

Max, Arthur, *Forgotten Voices of the Great War*, Ebury, 2002

Maze, Paul, *A Frenchman in Khaki*, Naval and Military Press, 2004

McKee, Alexander, *Vimy Ridge*, Souvenir, 1966

Middlebrook, Martin, *The First Day on the Somme*, Allen Lane, 1971

Montague, C. E., *Disenchantment*, Chatto & Windus, 1922

Moorehead, Alan, *Gallipoli*, Harper and Bros, 1956

Moran, C. McM. W., *The Anatomy of Courage*, Constable 1945; Constable & Robinson 2007

Mosley, Nicholas, *Julian Grenfell: His Life and the Times of his Death 1888–1915*, Weidenfeld & Nicolson/Holt, Rinehart and Winston, 1976; Persephone Books, 1999

Motion, Andrew, *First World War Poems*, Faber, 2003

Moynahan, Michael (ed.), *People at War 1914–1918*, David and Charles, 1973/1988

Nash, Paul, *Outline an autobiography and other Writings*, Faber

Panichas, George A. (ed.), *Promise of Greatness: The War of 1914–1918*, Cassell, 1968

Pankhurst, Sylvia, *The Home Front*, Hutchinson, 1932

Playne, Caroline, *Britain Holds On 1917–1919*, Allen & Unwin, 1933

Playne, Caroline, *Society at War 1914–1916*, Allen & Unwin, 1931

Pitt, Barrie, *1918*, Cassell, 1962

Powell, Anne, *A Deep Cry*, Palladour, 1993

Price, Evadne, *Not So Quiet*, Feminist Press, 1989

Purdom, C. B. (ed.), *Everyman at War*, J. M. Dent, 1930

Pym, T. W., and Gordon, Geoffrey, *Papers from Picardy, by Two Chaplains*, Constable, 1917

Read, Sir Herbert, *In Retreat*, Faber, 1930

Remarque, Erich Maria, *All Quiet on the Western Front*, Putnam's, 1926

Revell, Alex, *Brief Glory, The Life of Arthur Rhys Davids, DSO MC & Bar*, William Kimber, 1984

Richards, Frank, *Old Soldiers Never Die*, Naval & Military Press, 2001

Richter, Donald C. (ed.), *Lionel Sotheby's Great War*, Ohio (Athens), 1997

Rogerson, Sydney, *Twelve Days on the Somme: A Memoir of the Trenches, 1916*, Greenhill Books, London, 2006

Seeger, Alan, *Letters and Diary of Alan Seeger*, Scribner, 1917

Sheffield, G. D., and Inglis, G. I. S., *From Vimy Ridge to the Rhine, The Great War Letters of Christopher Stone DSO MC*, Crowood, 1989

Skidelsky, Robert, *Oswald Mosley*, Macmillan, 1975

Smart, Sue, *When Heroes Die, A Forgotten Archive Reveals the Last Days of the Schoolfriends Who Died for Britain*, Breedon, 2001

Spender, J. A. and Asquith, Cyril, *Life of Lord Oxford and Asquith*, Vol. II, Hutchinson, 1932

Stallings, Laurence, *The Doughboys, The Story of the AEF, 1917–1918*, Harper & Row, 1963

Stallworthy, John (ed.), *Wilfred Owen: The Complete Poems & Fragments*, 2 vols, Chatto & Windus, 1983

Tawney, R. H. *The Attack and Other Papers*, Allen & Unwin, 1953

Taylor, A. J. P., *The First World War, An Illustrated History*, Hamish Hamilton, 1963

Taylor, A. J. P., *English History, 1914–1945*, OUP, 1965

Terraine, John, *Impacts of War, 1914–1918*, Hutchinson, 1970

Thomas, Helen, *World Without End*, Harper, NY, 1931; Faber, 1972

Toller, Ernst, *I Was A German*, Bodley Head, 1934

Tuchman, Barbara, *1914*, Constable, 1962

Turner, William, *Accrington Pals*, Wharncliffe, 1988

Vaughan, Edwin, *Some Desperate Glory*, Warne 1982

Ward, Mrs Humphry, *England's Effort*, Smith Elder, 1916

Williams, John (ed.), *The Home Front*, Constable, 1972

Williamson, Henry, *The Patriot's Progress*, Sphere, 1978 (first pub. 1930)

Williamson, Henry, *The Fox in the Attic*, Macdonald, 1955

Williamson, Anne, *A Patriot's Progress* and *Henry Williamson and The First World War*, Sutton, 1998

Wilson, Jean Moorcroft (ed.), *The Collected Letters of Charles Hamilton Sorley*, Cecil Woolf, 1990

Winter, Denis, *Death's Men*, Allen Lane, 1978

Witkop, Philipp (ed.), *German Students' War Letters*, University of Pennsylvania Press, 2002

INDEX

Songs are indexed under title. Titles of books and poems may be found under author's name.